Adirondack Camps

Adirondack Camps

Homes Away from Home, 1850–1950

CRAIG GILBORN

With a Foreword by

PAUL MALO

The Adirondack Museum / Syracuse University Press

Publication of this book is made possible by a grant from FURTHERMORE ...
the publication program of the J. M. Kaplan Fund.

This book is published with the assistance of a grant from the John Ben Snow Foundation.

The paper used in this publication meets the minimum requirements of American
National Standard for Information Sciences—Permanence of Paper for Printed Library
Materials, ANSI Z39.48-1984.

LIBRARY OF CONGRESS CATALOGING-IN-PUBLICATION DATA

Gilborn, Craig A.
    Adirondack camps : homes away from home, 1850–1950 / Craig Gilborn ; with a
foreword by Paul Malo.—1st ed.
        p.   cm.
    Includes bibliographical references and index.
    ISBN 0-8156-0626-5 (cloth : alk. paper)
    1. Outdoor recreation—New York (State)—Adirondack Mountains—History.
2. Summer resorts—New York (State)—Adirondack Mountains—History. 3. Vacation
homes—New York (State)—Adirondack Mountains—History. I. Title.

GV191.42.N7 G54 2000
643'.2—dc21   99-086676

Book design by Christopher Kuntze
Manufactured in Canada

To Alice,
who lived this book before she edited it,
and to Lex & Amanda

Craig Gilborn, for twenty years the director of the Adirondack Museum, is author of *Adirondack Furniture and the Rustic Tradition,* a book that introduced the public to a craft little known or appreciated before its publication in 1987. He started writing this book on Adirondack camps in Dorset, Vermont, and finished it at his home on Long Lake in the Adirondacks.

Contents

Color Plates

Illustrations

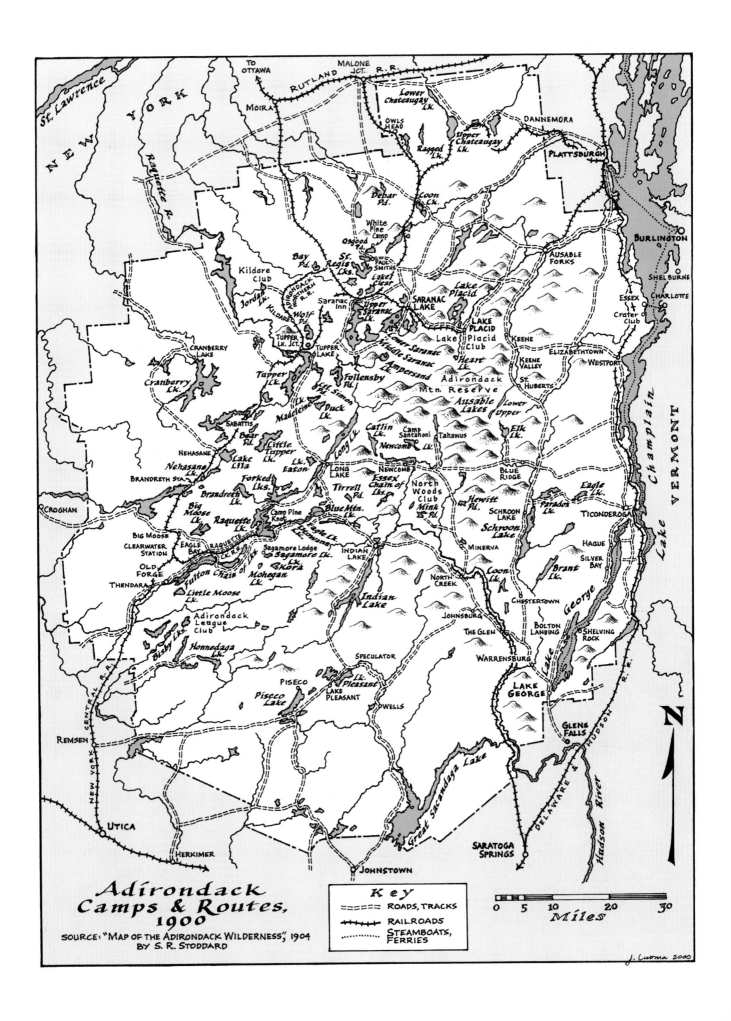

Adirondack
Camps & Routes,
1900

SOURCE: "MAP OF THE ADIRONDACK WILDERNESS", 1904
BY S. R. STODDARD

Key
ROADS, TRACKS
RAILROADS
STEAMBOATS,
FERRIES

Miles
0   5   10   20   30

Beyond the Blue Line

Paul Malo

GREENER, as June approaches, is the other side of the fence—beyond the Blue Line. At the season when suburban mowers refuse to start we yearn for a place where no grass demands mowing, but where woodland trails wait to be explored, streams to be paddled, mountains to be climbed—a place with few urbane amusements, but many serene lakes. Who is not still thrilled by the first glimpse of the distant mountains? Who does not still react with childlike anticipation, approaching the Blue Line, awaiting the familiar sign: Entering the Adirondack Park?

Old camps, opened in the spring, emit familiar smells—of smoky hearths, musty books, mosquito repellent. Alien cockroaches despised elsewhere are less repulsive when recognized as familiar Cedar Bugs. Rodents are more welcome with furry tails. The first hum of the refrigerator, the first cry of a loon, but mostly it is the quiet that speaks to us—the silence, except for the continuous lapping of water, the rustling of leaves overhead. We are back.

The character of a beloved place may be as compelling as the idealized features and foibles of a cherished person. The heart grows fonder with fall closing of the camp. Absence occasions not only grief but a long winter's longing. The image in the mind's eye, the Edenic vision, may be illusory, but as desire becomes anticipation, it is palpably real.

People and place bond. We are related, as in a good marriage, when over the years partners become more like one another. We leave our mark on the land, but the land leaves its mark on us. Children who have paddled up wild creeks may later drive on highways, but those roads will bring them back, not so much to trendy villas or luxurious summer homes, as to camps—plain camps, where on the log mantel over the stone fireplace their childish drawings, like rock markings of an ancient people, still are discernible on browning fungi. Summers of 1954, 1938, 1913, 1902. Mother's curtains. Grandma's china. What would the porch be, without that old chair, the one with the rattan unraveling—or even that ugly, bent aluminum folding job, which someone rewove one summer with too-bright plastic strips?

In the woods, something common links the rudimentary hunter's shanty and the Great Camp, even though the landed establishment may have scores of imposing structures. As William Randolph Hearst required ketchup bottles at each San Simeon dinner setting—because his baroque hacienda was "camp"—so Mabel Brady Garvan made her guests, although required to dress for dinner, sit on backless benches at a long picnic table—presidents and archbishops —because Kill Kare was a camp, even if spelled with a K.

Inherent in the mystique of the Adirondack camp is a patrician disdain for pretension. Whereas the New Rich may resort to showplaces, Old Money prefers to hide away in the deep woods. As a general rule, the more established and socially secure a family, the more remote and invisible its camp. Estates such as Sagamore, about a thousand acres, were relatively small, compared to larger establishments, such as Santanoni Preserve, at about thirteen thousand acres, Litchfield Park at twenty-eight thousand acres, Whitney Park at about seventy-nine thousand acres, and Nehasane Park at one-hundred-and-twelve thousand acres. Although cottagers elbowing along communal lakes live somewhat differently from occupants of large country houses on vast estates, Adirondackers generally have shared a wilderness ethic and a conservative aesthetic. The lakeshore cottager and great camper may feel more at home in one another's genteely shabby digs than at a Hampton beach house or grandiose Newport villa.

Few interior decorators have found clients in the Adirondacks. Although local crafts people export rustic furnishings, local residents import few fashions from without. Few chic boutiques line village streets; few restaurants serve cuisine that is *nouvelle*. There are few golf clubs, few social events of consequence. Campers come to escape all that. They are indeed at home, in their homes away from home.

Camps are old clothes, fishing poles, wooden boats, creaky buildings, moss on the roof, and critters under the porch. Nevertheless, for all their homeliness, despite their deftness with the common touch, it would misrepresent many Adirondack campers to introduce them as Just Folks. The Adirondack camp is not rural, but exurban. Virtually all of the families that built the Great Camps came up the Hudson River, from Manhattan and the Hudson Valley, to its source, the Adirondack Mountains. Some families once came by private railroad car; some owned their own railroads. Now some fly in by their own jet. The second and subsequent generations privileged by wealth generally have been privileged culturally as well. The apparent artlessness of their camps is artful.

Craig Gilborn speaks with authority about the art of rusticity. Devoting a long career to collection and conservation of the material culture of the region, particularly its rustic architecture and decorative arts, Craig Gilborn has become its preeminent historian and interpreter. His involvement has been neither merely institutional, while director of the Adirondack Museum, nor merely scholarly, as author of unsurpassed studies, but also has entailed activism. Craig Gilborn has championed folk crafts and advocated historic preservation of landmark buildings.

Craig's initial call to save Camp Sagamore has evolved into a broad-based movement to preserve historic buildings of the region. Books, articles, and frequent public lectures have created a constituency for historic preservation. Adirondack Architectural Heritage, an organization founded in 1990, has become well established as regional advocate and interpreter of historic buildings. The older Adirondack Museum at Blue Mountain Lake likewise is institutional steward of the regional heritage. Many writers and artists have enriched the regional literature and continue to interpret this special place.

Regional traditions evolve from interaction of people and place. Distinctive character requires neither that the people nor the place be unique; it is the particular combination of peoples and their place that determines character. There is an identifiable Adirondack culture; it is not the same as that of the nearby Catskills, of the Green or White Mountains. This is neither because the Adirondack Mountain region of New York State differs naturally (an extensive and celebratory literature notwithstanding) in geology, flora or fauna from the other forested mountains of the American Northeast, nor because Adirondackers are special; very similar people live elsewhere in North America. Rather, the particular mix of people and place has been distinctive here, and from this ferment has evolved a regional reflex consciousness, a sense of Adirondack identity.

Three major groups of people have brought traditions to merge in the Adirondacks. Habitants came from the north, Yankees from the east, and Yorkers from the south. Contact between historically different cultures of Quebec, New England, and New York stimulated creative interaction. After two centuries, the result is not a homogenous Adirondack tradition. Rather, fibers from the several constituent traditions have become woven into two main strands: elite and vernacular. Generally the elite or "high style" Adirondack subculture is Yorker in origin whereas the vernacular is Yankee and Habitant.[1]

Historically anglophile, conservative, and conservationist, Yorkers adopted English poets' Romantic reverence of Nature. The Hudson Valley elite of the nineteenth century contrived artful "wilderness" gardens on their estates, embellished with rustic follies. In contrast, as Perry Miller observed, "Anyone who knows the New England peasantry—whom we never call peasants but always "natives"—knows that you can never get an authentic Vermont farmer to admire the view."[2] The Adirondacks were settled in the early nineteenth century largely by Vermonters, followed shortly by French-Canadians. Trees were for felling, woods for clearing.

Because the public far beyond the region identifies rustic buildings and furnishings with the Adirondacks, and because these artifacts intentionally appear naïve, those unfamiliar with the subcultures of the region may equate Adirondack rusticity with folksiness. To the contrary, rusticity has been cultivated by an elite that has been largely alien to the region. Their camps were consciously theatrical. Some rustic buildings and furnishings of the Adirondacks do indeed qualify as art, but they should not be mistaken as folk art.

The Hudson River, originating on Mt. Marcy, the region's highest peak, has connected the Adirondacks historically as well as geographically to New York City. Yorkers, coming up the stream into the mountains, have brought an elite culture that has been cosmopolitan. One of the great patrons of rustic architecture, William West Durant, was educated as a youngster in England, and as a young man on the continent. He knew naturalistic English landscape art, and experienced the Swiss-German alpine mystique. Durant brought to the region an educated appreciation for the European Romantic tradition and a cultivated taste for inventive craft. Another Great Camper, Robert C. Pruyn, likewise a Yorker, but of old Dutch lineage, as a youth had lived in Japan, where his father was President Lincoln's ambassador. Pruyn retained a life-long appreciation for Japanese culture, integrating in creative synthesis Buddhist iconography, villas and log treasure houses of Japan, and Adirondack lumber camps. Elite Yorker clients engaged accomplished architects from New York City, as well as skilled local craftsmen. The synthesis of elite and vernacular models, representing European, Asian, and American ideals, resulted in a regional school of design that was distinctive. The Adirondack rustic style was both *gemütlich* and *shibui*. It integrated the cozy chalet and the elegant tea house—as well as the rugged lumber camp.

The Adirondack rustic villa is best appreciated in context of what affluent Americans were building elsewhere in the late nineteenth century. Compared with florid showplaces of the period that lined suburban avenues and resort waterfronts elsewhere, the Adirondack rustic villa is remarkable for its divergent aesthetic. Its secluded primitivism was antithetical to palatial display and chateauesque grandeur. The naïveté of the woodsman was contrary to the knowing stylism of the academy.

The rustic style was not invented in the Adirondacks. What is uniquely Adirondack is something else. There was no Japanese equivalent, no European or American model, for that remarkable invention of the Adirondacks: the rustic log villa.

The painter Alan Gussow, in his beautiful book *A Sense of Place: The Artist and the American Land,* observed a growing consciousness not only of environmental degradation, but also loss of place.[3] The environment, he noted, "sustains our bodies. But as humans we also require support for our spirits." Sense of place is appreciation of how a locale "has been claimed by feelings."

The Adirondacks are more than a geological and geographical notion. The Adirondacks have acquired a cultural identity. They have been "claimed by feelings," enriched by a remarkable regional literature, art, and architecture. As much or more than major works enshrined in museums and canonized in libraries, the feelings that have made the Adirondacks a special place may be most intense about that quintessential Adirondack work-of-art-in-progress, the "camp."

Preface

THIS BOOK looks at Adirondack camps in all their variety, generally between 1850 and 1950, and in chronological order, beginning with improvised shanties and cabins in chapters 1–4 that signified a region without boundaries, where people roamed and even settled outside towns without title and little or no opposition. This freedom changed in the 1870s as the public, encouraged by the prospect of rail travel and cheap land, bought large tracts with forests and lakes and called them preserves. A state law passed in 1871 gave owners, including clubs, the right to post the land and prevent trespass on it. Land and the formation of preserves and clubs is examined in chapters 5–6.

The remainder of the book looks at the camps built for these newcomers, the majority of whom came as families and were from the city, setting in place the dynamic that prevails to the present day, that of Adirondack resident and the camp owner who pays taxes like the resident but resides somewhere else. Chapter 7 identifies a few early efforts at gentrifying the log cabin, chiefly at Camp Pine Knot on Raquette Lake and in the first camp buildings on Brandreth Lake. These transitional camps are followed by an examination of architect-designed camps, in chapters 8 through 12, called Decorous Camps by the author in preference to Great Camp, the limitations of which are discussed in Appendix A.

The idea underlying the Decorous Camp as an enclave designed and built pretty much at one moment in time was expressed almost simultaneously at two camps, Santanoni and Nehasane, in 1892–93. Both camps were designed by the same architect, Robert H. Robertson, a New York City architect with family ties to the iron mine and smelter at Tahawus. There followed a succession of camps, three by William West Durant, each with its principal camp buildings and service dependencies and a farm for a supply of fresh food in summer and enough left over for the caretaker and his wife and family, and perhaps a few employees, in winter.

A boom in the construction of decorous camps started in the late 1890s and continued into the 1920s. If the Adirondacks lacked Newport's social cachet at this time, it was only because its fashionable people vacationed in camps and clubs in a region into which six Rhode Islands would fit with room left over for a third Newport. This world of fast boats and endless summers came to an end with the Crash of 1929 and the decade-long depression after it.

Chapter 12 focuses on one camp, Kamp Kill Kare, where the author and his wife were guests in 1979 at what was ostensibly an informal gathering of former students and colleagues of Tony and Bea Garvan; in actuality, it was Tony's farewell to the camp where he had been born, upstairs in the Boathouse with a physician in residence, and where he had spent many summers and a few winter visits as a boy and young man. His mother had died the year before, and the camp was on the market along with other properties, and the goodbye for the group—historians all of them—was to the style of life that had passed with her.

The importance of Kill Kare—the reason for giving it a chapter of its own—lies in its marriage of vernacular building and formal architecture, of native builders and trained architects. Kamp Kill Kare was not unique in this respect, but what is notable was the broad canvas on which rustic detailing and stone work were expressed or played out. Kill Kare did something done by few other camps in the Adirondacks—it was visionary, not so much in the sense of looking to the future as in suggesting that designers and architects have far to go before they exhaust the possibilities of an authentic rustic art.

Finally, familiarity with a lake and the camps on it can embrace three generations in one family, and it is from this group that criticism of neglect of their beloved place can be expected. The author concedes their claims, and apologizes for his oversights, not just of their camp but perhaps of a neighbor, or, indeed, of constellations of deserving camps on any of hundreds of lakes. He asks that critics see the book as he did, as a beginning and a foundation for further work, and not the last word in our understanding of Adirondack camps.

Acknowledgments

THIS BOOK contains written and visual material the author began accumulating in 1972–1973, when Marcia Smith, the first librarian at the Adirondack Museum, introduced him to a few camps she knew from driving the region's back roads in an effort to wheedle items for the research library she was developing at the new regional history museum at Blue Mountain Lake, N.Y. Ms. Smith is no longer alive, as might be expected in a project twenty-five years in the making; but alive or deceased makes no difference for those who contributed to this book and others like it. The author thanks to all, but with the disclaimer that the name of a person does not imply their approval of what he has written.

At the Adirondack Museum: Jacqueline Day, director; Jerold Pepper, librarian, Tracy Meehan, collections manager; James Meehan, historic photographs. Editor for Syracuse University Press was Alice Wolf Gilborn, who also is editor of publications for the museum. I would like to thank Robert R. Worth for his support and editorial help, and Richard W. Longstreth and Paul Malo for their comments. *Furthermore . . . ,* a publication program of the J. M. Kaplan Fund, made a grant to Syracuse University Press. Thanks to Joan K. Davidson, Fund president, for her confidence and her long-standing interest in New York's cultural heritage.

The strength of the museum's holdings owes much to the museum's early years, beginning with the book *Township 34,* written by Harold K. Hochschild and published by him in 1951. Containing personalities, events, and illustrations of artifacts later exhibited at the Adirondack Museum, the book's credibility induced Adirondack residents, camp owners, and their descendants to contribute Adirondackana to the new museum, which opened to the public in 1957. An instance were members of the Durant family who severally donated materials relating to the family's camps and business interests in the Adirondacks. Some of these documents had been consulted by Mr. Hochschild in the 1930s and perhaps earlier, in anticipation of a book; and others drifted into the museum from employees and the dead files of law firms. Entries under "Durant" in the index will give the reader an idea of the importance of these papers to this book, and two other books by the author, *Durant: The Fortunes and Woodland Camps of a Family in the Adirondacks* (1981), and *Adirondack Furniture and the Rustic Tradition* (1987).

The following persons, listed alphabetically by organization or family, also helped in the preparation of this book: Steven Engelhart, Adirondack Architectural Heritage (AARCH). Edward Comstock, Jr., of the Adirondack League Club, as well as Mr. and Mrs. J. Mabon Childs, Mr. and Mrs. Arthur B. Lawrence, David C. Squier, Mark C. Webster, the late Barton A. Cummins, also of the A.L.C., and members of the Hochschild family, including the late Lynn H. Boillot.

Thanks as well to: Harriet Barlow, Blue Mountain Center, Eagle Nest Park. Franklin B. Brandreth, Eleanor Brandreth Wunderlich and the various members of the Potter and McAlpin families, Brandreth Park Association. Joseph K. Pierson and George C. Fuge, Cortland College Camps (Camp Pine Knot). Richard Nason, Finch Pruyn and Co. and Bruce Kirkpatrick, Gooley Club. Peter Benson, Ro Woodard, and Julie Fevreau Schwartz, Eagle Island (Girl Scout) Camp. Raymond D. Masters, Huntington Wildlife Forest and Newcomb Historical Society. Mrs. E. N. Asiel, Mr. and Mrs. Robert Friedman, as well as Basil Cheney, Kildare Club. Mrs. Edward S. Litchfield, and Pieter Litchfield, as well as Edward McMahon, Jr., Litchfield Park. Leila Fosburgh Wilson, John E. Olsen, Sherman Gray, and the late Mr. and Mrs. E. I. du Pont, North Woods Club. Katie Case, Putnam Camp. Mr. and Mrs. Peter B. Read and Curtis S. Read, Read (Three Star) Camp. Beverly Bridger, Sagamore Conference Center. Michele Tucker and Barbara Parnass, Saranac Lake Free Library. Carolyn A. Davis, Syracuse University Library. Ronald H. DeLair, Wareham DeLair Architects. Dr. Howard Kirschenbaum and Lyn Witte, White Pine Camp. Robert Perkins, George Rehm, and Kenneth Gochnaur, Young Life–Saranac Village.

The following individuals: David Ackermann, Winthrop Aldrich, Mr. and Mrs. Mark Barlow, Ralph Bennett, Mr. and Mrs. Thomas T. Bissell, Mrs. Morison Garrett Brigham, Sarah Cohen, George Canon, Thomas and Lisa Chapin, Arthur M. Crocker, Mrs. J. Richardson Dilworth and the late J. Richardson Dilworth, Mr. and Mrs. William Distin, Jr., Robert Engel, Richard Fay, Dr. and Mrs. Robert F. Fisher, Mrs. Bea Garvan and the late Dr. Anthony N. B. Garvan, Robert T. Gates, Barbara Glaser, Karen Halverson, Dr. and Mrs. George G. Hart, Janet Hosley, Mary B. Hotaling, Mrs. William H. Hudnut, Jr., Harry A. Inman, George L. Jacques, Dr. Mark C. Johnson, Mr. and Mrs. George D. Kirkham, Mr. Walter Kirkham, Hon. Mary Ann Krupsak, Peter and Rosine Lemon, Richard Linke, Coy Ludwig, Dr. Karen Lux, Ann Mallinkrodt, Mr. and Mrs. Paul Maloney, Mr. and Mrs. Anthony Moro, Mr. and Mrs. Gerhard Neumaier, Ms. Tam Nevil, Robin Pell, Mrs. James A. Perkins, Edith Pilcher, Ian M. G. Quimby, Mr. and Mrs. Whitelaw Reid, David Fitch Remington, Mrs. Lewis Spence, John W. Stock, James Swedberg, Dr. Philip G. Terrie, Ms. Dorothy Triesmann, Norman VanValkenburgh, Mr. and Mrs. Carter Walker, J. Watson Webb, Samuel Webb, Jr., Sidney S. Whelan, Jr., Mrs. C. V. Whitney and the late Cornelius Vanderbilt Whitney, Mr. and Mrs. Richard Winn, Hon. Dana Winslow, Mr. and Mrs. Richard Youngken.

INTRODUCTION

Camp—E Pluribus Unum

CAMP is a *place* more than it is a cabin or tent. People said to be in camp are sojourners who stay a day or a week or even a summer but in time move on for another destination or to resume a workaday life at home. War and peace each claim a part of the camp dating from pre-history times when tribes lived in camps to hunt and fish and perhaps cultivate and graze their cattle and sheep before moving on to fresher territory and pastures elsewhere. Warriors left women, children, and old men in camps while they marauded afield and, incidentally, spawned overnight camps.

Agriculture and the appearance of towns and cities in biblical times, which presupposed pacification of the greater countryside, introduced recreational camps for those who could afford a "retreat" from the noise and pestilence of the city. Native

Kickapoo mat house of bark and saplings, late nineteenth century, Illinois. Photograph courtesy Smithsonian Institution National Anthropological Archives.

Americans migrated in summer from lower elevations to the Adirondacks where cooler temperatures, fresh game, and berries were found. Seasonal migrations were vacations of a sort, as obligatory as they were: shepherds took sheep, goats, and cattle to greener pastures on mountain slopes in spring or summer, staying in huts. Laplanders followed reindeer in their migrations and occupied tents.

Breaking the daily round of work has been very nearly universal, festival days for the poor being brief substitutes for the longer holidays of the better-off and privileged. Sometimes the journey from one place to another was largely symbolic, such as sleeping on a porch instead of a bedroom, or cooking in a summer kitchen, or perhaps moving the stove under the house, in order to keep the house cool in hot weather.

Adirondack residents did not abstain from Adirondack vacations: often they had, away from their homes in town, cabins or cottages where they stayed, occasionally renting to city people in summer or to hunters in fall. Outsiders might perceive a house in town and cabin a few miles distant both to be vacation homes. And so they were, since the Adirondack resident moved to one to rent the other, perhaps occupying the cabin in deer season when things were quieter. In these ways, vacationing is a state of mind as much as it is a substitute of one life for another.

In ancient Rome the *campus martius* was a level field where military drills and athletic games were conducted, sport being both a substitute for battle and preparation for it. (Definitions are derived from *The Compact Edition of the Oxford English Dictionary.*)[1] "Encampment" captures the dual meanings of camp as an amorphous staging place for people on the one hand and the buildings and materiel needed for their occupants' support on the other, culminating in some ultimate or final test,

During the long siege of Petersburg, Va., in 1864–5, engineers from New York used sapling rods and log slabs with the bark still on for headquarters buildings like these, as well as for a church with steeple. Notice the cribbed chimneys and attached columns of the two buildings to the right in this photograph taken by Timothy O'Sullivan, March 5, 1865. Collection of the Library of Congress.

Bungalow, near Lake Okara, Thendara, N.Y., H. Van Buren Mogonigle, architect. This was one of a number of cottages allusively Japanese in style, in a real estate development of c. 1919. Photograph by Craig Gilborn, 1998.

competition in the form of battle or its substitute, games, or a demonstration of one's personal best performance. The word has a kinship to the German "kampf" and Scandinavian "kamp," both places of combat. The word "champion" is derived from "camp."

Camp Dudley, formed in 1881 and the oldest summer camp for youths in America, initiated boys to the trials of manhood as a team and individual effort. Located on a bluff above Lake Champlain, a few miles south of the Adirondack town of Westport, N.Y., Dudley has seen its campers serve in every American conflict in the twentieth century. Like other summer camps, Dudley has harbored a peculiarly American contradiction between personal expression and group discipline: self-reliance in the outdoors was secondary to instilling team spirit among boys and young men, introducing them to the regimen they would find in the adult world. This included competition and even combat, which takes us back to camps as grounds where men stay while they train, compete, hold a strategic location, or wait out the winter or for orders to move on. Strings of forts in the valley between Montreal and Albany were fortified camps—garrisons—variously held by the French, English, and Americans. Tens of thousands of Americans got their first taste of military life at boot camps in the twentieth century.

The camp is impermanent and bears its mortality like the summers which were its reason for being. The word "cabin" derives from the French "cabane," though

English also has a counterpart in "cabana," meaning a temporary shelter of slight materials. E. B. White, in an essay whose title the author now forgets, said of an abandoned camp in the late 1930s that it had the "faintly disreputable air which pervades any woodland rendezvous where the buildings stand unoccupied for most of the year, attracting woodpeckers, sneak thieves, and lovers in season." As a boy, White had summered with his family on a Maine lake at a cabin owned by a farmer in whose farmhouse they ate their meals. These summers were "infinitely precious and worth saving" in their "jollity and peace and goodness," he wrote in a second essay, of August, 1941, when he was sure that America would enter the war against Germany.[2]

"Bungalow" is an Anglicized term from India referring to a one-story house enclosed by a veranda for shade, catching breezes, and fending off monsoon rains in hot, sultry Bengal. The earliest printed reference in English to bungalow is dated 1676: "It was thought fitt . . . to set up Bungales or Hovells," which suggests temporary shelter. The word came into wide use by 1900 and generally meant a smaller house in which bedrooms were on the first floor with the living room, with one or two bedrooms above if there was a second floor. Writers applied the word to so many kinds of houses, including quite large residences, as to render it useless.[3] For example, the defining element of the bungalow was the veranda or porch, which is why the type was adopted in vacation places in the United States and Canada. But the porch disappears altogether in picturesque tourist cabins after the First World War.

The "hut" was a structure of rude construction, as were "shack," "hutch," and the more pejorative "hovel." Military men expected to bivouac in huts for the winter. The expedition led by Meriwether Lewis and William Clark, of 1803 to the fall of 1806, included three winterings-over, the first in St. Louis and the others in unexplored territory in the northwest. There the party of about twenty-two was forced into camp between December and the spring melt in April or May when conditions allowed them to move once again. The two men, Lewis and Clark, were friends who knew what all army officers knew, that their winter camp must be in a place with water and game, which meant it should be close to an Indian village. Among the trade items and provisions, which were carried by wagon and boat to St. Louis and from there up the Missouri River, over the Rocky Mountains and down the Columbia River to the Pacific, was an iron stove. The expedition lived off the land and, as snow approached, settled for the winter in fortified huts near Indian villages, where they obtained guides—one of whom, Sacagawea, was a woman—and even food when the Indians themselves were going hungry.[4]

The word "shed," meaning an attachment to a main building or a dependency nearby, was derived from the Old English "sced," which meant shade or shelter. The shed might be open on one or all sides, or it might be enclosed, but its defining feature is a roof that slants from front to back—a "shed roof"—which protects what is beneath it from rain and sun. What came to be called a "summer house" in England, a roofed shelter open on the sides, had been called, more appropriately, a "shade house" in Italy. "Pavilion" is another name for a more elaborate type of garden or park structure with sides that can be opened as, for example, with French doors off a porch, deck, or lawn.

We have saved terms with a forest identity for last. The "log cabin" hardly needs explaining, remembering that this meant log construction, even though planks, boards, and log slabs were incorporated in many or most log cabins. Shanties usually combined log walls with bark roofs. The word "shanty" is French for a forest dwelling and derives from the French "chantier," or a staging area in the woods where, according to an 1894 definition, "woodcutters assemble after their day's work." Mrs. Traill, in *Backwoods of Canada,* published in 1836, said that "The shanty is a sort of primitive hut in Canadian architecture, and is nothing more than a shed built of logs."[5]

Of all terms, "lodge" is perhaps the most apt for our purposes. The *Oxford English Dictionary* traces the word to early German, French, and English words sharing a common reference to the tree. Variant spellings in English were "loge," "logge," "luge," "lodg," and "logges," a rustic enclosure or bower being implied. The "loge" as a small box at the theater is derived from lodge, as is "box," another theatrical term, used by polite society for a small and remote shelter for hunting or fishing, as in a fishing or hunting box.

Lodge comes closest to embodying the equivalent meanings of forest, logs, and lodge—a residence in a remote place where people indulge in activities in the outdoors or always in proximity to it. Privilege seems implied in lodges from early times, albeit by a qualifying adjective, as in "a grete lodge" of 1465 and "He . . . retired . . . into a certaine forrest . . .where he hath builded two fine lodges" of 1586. The Adirondack camp or lodge was not a "country house," which in England was a pretentious and sumptuously furnished residence on an estate of hundreds to thousands of acres and maintained by dozens of workers, servants, and tenants. An exception to this is the stone Castle at Litchfield Park, which comes closer to the idea of the English country house than any other house in the Adirondack Park.

The lodge retained contradictory identities. On the one hand it was democratic, undifferentiated by considerations such as size, the quality of its furnishings, or the class of its owners or occupants. "Oh, for a lodge in some vast wilderness," a line from a poem by the eighteenth-century English poet William Cowper that was used as a motto by the North Woods Walton Club, likely was closer to a simple building in the woods, the poet seeking a haven "Where rumor of oppression and deceit . . . might never reach me more." A lodge today is construed to mean a hotel or camp of a larger and better sort in a remote or country setting, but it retains the idea that the occupants—lodgers—are there temporarily.

The frontier was a great equalizer in America, and Americans can be seen to have used language to blur very real underlying distinctions of class that did not fit comfortably with the preferred notion that one person was as good as another. Thus the sportsman or employer could indulge in familiarities that could not be reciprocated by his guide or caretaker. A "cottage" was a home for a wage earner, but it also became a euphemism among America's rich after the Civil War to distinguish one property

"Living Room Cabin," Camp Wild Air, built c. 1895, burned in 1916. The family had cabins and sleeping tents elsewhere, but met here evenings and for some meals. William R. Mead of McKim, Mead and White designed the replacement for this camp, so he may have designed this earlier building as well. Photograph, 1895. The Adirondack Museum (P11417).

from another—the home in the country as opposed to one in the city or suburb. Mrs. Merriweather Post referred to the "small cottage" she was building in Florida between 1923 and 1927, even though it would have over a hundred rooms and cost two and a half million dollars.

Locutions were code terms for insiders to set outsiders apart from themselves. At Mount Desert Island off the coast of Maine, one of America's oldest summer resorts, the distinctions were subtle but understood by old-timers high and low on the social ladder: visitors to the island were called "boarders," while camp owners were "cottagers," according to the historian Samuel Eliot Morison, a long-time cottager. A house, he said, was a permanent residence while a building without interior sheathing and plastering was called a cottage no matter how elaborate it was.[6]

By the eighteenth and nineteenth centuries, according to Clive Aslet, quoting Sir Gilbert Scott, the largest room in the manor house, called the hall, was the scene of tenants' dinners, hunt meets, and meetings related to the estate and shire.[7] This *noblesse oblige* was echoed distantly in the Adirondacks in 1899 when Lieutenant Governor Timothy Woodruff entertained political cronies from Albany at his new camp, Kamp Kill Kare. The weekend was reminiscent of the "congresses" held by Sir Robert Walpole, Prime Minister of Great Britain from 1721 to 1742, who invited his political allies to his hunting lodge, Houghton Hall, in Norfolk. The similarity ends there, for Walpole's house was a Palladian monument, while Kamp Kill Kare was a rustic camp, perfect in its way but not pretentious.

Harold and Mary Hochschild entertained men and women from many walks of life at their camp on Eagle Lake, as close to a literary salon as one would get in the Adirondacks, except for the Putnam Camp and clusters of artists, educators, and other intellectuals in Keene Valley at the turn of the century. Eagle Nest was memorable not solely for celebrities like George Kennan, Harrison Salisbury, and Norman Thomas, but for the mix of others who shared a curiosity about the world regardless of age and affiliation. These gatherings came to an end with Harold's death in 1981.

Adirondack connections to the word "camp" have a sound historical foundation. The noun "camp" means much the same today as it did a century and longer ago— it is a place in the outdoors for visiting but not residing. In camp people behave in atypical but socially sanctioned ways. When one says he or she will be "in camp," a common expression, a special place is designated, and the speaker has been set apart because going to camp is a kind of pilgrimage: being in camp partakes of ceremony and communion, the camper entering nature as an outsider and expecting to undergo some change there. That this partakes of ritual goes without saying. The hunter's skills and fortitude are rewarded by trout and venison, evidence of which are displayed on walls in camp or in the hall or study of his home in the city, as mounted trophies.

Sanctimony about camp must be balanced by knowledge that going to camp may be less ritual than license for men to drink, play cards, tell dirty stories, and behave as louts, as parodied so aptly by the lyrics to "Deer Camp." Camp buildings may enhance the experience but are secondary to the *process* of what takes place in and around the camp. While the camp is "real property," its value inheres in the transformation of body and spirit that takes place there.

Building a pretentious camp in the Adirondacks risked an accusation of poor taste and ignorance of the reason for coming to its lakes and forests in the first place. The so-called great camp, or, as is preferred here, the decorous and trophy camp, was a

A few "surprise dens" were built in city and suburban houses, so this amusing illustration, from D. C. Beard's book Shelters, Shacks and Shanties, *first published in 1914, was not pure fantasy. Outside the door is a male as anemic as the neoclassical interior, but see the transformation when he enters the den.*

phenomenon of the 1890s and after. These later camps were singled out by journalists delighted to expose the irony of an outdoor life that depended on cooks and servants. What they often did not see was that despite the luxuries, character and acumen counted for more than money in the bank in the Adirondacks. That was why the Adirondack guide was deemed the equal of the millionaire, and the guide's shanty qualitatively equal to the rich man's lodge. As all men are equal in the sight of God, so all camps were equal in the sight of men.

Adirondack camps that had gotten too big or civilized, in part because of the brief custom of Victorian and post-Victorian families for large staffs of indoor and outdoor help, spun off remoter camps where men and women might reclaim the simple life that had brought them or their parents to the Adirondacks in the first place. There were many of these camps-away-from-camp, at the Adirondack League Club and Ausable Club, where log cabins were retreats from the clubhouse and camp where life too much resembled the life of house and country club back home. Outlying cabins or cottages were also built apart from the main lodges on preserves at Nehasane, Whitney Park, and Litchfield Park.

The human drive to improve and tame wilderness and domesticate the camp is universal, as illustrated by experiences from ancient Rome to the Versailles of pre-Revolutionary France. Martin Ives could find little to criticize at the Prospect House on Blue Mountain Lake except that it had "too much civilization." Writing of a visit about 1898, he added that "One has but to shut his eyes to imagine that he is in Newport or Saratoga" because the architecture and services were so much alike.[8]

But seclusion is as much an idea as it is a condition arising from the people and things around them. Seclusion is both a social and literary convention, the latter giving rise to a body of imaginative literature known as *belles lettres,* often originated by a person observing past and present from the vantage of new or fresh surroundings. Moving to his summer-house from his villa led Pliny the Younger (A.D. 62–113) to fancy he was "a hundred miles away from my villa," though the distance might have been a hundred yards.[9] Identical language has been used thousands of times in letters and diaries. The Prince de Lique, referring to the make-believe farm and English garden fashioned for Marie Antoinette on the grounds of the palace at Versailles, remarked that "One might believe oneself a hundred leagues from court."[10]

Indeed, backsliding seems to be a part of our humanity where seclusion and the simple life are concerned. The Roman poets and satirists Horace (65–8 B.C.) and Martial (A.D. c. 40–c. 103) advocated a return to the simple life of the *villa rustica,* the true country home, as opposed to the *villa suburbana.* Both have their counterparts in the Adirondacks, in the camps of 1875–1900 and their successors of the 1890s and after.

Adirondack Camps

Living room, Blue Mountain Lake. Built in 1924, the cottage has been renovated over the years for Richard Fay. Photograph by Peter and Rosine Lemon, 1980.

Octagonal dining room, Eagle Nest Park, Blue Mountain Lake, N.Y., 1938. William G. Distin, architect. Photograph by Craig Gilborn, 1984.

Bunk in Noah John Rondeau's small log cabin, 1920s or after. Installed at the Adirondack Museum. Photograph by Craig Gilborn, 1986.

Cottage (detail), Big Moose Lake, late nineteenth century. This part of the Adirondacks utilized palisade log construction, in which exterior walls were half-logs stood on end, bark-covered on the outside and smooth inside. Photograph by Craig Gilborn, 1999.

Great Hall, Wonundra (The Point), Upper Saranac Lake, 1933. William G. Distin, architect. Photograph by Craig Gilborn, 1982.

Living room, Bull Cottage, c. 1910. Gallery displays rustic furniture in a cottage adaptively restored for public access at the Adirondack Museum. Photograph by Craig Gilborn, 1987.

Open Camp, watercolor, artist unknown, 1888. Adirondack Museum (88.113). Photograph courtesy of the Adirondack Museum, Eric Borg, photographer.

"Bishop's Palace," Camp Wild Air, Upper St. Regis Lake, c. 1895. The Whitelaw Reid family named the small cottage for Episcopal clerics who sometimes stayed in it. Photograph by Craig Gilborn, 1989.

Residence for caretaker and family, Sagamore Lodge, Raquette Lake, N.Y., by 1915. It is called "The Chalet" by Sagamore Lodge and Conference Center. Photograph by Craig Gilborn, 1982.

Mrs. T. C. Durant's cabin, left, c. 1876, and Nursery (Annex), built c. 1890, Camp Pine Knot. The photograph was taken before the fire of 1983 that destroyed the cabins. Photograph by Craig Gilborn, 1981.

Log cabins, Utowana Lake, 1930s and after. Built by George Baekeland. Photograph by Craig Gilborn, 1977.

"A Sportsman's Favorite Things," Adirondack Museum. The chair was made c. 1875 by Reuben Cary for Benjamin Brandreth (see page 26). Photograph by Craig Gilborn, 1981.

Cottage interior, before 1915, part of Blue Mountain House (hotel), now the site of the Adirondack Museum. The cottage was used as a painting studio by Gustav Wiegand. Photograph by Craig Gilborn, 1981.

Minnewawa, Blue Mountain Lake, c. 1913. C. E. Schermerhorn, architect, Philadelphia. Built for Clifton Maloney, the cottage is still in the Maloney family. Photograph by Craig Gilborn, 1999.

Moodie Cottage, one of a number of summer cottages built on the hill overlooking Blue Mountain House, 1900–1915, adaptively restored by the Adirondack Museum.

Bedroom, Camp As You Like It, Brandreth Lake, 1890s. Photograph by Karen Halverson, 1986.

Lodge, Long Lake, c. 1904. Two chalet-like cottages were built for Dr. Arpad Gerster, one on Raquette Lake in the 1880s and a later one, shown here, called Kwenogamac. Photograph by Craig Gilborn, 1999.

I love the rough Log Cabin—
It tells of olden time,
When a hardy and honest class
Of freemen in their prime,
First left their father's peaceful home,
Where all was joy and rest,
With axes on their shoulders,
And sallied to the West.

—*The Log Cabin Song-Book*, 1840

CHAPTER I

The Log Cabin as American Symbol

THE STRENGTH of the log cabin as an American symbol lay in the prevalence of log construction on the frontier and in backcountry regions of states in the East. The attributes of a frontier could be found in the Adirondacks in the nineteenth century, including log cabins and clusters of humanity in towns surrounded by a sea of forest. The Adirondack region, including Tug Hill to the west, is at the western end of a largely unbroken forest that covers more than half of Maine, much of northern New Hampshire and Vermont, and about a quarter of New York.

In eastern American cities and towns, the log cabin was becoming an object of curiosity and antiquarian interest in what was now part of the past—of one's grandparents or parents but not of one's own memory. An artifact of a vanishing way of life in settled parts of the American East, the log cabin's potency was fed by a stream of articles and illustrations in the popular press—in periodicals and books, but also by printmakers like Currier and Ives whose tinted lithographs of paintings were framed and hung on home and office walls, and by stereoscopic photographs of the same period, in the 1850s and after.

Log dwellings were temporary residences for families looking for a better life; for others, however, the cabin was a commentary on the impoverishment within. Whichever, as the first rung up the ladder to a better life or as a trap of perpetual poverty, the log cabin represented risk and a hardscrabble life that few would wish for themselves. For brief stays, however, the log cabin in a clearing at the edge of a lake or stream was worth the insect bites, chill, and limited diet in return for solitude, beauty, and a quest for game. Austerity of this kind was not the wolf at the door, but it was salutary to body and spirit and was deemed worth revisiting for all those reasons adduced by Henry David Thoreau in *Walden*.

The accessibility of log construction contributed to its success as a symbol for frontier living. Readers need only consult their limited skills to realize, as their colonial and pioneer predecessors frequently discovered from experience, and as all children try doing at least once, that serviceable shelter can be built by anyone who has an axe or bucksaw and nothing else. Confronted with an abundance of trees and land that needed clearing, settlers dealt with their predicament the only way they could—they cut and limbed trees, stacked the logs, and filled spaces with a mix of moss and clay or mud.

These were not log houses that reflect a tradition of log construction from Europe, principally of German and Swedish influences; they were, more often, thrown up, the urgency being clearing the ground and seeding it and getting a roof overhead by early summer and harvesting the crops and sealing the walls before the first frosts. These were subsistence shelters, as much shanty as log cabin, often leaking rain and drafty in a wind, and requiring occupants to continuously plug up holes in the roof or in walls.

All Americans were putative log cabin builders, and each had a claim to the myth surrounding the log cabin about self-reliance and getting a new lease on life. Reality on the frontier and in hinterlands like the Adirondacks refreshed the myth, which has hardly lost any of its appeal to judge by the build-your-own log cabin articles and books that have appeared to the present day, ratifying an existing dream more than they signified the birth of a new one. The bibliography at the back of this book is far from complete, but it is evidence that the log cabin still lives in the minds of many Americans.

America had other symbols, in Columbia and Uncle Sam, each a personification, the former a likeness of a Roman goddess and the other a roguish man with a beard and stovepipe hat, an outgrowth of the War of 1812 and the American counterpart to John Bull as representative of England. But the log cabin, which was to appear perhaps as early as the 1830s in connection with Andrew "Old Hickory" Jackson, was familiar where trees grew, which in America was every place east of the Mississippi and most of what lay west of it. Rooted in the American experience, the cabin was seized by the press and campaign managers for politicians as a symbol of an ideal American character that was manly, honest, and fair-minded.

The cabin was democratic, sheltering people in all walks, the rich as well as poor. It was the farmer's first abode, and home in the gold fields of California and Colorado. It conformed nicely with the view held by many that vacations should not be an extension of one's home in another place but a wholesome and revitalizing alternative in proximity to nature. The resort at White Sulfur Springs in West Virginia, which is one of the oldest spas in America, had a lawn at the edges of which were cabins of squared and whitewashed logs. They gave the grounds an "air of a rural village," according to J. R. Paulding, in *Letters from the South,* published in 1835.[1]

About this time, in the 1830s, residents of the Catskill Mountains who traditionally supported themselves by farming and cutting trees for lumber and bark for tanning hides were picking up extra cash by renting to summer boarders. They opened their homes and log cabins to guests, and soon some found themselves in the hotel business. Tourists rather than trees became the chief cash crop.[2] The Adirondacks witnessed a similar sequence of events at about the same time, although tourism there augmented and did not replace logging.

Adirondack loggers and guides and especially their wives opened their homes to boarders and found it hard work but a source of hard cash as well. Jonathan Bellows was a farmer who built and kept a hotel on Chateaugay Lake. His log house—likely the first on the property—appears in a painting of 1854 that was reproduced two years later as a lithograph by Currier and Ives. Titled "Arguing the Point—Settling the Presidency," the scene shows three men in a political discussion. The men appear deaf to the call to dinner by Sophrone Thurber, a hired girl.[3]

One of the earliest depictions of the log cabin as a symbol is the engraving "The Beginning and Completion of an American Settlement or Farm," published in London in 1761 from a design by artist Thomas Pownall. Settlement's first phase is shown in the farm still being cleared by a pioneer farmer. Trees from the forest around the farm have been cut in the sawmill powered by the stream and are ready as lumber for shipping to a distant buyer in a boat like the one in the distance. The scene is a visual metaphor on mercantilist ideas about trade and the expansion of markets and the reward of personal effort as illustrated by the fine mansion on the hill.

The log cabin as the quintessential American political symbol appeared in the campaign between William Henry Harrison and the incumbent, Martin Van Buren. Sometimes called the "Log Cabin Campaign," the cabin's role materialized when one

Lithograph, hand-colored, by N. Currier, 1855, after the painting by A. F. Tait, Arguing the Point— Settling the Presidency, *1854. Tait depicted a log cabin instead of the newer hotel building nearby because the log cabin was identified with democracy. Mr. Bellows, the owner, stands between two men. The locale is Lower Chateaugay Lake. The Adirondack Museum (65.042).*

of Van Buren's journalist supporters speculated that Harrison would be happy if he spent his days in a log cabin drinking hard cider and collecting his government pension. Harrison had been an army officer in the Old Northwest Territory for eight years, and he had held offices there and in Washington as a congressman and then a senator from Ohio. Rather than deny his frontier identity, his campaign turned it to advantage, soon distributing miniature log cabins and setting new words to old tunes. Among the lyrics sung at rallies in support of Harrison was one set to the tune of "Old Lang Syne."

> Should good old cider be despised,
> And ne'er regarded more?
> Should plain log cabins be despised
> Our fathers built of yore?

Harrison, raised and educated in Virginia, was a member of the Virginia aristocracy. His grandfather built the house at Berkeley Plantation in 1724, and his father was in the House of Burgesses in Williamsburg. This history was lost on the majority of voters, who saw Harrison's Ohio homestead, on which there may or may not have been a log cabin, as sufficient to elect him in 1840, when a record 80 percent of eligible men voted, giving him 234 electoral votes to just sixty for Van Buren.

Abraham Lincoln's boyhood in a log cabin and his election in 1861 and 1864 sealed the log cabin as an icon of the American experience. The humble but sturdy home of logs imparted human virtues to "Honest Abe," enabling him to lead a nation at war with itself. The Lincoln legend is as durable as that of the log cabin on which it

The origin of the log cabin as a symbol of the American experience may be said to begin with this engraving of 1761 after a design by Thomas Pownall, a British administrator in New York and Massachusetts between 1753 and 1760. The title—A design to represent the beginning and completion of an American Settlement or Farm—*traces the rags-to-riches myth in which the pioneer's sacrifice will be rewarded by a fine mansion and farm like the one in the distance. Courtesy of The New-York Historical Society.*

Henry David Thoreau based his book Walden on his "experiment," in which he built a one-room cabin above Walden Pond and lived in it for twenty-five months in 1845–46, keeping a journal that he used for the book that was published in 1854. The book has inspired thousands of others to follow his example, including Karl Henck (p. 19). A replica of Thoreau's "house," based on a small and unclear woodcut, was once sold in kit form. This one, in the state park near Walden Pond, is likely too tidy, since Thoreau boasted that he talked an Irish worker on the railroad into selling his "shanty" for $4.25, salvaging what was not too rotten. Photograph by Craig Gilborn, 1995.

is partly founded. The dedication of *The Real Log Cabin*—"To Abraham Lincoln, Who Has Enriched the Log Cabin in the Hearts of His People"—was written in 1928 by Chilson D. Aldrich, a professional architect who designed log houses for a factory in Minnesota where they were manufactured.[4] The log cabin touched the American soul: buying land, and cutting trees and using them for building a home in the clearing, came as close to sacred as one could get.

Henry David Thoreau gave a hard-headed assessment of plain habitations like the one he built from boards scavenged from a hut he purchased from the occupants, a poor family ready to move on. One room with fireplace and bed, table for writing and eating, and a chair, it met his basic needs during his "experiment," in which he devoted himself to a study of nature and writing between July 4, 1845, and September 6, 1847, living only partly in seclusion since he often ventured into Concord a mile or so away for visits and occasional meals.

Thoreau understood why artists were attracted to cabins and other unpretentious habitations: "The most interesting dwellings in this country, as the painter knows, are the most unpretending, humble log huts and cottages of the poor commonly." He refuses to patronize the occupants by treating the houses of the poor as if they were props on a stage: it is, he says, "the life of the inhabitants whose shells they are, and not a peculiarity of their surfaces merely, which makes them *picturesque*." Thoreau's moral clarity held the log cabin to be more than the sum of its visual qualities; it was, instead, an expression of the dignity of its inhabitants.[5]

Some American observers thought that architects in America might turn to log construction for a style closer to America than Europe. Clarence Cook, a critic who advocated the establishment of public parks, echoing the ideas of A. J. Downing, his brother-in-law, thought the "Western log hut" deserved attention from American architects so they might develop from it a "more refined and graceful form."[6]

"Birds Do Not Sing in Caves"

Practicing what he preached, Henry David Thoreau spent twenty-six months in a one-room house he built on a site a couple of hundred feet from Walden Pond. From this elevated spot, he observed nature and kept notes in a journal, later using them as the basis for his book *Walden*, an American classic of personal independence from a society he found to be mindlessly acquisitive. Not a recluse, he referred to his stay on the pond as an "experiment."

"From the cave we have advanced to the roofs of palm leaves, of bark and bough, of linen woven and stretched, of grass and straw, of boards and shingle, of stones and tile. At last, we know not what it is to live in the open air, and our lives are more domestic in more senses than we think. From the hearth is a great distance. It would be well, perhaps, if we were to spend more of our days and nights without any obstruction between us and the celestial bodies, if the poet did not speak so much from under a roof, or the saint dwell there so long. Birds do not sing in caves."

The dream of building a cabin and living in it in the woods did not originate with Thoreau's book, but its ideas were so convincing at several levels as to make it the best of all back-to-nature books.

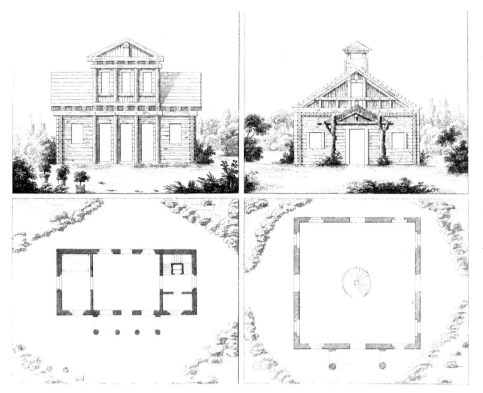

Calvert Vaux, a partner of Downing's who joined Frederick Law Olmsted in planning Central Park, thought that a log house "might be raised in character . . . without sacrificing in any way its primitive expression." Despite this statement, which appeared in *Villas and Cottages,* published in 1857, Vaux offered no credible example of what he meant. Illustrated was a lone building, a "simple log house" intended for "a well-to-do settler and his family," with a "rustic outbuilding." His inability to demonstrate a new rustic style was a failing among other architects who were aware of log construction and its appropriateness to a frontier nation but found it impossible to translate that into designs that would meet Clarence Cook's call for a more refined and graceful form.

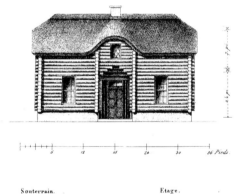

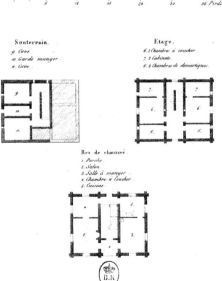

Critics hoped America would produce a log style expressive of its frontier heritage. A lodge of logs built about 1837 above a gorge of the Genesee River, shown here in a pencil sketch by Thomas Cole in 1839, came closest to fulfilling that vision. No longer standing, Hornby Lodge was a Gothic essay with a castellated tower, clustered chimneys, label moldings above windows, and six clustered columns on the entrance porch. The architect or builder did not conceal its log character, which largely dictated both plan and elevation. Courtesy of The Detroit Institute of Arts, Founders Society Purchase, William H. Murphy Fund.

Two other architects known to have made designs for log houses and houses with rustic trim were Alexander Jackson Davis and J.-J. Ramée. Davis's plan for Llewellyn Park in New Jersey, within commuting distance of Manhattan and the first planned garden community of its kind in America, included rustic detailing on houses and summer houses and other garden accessories, but he had no log houses. Ramée, who designed Union College in Schenectady, N.Y., published a design for a log house following his return to France. Cook and others looking for an exemplary American style of rustic design might have chosen a building already standing—Hornby Lodge, which was erected about 1837 at the edge of a gorge high above the Genesee River in western New York.

To artists and sophisticated travelers, log structures such as cabins, shanties, sawmills, and even corduroy roads and bridges were regarded not as intrusions on the landscape but as evidence of early human contact and travail in the wilderness. Contained in this was the paradox that the forest must be felled if commerce and civilization were, in that order, to follow. Timothy Dwight, president of Yale College, saw the change from forest to farm as a good and natural progression of steps. Seeing the man-made clearings on the slopes above Lake George, he predicted that the simple habitations visible from his boat would be replaced by "villas of opulence and refinement," thereby adding the "elegancies of art" to the "majesty of nature."[7]

Dwight's was a familiar view of a pastoral landscape of pastures and woodlots on which a mill or farm buildings might also be seen. But the generation that followed was less optimistic. Thomas Cole's paintings reveal civilizations that flowered but fell, their cities and monuments turned to moss-covered ruins. Cole, who traveled to Schroon Lake in 1837 with his wife and fellow painter Asher B. Durand and Mrs. Durand, sketched a log cabin in a clearing with forest and mountains behind. The farm occupied what Cole called the "middle landscape," a term that nicely demonstrates how artists like Cole searched diligently for fragments and scenes that they would sketch and work into finished paintings back in their studios. The cabin, which Cole placed at the focal point of a painting now at the Adirondack Museum, was less a harbinger of future development, as Dwight had predicted a generation earlier, than it was a melancholy perception of a condition in which humanity—the occupants of the log cabin—was adrift on a sea of forest and mountain; life was precarious in a lonely and enigmatic universe.

Karl Henck built this one-room cabin near Fort Ann, N.Y., in 1992, in the woods of an abandoned farm. Of college-age and from Massachusetts, he lived in it in all but the coldest weather while he worked on a larger cabin nearby. This cabin could sleep and sit two, but it was too small for two standees. Photograph by Craig Gilborn, 1993.

Bark in My Soup

The following excerpt is from "A Mountain Air," a memoir by Lewis Spence of four summers which he spent in the early 1930s at his grandfather's camp on the north shore of Upper Saranac Lake. The camp had been built in 1926 for his grandfather and is said to be standing. The passage, used with permission of Mrs. Lewis Spence, speaks of his grandfather's pride in his rustic lodge.

"But this artfully contrived rusticity that was Grandfather's loudest boast had its price: despite all the advice, concoctions, and sprays, and state forestry experts, the woodbugs got into the magnificent spruce trusses and split-pine stair treads, so that summer evenings over cribbage or dominoes were periodically punctuated by the grinding crunch of the woodbugs munching their way under the bark. There was no danger, Grandfather was assured, of the buildings collapsing in a spectacular powdery 'whoomph' of sawdust.

"But each spring when we arrived hours were spent by Oscar—Grandfather's guide—retacking the bark. Of course, the grind of those woodbugs' mandibles was an unpleasant counterpoint to Grandfather's grandiloquent explication of authentic Adirondack architecture."

Samuel H. Hammond, author of two lively books in 1854 and 1857 which envisioned the loss of the Adirondack forest, co-authored an earlier book, of 1849, with L. W. Mansfield, in which "a log house and a frame one conjoined," said to constitute an American "composite order of architecture," spells the doom of the forest. The "new sounds in the forest" tell the "old woods" that its end is near, as yet another "hardy settler puts up his cabin and makes war on the ancient trees." The woods are "pushed back" until "settlement meets settlement" and "painted houses have succeeded the log-cabins."[8]

The pace of log house construction has diminished little if at all in the twentieth century. Thousands of log houses are erected annually in the United States. The popularity of these modern log houses has much to do with their convenience and economy, since complete houses with a variety of floor plans can be purchased in kit form and assembled by the buyer or by workmen from the factory.[9] But the acceptance of log houses is a factor that has less to do with utility than with the comfort felt by Americans with the idea of living in a log house. This acceptance, for most a notion more than a tested experience, derives from a grab-bag of abstractions inculcated in Americans about self-reliance, home, and nation.

Born and bred, as many of them were, in this
wilderness, skilled in all the lore of woodcraft,
handy with the rod, superb at the paddle, modest
in demeanor and speech, honest to a proverb, they
deserve and receive the admiration of all who
make their acquaintance.

—William H. H. Murray, 1869

CHAPTER 2

Adirondack Guides and Caretakers

THEIR FAMILIARITY with the woods, as trappers, hunters, and loggers, turned woodsmen into guides for sportsmen habituated to city ways; Adirondack guides, like Dante's Virgil, escorted their clients, middle and upper class men and a few women, through the forest and across its lakes.[1] A few guides were Indian and the majority were not, but much of the guides' knowledge—for example, in the uses of peeled bark for boats, shelter, and dinner plates—had been common practice among Indians centuries before the arrival of Europeans in North America in the sixteenth century.

Forerunners of the nineteenth-century guide were scouts for contending French and British military units in the colonial period and the American Revolution. They carried messages between outposts and escorted units in their passage along the corridor formed by the Hudson River and Lake Champlain. Descendants of these early scouts found their services in demand by adventurous city dwellers who, starting about the 1820s, turned to forest and lake country as a destination in itself.

Guides were familiar with sites for camping and carries or portages on which they carried their canoes and guideboats from lake to lake. The challenge was to live off the land or the forest along the way, and it was the success and failure of this experience that would be memorable, recounted in the city and preserved in one of the growing number of periodicals and books that were outlets for this special branch of reporting—outdoor travel and sport. Men were in the care of the guide, and many returned home, to clubs and offices, full of praise for the guide or guides who had escorted, transported, and fed them in the wilds.

The guide supplied the boat and tent, as well as cooking utensils, sometimes called "camp kit" in books. The sportsman was expected to provide the provisions—pork, tea, cornmeal and other groceries, in addition to his bedding, gun, ammunition, rod and angling equipment. Much of this could be shipped ahead for the guide to hold for his arrival. Guides did most of the real labor, though clients pitched in when needed. The pay for guiding was good—three dollars a day in 1873—which was more than a logger could make in a day, according to Hallie Bond in *Boats and Boating in the Adirondacks*.[2]

OPPOSITE: The Lazy Guide, *as caricatured by Charles E. Whitehead for an article by F. S. Stallknecht in 1858. Guides were admired for resourcefulness and poise in the wilds, but a few were less than heroic.*

Log House at Head of
Third Lake, *by R. Fred
Bowdish, photographer,
Boonville, N.Y., 1869.
Perhaps the earliest photograph of sportsmen and
guides in the Adirondacks.
Deer and fish were prey year-
round at this time. The man
with hands on hips may have
been the proprietor of this
camp, and the man with
white beard and another
with a rifle on his shoulder
were clients, which leaves
heavy lifting to four guides.
The Adirondack Museum
(P28631).*

Guides who impressed their clients were employed to work at the permanent
camps that are the subject of this book. Most guides had carpentry skills, so it was
they who built many of the camps and hotels before 1900 and kept them in repair, as
well. Relationships between the client and guide and families became close when
guides became employees, exchanging independence for shelter and a small but relatively sure wage.

Professional travelers who lived from their writing and lecturing found in the
guide a rich source of anecdote for coloring their written accounts, finding a parallel
between the guide and Natty Bumppo, the fictional hero of James Fenimore Cooper
novels, who preferred the moral code of the Indians to the selfish exploitation of nature by white settlers in the Champlain valley of New York. Adirondack guides came
closest to Natty as real-life heroes.

The guide, like the log cabin, was interpreted by others, by men and women who
were outsiders and often were journalists for newspapers or periodicals back home.
The guide was praised for his many qualities, as typified by the quotation at the beginning of this chapter; he was admired for his ability to follow a deer and unerringly
return to camp, where his special skills might be displayed, in building or repairing
a lean-to, preparing tasty meals at an open fire, and telling stories. He was often admired for his modesty, laconic ways, and philosophy of life.

The guide's sportsmen-clients—Hallie Bond called them "sports" in her book
Boats and Boating in the Adirondacks—were not always duffers; some were as com-
petent in outdoor skills as their guide but needed the guide to find the game and

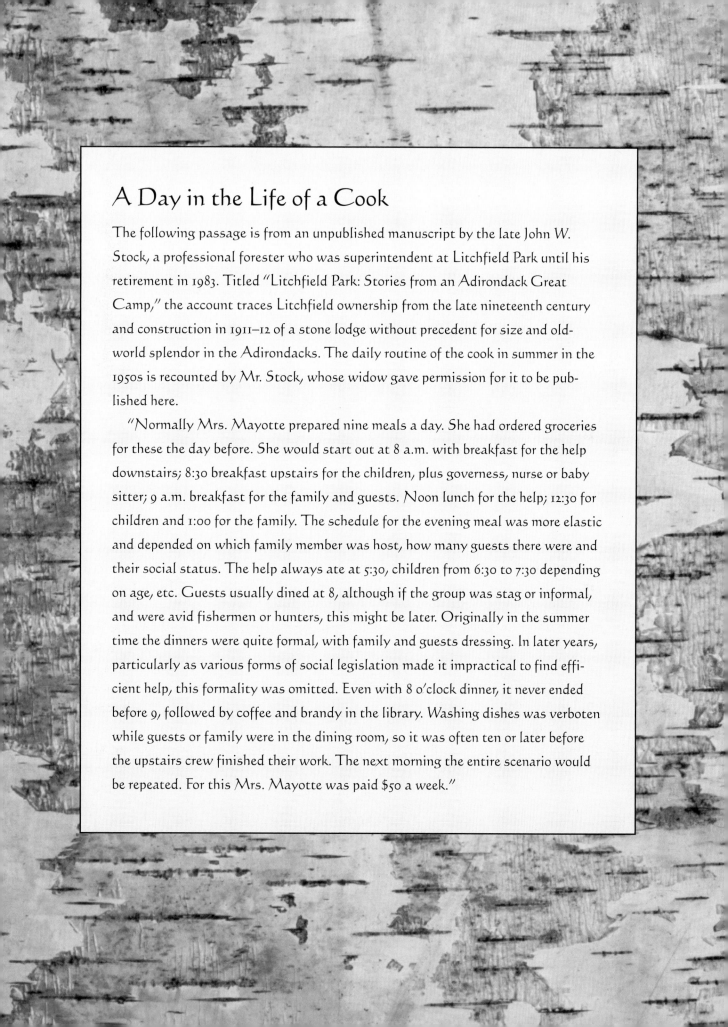

A Day in the Life of a Cook

The following passage is from an unpublished manuscript by the late John W. Stock, a professional forester who was superintendent at Litchfield Park until his retirement in 1983. Titled "Litchfield Park: Stories from an Adirondack Great Camp," the account traces Litchfield ownership from the late nineteenth century and construction in 1911–12 of a stone lodge without precedent for size and old-world splendor in the Adirondacks. The daily routine of the cook in summer in the 1950s is recounted by Mr. Stock, whose widow gave permission for it to be published here.

"Normally Mrs. Mayotte prepared nine meals a day. She had ordered groceries for these the day before. She would start out at 8 a.m. with breakfast for the help downstairs; 8:30 breakfast upstairs for the children, plus governess, nurse or baby sitter; 9 a.m. breakfast for the family and guests. Noon lunch for the help; 12:30 for children and 1:00 for the family. The schedule for the evening meal was more elastic and depended on which family member was host, how many guests there were and their social status. The help always ate at 5:30, children from 6:30 to 7:30 depending on age, etc. Guests usually dined at 8, although if the group was stag or informal, and were avid fishermen or hunters, this might be later. Originally in the summer time the dinners were quite formal, with family and guests dressing. In later years, particularly as various forms of social legislation made it impractical to find efficient help, this formality was omitted. Even with 8 o'clock dinner, it never ended before 9, followed by coffee and brandy in the library. Washing dishes was verboten while guests or family were in the dining room, so it was often ten or later before the upstairs crew finished their work. The next morning the entire scenario would be repeated. For this Mrs. Mayotte was paid $50 a week."

move expeditiously from place to place. In addition, the guide performed jobs that city men ordinarily did not want to do. An able city sport was Arthur Fitzwilliam Tait, an artist from England who opened a studio in New York but began visiting the Adirondacks when he was in his early thirties. The region offered subjects rich in anecdote and detail for patrons in the city who could pay the $50 to $200 fetched by Tait's paintings in the 1850s. He put companions, guides, and occasionally himself in paintings that he finished back in the city. Scenes of men stalking deer or resting in the woods provided reportage of the most vivid kind before the Civil War and the advent of photojournalism. Tait came by his subject matter honestly, for, like Winslow Homer, he depicted what he had done himself. A hunting knife and sheath which belonged to him, now at the Adirondack Museum, were not merely props for a painting but survival tools in the woods.

Guides were subjects and tellers of countless stories, the majority of which have vanished with the telling. Alvah Dunning, barely five feet in height, allegedly shot holes in Ned Buntline's boat, in response to which Buntline, who had served one year in prison for fomenting a riot in New York City, shot Dunning's dog at Dunning's feet.[3] Some time later, in 1879, Dunning, brandishing a weapon of some kind and telling them to "skedaddle," forced several men to retreat from Osprey Island, where they were to locate the site of a camp for Charles Durant—Camp Fairview. Dunning, who had several shanties on the island, had not been consulted. He was placated by Mrs. Thomas Clark Durant who owned Camp Pine Knot not far distant, signing a quitclaim deed in return for $100 and a like amount the year after.[4] Dunning had a beaked nose and flinty eyes and behaved like the character he appeared to be. An

Adirondackers. Brandreth Park, c. 1895. Noted guides John Plumley, third from right, and Reuben Cary, far right, were among those finding employment at Brandreth Park. The Adirondack Museum, gift of Franklin Brandreth (P41967).

etching of him was made from a sketch by Dr. Arpad Gerster, New York surgeon and camp owner. And he was photographed several times by the photographer Seneca Ray Stoddard.

"Adirondack" Murray, whose *Adventures in the Wilderness* is the source of the passage at the start of this chapter, did warn readers that there were guides to avoid—the incompetent or lazy ones, or those convinced they were smart or witty and who liked to chat.[5] Even at this early date, guides attached to hotels had a poor reputation, being less motivated than "independent" guides, whom he characterized as "quick, inventive and energetic," qualities essential to any guide.

Having cast doubt on one category of guide, Murray held the remainder as worthy of public esteem. Guides were, he said, better than most men: "a more honest, cheerful and patient class of men cannot be found the world over. . . . Bronzed and hardy, fearless of danger, eager to please, uncontaminated by the vicious habits of civilized life, they are not unworthy of the magnificent surroundings amid which they live." He listed Long Lake guides, among whom was the name of John Plumley—he spells his name "Plumbley"—who had been his guide for the incidents related in his book, which became a best-seller and led, allegedly, to the "rush to the wilderness" by "Murray's fools" the summer of its publication, in 1869. He would later eulogize Plumley, who had become a long-time employee of the Brandreth family at Brandreth Park, as "Honest John."[6]

An all-bark shanty, possibly built for men working on the survey for Verplanck Colvin sometime after 1871. The Adirondack Museum (P9581).

Lodge Run by Three Sisters

Crane Point Lodge on Blue Mountain Lake was run by three daughters of Henry C. Crane, who rarely visited it after his wife's death in 1881. Each sister had a set of chores suited to her preferences: Emily handled "general entertainment," Helen was the bookkeeper and handled accounts, and Gertrude supervised housekeeping and perhaps the kitchen. Gertrude used her savings from the hotel to buy her trousseau for her wedding to George D. Kirkham, in September 1888. Food for the lodge was raised on the farm nearby, its pasture affording a view of the lake from the road, now obscured by trees. After Mr. Crane's death in 1890, the lodge was run by the sisters and then by a brother. A business downturn hurt the hotel, and it was sold to Gertrude's husband, George D. Kirkham, about 1900. The original log house of 1875, and its addition, burned in 1926; its replacement, called Carenaught Lodge, remained a summer home and family hotel until about 1965 when it was sold and renovated.

Remnants of the farm could be seen in 1998 in a cottage, workshop, and other weathered buildings on Blue Mountain Lake, owned by the grandchildren of George and Gertrude Kirkham.

PICTORIAL GRAVURE SECTION — THE POST-STANDARD — SUNDAY JULY 4, 1920

Old-time guides. Fulton Chain of Lakes region, published in Syracuse Post-Standard, *July 4, 1920. Like most guides, these men were carpenters and helped build many camps between Old Forge and Eighth Lake. Reuben Cary, upper right, is said to be the veteran guide of the bunch. Cary is pictured on page 26. The Adirondack Museum* (P20070).

How guides came by their techniques and woodcraft is a subject of interest because the majority of Adirondack guides in the nineteenth century may be presumed to have been first generation guides, not long off the farms and out of villages of New England from which many had migrated. Some worked as loggers, in itself an education in self-reliance in the woods. Still, not all settlers and their offspring came from a forest culture, so their knowledge must have been the result of trial and error and observation, by emulating other guides, among whom the best were Indians familiar with the northern forest between Maine and the Great Lakes. An Indian whose reputation extended beyond the territory around Long Lake where he lived was Mitchell Sabattis, an Abenaki said to hear and see in the woods with, in historian Alfred Donaldson's words, "a refinement that was uncanny." He was reticent and gentle but he had "the strength and endurance of tempered steel in action."[7]

Guides were versatile at many jobs, from carpentry and kitchen cooking to felling trees and other work as members of a crew in a logging camp. Many worked at hotels and clubs, to which they became attached as house guides. Others were independent guides but gradually worked themselves into jobs at family camps as resident guide and factotum. Many stayed in what was called the "Guide House" at camps and clubs, their wives remaining at home. Some guides were caretakers at camps, a job that offered a measure of security and a measure of independence for all but the one to three months that the camp was occupied. As caretaker, the guide got a residence or an apartment for himself and his family.

The competence of the Adirondack guide is suggested in this photograph of Fred Barnes, seated, and Fred Jarvis in the boathouse at Camp Wild Air on Upper St. Regis Lake. A guide, Barnes put up all the buildings and was caretaker at the camp between 1882 and 1930 (see p. 151). Fred Jarvis ran a freight and delivery service at the time of this photograph, about 1890–95. Courtesy Whitelaw Reid.

Hardened guides were hired by Verplanck Colvin in 1873, approximately fifty out of the hundred men who assisted Colvin in conducting a topographical survey of the Adirondacks, an endeavor that would occupy him to the end of the century. Surveys were strenuous, but this one posed special hardship given the size of the territory and forested mountain slopes without trail or road, up which surveying instruments were carried in heavy wooden crates. The guides, Colvin said, were "skillful hunters and trappers" who were useful even in areas unfamiliar to them. Fifty to sixty pounds of provisions, blankets, and camp equipment were carried by each guide. At the campsite, they were expected "to build huts or shanties . . . cut timber, build and keep up camp fires during the night, act as cooks, and perform such other labor as was necessary."[8]

Marc Cook, whose *The Wilderness Cure* recommended outdoor camping as therapy for tuberculosis patients, said a guide possessing the "usual ingenuity of his class" would be needed to build the camp and furnish it with tables, chairs, lounger, and other articles of furniture.[9] Another author advised his readers to avoid second-guessing their guides while they put together the camp. A "singular product," the guide "knows what has to be done" and should be left alone.[10]

Men in the Adirondacks did so many jobs that it was easier to call themselves guides even if they had guided little or not at all for years. The Adirondack Guides Association was formed in 1887 with Verplanck Colvin as Honorary President. Membership required the guide to be a resident of the Adirondacks for at least fifteen years and have had a minimum of three years experience as assistant guide.[11] Guides were not always disposed to get somebody's approval, other guides included.

Men seem to have been called guides whose experience in the woods was construed as earning them the title. Eligibility was slippery, but stretching the meaning was tolerable because calling oneself a "guide" was easier than saying one was a lot of other things—carpenter, farmer, logger, wagon driver, cook, hotel proprietor, and the like. "Guide" filled a role similar to that of "farmer," the term that seems to have been preferred to any other, such as laborer, to judge by Federal census reports.

Testimony for several civil trials centering on Raquette Lake point to this preference. William Ballard, who in the 1880s had helped build a camp for Frederick Hasbrouck, demurred when asked if he was "a carpenter and builder?" to which he replied, "No sir, I am not. Just simply a guide. Most every man in this country is the mother of invention. Most every man is a carpenter."[12] Osmond Hough, another witness, responding to the question, "You said that Plumley's business was hunting, trapping and farming?" replied, "Yes, sir. Worked at all trades. Same as I did in those days."[13]

Friendships between guides-become-caretakers and camp owners lasted two generations and sometimes three, and included sons and even grandsons on both sides. Fred Barnes worked as a guide, carpenter, and caretaker for the Reid family at Camp Wild Air on Upper St. Regis Lake for fifty years, from the early 1880s to the time he retired early in the Great Depression. He did most of the construction at the camp. Basil Cheney, when interviewed at the Kildare Club in July 1998, said his father and grandfather had worked at the camp before him. Now elderly, he was at Kildare off and on between 1942 and 1988, returning recently from retirement until he could break in a new replacement.

Continuity at Adirondack camps often is vested in employees more than those who own and occupy the camp. Matamek, the family corporation that owns a camp on Ragged Lake and a preserve around it, had three caretakers from one family, beginning in 1931 with Joe Gagnon and continuing through Angus and his grandson, Angus, Jr. Arthur Gates was a guide and caretaker for the Kirkham family of Cleveland, Ohio, continuing to his death at ninety in 1989. His son Robert worked at an adjoining camp formerly belonging to the Kirkhams and added his father's job to the one he already had.

The guide was seen but not heard. He did not bunk down with his clients except under exigent conditions; he and his fellow guides had shelter of their own in the

Basil Cheney was chore boy at the Kildare Club in the 1940s, emulating others in his family who found work at the remote camp on Jordan Lake. Later superintendent, his family and one other lived year-round at the camp, thirteen miles from the nearest highway. He had come out of retirement to assist a new superintendent when this picture was taken in 1998. Photograph by Craig Gilborn, 1998.

vicinity, even if that meant stretching out beneath a guideboat. Guides busied themselves setting up camp and preparing meat and other food for the meal, looking to others' needs before their own. A respectful distance was maintained between guide and client, despite a relationship that might be close. The order and conduct of the outside world was preserved in the Adirondack camp.

Advantage lay with the employer, who had choices undreamed of by his guide. Caretakers were fired and they quit, some were slackers and managed to bamboozle the owner, or even intimidate him or her. Even so, the owner always held the trump card and everyone understood that, some more graciously than others. Tension inherent in the relationship from the start was best expressed by Marc Cook about 1880, when he said that the "pith of backwoods logic" lies in the conviction of the guide that "every man is a sportsman because he is rich, and that he is rich because he is a sportsman, and that he is both because he is not a St. Regis guide."[14]

Cook found the Adirondack guide to be justified in being peevish since he typically was forced to "drag through seven or eight months of the year waiting for the other four or five months to come round." The guide's impecunious life style rendered him indifferent to money and material possessions and appearances: "Oddly enough, the want of money here, while it may enhance its value as a personal possession, seems to give the native a supreme indifference to the wealth of others." His use of the word "seems" left open the possibility that indifference was a mask, a human response to a condition without remedy.

City and Country, 1896. Grizzled Adirondackers look skeptically as a fashionably dressed lady heads for the water, a fly rod on her shoulder. Her debonair companion follows with a paddle, and behind him is their guide, who totes a picnic basket and wears a scowl. The illustration, drawn by J. M. Gleeson, appeared in Munsey's Magazine *for June, 1896.*

Bloomers and Other Articles of Freedom

Kate Field called on women to enjoy the wilds as their brothers and husbands had been doing. In 1870 she published an article in which she cites Thoreau and even, in her forthright comments, seems to be trying to write with his directness. She wore a trouser-like garment called "bloomers," and advised other woman to do likewise, for the same reasons that led to its being invented by Amelia Jenks Bloomer in about 1850, for the freedom it afforded in movement. Arriving at Martin's Hotel after a day-long wagon ride, Kate Field looks at the happy clutter and informality of men, finding lessons in this for women:

"Trunks lie about in hopeless confusion, guns peer from every corner, fishing rods bow from every window, flannel shirts and ambiguous boots proclaim the downfall of that tyrant Fashion, and everybody looks as if the business of life were to lounge and despise 'store' clothes. At least this is the impression produced by everybody of masculine gender. Men know the meaning of personal comfort. . . . Women glory in discomfort. . . . [They flaunt] their muslins in the face of backwoodsmen, [and] hover on the outskirts of the Wilderness . . . while fathers, brothers, husbands, and sons grow away from them as they grow into sympathy with outdoor life."

Dressed in bloomers, stout boots, and felt hat, she takes her place in the bow of a guideboat and watches as women on the dock watch her, aghast at her madness. She, however, is pleased that she is prepared now to be "a helpful human being."

Few "old woodsmen" of the type praised in books could be found in 1902, said Thomas G. King in his article on guides in *Recreation* magazine. Guides now followed "beaten paths" between hotels and lakes and knew little else.[15] William H. H. Murray had said something like this in 1869, but visitors to the region had very different interests by 1900: cross-country travel was less common and that was due both to the posting of camp sites and to outings that now included the entire family. For an experience in outdoor camping old-style, Dr. Arpad Gerster and his family left their cottage on Raquette Lake and took a boat to the south end of the lake and went two miles up the outlet to a landing, where they either took a wagon or walked several miles to Sumner Lake (renamed Lake Kora). The surgeon and his wife and young son slept in a lean-to, while their two guides stayed in a tent. But the Gersters became the exception.

The change to a life that was busier but less strenuous took place rather rapidly, as symbolized by the fact that skill and luck were no longer needed by campers in order to eat a decent meal of venison and trout. Earlier, when a hunting party got its meat from the forest and lake, energies were focused on getting game. But by the turn of the century, hotels offered a menu of activities such as swimming, tennis, cruises in a launch or power boat, afternoon tea, and even amateur theatricals.

These changes, King said, had taken place in the Adirondacks in twenty years, which would trace the start of change to the early 1880s. Outdoors had become scenery for the new generation, and this could not help but affect the quality of the guides: in King's words, "no one wants to visit the real wilderness and forego the luxury and social pleasures of the hotels." Guides had no choice but to go along with the shift to passive outdoor recreation.

The movement continues to this day as the generation that came of age in the Vietnam era and after is less inclined to fish in spring and hunt in fall, far less than their grandfathers and fathers before them. The grandson of an early camp owner told the author that the camp was visited less often before and after summer because his generation was less passionate about fishing and hunting, and in perpetuating the rituals of returning to the Adirondacks in spring and fall.[16] Peter Benson, who has been caretaker at a Girl Scout camp for fifteen years, thought that campers and staff were less disposed to the kind of climbing and hiking he had done as a counselor, even on his days off.[17]

The Adirondack guide was a pivotal figure as a camp builder, first of "squatter" or field camps of about 1830 to 1890, but also of the permanent camps that followed, starting in the 1880s. Permanent camps would not have been feasible without guides and caretakers to keep an eye on them, make repairs, open and close them, and keep interlopers away. Before 1950, camps had rooms and buildings for employees and a garden or even a farm for fresh food. Today a camp can be operated with virtually no one save the caretaker, who remains as indispensable today as a half-century ago. Owners must still have a year-round presence at their camp, even if that means, as it does at remoter camps, a winterized cottage for the caretaker and his family.

Guides became caretakers of camps in the twentieth century. Whether they lost prestige in this changeover was likely less important to them and their wives than the happy prospect of a monthly stipend and snug residence for them and their children. At large camps where the job called for managing other people, the title "caretaker" was supplanted by "superintendent."

At Ragged Lake the duties of the caretaker were spelled out in a letter of December 6, 1930, from Morton Fitch to Joe Gagnon, whose son and grandson would follow him in the position. Morton Fitch, speaking for his family, said that the job paid $50 a month and that either party could end the relationship on "reasonable notice." The caretaker was expected to live on what was termed a "private estate" between April and December, but he would be allowed to live in Owl's Head, N.Y., the nearest town, for the remaining four months as long as he visited the camp at least once every week.[18]

An energetic caretaker could earn more than his monthly wage, Mr. Fitch said; the amount depended "largely on how useful he can make himself to the family." Thus, the caretaker was expected to make two trips into town each week at his own expense, after which he could charge five dollars for each round trip. Putting in firewood and filling ice houses at the club house and main camp were part of his regular duties, as was supplying ice to the Ostby and Dickinson camps; but the latter camps could be charged for firewood, repairs to buildings and boats, and in "planting trees."

An imperious tone of a kind not lost on Adirondackers like Mr. Gagnon insinuates itself: it was "very necessary," Fitch said, that the caretaker have a cow at camp to "supply fresh milk" when the owners were in residence. In addition, he would need to have horses for getting people in and out of camp and for heavy loads when the road was too muddy for a car. The estate had a wagon or two and a buckboard in the stable, but it owned no horses and "doesn't ever intend to." An allowance would be paid by the estate for horse feed.

Here Mr. Fitch delicately steps around the issue of an automobile, still a novelty at many camps in 1930. He proposes a "thought," that the caretaker have a car and use it for his work at camp; or, if not, that he be able to drive a car or find someone who could drive in his place.

At the end of his letter, Fitch reveals a role for Mrs. Gagnon, Joe's wife, who is presumed to be a part of the deal: "From what I hear, you and your family would suit us," adding, "It is quite important that your wife be able to cook fairly well and be willing to help at all times." Joe Gagnon accepted and served as caretaker until October 1944, when he quit believing he could make more money elsewhere.

Watson Boyea, his replacement, received a letter that offered similar terms, except the monthly wage was $55 in 1944, an increase of $5 a month in fourteen years. Mr. Boyea could earn additional money for some services: $15 for each ice house he filled. He was not to charge for minor repairs, but major work, such as planting and cutting of trees, painting boats, and the like, were to be paid as labor at the rate of 50 cents per hour, up to $4 for a day's work. In summer, vegetables and milk might be sold to the family, though the prices "should not be more than those current at Owl's

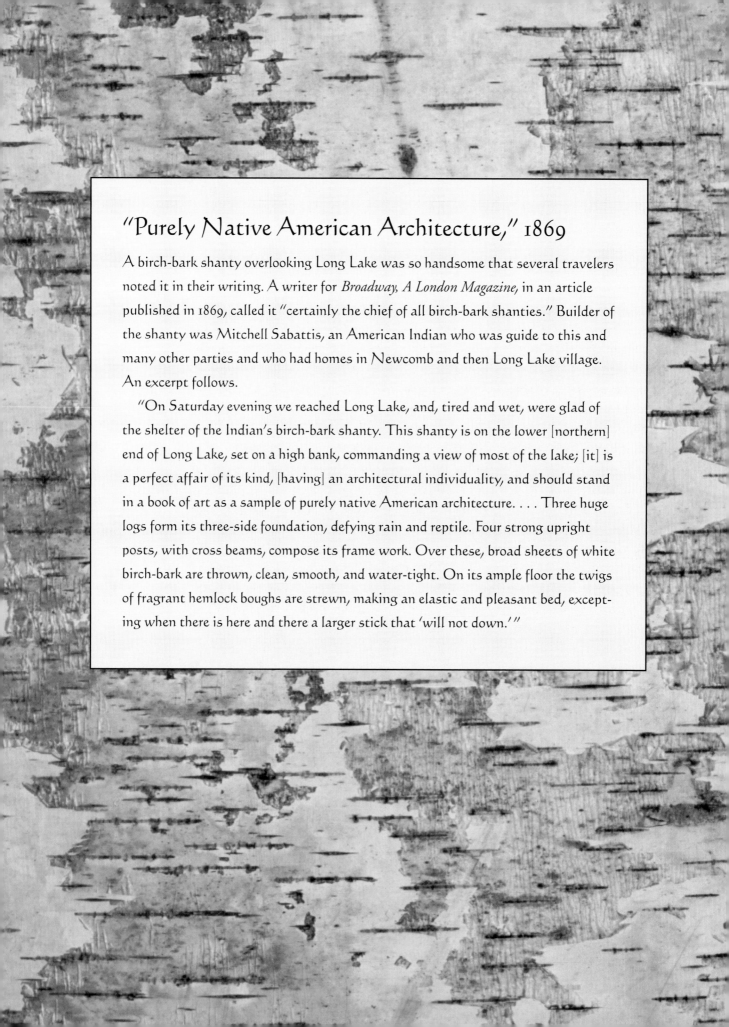

"Purely Native American Architecture," 1869

A birch-bark shanty overlooking Long Lake was so handsome that several travelers noted it in their writing. A writer for *Broadway, A London Magazine*, in an article published in 1869, called it "certainly the chief of all birch-bark shanties." Builder of the shanty was Mitchell Sabattis, an American Indian who was guide to this and many other parties and who had homes in Newcomb and then Long Lake village. An excerpt follows.

"On Saturday evening we reached Long Lake, and, tired and wet, were glad of the shelter of the Indian's birch-bark shanty. This shanty is on the lower [northern] end of Long Lake, set on a high bank, commanding a view of most of the lake; [it] is a perfect affair of its kind, [having] an architectural individuality, and should stand in a book of art as a sample of purely native American architecture. . . . Three huge logs form its three-side foundation, defying rain and reptile. Four strong upright posts, with cross beams, compose its frame work. Over these, broad sheets of white birch-bark are thrown, clean, smooth, and water-tight. On its ample floor the twigs of fragrant hemlock boughs are strewn, making an elastic and pleasant bed, excepting when there is here and there a larger stick that 'will not down.'"

Head or Malone." Mr. Boyea's family were to occupy the north wing of the club house and even to have family and friends visit there, but under no circumstances could they allow anyone in rooms reserved for the family.

Caretaking still meant a wife. She was expected to "be able to do good plain cooking" in the clubhouse and to clean, for which she would receive $65 a month. She would get extra for doing laundry. Club members "provide" food for themselves. An allowance of three tons of hay was offered for the use of Mr. Boyea's horses in 1944. However, a car remained an issue: Fitch offered to put up the money to buy a second-hand station wagon but made it clear that Mr. Boyea would pay for it out of his monthly wages. Watson Boyea, his wife, and his two children moved into the club house in October, but Watson was inducted into military service the following February and was replaced by Alvin Boyea, his brother.

While the advantage seemed to have rested with camp owners, it must be said—and undoubtedly was—that caretakers and their wives were their own bosses most of the year. They were surrogates for the owners, and the two sides exchanged authentic feelings for one another in the course of time. Like other camps, Matamek was fortunate in having the Gagnon family—father, son, grandson—in the caretaking position for more than fifty years. Joe was succeeded by Angus following the hiatus filled by the Boyea brothers. Angus, dying in 1987 at the age of 74 after caretaking for 29 years, was replaced by a third-generation Gagnon, Angus, Jr., who in 1997 lived with his wife in town, commuting to Ragged Lake in his own car.

The reality for both camp owner and Adirondack resident has always been—and still is—that the relationship is symbiotic and that both must get along above all else. Those of the Boomer generation may be indifferent to this unwritten rule: as employer they feel the prerogatives belong to them, in the Adirondacks as in the offices where they work in the city, where employees are ordered about and cashiered without qualm. If the owner is smart and wise, he will accept the reality of life for the absentee owner, that he needs the caretaker as much as the caretaker needs him. The caretaker may also be the owner's representative to the community. More than one owner who had alienated himself with townspeople was partly redeemed by caretakers who were liked in town, smoothing matters or explaining the owner's side of the story.

The psychology of the resident in a woodland setting inclines him to attend to things he can control and ignore the rest: home expenses and budgets of school and town concern him, but matters farther away, such as county and state governments, are less important, which may, by reason of their remoteness, be why they make good targets for daily ridicule. Government always must be criticized, despite the fact that the region gets upwards of half its infusion of money from local, state, and Federal governments.

The preference of rural people for the tried and tested—their conservatism—persists today as it did a century ago, and for much the same reason: community cohesiveness is a shield to the unfamiliar or alien. Residents will put aside local feuds when a neighbor seems unjustly threatened by outside authority. The laconic reserve of Adirondack residents has been a mechanism for biding one's time in taking the measure of people on whom they are dependent for a livelihood.

CHAPTER 3

Open Camps and Shanties

"OPEN CAMP" is synonymous today with the lean-to, but it also had a
more general meaning which embraced any number and type of improvised shelters in combination, referring to shelters open on one side, but
also to the ground and space around them. In the passage above, Murray did not
characterize the buildings or tents or combination of shelters at these sites. What was
open was the campground.[1]

The humble huts and cottages alluded to by Thoreau in chapter 1 are *vernacular*
houses; following the dictionary meaning, they were native, originating in the place
where they occurred. By this definition, the buildings in this chapter were certainly
vernacular. Whether they were traditional or not remains to be seen, since they were
as often as not improvised on the spot and were less constructed than assembled in
response to an exigency of some sort. Folk historians speak of tradition in connection with the building arts and handcrafts of New England and Pennsylvania.
Vernacular buildings of the Adirondacks may express a tradition, but most, to the author, seem to reflect not settled habits so much as hasty solutions to the fundamental animal need to get dry and stay warm.

The illustrations of lean-tos and shanties and log cabins with this chapter are
clearly vernacular in that they originated and were used in a place—the Adirondacks;
but they are not traditional as the term is usually used—a transmitting of technique
by one generation to another. An analogy might be Robinson Crusoe, who built hut,
stockade, and furniture, but not from what he already knew about carpentry and
building, which was very little at the time he was shipwrecked. Defoe's readers were
excited at Crusoe's predicament and charmed by his successes, not just at surviving
but by prevailing, as he eventually does, alone on an island.

Readers of this book might, like their counterparts nearly 300 years ago, imagine
themselves, with nothing more than an axe, cutting and tying a frame of saplings and
layering boughs over and around it to form a lean-to that shuts out rain and wind.
Frontier conditions made book learning appear to be irrelevant, but then physical ex-
egency adversely affects all the arts, including the building crafts.

OPPOSITE: Lobb's, *Lake
Piseco, Hamilton County.*
Stereoscopic photograph,
1880s. Floyd Ferris Lobb used
this open camp for thirty-five
years and caught thousands
of fish from Lake Piseco.
Here he is seated in a plank
chair with rod, fish net, and
rifle to his left, together with
fresh-caught fish. He was a
fiddler. The Adirondack
Museum (P37828).

The Lean-to

Men and a few women from the city regarded an Adirondack visit as an adventure; they accepted rain, bugs, and other discomforts for the leap of a deer or other beauties that might lie around the next bend in the trail or stream. W. E. Wolcott described travel in the region before the Civil War, in an account of the North Woods Walton Club in 1858:

> Those were the days of long wagon rides over rough and rocky roads, long carries with heavily laden pack baskets and camping accessories, primitive log rafts and open bark camps. In those times, none but true sportsmen cared to visit the woods, for it was only the lover of nature who could find there sufficient reward to compensate him for the deprivations and hardships incident to a wilderness trip.

Writing of a distant past in *Forest and Stream* magazine for 1897, he contrasted those primitive conditions with those of the present day, when "the percentage of people who spend their vacations in bark shanties is very small."[2]

An early reference to both Adirondack guide and his lean-to appeared in a magazine in 1838, in which William Charles Redfield, member of a party visiting the mining settlement at McIntyre, wrote, "A shelter, consisting of poles and spruce bark, was soon constructed by the exertions of our dexterous woodsmen."[3]

"Lean-to" and "open camp" are equivalent terms meaning a shelter open on one end or side. However, the lean-to is a specific type of structure, while the open camp applied both to the lean-to as well as to an undifferentiated assemblage of shelters. This wide meaning seems to have fallen into disuse, perhaps with the passing of an Adirondacks where guides and sports threw up camps when and where they wished. Just as one means the ring and not the hole in the doughnut, so guides thought of the open camp in terms of a specific building rather than the space and ground around it. Jeremiah Plumley, in testimony given in 1906 concerning Raquette Lake

in the 1860s, recalled that Osprey Island "had what you call a lean-to," to which he added, "Used to call them open camps."[4]

The additional meaning is important because, as will be seen below, enclaves of shanties and cabins assembled by guides may have been a model for the developed Adirondack camp of the 1870s and after. Examples of early camps that may be seen to have borrowed from temporary camps are the camp buildings of Benjamin Brandreth on Brandreth Lake and Camp Pine Knot on Raquette Lake, both dating from the 1870s.

The origins of the lean-to are unknown but can reliably be predicted to be found in the forests of North America and Europe in prehistoric times. A hut with a sloped

ABOVE: *Open Camp,*
1875–90. The photograph is
an inventory of a field camp
and attire of sportsmen and
guides. The bigger lean-to is
for sleeping, but the one
opposite appears to be for
keeping provisions dry and
secure from varmints. Notice
the animal skins, banjo, leg
puttees (or gaiters), and pack
baskets. The Adirondack
Museum (P20738).

LEFT: *Hermit's hut in the*
form of a shed. J. Groh-
mann, Ideen Magazin,
c. 1800.

or shed roof appeared in Johann Gottfried Grohmann's *Ideenmagazin,* an unsystematic collection of images lifted from various sources in Europe and England in the 1790s and early 1800s. Instead of being open in front, as in the Adirondack lean-to, the front is a log wall with a door in it.

The lean-to was quickly built from conifer trees, usually spruce, hemlock and cedar. An axe was all that was needed. Lean-tos held anywhere from two to a dozen or more campers, and they differed in quality and permanence. They were found along well-traveled routes and on sites good for stays of a few days. An unoccupied lean-to could be claimed by anyone. Being made of bark and boughs laid over a frame, a lean-to usually needed refurbishing as these materials dried in the sun and air, exposing openings that needed to be plugged in rainy weather.

A lean-to of the 1880s was described by A. Judd Northrup in an article he wrote for the Forest Fish and Game Commission about 1902, edited here for easier reading:

> First, we laid logs two or three feet high on three sides (sometimes we omitted the logs), leaving an open front; then we put up crotches to carry a pole in front, seven or eight feet above ground from which poles were laid sloping to the logs or ground in the rear, as a framework for the roof, on which were laid broad sheets of bark. . . . A heap of stones, if obtainable, was placed in front . . . for the fire of logs, to warm the camp at night. The bed was composed of the finer twigs of balsam boughs, or hemlock.[5]

Decades of girdling trees for their bark resulted in dozens of popular campsites marred by dead trees. Northrup admitted his contribution to a practice he called "fearfully wasteful," but he said it seemed excusable at a time when bark was the only procurable material in the woods. Light canvas tents, cheap papers for roofing, and improved transportation have eliminated the rustic lean-to. Even so, he said, the old-timer "still laments the passing of his open camp."

The Bedroom/Feb. 9, 1894, pencil on paper, by Arpad G. Gerster. Dr. Gerster, a New York surgeon, was not deterred by winter. Sketchbook: The Adirondack Museum, gift of Dr. John W. Gerster (81.26.53. Book no. 7).

Bark was preferred because large sheets quickly covered roof and walls of the lean-to. Many barks would do—spruce, cedar, and birch were used, though spruce was the most common. Bark was easily peeled as long as sap was still running, from early March through July. However, when the sap began migrating to the roots, the bark was impossible to peel, so layers of evergreen boughs tied down by saplings were used instead. Both bark and boughs, if properly laid, were effective in keeping the interior of the lean-to dry.

Configuration, size and imperviousness to rain depended on circumstance and the mood of the guide. Orient the camp, Northrup advised, toward the prevailing breeze, which helps drive away punkies, black flies, and mosquitoes. Smoke from a fire and a smudge helped keep insects at bay, and sunshine kept the camp dry. The camp should be placed away from trees so it could not be hit by a falling tree or by broken limbs lodged in a tree and ready to fall. Loggers called the latter "widow makers."

Kate Field, a writer and lecturer, mildly complained at having "to dispatch your guides in advance" when there was no camp at the end of a day's trek. Otherwise, she said in an 1870 article, you will be forced to "sit down in the woods with the sky for a roof" while the guides put it together. A shawl separated two gentlemen and two women who shared a single lean-to, in Lady Amelia M. Murray's account of her trip across the Adirondacks in 1855.[6]

By 1900, the lean-to as a log, bark, and bough shelter was disappearing due to criticism of the depredation to trees and its unsightliness. However, it acquired a new lease on life by becoming an accessory of the permanent Adirondack camp. Logs were

Mr. and Mrs. Laurence Turnure, Jr., on Raquette Lake, as photographed by Alonzo Mix, August 1893. A handsome couple in fashionable summer attire. At her side is a dog more suited to a lap than deep forest; nearby is a rustic table with tea for two. The Adirondack Museum (P11559).

"Dog Kennels," book illustration, 1889. Adirondack Museum Library.

Dog Kennels

The architect William S. Wicks wrote what may have been the most widely read "how to" book on seasonal homes ever published. *Log Cabins and Cottages,* reprinted many times after publication in 1889, used small drawings of camps in margins and text. Wicks made free-hand drawings from photographs in some instances, as suggested by these pictures. Hunting deer with hounds was suspended and then abolished by law, 1896–1901.

Dog kennel, dogs, and handlers, c. 1890. Adirondack Museum Library.

used as before for sides and the back wall, but roof and platform were built from lumber and shingles; the floor was raised well off the damp ground, so occupants were able to sit on the edge with their feet on the ground, facing the fire, and the roof overhead extended beyond the platform so as to keep sitters dry in a rain. Developed lean-tos such as these were built by carpenters (who may not have been guides) in a couple of days rather than a couple of hours depending on their size. Architects and camp owners often left construction to the builder or contractor who could be counted on to employ at least one carpenter who could build a lean-to without a blueprint.

Ready to make a bough bed, *Raquette Lake locale, album of snapshots, c. 1897. Original is unfocused. The Adirondack Museum* (P32116).

Boughs were placed in lean-tos of all kinds for cushioning and fragrance. A few lean-tos had interiors that were entirely lined with boughs, resembling a burrow or nest—a bower in the literal sense—"a leafy shelter or recess." Charles C. Hiscoe, reporting on preparations in June for the opening of Kamp Kill Kare the summer of 1917, referred to the guide Mossy Maxam in a letter to Francis P. Garvan: "Mossy is busy boughing up the lean-to's at the bottom of the hill."[7] The fragrance of balsam, or of hemlock or cedar, invariably aroused surprise and favorable comment. As for the mattress of boughs, unless laid properly, with the woody ends pointed down, sleep could be difficult. A McAlpin family member, writing in 1882, said that "hemlock boughs look soft and smell sweet, but after you have lain on them for an hour, you are glad to sit up again."[8]

Early Open Camps

Early camps built by guides consisted of several structures in clearings or openings in the woods, near water, usually on a lake or sometimes by a stream. The Stickney Camp represented a semi-permanent enclave where sportsmen boarded in small parties for a few days. It was situated on a point between First and Second Lakes, so, in the words of a visitor of about 1879, "one could look upon the waters of two lakes, and hear the 'lap lap' on either shore" from the open door of the dining room. The camp had two log houses with shingle roofs that nearly touched at their corners, each a story and a half high and measuring about twenty-five by twenty-eight feet with a veranda or porch that extended "nearly around" each house. One house had a kitchen and dining room where "twenty hungry men might sit at ease," with the upstairs di-

SLIDING ROCK FALLS.

vided into two sleeping rooms, one for "the party" and the other for guides. In the shade of trees was the ice house. On Second Lake was a framed boathouse with a store room above. The second house, which is not described, may have belonged to the Stickney Camp owner.[9]

A camp on Upper Ausable Lake was described in a diary, possibly of Susan McAlpin, who was camping out with her family and their guides in the summer of 1882.[10] The entry says of the approach to the Trumbull Camp: "The ground rises steeply from the lake, and the log shanty stands under high trees. Near it is a dining table with a smoothed log on each side for a seat, and a birchbark roof over it. High up in the clearing stands another log shanty where the guides sleep, with its own campfire in front of it, and near this a kitchen fire with a birchbark covered enclosure, that one might call a pantry." Susan McAlpin, whose family had a camp on Hewitt Lake near Minerva, N.Y., later married James Fenimore Cooper, who was grandson of the novelist.

Chauncey Hathorn had several camps on Tirrell Pond, Blue Mountain Lake, and Raquette Lake, the last described as "a series of tents and of bark, board and log shanties . . . and a dining room for general use—simply a rustic canopy supported by pillars but not enclosed."[11] Hathorn had moved his camp to Raquette Lake, squatting on Golden Beach, since the township to which it belonged was owned by Dr. Durant, who seems to have let Hathorn lodge guests there.[12] Meals were served in Hathorn's log house where the main floor was a combination living room, dining room, and kitchen. To the left of the entrance was a long table with benches for three or four on each side. Food prepared by Hathorn for his guests was venison, salt pork, fish, potatoes ("the only fresh vegetable"), a canned vegetable, flap-jacks, bread and butter, cheese and "canned sauce."[13] In his travel guide, Edwin R. Wallace said Hathorn was "thoroughly familiar with the special haunts of deer and trout for dozens of miles around."[14]

Alvah Dunning had two camps on Raquette Lake and one to the west on Eighth Lake, none of which he had actually purchased. Two of the camps were subject to ejection suits by the state, one in which Dunning's claim was rejected. The third camp, on the west shore of Raquette Lake in the vicinity of the present-day village, was sold when Dunning signed a quitclaim deed in exchange for two hundred dollars. Squatting was overlooked until land began to acquire greater potential value in the Adirondacks, starting perhaps in the early 1870s, for reasons discussed in the chapter on preserves.

Lean-tos were on water as a rule, but a few were on mountain tops. One, on Black Mountain, belonged to Horicon Pavilion, a resort hotel and dining room on the eastern shore of Lake George. Reached by boat and not from land, the hotel got its business from tourists who arrived by steamboat and lunched in the restaurant and strolled on paths on the grounds. Horse-drawn wagons carried guests on the toll road to the top of Black Mountain, where the lake and the country could be seen for miles around. A large lean-to was built on the summit for the more adventurous who wanted to watch the sun set over the Adirondacks in the west and see it rise the following morning in the east, over the Green Mountains of Vermont.

Open camp and shanty. Two ladies and a gentleman are served in a dining pavilion with a roof of bark laid over a ridge pole in tree crotches. The stump to the left may have been a first-growth softwood cut two or three generations prior to this photograph of c. 1890–1900. A frying pan is on the table. The Adirondack Museum (P 20736).

Another mountain lean-to was described in a letter written in 1873 by Dr. William Watson Ely, a physician from Rochester, N.Y., who six years earlier had published the first of many editions of a tourist map of the region. In the article, Ely described a shelter on Ampersand Mountain that took in "views of great extent and interest" of the surrounding country of lakes and mountains.[15] His purpose was to take elevations and positions of various points from this summit, perhaps to update his map. (Verplanck Colvin had just begun an official survey for the state in 1872–1873.) In Ely's party of ten were five guides and five observers. Having reached the top and eaten lunch, the guides began clearing trees that obstructed the view and using some of the logs to build a lean-to. The party spent three nights in the lean-to, which faced the Saranac Lakes and the high peak mountains to the southeast.

Very large lean-to's were built. An anonymous writer in *Frank Leslie's Illustrated Newspaper* recalled coming across a spacious bark shanty "quite open in front" sixteen years earlier, which would have been 1858. On Fourth Lake, it was "the largest and best built shanty I have ever seen in the woods," capable of "accommodating thirty men side by side in their snoozes," for "there they reposed." He had stumbled on members of the North Woods Walton Club, which had been formed the year before, in 1857.[16]

The Adirondack lean-to was an adjunct to the "wilderness cure" introduced to the region by Edward Livingston Trudeau beginning in the early 1880s. Two lean-tos were built at Loomis Sanatorium, each with eight or nine convalescent recliners, and a more elaborately built version, perhaps constructed for Henry B. Auchincloss on an island in Lake Placid, had a large central sitting-room connected to the lean-tos by Dutch doors, to be used in inclement weather.[17]

Nearly all older Adirondack camps have an Adirondack lean-to. They are used less often than before, partly because the belief that fresh air was good for children and teens has disappeared everywhere, except perhaps at some Boy Scout camps where tents are still used. Today the lean-to may introduce children to overnight sleeping under the stars; and their older brothers and sisters may find the lean-to, which faces toward the lake and sometimes is oriented so no one can look into it except from the water, a fine place for smoking, drinking, and kissing. A lean-to may be the center of a picnic once a year, renewing ties to the past in the one artifact everyone agrees is an anachronism.

A small crisis arises when word is circulated that a tree or limb has fallen on the lean-to, the issue being whether to repair or expunge it. Each family member must examine feelings that are as much about his or her life at the camp as about the lean-to itself. One faction, citing rot and moss, votes for its demolition. The sentimentalists plead for its resurrection. In staying the destruction of the lean-to, as usually happens, each person believes that his or her dissolution, and that of the family, has been delayed. Seldom used as it may be, the lean-to's presence is an object lesson in mortality.

Leaking Roof of Open Camp

Young men and ladies on an outing in Keene Valley, marooned by rain in an open bark shanty, busied themselves sketching, sewing, playing cards, and writing letters. Then their shanty began to leak. The excerpt below has been edited and abridged.

"So all went well for a half hour or so, and we rather enjoyed the security of our bark roof, when, to our dismay, a few drops began to trickle through in various spots, followed by unmistakable streams of water. With the rising wind, the smoke was driven in so as to almost blind us. The roof was an old one, and the bark had shrunk. Unluckily, the guides, having washed up the breakfast things and trimmed our fires, had supposed we no longer wanted them and had gone off in their boats. The only thing to be done was for the whole party to stand up with tin cups in hand and catch the water as it now came sneaking through. The guides returning, we soon had our roof covered with our rubber blankets [while] the guides . . . brought a boatload of splendid bark. It was too wet to cook dinner, so we made ourselves very comfortable with ham, tongue, sardines, and claret, which we dispatched seated 'a la Turque.' One of the young ladies did the best she could by singing and laughing to make herself think that she was happy."

The incident is from Charles Holt's *Adirondack Frontier: Stories of Keene Flats after 1776,* published in Elizabethtown, N.Y., in 1976.

Shanties

Lean-tos and log cabins were termed shanties: the *Oxford English Dictionary*, in a line from a book by Mrs. Traill in 1836, gives, "A primitive hut . . . a shed built of logs." However, shanty in this book means what historic photographs seem to suggest, that the shanty was a cold-weather habitation if need be, irregular in plan and configuration.

Wood's Cabin on Rackett Lake, *pencil on paper, Jervis McEntee, 1851. Bark, irregularity, and shelter habitable in winter describe the shanty. Billy Wood, a guide, prevailed despite having lost both legs below the knees to frostbite before moving to the Adirondacks. The drawing was copied as a woodcut in* The Great Republic Monthly *for April 1859. The Adirondack Museum, Gift of Mrs. Jacqueline Schonbrun and sons (76.77).*

Alvah Dunning's Camp, VIIIth Lake, May 17, '92, *pencil on paper. Arpad G. Gerster, 1892. Dunning had dubious claims to land on which he built three separate camps. The site of this camp, on Eighth Lake, now belongs to the state. Dunning cut and stacked firewood in the outer room. The Adirondack Museum, gift of Dr. John W. Gerster (81.26. Book no. 23).*

Shanties are the most interesting and original of early housing in the Adirondacks. They had one room or perhaps two depending on one's definition of "room," which meant two occupants in one was fine, but a third, except in an emergency, was a crowd. They were all-season shelters, thanks to their being enclosed and having a fireplace or wood stove. Shanties were made of materials cut on the site, although boards or a window scavenged in the locality and brought by boat or on one's back were incorporated in some shanties. Bark for roofs and even walls on occasion seems to be an attribute of the shanty. Large shanties at staging grounds in the woods included bunkhouses holding one to three dozen men, so not all shanties were small. Bark seems to have been used as often as logs in the Adirondacks; a few shanties employed nothing but bark applied to a pole frame. Some had shed roofs—flat and higher in front than in back. But small log cabins with bark on a gable roof might be termed a shanty.

Haste or carelessness characterizes shanties. Shanties were temporary houses for single men who by choice or necessity lived off the land and were squatters, subject therefore to being ejected by whomever owned the land. Habitations likely to be abandoned did not have a place in human society, and their remote location, together with their ramshackle appearance, confirmed their marginal character. Trappers used shanties in winter and spring while setting and checking trap lines for a spell and then moving on, perhaps to another shanty.

Shanties followed no rule save the builder's need for shelter from weather and wildlife, together with his skills, tools, and the material at hand. Shanties were never

Improvisation describes this shanty. Gravity, rather than nails, may have held the cabin together, except for the door, which may or may not have been hinged. The Adirondack Museum (P455).

ABOVE: Camp Rockwell,
c. 1880. Sports and guides
were evenly divided in a
photograph showing six men
with a day's catch of deer
and fish, posed outside a log
shanty with boards for a
chimney. The Adirondack
Museum (P37832).

TOP RIGHT: Adirondack
Home, *1875–80. Seneca Ray*
Stoddard, photographer. A
woman stood in the doorway
of a shanty located on the
carry between Raquette and
Utowana Lakes. The cabin
appears to be two lean-tos at-
tached face-to-face, con-
nected to a lean-to by a
bark-covered breezeway. The
Adirondack Museum
(P19197).

RIGHT: *Field shanty, part of*
Forest Lodge, a popular
hunting camp on Jock's (now
Honnedaga) Lake belonging
to "Dut" Barber. The Adi-
rondack Museum Library
(MS63-269, box 4).

exactly alike, which may be why travelers so often mentioned them in diaries and journals, since they were picturesque in appearance but also because each contained a tale or two about its maker and occupant and was a commentary on how precarious life was in the forest apart from human society. A journalist conjured a pathetic tale on coming upon a shanty or cabin near Tupper Lake: "With no companion but his dog, he had probably spent two or three months, and very possibly more, in this lonely cabin."[18] A shanty said to have been built by a man "from the East" had potatoes a foot and more deep on half the floor and under the bedstead, which was covered with a bearskin and blankets on a mattress of evergreen boughs. The account was of a trip taken by two young men in 1843 near Tupper Lake but not published until 1881.[19]

Forest Shelters, 1853

Early visitors to the Adirondacks kept diaries of their travels as though they were explorers of a new land. One account was written by Henry Smith Huntington, a student at Princeton Seminary, of a trip taken in 1853 with three companions and an uncertain number of guides. Moving in a westerly direction, they never seem to have lacked for shelter along the way. They exited at Lowville, N.Y., where they caught a stage to Huntington's home at Rome. The excerpts below have been edited.

"After dinner we peeled bark for our shanty, before which a huge bald high rock formed an excellent fireplace. We 'turned in' to an old shanty after laying it with new fresh boughs, which furnish a clean, neat bed for limbs worn out with travel. . . .

"We pass the farm & home of Mitchell [Sabattis], the Indian huntsman. It is of log, the nomadic peculiarities of the hunter preventing the cultivation of his farm, though reports award him the credit of being 'the smartest woodsman' of the North. We found a little way upstream [Cold River, where it empties into Long Lake] the best log shanty fortune had thrown our way. Its roof is low but snug and tight. It is probably 14 by 12 feet large. A huge stone fire hearth and chimney occupy most of one end, while about the apartment are benches or stools & crotched sticks in which to suspend the rifles above the head. The cabin is of hewn hemlock logs with a large ridge beam for the roof which is highest in the center like that of an ordinary house. A wooden whittled latch secures the door. The room has no windows or flooring; & for beds fresh boughs have been strewn around. . . .

"We came to Eldridge's cabin on the west side of Raquette Lake. We found the occupant absent & had to take unbidden possession of his log & bark shanty—turning that night 3 in a bed. . . .

"Billy [Wood] takes my buck home to his shanty [which he] seems to be delighted to show me. Rough & uninviting, it lacks no comfort essential to woodland convenience within doors. A bark portico rudely graces the front, where at times, during the heat of summer, our hermit sips his tea (p. 50). Within, a bed decorates one corner, besides which is a window. The furniture is simple but useful—consisting of a few rough chairs, a chest, cupboard & table. Deer horns, pelts, snow shoes hung about the walls. The fireside is ample."

Billy Wood, who had resided in this shanty a decade or so by this time, served gooseberry pie, maple syrup, and sour bread to his guest. The Huntington diary is on microfilm in the Adirondack Museum Library.

Bark shanty, Jack Leadley, builder, Speculator, N.Y., c. 1990. Located in a sugarbush behind his home, the shanty is used by Mr. Leadley in summer and for demonstrating woodcraft to school groups. Fires can be laid against the boulder opposite the entrance. Photograph by Craig Gilborn, 1993.

More permanent shanties had log walls and roofing of bark laid over poles. Less permanent shanties were largely of bark sheets laid over a pole frame. By 1882, Floyd Ferris Lobb had spent thirty-five years in a "rude bark shanty" which was "comfortable in both winter and summer." The article, in *Forest and Stream,* implied that Lobb lived in it year-round, although he likely had a home near enough for him to visit the shanty in all seasons. Lobb was photographed outside his shanty at about the age of seventy. He was a fiddler and caught thousands of fish on Lake Piseco and its tributaries.[20]

The word "shanty" derived from "chantier," the French term for a staging area related to an industry, such as a coal or rail yard, where workers, tools and by-products of their labor were concentrated. Chantier was closely identified with the forest, being an "establishment regularly organized in the forests in winter for the felling of trees." The arrival of French-speaking migrants from Canada in the 1830s and after certainly had much to do with its currency in the nineteenth century, since many had worked in the forests and mills of French Canada prior to their move into northern New England and upstate New York.

Shanties were used as evidence for later claiming ownership of a piece of land such as an island by right of "adverse possession," on the legal ground that the shanty—or any structure for that matter, such as a fence—had been flagrant but unchallenged for a period of years. The occupants of Osprey Island traced their claim from the log cabins or shanties that had been on the island since about 1868. According to common law, a lowly shanty or cabin could be cited as material evidence of ownership in a trial. Alvah Dunning's shanty on Eighth Lake was relinquished to the state. But the contest between the state and the occupant of Osprey Island on Raquette Lake at the turn of the century eventually favored the occupant, Harvey Ladew, on the basis of what Dunning had said was his "hum" from about 1870. Accounts of eyewitnesses vouched for Dunning's presence on the island, and the state's problem, according to one judge at least, was that this hearsay evidence was better than anything the state was able to muster to support its claim to the island, which today is in private hands.

Dunning's Eighth Lake shanty was described in the trial record. It was log, 13 feet wide and 26 feet deep, the side walls 5 to 6 feet high but about 10 feet high in the center, under the roof peak. It was divided into two rooms inside; a front room had a dirt floor and was a woodshed, while the living quarters, measuring 12 by 13 feet, "contained a hunter's bed, three or four camp stools, a stove with a pipe going through the roof," as well as lesser items—a frying pan, several kettles, and some dishes and utensils. The ground around the shanty was not cultivated.[21]

A shanty on Raquette Lake owned by William Wood did have a garden, as Jervis McEntee recounted in an 1851 entry in his journal. "We took our folios and boxes in the forenoon and rowed down to Wood's to get a sketch of his cabin," he wrote, alluding to a fellow artist, Joseph Tubby, who accompanied him.[22] The cabin was one of "two little log shanties" belonging to Wood, a bachelor who worked as a guide in spite of having lost his legs below the knees in a winter accident some fifteen years earlier.[23] The two young men spent an idyllic afternoon at the shanty, eating raspberries and making sketches, one of which, of the shanty, is at the Adirondack Museum. For two to three hours they lounged on a bench beneath Wood's crude porch. Nearby was Wood's "good garden, entirely free from weeds and a field of rye and potatoes growing."

The sketch shows bark laid over pole rafters for the roof and porch. The chimney, a mud or clay mixture enclosed by boards, was primitive. The irregularity of the shanty is apparent in McEntee's drawing, from which no conclusion can be made about the plan inside or even the appearance of the shanty on the side not shown.

Camp in the Wilderness, Hunter's Shanty, Adirondacks, Jan. 1888. *Three men, possibly members of the team surveying the region under the direction of Verplanck Colvin. The Adirondack Museum* (P7847).

Other visitors to Raquette Lake mention Wood's shanty, which seems to have been an early tourist attraction.

A shanty might be built against an erratic boulder. At Stillwater, northwest of Raquette Lake, McEntee wrote of "a log shanty about ten feet square built against a rock" which had a "hole two feet square" for a door and an opening in the roof "as an escape for the smoke." Elsewhere, on the Beaver River, he and his friend came across a bark shanty that was "such a poor one" that they pitched a tent "for the first time" in preference to spending the night in it.

The shanty shared a kinship with the cave or burrow, and it was strictly utilitarian, with little concern about outward appearances. In *Wild Northern Scenes,* published in 1860, the author Samuel H. Hammond mentions coming across "the winter hut of a martin and sable trapper."[24] It had, he wrote, "an outer and inner apartment, the latter almost subterranean" and "fashioned by leaning stakes . . . on the outside . . . filling the spaces between with moss, and covering the whole with bark." The "inner apartment," for sleeping, was reached from the "parlor" by an opening that one had to get down on all fours to enter. This bedroom was lined with "a plentiful supply of boughs from the spruce and fir tree."

A party of ladies and gentlemen were said to have made two "comfortable bark lodges" on Constable Point at Raquette Lake in 1851.[25] The bark lean-to on Constable Point painted by one C. Themmanen perhaps was one of these "bark lodges." A shanty or log cabin was built by a student at Hamilton College on the lake a little later. His father, citing the remoteness of Raquette Lake, refused to buy a piece of land for his son but agreed to pay for a "log house," presumably on land

Noah John Rondeau seated outside his log shanty, c. 1935–45. Noah welcomed hikers at his home on Cold River, near Long Lake on the north, where he squatted on state land for many years. He stacked firewood tepee-fashion. The Adirondack Museum (photographer unknown).

Rondeau chopping wood, pine carving by Robert Longhurst, 1978. Installation at the Adirondack Museum (William K. Verner and Edward Comstock, 1980). The Adirondack Museum: shanty, gift of Harvey Carr (67.128); sculpture, gift of the artist (78.58.1). Photograph by Peter and Rosine Lemon.

his son would not own, an indication of the free use of land in the Adirondacks and the small cost of building a shanty or cabin in the woods. A story high and measuring 12 by 14 feet, the cabin had windows and a doorway that were cut out of the log walls, the brothers Seth and Ed Pierce assisting. At the end of summer, the young man boarded up the shanty and returned to college "much improved in health." Coming back the next summer, he found leaks caused by "loose knots" in the roof, suggesting a bark roof. He covered the holes with flattened tin cans from the summer before. He also cut an opening for a stove pipe, laid a "proper floor," and squared up the door and window.[26]

A colorful squatter of the twentieth century was Noah John Rondeau, who had two small shanties or cabins on Cold River, near where it empties into Long Lake. A Canadian by birth, Rondeau lived alone in this remote spot for about twenty years. Barely five feet tall, Rondeau built his two one-room shanties high enough so he could stand in the center, perhaps stooping a little. One shanty was for storage, the other, brought to the Adirondack Museum in 1967, was Rondeau's residence. In it, he put his bunk on the wall opposite the entrance, a few inches off the floor; to one side was a table-top hinged to the log wall so it dropped out of the way, and to the other side was a small wood stove. Rondeau appeared at a number of annual Sportsman's Shows in New York City, taken there by the Department of Environmental Conservation, which knew he was the biggest attraction in the show.

Poverty made Rondeau reclusive, but he was not at all unsocial, for he welcomed hikers who sought him out and enjoyed calling himself the "Mayor of Cold River." He was given food and gifts, among which were birthday cakes carefully borne by members of the Adirondack Mountain Club. He moved to a retirement home in Saranac Lake, and his papers, rocking chair, and the ramshackle table that he built are at the museum.

Bunkhouse Shanties

Bunkhouses of logging camps, often called shanties, allowed between twelve and forty-five men to eat and sleep in them, depending on the size of the operation, according to Harold K. Hochschild in *Township 34*. Some had two floors, with that at ground level containing a "cook room," combining kitchen and dining hall with long board tables at one end and the "men's room," for relaxation, at the other end. The cook, man or woman, had a room off the kitchen. The floor above had tiered bunks for sleeping, in what Hochschild called the "attic."

Logging camp buildings might all be called shanties. These were always of log and frequently had bark roofs before the First World War, when mechanization began to alter how loggers worked and lived in the woods. Shanties besides bunkhouses were built for a variety of purposes essential to maintaining an "establishment" of men and horses in the forest: these were for keeping food and supplies, stabling horses, and perhaps keeping pigs for fresh pork, repairing tools and equipment and shoeing horses. Logging camps were as purposeful and hierarchical as any military unit.[27] A photograph taken about 1920 at the Emporium Lumber Company's mill at Childwold reveals a complex of seven log shanties and a team of thirty-six men and two women. When a locale was harvested, loggers might, depending on the location of the next site, dismantle the shanties—easily done in log construction—and load logs and planks or boards, along with cook stoves, onto sleds, wagons, or even rafts to be hauled elsewhere.

Logging shanty, c. 1900. Staging areas for loggers consisted of bunkhouses, stables, and sheds made from logs and sheets of bark. Women worked in the kitchen and dining room and were segregated from men. The Adirondack Museum (P491).

Logging shanties were abandoned in time, for travelers who mentioned seeing them do not ever speak of them as occupied. A logging camp on the Raquette River was "deserted now," like others that S. H. Hammond had seen "every few miles along the banks . . . [constituting a great feature of this region]." In the center of one shanty was a "rude fire-place of stone" and a hole in the roof above for the smoke to exit, while another had "immense cooking stoves" in their centers. In a corner of one were "piled up axes, crowbars, log chains, iron dogs," and on a shelf were two casks, one smelling of vinegar and the other of whiskey, plus "a great pile of codfish, and bread hard and dry enough to answer for cannon balls, pewter dishes, knives and forks."[28] One wonders whether Hammond or his co-author were embellishing their account, since bears for miles around would have come running, attracted by the fish scent.

Abandoned shanties made good hunting and fishing camps. Dr. Arpad Gerster noted in an entry in his "chronicle" for 1898 coming across "an old landmark" while headed south to the Moose River, where deer and trout were plentiful. A logging shanty, he called it "Rousseau Shanty" after Jean-Jacques Rousseau, the eighteenth-century French philosopher who linked nature and the education and rearing of children. It was, perhaps like Rousseau's theories, an "untidy, spidery . . . abandoned lumber shanty" that had become "habitation of a huge colony of blue hornets, whose nest is attached to one of the rafters." Two "rather grimy looking hunters, who were a sight of dirtiness," emerged from it and "begged us for a piece of soap, which we furnished." Gerster's companion was Jerome Wood, a guide and nephew of William Wood, whose shanty is described above.

Logging shanty, c. 1900. When a district was cut, the shanties might be abandoned or salvaged in part and hauled by wagon or sled to a site somewhere else. Windows, kitchen stove, and planks for tables and benches would be saved. The Adirondack Museum (P7139).

We must move next Spring down to the village
And build a fine frame house with good windows
And never say we lived in a log one
'Way up here at the far end of no-where.

Jeanne Robert Foster, 1916

CHAPTER 4

Log Cabin, Log House, Home into Hotel

Log Cabins and Log Houses

LOG SHANTY, log cabin, and log house in the nineteenth century were undifferentiated, so the same building might be referred to as shanty, cabin or house in a single instance. The distinction in this chapter comes less from what people said or wrote than from inferences in historic photographs and imaginative writing like Jeanne Robert Foster's blank verses, from her poem "Transition," quoted above.[1] A modern housewright in 1977 wrote that a cabin was one to one and one-half stories high and twenty by twenty feet in plan. Anything larger, he said, "is a log house," which was "fully developed" as a type by about 1750 and little changed in basic structure down to the 1930s.[2]

Photographs of log shanties, cabins, and houses suggest that while the log shanty may have sufficed for a single man, it was unsuitable as housing for a family for very long. The shanty, as seen in the preceding chapter, was small, with one or two rooms, while the log cabin had two or three rooms and additionally was more regular in elevation and was better finished inside, as with a plank floor. The log cabin, less primitive than the shanty, was an interim habitation for a family until a bigger house—or an addition to the cabin—could be erected.

The log house, as distinct from the log cabin, was respectable housing, but barely, being on the bottom rung of the community ladder, but positioned to be clapboarded over so it more closely resembled the framed houses that townspeople took as a measure of their town's level of development. A log house had two full floors in contrast to the cramped, head-ducking loft of the cabin, and its uprightness contrasted with the earth-bound posture of the cabin. Cabins with eaves near or at eye level usually had the door in a gable end, so one could enter without stooping. The log house could have a door in any wall, and people could stand straight in all rooms on two floors, except in the attic, if there was one.

Log houses often had walls of hewn logs, which made it easier to make improvements later on. Usually this meant a siding of some kind—clapboarding, boards-

OPPOSITE: *Diminutive but neatly built, this cabin with shingle roof was too small to hold kitchen utensils inside. One hunter naps and the other smokes a pipe with the same droop as his mustache. The Adirondack Museum* (P37827).

French Louie was a Canadian who moved to Herkimer County, where he hunted and trapped. This was his cabin, but the children may have been rounded up by the unidentified photographer for this picture. *The Adirondack Museum Library* (MS 63.269).

Adirondackers regarded log cabins as temporary habitations. This family of taxidermists share the same stoic expression. Rev. Osmund Putnam, an able amateur photographer, took this and other pictures of his neighbors in the Johnsburg, N.Y., township. *The Adirondack Museum* (P24240).

A cabin like this one could accommodate as many as four—two on the ground floor, opposite the stove, with one or two squeezed into the loft, if one had been built. The Adirondack Museum (P601).

Log house. Terrel [Tirrell] Pond, photograph c. 1900. LaPrarie House, a popular hotel for fishermen and hunters, was built by Henry LaPrarie in 1895. A game warden, claiming the family disregarded warnings that the hotel was on state land, burned the buildings in 1917. The Adirondack Museum (P22892).

and-battens, or shingles on the outside, painted white as a rule; inside rooms had boarded or plastered walls, or adopted a combination of both. Eventually the majority of log houses disguised their underlying log construction, so passers-by thought they were of frame construction like the other houses. So effective was this cover-up that long-time occupants were amazed to discover log walls at the start of a construction project.

Log cabins and log houses reeked of rural deprivation, as Foster, who was born and raised in the Adirondacks, says through the voice of a long-suffering wife in her poem. Isolation—"'Way up here at the far end of nowhere'"—was as hateful as poverty, especially for women and children. Artist Thomas Cole placed a log cabin at the focal point of a landscape painting now at the Adirondack Museum. When he saw people at a cabin (not necessarily the one in his painting) in the same locale, he

Parents and two small children posed at the doorway of a log cabin that appears older than the marriage. Migrating families often stayed in cabins abandoned by people who had themselves moved on. Photograph by Rev. Osmund Putnam, Johnsburg, N.Y., c. 1900. The Adirondack Museum (P24241).

described them as "half-civilized inmates."[3] Although called a romantic painter, Cole was unsentimental about the cabin and the way of life that he and his contemporaries knew it represented.

Log buildings were expected in new settlements, but they became less prevalent as sawmills began producing lumber—timbers, boards, and other lumber—for frame construction. The logging town of Brighton had twenty-six log houses and twenty-two frame houses in 1875.[4] About five years later, the "miserable hamlet of Saranac Lake" was said to consist of "about fifty or sixty log and frame houses," according to a convalescent minister impatient to return to Philadelphia.[5] In 1855, when it was the least populous county in New York (it still is), Hamilton County had 147 log houses, 273 framed houses, two houses of stone and none of brick.[6] At this time, Long Lake, barely twenty years old, had thirteen log houses and thirteen framed ones. At the Lower Works of the Tahawus iron mine, in 1851, Jervis McEntee reported seeing "about a dozen log houses" and one frame house.[7] Two Essex County towns, Essex and Newcomb, offer somewhat contrasting pictures. The former, a ferry town on Lake Champlain, is older and was oriented to the sizable carrying trade on the lake and its tributaries between Albany, Vermont, Canada, and communities on the St. Lawrence River. In 1855, Essex recorded 356 houses of which 298 were frame, thirty-six brick, seventeen log, and five stone. Newcomb, in a remote corner of the county and settled decades later, in the 1820s, counted seventeen frame houses and seven log houses, with one house of brick.[8]

Adirondack Porches

The excerpt below is from "On Adirondack Porches" by Alice Wolf Gilborn, in *Blueline* for 1980, a literary magazine founded by her in 1979 and published by the English Department at Potsdam College since 1988.

"The grand Adirondack hotels of the 1890s were noted for their verandas, or promenades as they were sometimes called. Here the city-born merchant and his family gathered to take tea, play games, and stroll their afternoons away. The veranda not only allowed for social pastimes and perhaps a courtship or two, but also served as a border between the wilderness . . . and the familiar, civil world of the hotel. . . . The porches [of homes] in these mountains cautiously invite the stranger to enter by degrees into the intimacy of the home—but not before he has wiped his feet and discarded his boots. The porch is protector of the house, a zone of moderation allowing its owner to emerge by similar degrees from the warmth of his stove into the chilled and windy landscape. It is both a barrier to raw nature and a conditioner for those who have grown too soft within."

Cranberry Lake Inn (Bishop's Hotel). The sequence of construction by Riley Bishop can be traced in this photograph—log cabin, then the annex next to it, followed by the two-and-a-half-story frame hotel building with a double porch. Other hotels, including Wilbur's Raquette Lake House (1856–73), followed this progression. The Adirondack Museum (P250).

The progression from log to frame construction can be seen in historic photographs and is further supported by testimony given by Reuben Cary about 1904. Referring to Wilbur's Raquette Lake House, a hotel which opened in 1856 and was run by Julian Wilbur, Cary said the first house was "a log cabin—log house—just large enough for his family." The family lived in the cabin while Julian worked on a second house, which, in Cary's words, was "a frame building—two stories high."[9] Bishop's Cranberry Lake Inn followed the same progression.

Wilbur's frame building was unfinished but taking guests when a visitor stayed in it in 1858. It was, he said in a later article, a "roomy, commodious house, only it is not yet clapboarded and plastered, but simply lathed, and you can take a peep from room to room through the chinks." Blankets were hung for doors in the rooms upstairs.[10] The hotel closed in 1873 and was moved in 1878 to the opposite end of the carry between Raquette Lake and Forked Lake, where it reopened as the Forked Lake House under the management of George Leavitt, who worked for Dr. Thomas Clark Durant on railroad matters.

That framed buildings were preferred to log ones seems supported in *Long Lake* in which its author, John Todd, told of missionary visits to the town between 1841 and 1844. On his first visit, he found eight or nine families "here alone, shut out from the world." A Congregational minister, Todd first preached in a "little log house, covered with hemlock bark," but on his return he found the congregation had made a critical decision, with the emphasis his own: "They have already got so far that they think they had better have a *framed* meeting-house instead of the log one proposed."[11] Log construction implied a lack of vision to Long Lake residents.

The bias against log cabins carried with it a prejudice against poor people or an ethnic group. In 1847, a couple whose memories of Washington County dated from the eighteenth century told a local historian, Asa Fitch, of their irritation with Scotch-Irish settlers moving into Washington County, a portion of which is in the Adirondack Park:

> A Scotch family would come into the town and a day or two after would have a little hut or cabin built of logs and covered with bark—without floor, door, or chimney—and would thus become resident citizens in a house of their own the day after their arrival.[12]

Drawings by Seth Moulton, 1960–75. Log houses in Winthrop, N.Y., when Mr. Moulton was a boy. Mr. Moulton's caption, about the George Searles's house being the "first log house to be covered with boards," is evidence that the intent was to mask the log origins of some houses behind siding. The Adirondack Museum (76.83.203).

The couple viewed the newcomers and the log huts and cabins they threw up in a day or two the way some Americans greet the arrival of a mobile home on a vacant neighborhood lot today.

Travelers seldom mentioned frame buildings, though they often singled out log ones, perhaps because frame houses were so familiar to them back home; log cabins and houses were becoming a novelty by the 1850s for Americans from settled parts of the East. The advantage of frame construction was its versatility. It was amenable to alteration and infinite variations, as people who travel through upstate New York and New England can readily see from their cars: raise the roof, punch in dormers, add a porch and later enclose it for an extra bedroom, and so on. Frame construction allowed homeowners to alter a house quickly and cheaply, to partition one room into two, or turn two into one, and to build up, out, and even down, below grade.

Log cabins were low-tech, low-skill habitations. They were built by one or, preferably, two men, which largely accounts for their small size, which was based on logs of a manageable size. The men and families in them lived off the land in a combination of occupations which were seasonal and sometimes carried out simultaneously—farming, hunting, labor, perhaps with a horse.

Cabin material was usually spruce logs eight to twelve inches in diameter without a discernible taper. These were laid alternately, top end to bottom end, to form four walls high enough for head room for someone standing inside. Logs might be left round or hewn on two, three and four sides depending on the effect desired, the time available and the ability of the builder in making the structure rigid, usually by a joint at the corners where the logs met or by splines, pegs, or spikes. Hewing tops and bottoms made for snugger fits and eliminated the labor of filling the spaces between the logs with chinking. The inside face of the log might also be hewn with the intention

of concealing it eventually behind plaster and lathing, boards, or wainscoting. A flat
exterior wall made it easy to apply siding to the house for the sake of appearance and
to protect the logs from weathering and insect borers.

Openings between logs of some cabins or houses were wide enough to allow a
man's hand to slip between them, possibly a technique for throwing up the walls
quickly in order to get the framing of the roof and floors finished that much sooner.
Artistic effect might have been a factor, since travelers liked the banding of white
caulking and dark stained logs. The best chinking was sphagnum moss or oakum
pressed between logs and held securely in place by mortar or a cement mixture.[13] Abel
Edgar Leavenworth mentioned seeing a "little log hut school house with a chair, two
benches, shingles stuck in the cracks for shelves," on his passage through Newcomb
in 1851. Moss, he said, was used "in place of mortar."[14]

Caulking sealed the log building from vermin and drafts, but, as said, city people
liked its banding. A girl in her teens from Glens Falls, on a church outing with girls
and boys and an adult chaperone, was pleased by the striped walls of the log cabin—
she called it a "habitation"—which the group occupied for two or three days on the
Cedar River outside Indian Lake, N.Y., in 1859. The walls inside were flat, and she
speculated this had been done "for the sake of giving a somewhat smoother, more
even appearance" to the interior. Partitions separating the rooms were "boarded up
with white, nice looking boards," a reference to whitewash which brightened interi-

ors darkened by an outside porch. An attic partition created two bedrooms and a "large dormitory" in which there were seven beds. The boys slept in the dormitory, and girls other than the narrator took the bedrooms. The chaperone and the girl who wrote the account got the two bedrooms on the first floor, which also had a parlor and a dining room with a table "nearly as long as the room, painted blue," with benches of the same color on either side. On the table were four or five tallow candles in tin candleholders, together with bouquets of flowers in "a tin measure, a pitcher and tumblers" for vases. The account was published in *The Glens Falls Republican* for 1859. A typescript is in the library at the Adirondack Museum.[15]

An example of the log house as distinct from the log cabin may be seen at the Adirondack Museum in the Log Hotel which was built in 1876. With a roofed porch in front and along one side, the main entrance to this hewn log house is in a gable end. Opposite the front door is a stairway and a front room which contains a reception desk and office for the hotel on the site between 1875 and about 1954. In the back are several small rooms. Upstairs are two front bedrooms and a third in back, each off a narrow hallway at the top of the stairs.

The layout is similar to small frame cottages of the nineteenth century, in which the living room and stairway share the front room, ordinarily the parlor or sitting room. Although it is a story-and-a-half tall, the second floor rooms are small but finished with ample headroom, plastered walls and ceiling, and varnished floors.

The museum also has a log cabin which was built in a remote spot in the northeastern corner of Herkimer County by Mike Virkler and his wife, Hilda. As the only concession to mechanization, Mr. Virkler, a businessman in Castorland, N.Y., who

At Blue Mountain House. Sept. 12, 1879. Seneca Ray Stoddard, photographer. Built in 1876, the log building was part of the hotel on this site. In 1954 it became the site of the Adirondack Museum, Blue Mountain Lake, N.Y. Logs were hewn against a time when the house would be covered in a siding of some kind. The Adirondack Museum (P37888).

Mike Virkler's log cabin, 1962–65, built on club land leased from a paper company. A chainsaw was Mr. Virkler's sole concession to technology: he used tongue-in-groove spruce floor boards and hand-cut pine shingles that were held by pegs and dowels. Mr. and Mrs. Virkler gave the cabin to the Adirondack Museum in 1991 after the state bought the land. The cabin was being reassembled when this photograph was taken in 1998. Photograph by Craig Gilborn.

was also a licensed guide, used a chainsaw when he built the cabin in three years, beginning in 1962. It uses wood pegs and dowels, eschewing nails, which made dismantling and reassembling easier and less destructive. The round spruce logs are held by tongue-in-groove which requires no chinking. The pine shingles are hand-cut and fastened by pegs, and the floor is made of planks doweled to horizontal timbers called "sleepers."

The cabin, on Buck Lake, was on a 16,000 acre tract owned by the International Paper Company. In 1986, the company sold the land to the state, and the Virklers and other owners of cabins were given until September 1, 1991, to remove what were soon to be non-conforming structures on Forest Preserve land.[16] Tom Brown of the Department of Environmental Conservation contacted the museum for Mr. Virkler, and Mark Schisler, a graduate of Paul Smith's College and a museum staff member, was asked by the author to accept it if it looked good to him. Mark camped out in a lean-to for five nights in January while marking the components of the cabin. Later it was disassembled and brought out by truck while the road—a logging road—to the tract was still frozen. Included were stones for the fireplace, collected by the Virklers on travels around the United States.

Homes as Hotels

Homes in the Adirondacks became hotels sometimes by luck—campers seeking a bed for the night asked for a room and children found themselves displaced. "Half home, half farmhouse and the rest 'hotel'" was how Arpad Gerster described the Kenwell home that was also a hotel a dozen or so miles south of Raquette Lake. Builder-owners selected their sites more often by choice, on a well-traveled route, as Julian Wilbur did in 1856 when he and his family built a cabin and then a house for a hotel on the carry between Raquette Lake and Forked Lake. Their log cabin was a first step of a plan to expand to a more ample building, which followed a basic plan for a boarding house two to three times as wide as it was deep, two stories high, perhaps with a half-story under the roof. Located on carries and lakes, these were family-run hotels, in contrast to resort hotels like the Prospect House that had a professional manager the moment it opened on Blue Mountain Lake in 1882. The latter, which took two years to plan and construct, dwarfed the small hotels on the lake with its three hundred rooms.

Family establishments filled an important niche, offering bed and wholesome food for $7 to $10 for the week. They could be run by women who likely would be at home while their husbands were often absent at work in the woods or at a camp or hotel elsewhere. Renting out rooms was a boon to many a wife and mother, who could move children to a shed or a relative's home. Jack Leadley recalled losing his room in Speculator to deer hunters as a boy in the 1930s.[17]

The frame houses that can be seen on the high east bank of Long Lake were big to accommodate guests in summer. After summer, and perhaps with a hiatus that was followed by hunting season, families reclaimed their homes and the views and proximity to the lake that appealed to outsiders. Part of the house was closed off, and the family lived in a few core rooms around the kitchen with its perpetually warm stove. Even so, family members jumped out of bed on winter mornings in rooms with temperatures close to freezing.

Heat came from wood stoves and later from furnaces that burned wood and coal. Fireplaces were fine for taking the chill off in summer and early fall, which is why they are found in guest rooms and cottages. But Adirondack residents knew that the heat in a fireplace mostly went up the chimney; they preferred stoves and furnaces for their efficiency and because smaller chimneys were required, as may be seen by anyone who drives through the region today.

Small hotels and boarding houses grew in stages, as photographs and a few written accounts indicate. First built was the log house or cabin for the owner and his family. To this a second structure, two stories and usually of frame construction, was added, perhaps connected to the original by a porch or breezeway, so one kitchen would serve both household and guests. This produced what one writer called a "house of the composite order," which was a "log house and a frame one conjoined."[18] Food was brought from the kitchen into the dining room where guests served themselves and sat on benches or plain chairs at long tables. Upstairs might be

Blue Mountain House. Built in 1874, it appears to have had a bunkhouse for loggers as its model. It burned in 1880, to be replaced that summer by a conventional hotel building. The Adirondack Museum (P6968).

partitioned into bedrooms. Privacy in hotels and inns was not expected by travelers for much of the nineteenth century; men often slept on cots or bunks in a dormitory-like arrangement, a custom whose end was likely hastened when women began reaching remoter hostelries by the middle of the century.

Boarding houses and resort hotels catered to guests of differing means and expectations, and they seem to have cooperated as a rule, perhaps in accordance with the custom of the frontier that neighbors help one another: everybody, even the hotel manager with his city ways, was in the same boat. A hotel that was full, or which had a minimum number of nights before it would take a reservation, referred travelers to boarding houses or another hotel nearby. Perishable foods such as dairy products, eggs, meat, and fresh vegetables came from the locality, perhaps from someone selling a surplus from his own hotel operation. In 1886, the author of *The Adirondacks as a Health Resort* said that travelers no longer were so dependent on getting game since "guides have built log houses, and small farmers have settled not far from many of the lakes" in recent years.[19]

An example of the accidental hotel may have been Blue Mountain House, on a site that was later, in 1957, occupied by the Adirondack Museum. In 1874, Miles Tyler Merwin was approached by Vincent Coffin who asked Merwin for a room for himself and his son. Merwin declined, saying his was a lumber mill and not a hotel, but he let the two—the senior Coffin became governor of Connecticut two decades later—spend the night in his hayloft.[20] The next year Merwin built a two-story structure clearly modeled from bunkhouses of loggers and opened it as a hotel.

The Jonathan Bellows family on Lower Chateaugay Lake took boarders at what had originally been a farm of about 1818. An anonymously written account in the July 15, 1848, issue of *The Spirit of the Times* gave the history of the hotel in a nutshell: "We found a small but pretty good frame house, a modern improvement on the log cabin, built by the present occupant, a son of Mr. Bellows, who settled himself in this wilderness about thirty years ago."[21]

The Bellows family's cabin but not their "modern" frame house was depicted in "Arguing the Point," the title for a Currier and Ives lithograph of 1855 from a painting by Arthur Fitzwilliam Tait. Tait had come from England less than four years earlier and was then beginning to make sporting and animal paintings a specialty, probably because many businessmen were sportsmen and potential clients, and the artist was an outdoorsman himself. The log cabin comported better with the political talk of the three men in the foreground than the twelve-room hotel, where Tait may have stayed during his visit to the farm in 1854. Americans liked rustic genre scenes, as Nathaniel Currier, joined by James Merrit Ives in 1857, knew when he began selling lithographic prints in the 1830s. Tait, in his association with Currier and then with the partnership, had forty-two of his paintings reproduced as lithographs between 1852 and 1864.[22]

Blue Mountain House and Cottages at Blue Mountain Lake, *1889, Seneca Ray Stoddard, photographer. The frame hotel erected in 1880 by Tyler Merwin offered guests fine views of Blue Mountain Lake and the surrounding countryside. It was demolished in 1954–55 to make way for a modern museum building, but the log hotel of 1876 and its attached cabins were preserved. The Adirondack Museum* (P37808).

Two Cottages

These two cottages, among eleven similar privately owned camps on tiny lots, got water and some meals from Blue Mountain House nearby and may have been dependencies of the hotel. Built between 1900 and 1920, the cottages had front porches a dozen feet or so off the steep slope, supported by posts in cement footings pinned to ledge. The two camps are overtly picturesque in style, one English and the other allusively Swiss. Despite their English and Swiss masks, both adopted a bifurcated plan inside—half large family room open to the rafters and half bedrooms set off by a railed balcony overlooking the family room below. Both cottages were built for the Rev. Archibald Bull, who for many summers was minister at the log church illustrated elsewhere (p. 218). The English-style Bull Cottage was adaptively restored for the Adirondack Museum by Richard Hanpeter of Wareham DeLair Architects, Saranac Lake. Photographs by Craig Gilborn, 1998.

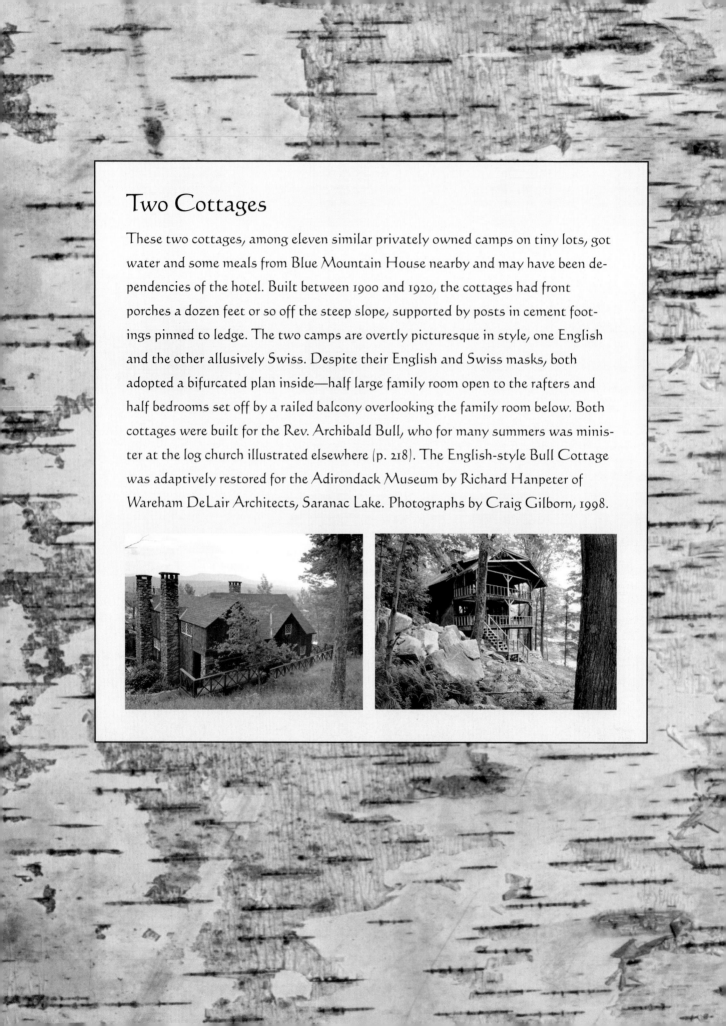

Nineteenth-century travelers experienced the Adirondacks far differently than did their counterparts of the twentieth century, in which access devolved to trails that could be reached by car on paved roads. The result is a tunnel vision in which the wilderness experience is largely dependent on well-traveled roads and trails. People in the nineteenth century moved as much by water as by land; the routes taken by early travelers meandered because they followed streams and lakes in any of the seven watersheds that drain the Adirondack Park. The most-traveled river was the Raquette because its watershed abutted six other watersheds and was not far from the seventh.[23]

A favorite stopping off place was Mother Johnson's on the Raquette River north of Long Lake. A midnight visitor to this boarding house about 1868 was William H. H. Murray and his guide, John Plumley, who would figure in the book Murray would publish in 1869, *Adventures in the Wilderness.* They roused Mother Johnson, the proprietress, who had been at this location as early as 1858. She welcomed them and prepared a meal of griddle cakes, which the two men ate, one plate after another, after which she returned to bed.[24]

The hotel, which Murray called a "half-way house," was a log structure, indifferent as to looks but known for its good food and hospitality to sportsmen and guides seeking a hot meal and a night's rest. At the end of the carry from Long Lake,

Mother Johnson's, Raquette Falls, c. 1875, Seneca Ray Stoddard, photographer. This L-shaped house appears to have a framed roof and gable end above log walls. William "Adirondack" Murray praised Mother Johnson, shown in an apron on the porch of her inn, half-way between Long Lake and the Saranacs, for her pancakes. The Adirondack Museum (P15188).

The proprietor, in an apron, was sketched by "Our Artist in the Adirondacks," along with city travelers in Appleton's Journal *for September 21, 1872.*

OUR ARTIST IN THE ADIRONDACKS.

it long since has disappeared, surviving in references in travel guides and perhaps a hollow that marks a former cellar.

Family-run hotels and boarding houses were personal and adaptable: if they satisfied their guests they could, with a little luck, remain in business for years. Some were sold, and their buyers spent an anxious year or two waiting for guests to reserve rooms and cottages as they had been doing for years before. Friendships were exchanged by loyal regulars and owners; a few were sealed by a marriage and then by celebrations of anniversaries that followed.

Running the boarding house often fell to women. This meant the care and handling of guests and supervision of hired help, along with managing the family and even the garden if there was one. They got little time off and often carried on in the absence of a husband or father, though most might have said they had been doing just that anyway. But they got valuable experience denied to other women and wives, yielding a dividend in independence: as managers, they learned how to supervise help, keep books, handle money, and pay bills. In addition, they came in contact with people from places and circumstances vastly different from their world.

Juliet Baker Kellogg and guests at Baker's Clearing, where her mother opened a boarding house, was an instance of a friendship shared by a resident and visitors in summer and fall.[25] A hired man and Juliet's father, Thomas Baker, started what became a seventy-acre farm in 1854. Juliet ran the boarding house and farm for about twenty-five years, moving in 1881 to a house nine miles closer to Minerva but almost as remote as the farm she had left. She began keeping a diary in 1862, and between that and exchanging letters with guests who now were friends, she kept loneliness at bay. The farm was purchased from her by boarders who wanted to form a club, today's North Woods Club.

The intimacy and simplicity of life in the Adirondacks seemed superior to people who lived somewhere else, often in a city. A glimmer of this was afforded by Arpad Gerster during one of his stays at a boarding house run by Mr. and Mrs. Wellington Kenwell in the vicinity of the Moose River, where fishing and hunting were good. The New York surgeon, in an entry in his diary for August 16, 1898, spoke admiringly of the house as a "genuine old fashioned Adirondack 'place'."[26] Its construction was plain: rough boards were used for floors, walls, and ceilings, and the rafters, which presumably supported the second floor, were peeled.

What he found especially charming was the activity around him. The dining room where he was seated was in "open communication with the kitchen," and he watched pleasurably as "the good housewife, having no reason to hide any of the mysteries of her art," went about her chores "honestly and publicly before our eyes." He noted that the "parlor"—the quotation marks were his—was furnished by "a few rickety chairs," stove and an organ. However, the dining room where he sat was "jamful" of happy confusion, as "Children, guests, dogs and hired girls roam where they please, and the air of the place is altogether delightful to . . . a despiser of the pretentious 'hostelry' of the day, which has the bad sides of both city and country hotel, and the good sides of none." Gerster railed against society's ceaseless search for comfort because this weakness was indifferent if not hostile to the unspoiled beauties and peace which he had taken some pains to find when he began regular visits—some when snow was on the ground—nearly two decades earlier.

Amenities did find their way into the Adirondacks in some of the most out-of-the-way places, reminding us not to jump to conclusions from appearances in old photographs. LaMont's was a "sportsman's lodge" managed by James LaMont on Smith's

Lake, now Lake Lila. Despite its ramshackle looks, it was said to have telephone service to Lowville, N.Y., in 1890, thanks to its owner, William Morrison, a Lowville merchant. Perhaps the telephone had something to do with the railroad that Dr. William Seward Webb was about to build in the Adirondacks at the time. Webb bought the property, renaming the lake after his wife, Lila Vanderbilt Webb, and building a lodge, cottages, and farm on the preserve, on which there were three station stops in 1892 when rail service began.

A traveler praised Mr. LaMont as "one of the fearless hunters and as genial a forest companion as one could find," preferring to stay in LaMont's own log house rather than occupy one of the "bark camps" on or near Smith's Lake which could accommodate about forty men. LaMont resided at the hotel for eight months, which likely meant he spent the months of December to April elsewhere, perhaps in Long Lake or Tupper Lake.[27]

Towns benefited greatly from small hotels and boarding houses, since cash from tourists was redistributed in the community before gravitating to Glens Falls, Albany, Utica, and other outlying cities where the banks and other creditors were found. Hard money was in short supply in Adirondack towns, which were usually at the bottom of the feeding chain. Residents turned to barter for goods and services, trading honey, trout, venison, and labor for groceries, kerosene, and dry goods. Cash paid by hotel guests was not large in absolute terms, but a thousand dollars circulating in a community with small hotels and boarding houses reaped visible rewards in countless ways, in healthy churches, decent government, well-kept homes, and schools that prepared some of its best students for college and careers in a profession or business.

Paul Smith was perhaps the only person who can be said to have gotten rich in the Adirondacks. He worked on the Erie Canal as a young man and hunted in the Adirondack wilds. He was said to be a superb outdoorsman and a talented raconteur, telling stories that entertained the city men he guided in the woods. In 1852, he opened Hunter's Home, an all-male camp which proved so popular that the men bankrolled Smith to a hotel which would admit their wives; built in 1858 on Lower St. Regis Lake, the hotel came to be called Paul Smith's.[28]

Fashionable people came, sometimes with their servants, and stayed for weeks and even an entire summer. Smith regaled his guests on the porch while his wife, Lydia, who was a graduate of Emma Willard Academy in Troy, ran the hotel and was said to have been the reason for its success among a clientele that included men and women who stayed in fine hotels in London and Paris. Smith became as rich as many of his guests, first by charging prices he knew his guests could afford, but also by buying and selling both land and timber and by generating electricity and providing telephone service in the region.

Boarding houses and hotels produced much of their own food, with extra to sell to other hotels or camps in the area. Lynn Galusha was two years old in 1915 when his parents bought a hotel that had been on Lewey Lake since 1850. Interviewed in 1987 by students at Indian Lake Central School, he recalled that the family grew carrots, beans, beets, onions, and turnips in two gardens. Root vegetables were stored in a root cellar for the winter, among which were fifty to seventy bushels of potatoes, the staple vegetable in the Adirondack diet.

The Galushas also had sheep, pigs, chickens, and turkeys, and they milked five to eight cows. Fresh meat—termed "fresh on the hoof"—was more of a problem, with periodic shortages alleviated by sharing among hotel owners.[29] The family also sold ice, firewood, fishing bait, and maple syrup to tourists, with some syrup bought by tobacco companies as flavoring for tobacco. The kitchen stove alone consumed thirty cords of wood each year. Mr. Galusha's mother did the cooking for guests, most of them hunters and fishermen. Once a week the family shopped in Indian Lake.

> The soil in these Adirondack mountains is unfit
> for cultivation. No man, no matter how industri-
> ous . . . can secure a livelihood from the soil in the
> Adirondacks. It has been tried, and it is a heart-
> breaking failure. The lands are fit for none other
> than public and general uses.
>
> —David McClure
> Constitutional Convention, 1894

CHAPTER 5

Land and the Formation of Private Preserves

Land

THE ADIRONDACK region was at a disadvantage when it came to competing for settlers against other regions in the state and the territories farther
west. This became evident as early as 1780, when New York and the
Continental Congress began offering land for settlement. A law in New York, in
1784, referring to the lands as "waste and unappropriated," implied a defect in
Adirondack lands, although the terms were equivalent, meaning the region lacked
boundaries and apparent ownership. Little was known about the region, except that
it was big, perhaps as large as Delaware depending on where the boundary was
drawn. Thomas Pownall, a geographer and former British official in the colonies, said
in 1784 that the region was reported to be "the Dismal Wilderness," a "high mountainous Tract," a "broken impractical Tract."[1]

Steep terrain and sandy soils made farming a marginal occupation in the
Adirondacks, as hardened farmers could likely have judged at a distance by looking
at the mountains. The growing season was short enough, but nearby mountains and
trees at the edge of clearings blocked one to two hours of sun each summer day in
places. Narrow valleys prevailed in the Adirondacks, in contrast to neighboring
Vermont, which had mountains to be sure, but separated by wide lake-bottom valleys with limestone soils that were easily plowed and mowed and higher slopes with
grass for grazing cattle and sheep.

New York's legislature passed several laws between 1784 and 1786 in a effort to dis-
tribute some seven million acres seized by the state in the war with England. The earliest law offered an acre of land for a shilling and established procedures for
auctioning forfeited estates. A more liberal law soon after provided for auctioning
unappropriated and confiscated lands, and an exemption from taxes for a period of
seven years. A third law in 1786 liberalized the exemption and provided free land to
men who could show they were veterans of the war. The last, called the Military
Tracts, were popular in New York—everywhere except in the region now known as

OPPOSITE: Modern
Invasion of the Wilds,
*illustration from an annual
report of a commission for
the State of New York for
1907–8. Starting in the 1880s,
telephone lines run from pole
to tree connected camps and
hotels with distant towns
and cities. Wildlife chewed
at the wrapping around the
wire, and that, together with
falling limbs, produced frequent interruptions. Today's
wireless phones represent a
leap forward in this regard,
although the issue of intrusion, as imparted by an illustration nearly a century ago,
remains the same.*

Robert Pruyn is next to Theodore Roosevelt in a picture taken with Pruyn family members and friends on the steps of Santanoni Lodge, c. 1899. Roosevelt may have been governor at the time. The Adirondack Museum (P 64570). This and the other photographs of Santanoni that follow were given to the Adirondack Museum by Susan King, a Pruyn family descendant, and her husband, Thomas King.

the Adirondacks. According to Norman Van Valkenburgh, not a single parcel was claimed in the Adirondack Military Tract.[2] The state, virtually unable to give Adirondack land away, sold its holdings to speculators for nine pence an acre.

Adirondack land was a poor commodity because it was difficult to exploit commercially. People were not fools: they knew the land had value—for recreation and not just extractive industry—but they preferred speculating in western lands, biding their time, perhaps, until others took the risk and began opening up New York's northern wilderness. Princely tracts of land were acquired at pennies an acre in the nineteenth century. Lumbermen and loggers cut hemlock bark for the tanning industry and white pine and spruce for lumber, and when they were done, they let the land revert to the state for taxes they perhaps had no intention of paying from the start. In the mercantilist view of the day, cut-and-run was not praiseworthy, but a defense could be made that the wealth it produced in such things as houses and jobs vastly exceeded lost taxes. Benjamin Brandreth bought all of Township 39 in 1853, or approximately 24,000 acres, at 15 cents an acre. The Adirondack Club, formed in 1858 in Cambridge, Massachusetts, paid $600 at the land office in Albany for some 22,000 acres of land around Ampersand Pond, which is about 3 cents a acre.

Unnamed until 1837 and not systematically surveyed until the last quarter of the nineteenth century, the Adirondacks correspond to the vernacular landscape of John Brinkerhoff Jackson, who, in *Discovering the Vernacular Landscape,* described it as a large amorphous territory lacking visual signals about underlying ownership.[3] The civilized good-twin was the bounded landscape, of which the bad-twin was countryside without walls, fences, and verges separating one property from another. If the bounded landscape signified stable social relationships, its opposite was a place outside the law. Elites in society, according to Jackson, prefer planned landscapes, and landscape painters from the seventeenth to the nineteenth centuries complied with paintings of tidy landscapes now hanging on museum walls.

Trees and water were essential to the region's well-being; logs were floated to mills downstream, creating jobs and material for construction and paper. Iron was abundant and contributed more to the Adirondack economy than historians have conceded; dozens of mining and smelting operations took place, mostly in the eastern part of the region. Tahawus and Mineville were scenes of sizable industrial mining activities for 125 years or so, until the 1970s or 1980s.

As important as trees were to the economy and culture of the region, the profits did not stay in the Adirondacks but enriched lumbermen and others whose businesses and homes were chiefly in Glens Falls and cities outside the region. Long-term economic growth depended on clearing forests rather than saving them, an expectation based on commonplace wisdom that cities and fortunes are not found in forests and that the miseries of poverty were worse in a forest culture than in a culture of farming. Forest residents do not necessarily want the forest destroyed, but they suspect that trees stand between them and the comfortable life they see outside the forest.

The forest is a resource on which the prosperity of a region may rest, though the wood-lot owner may chafe at being restricted from cutting where he pleases. In his book *A Forest Journey,* John Perlin presents his thesis that civilizations from ancient Sumeria to the present day rose on a resource base of forests. Wood was used in building cities, constructing ships for trade, as fuel for furnaces for smelting metals, and for baking brick.[4] As local forests were depleted, empires looked farther afield for a

Picnic, Santanoni, 1892. A box camera is on the corner of the table. The Adirondack Museum (63449).

supply of wood. Colonizing North America was justified by political economists in England for this reason. When they lost their forests and outside sources, empires slipped into decline, according to Perlin.

Forests have been regarded as unfriendly by the majority of peoples of the world, most of whom are accustomed to plains and wide valleys characterized by distant horizons and open skies. The forest is the setting for traditional fairy tales. Even in modern times, witches, vampires, and mad scientists still are depicted in stone castles on mountains surrounded by a deep forest. The forest is a place removed from human society. "I must tell you that there is something in the proximity of the woods which is very singular," wrote J. Hector St. John de Crèvecoeur (1735–1813), who, in his *Letters from an American Farmer* of 1782, theorized that men who live in the forest "are entirely different from those that live in the plains. . . . The chase [hunt] renders them ferocious, gloomy, and unsocial; a hunter wants no neighbor, he rather hates them because he dreads the competition."[5]

Prejudice about the forest was revealed in a story related by Dr. John Gerster about a camping trip his family had taken some sixty years earlier. In a letter of 1962, he said he and his parents stayed in an open camp accompanied by two guides, Jerome Wood

Ping-Pong, Santanoni Lodge, c. 1900. Young adults on the veranda, near a sleeping cabin. The Adirondack Museum (P63541).

and Mike McGuire, who liked to call himself the "King of the Adirondack guides." The Gerster family slept in a lean-to while their guides occupied a tent nearby. The cook, however, terrified of the woods, retired to a log cabin which had hinged iron shutters at the windows and a stout door from a walk-in icebox to keep bears from the meat and provisions inside: "Our cook . . . at night . . . retreated into this fortress—bolted the heavy door, went up a heavy ladder into the attic, let down a heavy trap door, and rolled a heavy block of wood on top to keep it down! In Hungary woods were supposed to harbor robbers!"[6] Arpad Gerster taught his son John to feel at home in the Adirondack woods, while Marie Papp, their cook, held to the European superstition of forests as places of villainy.

That Adirondack forests and waters require special consideration has seldom been an issue even among people opposed to regulation. Indians camped seasonally in the Adirondacks and are believed to have returned to their villages at lower elevations where weather and terrain were more temperate. The Adirondacks resisted domestication, being "fit for none other than public and general uses," according to the speaker of the passage that opens this chapter.[7] The region was retarded in other ways; it was late in being named, in 1837, when "Adirondack Group" was chosen by Ebenezer Emmons to identify mountains where the Hudson River originated, and it was not surveyed until the last quarter of the century, starting in 1873 with the issuance of Verplanck Colvin's first report of the survey he was to direct until 1900, when his position was abolished.[8]

In its first 100 years, New York State followed a policy of encouraging economic development for the entire state. This policy and its underlying philosophy was set forth unambiguously by the legislature in an Assembly Document for 1850:

> One of the first and foremost duties of the state is to subdue her soil to the culture of men, to remove the obstacles which nature and circumstances may have interposed, and to compel every part of her possessions to contribute to its full extent, to the support, comfort, and property of her citizens. [9]

The Legislature intended to spur growth by giving land away for pennies an acre and by granting privileges in charters, a kind of contract between government and private corporations authorized to do what the state could not itself do. Land by itself held little value until it could be exploited in some way—its trees cut, minerals extracted, waters harnessed. Setting aside land for posterity—a concept absent in the Assembly statement—was an unfamiliar idea at the time.

Land was necessary but not sufficient to development; the state knew it could make generous concessions in land, tax exemptions, and privileges at little direct cost to itself. Talk of a railroad through the Adirondacks had begun in 1848, but the charters granted by the state were not followed by actual work until 1863, when Dr. Thomas Clark Durant and several other men bought what became the Adirondack Railroad Company, obtaining a fresh charter from the legislature that was good for twenty years. Construction began in 1865, but progress was slow because Dr. Durant was busy with the Union Pacific Railroad and its affairs in the West and in

Dock, Santanoni, Newcomb Lake, 1911. The Adirondack Museum (P62957).

Washington, D.C. In 1869, when he was fired as its Vice President and General Manager hours after driving one of two gold spikes at Promontory Point in the Utah Territory, signifying completion of America's first transcontinental railroad, he turned his attention to what a reporter that year referred to as his "plaything of a railroad in the Adirondacks."

Dr. Durant introduced service as track crept northward to what became the terminus in North Creek, N.Y., on the southeastern edge of the core wilderness, reaching the hamlet in 1871.[10] No one knows for sure how much land was owned or controlled by the Adirondack Railroad. An editorial writer in 1865 thought it was upwards of a million acres; but in 1899 it was estimated to have been about 600,000 acres at the time of the sale in 1889. Whatever the extent, it was a lot of land, held in separate tracts and exceeding the railroad's need for a right-of-way for track through the Adirondacks. The surplus land presumably could be sold by the company to pay for labor, materiel, and rolling stock. The twenty-year exemption from taxes expired in 1883, and Dr. Durant was hard-pressed to find money to pay them.[11]

After his father's death in 1885, William West Durant continued his father's efforts to sell the railroad, which he did, to the Delaware and Hudson Railroad in 1889 for between $600,000 to $900,000, or about $4–6 million in present-day dollars. Actual cash exchanged cannot be known for sure, but the handling of land in the transaction is of interest, for it reveals how land was used as a commodity in the Adirondacks: the D & H, needing far less land than the railroad controlled, allowed

Durant to set aside unneeded lands in Dr. Durant's estate. The term used in the trial brought by his sister in 1899 was that the lands had been "stripped" from the railroad. William West Durant held powers of attorney for both his mother and his sister, and so controlled these sequestered lands.

What happened to approximately 370,000 acres can only be imagined. Durant may have allowed some to be auctioned for unpaid taxes; in the late 1890s he sold some of the land to the state for the Forest Preserve. Choicer tracts were

Fixing a flat tire, c. 1910. Possibly at Santanoni or somewhere between there and Albany, where the Pruyn family lived. The Adirondack Museum (P63152).

set aside as preserves of 1,000 to 1,500 acres each; he built camps on the shores of three private lakes, not counting the pioneering camp that belonged to his parents, Camp Pine Knot, which he sold to Collis P. Huntington in 1895. He sold Camp Uncas to J. Pierpont Morgan in 1895, Camp Arbutus to Archer Huntington in 1899, and Sagamore Lodge to Alfred G. Vanderbilt in 1901. His reason seems less to have been one of making a killing from these properties—it is questionable that he made much money on any of them—than to bring men of wealth and power to the Adirondacks and enlisting their help in developing the central Adirondack region into a year-round resort.

Reform

Cut-and-run logging practices of lumbermen and the passivity of the state as lands sold for less than a dollar an acre led to proposals that a state park be established, or what an editor of the *New York Times* called "a tract of country fitted to make a Central Park for the world," a characterization as apt today as in 1864, when it was made.[12] In 1872, the state appointed a citizens' commission that included Verplanck Colvin, who was to become one of the most eloquent and effective spokesmen for a park in the Adirondacks. The charge for the commission was to look at preserving part of the region for conservation and recreational purposes.

As if anticipating the state park to come, New York began exercising its right to preempt other buyers at tax sales rather than stand passively by. Land traders were furious when the state official at auction peremptorily removed more than 19,000 acres from a sale in 1877. A "chewing match" broke out between George Fowler, lawyer for Dr. Durant, and the state agent. The sale, which included most of Township 40 and all of Raquette Lake, was a major loss for the Durants because the lake was the crossroad for travelers from the four points of the compass.[13]

Hop Baron of DeBar Pond

Robert Schroeder and his wife belonged to beer-brewing families in Germany. In the 1880s they began amassing land on a pond named for a Canadian trapper, eventually owning 2,100 acres of which over three hundred acres were planted in hops. Using his own fortune and perhaps his wife's as well, Robert had a sixty-room mansion built to replace their residence that burned. The new building, in two sections of stone and wood frame, had a ballroom, mahogany staircase, furniture imported from Holland, and stained glass windows from Germany. The couple spent their fortune and moved to a tenement in Brooklyn, N.Y., where they separately took their lives. Their story was told by Maitland DeSormo in the fall 1959 issue of *North Country Life*. Vacant for years, the mansion was razed in 1940 and a log house with seventeen rooms erected for a couple from Palm Beach, Florida, according to an inventory of 1978 by the New York State Division for Historic Preservation in Albany.

Defenders of the Adirondacks, arguing that water supplies for downstream cities and industries needed to be husbanded, got three measures adopted into law within nine years—the Forest Preserve in 1885, the Adirondack Park in 1892, and the "forever wild" article of the State Constitution in 1894.

Preserves

Preserves in the Adirondacks date from the last quarter of the century for the most part. It was as though the spate of books and articles about the region between 1830 and 1870 finally led people to do what they had been putting off, which was to buy land themselves or in partnership with others. A law in 1871 sanctioning private preserves encouraged the formation of preserves that followed, many of which exist to this day. The object of the act was expressed in its title, "An Act for the protection of private parks and grounds, and to encourage the propagation of fish and game." It set no minimum on the amount of land, and owners had only to print a public notice of intent each week in an area newspaper for three months, after which "no trespassing signs" were to be posted on the perimeter of the property no more than forty rods apart (620 feet).

The legislature, which owned less than forty thousand acres in 1872, showed it was heeding calls to protect the region's forests, watersheds, and wildlife.[14] It was, in effect, enlisting private buyers to do this, a cost-free way of getting others to do a job.

The act gave preserve owners and their employees wide latitude in enforcing a state law, since an alleged trespasser could be arrested on complaint and quickly brought before a local justice of the peace. The justice could impose a fine of up to $25, of which half was earmarked for the county poor and the remainder for the informant so long as he was not an employee of the preserve owner. A sentence of thirty days in jail could be passed for destruction of fences, signs, or property, or the killing of fish and game, and a second conviction meant imprisonment in the county jail for up to a year.

The law's practical impact was not immediate, but its symbolic meaning was immense, sending a chilling message to sportsmen and (especially) guides. Previously men had hunted, fished, and traveled pretty much wherever they wished in what the 1792 measure had described as a wilderness of "waste and unappropriated" land. The act now made them law-breakers for doing what they had been doing for fifty or more years. Posted lands, including beaches and islands on lakes and streams, would now be closed to them.

Public reaction to the law requires further study, but the law was contrary to historic toleration of public access, and it additionally bore the taint of Britain's private parks as bastions of inherited wealth and privilege. Whether this impelled elected officials to create a state park is uncertain, but that is what happened, beginning in the 1870s when lands in arrears for back taxes began to be set aside by the state to itself. Money was first appropriated to buy land in 1885, which was the year the Forest Preserve was established. By 1892, when the Adirondack State Park was established

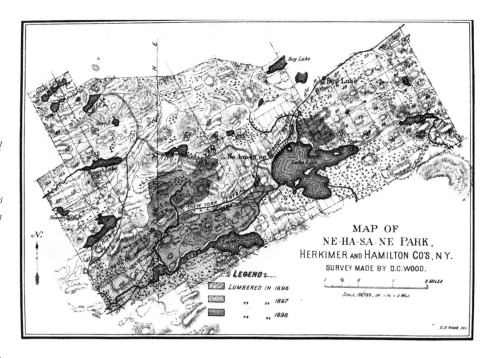

"Map of Ne-Ha-Sa-Ne Park," c. 1900. Nehasane Park, 34,700 acres in extent in 1901, was among forty-four preserves of 500 acres or more in the Adirondack Park. Married to a Vanderbilt, Dr. Webb owned a model farm in Shelburne, Vermont; in the Adirondacks, he amassed as much as 188,000 acres of forest land in the 1890s, the bulk sold in separate deals to the New York Central Railroad and to New York State. What he retained is shown on a map from a 1901 publication, indicating that lumbering was the chief business of the park, not counting recreation for family and friends. There were three station stops for trains crossing Nehasane Park, one being a depot for the family's camp on Lake Lila. Forest Lodge, the chief building, is illustrated elsewhere (p. 226). The map is from Henry S. Graves, Practical Forestry in the Adirondacks *(1901). The Adirondack Museum Library.*

and the state owned about 731,000 acres, the state had become the largest landholder in the region in under two decades. What this book calls "preserves" were termed "private recreational estates" in a doctoral dissertation by Roger Thompson.[15] By 1892 these estates numbered about forty-two and represented almost one million acres of land, according to Thompson.

Allowing lands to be posted put New York squarely behind private owners and ownership. Phineas Lounsbury, who had been coming to Echo Camp on Raquette Lake since the early 1880s, was dumbfounded when he received notice that he and others on the lake could no longer tie their boats at the dock on the Marion River Carry. Writing on stationery of the Merchants Exchange National Bank of New York, where he was president, he asked if a mistake had been made: he had patronized the Raquette Lake Transportation Co. for many years but now found himself barred from Blue Mountain Lake: "I think it is severe treatment after so many years," he said to George Thompson, the hapless superintendent who was only following orders.[16]

In an incident in 1896, a New York real estate dealer, John Golding, who owned a camp on the lake, accused local men of being too timid in crossing the log boom which Durant had placed across South Inlet of Raquette Lake. The next day, joined by his guide Ed Martin, Golding pulled his guideboat over the boom and fished upstream. A watchman posted at the boom wired Durant in New York, and Durant, replying by wire to Blue Mountain Lake, ordered Thompson to prosecute. Golding, brought before Tyler Merwin in Blue Mountain Lake, meekly paid a $25 fine. This further angered residents, two of whom, Charlie Bennett and Jack Daly, cut the boom with a crosscut saw. Durant had the boom replaced and stationed more men to enforce it.[17] The matter became moot the next year, in 1897, when William West Durant sold most of Township 6, including South Inlet, to New York, and the boom was removed.

State and private owners were potential adversaries and have criticised one another—private spokesmen especially—down to the present day. But both sides have a mutuality of interest, coming together in behind-the-scene negotiations seldom heard of by the public. Private buyers know that the state has deep pockets and is a serious buyer for lands no one else is likely to buy. A historical instance was the sale of Township 6 by William West Durant, who was land-rich but short of cash, selling the state nearly 24,000 acres in 1897.

There was conniving, however, since the purchase had been approved by the Forest Preserve Commission, of which Lieutenant Governor Timothy Woodruff was president. Removed from the sale was a thousand-acre preserve centering on Sumner Lake with a log cabin on it. Woodruff was the buyer of what became a private in-holding surrounded now by the State Forest Preserve. According to Harold Hochschild, Woodruff bought the property in February 1898, although Durant had informed Dr. Gerster the summer before, in August 1897, that Woodruff had "bought for himself the Sumner Lake property."[18] The exemption from the sale of what came to be Kamp Kill Kare was criticized in the *New York World,* but nothing came from a later investigation by the Moreland Commission.

Protected land went by names other than "preserve." If there are fundamental differences among the following terms, they elude people who have dealt in land in the Adirondacks: reserve, club, park, estate, and association. All appear in legal and quasi-legal documents. To preserve owners, the object boiled down to stewardship of forests, waters, and wildlife.

Preserves were managed conscientiously—no preserve owner has been called to account for abuses of a trust, to the writer's knowledge. The state's authority over private land was ill-defined and assumed importance only in an infrequent crisis, as when a rash of forest fires in 1903 and 1908 destroyed about 800,000 acres, roughly a quarter of the Adirondack Park at the time. Jeopardy to state lands showed that the state had a "pressing interest in what happened to forested land throughout the Adirondacks . . . public and private," according to Philip Terrie.[19]

Preserve owners adopted varying management strategies. The Woodruffs and the

Dr. William Seward Webb on the porch of Forest Lodge, his house on Lake Lila, 1902, T. E. Marr, photographer. Webb practiced medicine little or not at all, his marriage to Lila Vanderbilt enabling him to own a palatial home in New York City and another in Vermont, where a model farm and stable evolved under his supervision. He served in public life, and his descendants, a few of whom retain a reduced portion of the original preserve, went on to collect art, and to open and even run museums. Chief among the museums are the Shelburne Museum and Shelburne Farms, separately run but complementary educational facilities sharing the estate formerly belonging to Dr. and Mrs. Webb. The Adirondack Museum, gift of J. Watson Webb (P23720).

Log cabin (Stabbur),
Raquette Lake. Sidney
Whelan, Jr., whose first sum-
mers were spent on Raquette
Lake, bought twenty-five
acres on a remote corner of
the lake and had Robert
Waldron construct a
Stabbur, *a traditional*
Norwegian farm building,
in 1984. The upper room, for
sleeping (in sleeping bags), is
reached through a trap door
in the ceiling of the sitting
room below. Nearby is a
lean-to. Photograph by Craig
Gilborn, 1994.

Garvans who bought Kill Kare and its preserve left the forest largely untouched. The Kildare Club, which became a camp for several families when bought from a club that included William C. Whitney, divided its 10,000 acre preserve into two roughly equal parts, one where cutting was allowed on occasion and the other to be left intact and which today is a veritable virgin forest.

Of forty-two estates in the Adirondacks in 1893, the smallest was the Ragged Lake Club which had 350 acres but would have considerably more a century later. Most preserves were large, the average being about 23,000 acres, and the largest aggregate, 188,000 acres, belonging to Dr. William Seward Webb, of which 112,000 acres were held by the Nehasane Park Association and 76,000 by W.S. Forests. In 1895, Webb sold 75,585 acres to the state for $8 an acre, or $1.50 more than the prevailing price, in a settlement by the state with Dr. Webb after rising waters behind Stillwater dam flooded and destroyed some timber and prevented him from getting timber to market.[20]

Support for private preserves appeared in *Outing* magazine for August, 1898, in which it was conceded that "the charge brought against some of the private owners of large preserves, that they assume an authority far beyond what they actually possess," was just and true in many cases, an allusion to the deputizing of private owners to enforce state law. However, the writer added, the state "has been very remiss in protecting and preserving this matchless inheritance of the people from the destroying hand of the lumberman." For all their faults, wealthy individuals bestowed a public benefit by the "purchasing and careful preservation of this territory."[21]

Preserve owners were aware of their responsibilities and proud of their initiatives, which often were ahead of state conservation practices. They hired scientists and foresters and became partners in research by state agencies and colleges. Some preserves employed gamekeepers and other men to monitor and carry out management plans, and some embarked on the tricky process of restocking lakes and ponds, sometimes by raising fingerlings at hatcheries on the preserve. The Adirondack League Club has perhaps been more consistently committed to research than most clubs, except perhaps for the Ausable Club, through its land-owning component, the Adirondack Mountain Reserve.

Two preserves were stocked with wildlife. Edward Litchfield fenced in part of Litchfield Park and introduced moose, elk, beavers, and varieties of birds.[22] He also posted uniformed guards to watch for poachers.[23] William Seward Webb, a neighbor of Litchfield's, tried propagating large game animals at Nehasane, an experiment that proved unsuccessful.

Introducing big game seems foolish today, but at the time it came under the heading of "propagation" mentioned in the act of 1871 and was perceived as "scientific" conservation. Webb also brought in Gifford Pinchot to prepare a plan for managing the forest at Nehasane. Pinchot, a Yale graduate and pioneer student of scientific forestry in America, began his study for Webb in 1892; six years later, he took his ideas on conservation goals to Washington where he became chief of the Forestry Division in the U.S. Department of Agriculture.[24]

Preserve owners sometimes tolerated access and granted passage to local residents in an effort to mollify local opinion and to win their cooperation. While money and law were on the owners' side, locals were not without power of their own, as everyone knew. What if townspeople failed to come to help fight a fire? Raymond Hopper doubted that "the game laws will be enforced rigidly in the Adirondacks, owing to the immense territory" and because local law officers played favorites.[25] When preserve owners had a retinue of a dozen or more men working for them, it may have seemed to them that the estate was self-sufficient and free of dependence on the good will and help of townspeople in the nearest community. This attitude changed as labor costs rose and the number of employees steadily got smaller, to a caretaker and wife in some instances: most preserves rely on towns for their security today.

Innocent use of private land was tolerated at one time. Lumbermen knew that hunters and campers were little threat to their forests, which may be why the tradition of access remains strong in New England but less so in New York. Marc Cook made these cautionary remarks in *The Wilderness Cure,* which was published in 1881:

> The right to the ground [private property] is not, therefore, a legal one, with the camper-out. But so long as a proper regard is shown for the preservation of the property, and care taken not to maliciously injure the woodland, nobody need fear dispossession.[26]

Cook, who had built a temporary camp in the vicinity of Upper St. Regis Lake, might have found owners less tolerant a decade later. In New York, trespass has been

Litchfield Castle

Lake Madeleine, 1911–1913, Tupper Lake, N.Y., Don Barber, architect.

Edward H. Litchfield, an avid Brooklyn, N.Y., sportsman, acquired 8,600 acres in 1893, built a camp, and in 1901 erected an eight-foot fence around two tracts to propagate moose, elk, black-tailed deer, wild goats, jack rabbits, fox squirrels, quail, and (in a separate enclosure) wild boar. He replaced the old camp with a stone castle or schloss of steel and cement using laborers recently arrived from Italy. The Litchfields, including Pieter Litchfield, the builder's great-grandson, have kept the Castle and much of the Preserve of which it is a part. Replacing old tiles with new in the early 1990s meant finding a Wisconsin roofer able to work on steep-pitched roofs high off the ground.

Litchfield Castle, under construction, c. 1912. The entrance is the arched door to the left of the loggia. Courtesy of Pieter Litchfield

Door on lake side with scrolled pediment and Litchfield coat-of-arms. Photograph by Craig Gilborn, 1998.

Great Hall. The door in the preceding illustration is left of center here. Floors are concrete and tile, and heat is delivered by ducts incorporated into walls and floors. Photograph by Craig Gilborn, 1998.

Workmen, c. 1912. Workers lived at the site, which was five miles from the nearest road. There were more men than appear in this detail of a larger picture. Courtesy of Pieter Litchfield.

Outlying cottage, Duck Pond, Litchfield Park. Courtesy of Pieter Litchfield.

discouraged by forest owners who lease their lands to hunting and fishing clubs which allow access to members only.

One Preserve, Many Owners

A preserve was a territory to be saved—preserved—as an entity, yet ownership devolved into a number of sometimes conflicting interests. In time these invariably got more complicated as the founder left the estate to three children who then had children of their own. How should the interests of all these parties be divided without jeopardizing the integrity of the property itself? Shares, preferences, concessions, and buy-outs were used to prevent balkanization and dissolution. This meant that some in the family, whatever face was put on it, had to leave the nest, a legacy that rankled, not so much among those who had been paid as among *their* progeny, who viewed the perennial delights of a camp in the hands of a cousin as a treasure that might have been theirs.

Equity was also an issue when some undertook more of the thankless chore of managing the camp and preserve than did other family members. The workers believed their diligence made them first among equals. Less active members, sensing a subtle shift of power was afoot, were constrained to write the president—perhaps the eldest son or grandson of the founder—regretting (again) that they could not attend the annual meeting but asking that he and others not construe their absence as a reliquishment of their interest in the property.

The end of the Second World War saw Adirondack preserves and camps begin to pass into institutional hands, as gifts to colleges, Boy Scout and Girl Scout councils, children's camps, and religious and charitable groups that ran summer programs. The first such gift may have been made by Archer and Anna Huntington in 1932, when they gave a large preserve to the college of forestry at Syracuse University. They retained their camp on Arbutus Lake and a more remote camp on Catlin Lake until 1939, when they gave these properties to the college, as well.[27] Nine years later, they donated Camp Pine Knot to Cortland College, which has operated the camp as an outdoor education center.

Preserve and corporation are impersonal words, but behind them are human stories of struggles to save a world connecting people to particular places. Ragged Lake, where artist Arthur Fitzwilliam Tait painted a winter shanty and two men carrying a black bear in 1856, was a stage for one such family saga. In his history of the camp, David Fitch Remington, a grandson of the founder, looked on the family's 109 years on the lake and found that the substance of their enjoyment in the camp, and even many of its details, had changed little despite sea changes everywhere else.[28] It is Matamek's resistance to change that is cherished above all.

Matamek remains a place apart from the world of getting and spending. The cows and horses have gone, Remington says, and ice houses are in disrepair or have collapsed. Four camps have been added to the older buildings, the oldest of which dates from 1869. Occasionally an electrical generator can be heard. But the shoreline of

Ragged Lake is as it has always been, outhouses are still in use, motor boats banned, and no electric or telephone lines can be seen. The forest, he notes, is in good condition and is home for an abundance of wildlife. However, fishing for trout has deteriorated, as measured by declining catches.

Both lake and preserve, now about 3,000 acres in extent, demand family attention more than ever before. Previously, before the 1950s, the biggest problems faced by president and board revolved around money—how to pay for caretaker, upkeep, and taxes. Money was especially scarce in the Depression. But management in the 1990s requires an understanding of forest, land, and lake—the three pillars of the preserve, its watershed included.

Years ago, a couple of members proposed that the corporation sell most of the preserve to New York State. There were advantages to this: shareholders would get a windfall of money but retain the camp buildings and a portion of lake front, and a large part of the tax bite would shift to the state. Family members would share the lake with others, but this was a democratic value that was no real threat, except the possibility that power boats would be allowed where there had been none before.

It was against just such the possibility, that all or part of the property might be sold, that led Morton Fitch, a son of Matamek's founding patriarch, Ashbel Fitch, to seek to incorporate the property in 1928. The asset was consolidated in 500 shares with 100 each going to four siblings, while the fifth, for reasons that elude Remington to this day, got ninety-five, the remaining five shares going to a sixth party. Actual incorporation did not take place until 1933 under the not-for-profit law of the state.

The complications that can unfold as families grow were demonstrated here. The five brothers and sisters who shared ownership in 1933 numbered 39 by 1989, or, as loosely identified by Remington—"brothers, sisters, first, second, and third cousins, fathers, mothers, uncles, and aunts." In a letter to the family that year, Remington said that Matamek had become "a subtle blend of competing interests which reflect our shareholder diversity and balance the financial needs of the Corporation with the needs and circumstances of its shareholders." Keeping Matamek meant all should share equally even when some in the family might pay more than others: this was, he acknowledged with the emphasis his own, "a compromise of *equal rights based on unequal contributions* between users and non-users."[29]

The object of incorporation was to perpetuate an interest that had evolved from the personal possession of Ashbel Parmelee Fitch to the joint responsibility of his descendants. The preserve was deemed by the family to be indivisible, a vow by the living that the preserve would pass to their posterity in a condition as good or better as when they found it as children.

Environmental issues have intruded on Matamek's remoteness in the northern Adirondacks. Its directors can address matters at hand, as by the purchase of a pond that was a headwater for Ragged Lake. But they are powerless to stop pollutants drifting from cities to the west which have acidified the lake. Limestone gravel was placed at the inlet with the hope that this would reduce the acid and so make the lake more hospitable to trout.

Taxes, always a problem, doubled between 1940 and 1986 but rose, Remington says, 12 percent each year since then. He does not place blame for this but finds state policies contradictory or self-defeating: the state, he says, has advocated open space, healthy forests, clean water and air, and a self-sustaining wildlife population, all of which private preserves have been doing as well or better than the state itself. Yet it allows local governments to treat preserves like the fabled goose that laid the golden egg.[30]

CHAPTER 6

Clubs

Men's Clubs

THE FIRST of the men's sporting clubs in the Adirondacks may have been the Piseco Lake Trout Club which was formed by the late 1830s but became known to readers of sporting magazines which flourished in the 1840s and 1850s. The club did not seem to own land, and it rented a cabin, the members being as interested in fellowship as in sport, exchanging stories and fly patterns, and comparing the action of bamboo fishing rods. George Washington Bethune, a founder, was an early theorist on designing flies and angling in America, and he edited the first American edition of Sir Izaak Walton's classic, the *Complete Angler,* in 1847.

The men who formed and belonged to these early clubs were successful in business and other lines of work. Paul Schullery, in his fine book *Fly Fishing in America,* says that they were typical of the cultured and well-educated club members of sporting clubs elsewhere, of which the Schuykill Fishing Company, founded in 1737, was the first in America.[1] Among the members of the North Woods Walton Club were the Governor of New York, the editor of the *Albany Evening Journal,* and an army general, Richard U. Sherman, its first president. In 1856, when it was formed, the group called itself the Brown's Tract Association, but changed the name a year later.

Walton Club members fished streams and lakes in the large territory between Raquette Lake and Old Forge. Their first camp, on Third Lake, was humorously described and illustrated in wood engravings of a bark and pole lean-to, called "The Hotel," and an open shed of the same material, called the "Dining-Saloon," in *Harper's New Monthly Magazine* for July 1859.[2]

These early clubs soon passed from the scene, partly because they owned no land and were social rather than proprietary in character. But many streams and lakes where they had fished for two to three decades were depleted, as might have been predicted given reports and historic photographs of catches far in excess of what could be eaten. By mid-century, when declines were reported, blame was placed on too many anglers having access to the same streams. It was this, Schullery believes, that started the search for land and water that could be leased and purchased.[3]

A short-lived club was the Adirondack Club, formed in the fall of 1858 as a follow-up to the outing the previous July of ten Harvard and Boston luminaries to Follensby Pond. James Russell Lowell named it "Camp Maple," but the guides got the last word by calling it the "Philosophers' Camp," which stuck. Among its members were the philosopher Ralph Waldo Emerson, Harvard scientist Louis Agassiz, and Judge Ebenezer Rockwood Hoar, who would later be Attorney General in Grant's cabinet.[4] That winter, the painter William James Stillman purchased a 22,000 acre tract for $600. Adirondack Club members met on Ampersand Pond the following summer, but the outbreak of the Civil War obliterated what little interest there was in the club, and it came to an inglorious end.

Family Clubs

A second Adirondack Club, a separate venture, was formed in 1877 on lands leased from the former McIntyre Iron Company, the owners of which also became club members. Renamed the Tahawus Club, it was said to have a preserve of about 75,000 acres in 1901, when it had cottages at two locations about seven miles apart, both former sites of the mine operation. One of these, the Upper Works, was taken over by the Federal government in the Second World War, when titanium bearing ore was extracted and sent as a concentrate to a smelter. Club members with cottages moved from the Upper Works to the Lower Works, where the club is found today.[5] It owns some land but leases more, which formerly belonged to it, from the Finch Pruyn Company.

Two clubs started by a few wealthy men proved short-lived as membership clubs. The Caughnawauga Club was formed in 1894 and a clubhouse and other buildings erected on Catlin Lake, north of Newcomb. In 1911, a member, Archer Huntington, who owned the Arbutus preserve and camp, purchased the outstanding shares from the other members. Mr. Huntington did not use the camp, which did not have a road to it; still, he retained a caretaker and his wife on the property until the 1930s, their responsibility being to keep trespassers away.[6] The Kildare Club was formed by William C. Whitney and a handful of other men in the early 1890s, but it was sold before the end of the century to families from New York whose four descendants still owned it in 1998.

The North Woods Club initially called itself the Adirondack Preserve Association, incorporating in 1887 for the purposes of "boating, fishing, athletic and all manly sports and pastimes, and the preservation of game and forests." It switched to its present name in 1895 when it acquired additional lands and had a membership of fifty, mostly from New York City. A few, such as artists Eliphelet Terry and Winslow Homer, had been coming to Baker's Clearing years before there was a club.

The North Woods Club never lost the weathered character it had from these earliest times. By 1901, when it joined the Association for the Protection of the Adirondacks, the club was listed as owning 4,583 acres of land, most of it forest, and managed to help pay for a caretaker, taxes, and maintenance. The heart of the club was the clearing with its log boarding house built in 1863 serving as a clubhouse. Dues were $50 a year in 1897, and members who stayed in the clubhouse were charged $12

Rich individuals and socially prominent families were buyers of preserves, owners of lodges, and members of clubs in the Adirondacks in the last quarter of the nineteenth century. Most of them viewed the Adirondacks as an antidote to scenes like this one, but the majority accommodated both worlds, dressing up in the city and down in the Adirondacks.

Boarding house, built 1863, burned 1920. This photograph of c. 1900 shows the log building when it was a clubhouse for the North Woods Club, Minerva, N.Y. It was built by Thomas Baker and a handyman in 1863. Baker's wife and daughters took boarders from New York and other cities. The visitors purchased the property in 1886. Eliphelet Terry was a guest, and he introduced the place to Winslow Homer, whose Adirondack paintings became his finest work. The Adirondack Museum Library.

a week, or $10 if they took meals in the clubhouse but had cottages of their own. Before automobiles, members and guests were met at the railroad station in North Creek and driven eighteen miles to the club in a horse-drawn wagon over a road dug out of the hillside.[7]

The club had tough spells, partly as the result of erratic membership. The Johnstown Flood of May 31, 1889, produced a few new members from Pittsburgh. Seven Pennsylvania towns were destroyed and upwards of three thousand people lost their lives in the flood, which resulted when a rain-filled lake broke through an earthen dam and sent a wall of water for miles down the valley. The dam had been built for canal purposes earlier in the century, but subsequently the property was acquired for use as a resort by wealthy families from Pittsburgh, about sixty miles to the west. Members stayed in cottages and a clubhouse on the shore of the lake, which, because of its higher elevation, afforded cooler air in summer. In the fault-finding that followed the disaster, the accusing finger was most easily pointed at the club. The accusation was not altogether fair, as torrential rains had been falling for days prior to the flood. The club's membership, which included industrialists associated with labor unrest in Pennsylvania, was an easy target in the recriminations. One member was Henry Clay Frick, who joined the North Woods Club along with several other former members of the South Fork Fishing and Hunting Club. In violently breaking a strike at Homestead, Pennsylvania, in 1892, Frick ended trade unionism in the iron and steel industry for years to come.

Membership in the North Woods Club never got much above seventy and often it was far less. The nadir came in 1939–1941 when membership slipped from thirteen to eight, of whom several were in the armed forces. Helen Frick stepped in and saved the day. The daughter of Henry Clay Frick, she remembered her summers at the club when she was a girl. She purchased thirty-six club certificates and sent six English girls who were exiles of the war in Europe to stay at the club.[8] Miss Frick, who established the art reference library attached to her father's Frick Museum in New York City, paid for the restoration of equipment, boats, and docks at the club.

The Bisby Club was founded in 1878 by twenty-five men who had fished Bisby Lake, some of whom were former members of the North Woods Walton Club (not to be confused with the North Woods Club in Minerva), among them a Civil War general, Richard U. Sherman, who pronounced Bisby to be "the Canaan towards which my footsteps have trended the last forty years in the wilderness." The club leased 320 acres and nine lakes and ponds, purchasing the property ten years later, in 1888. Bisby Lake, like most other waters in the Adirondacks, had been open to all anglers, but no longer, as Gen. Sherman made clear: "By the law . . . all the fish and game in this tract are our own personal property, and the taking away from it by an unauthorized person, of any bird, four-footed animal, or fish, is larceny."[9]

The "law" cited, adopted by the state in 1871 and discussed elsewhere in this book, sanctioned private preserves and enforcement, giving preserve owners and employees authority to bring charges against poachers and have them quickly brought before a local justice to be fined and perhaps jailed.

A clubhouse was built in 1879 for Bisby Club members. The building had twenty bedrooms and "self-supported" housekeeping, which, according to Roger Yepsen in an article on social life at the club, meant that housekeeping was done largely by members. Food was ample at the lodge, since Yepsen calculated that each club member consumed an average of six pounds of food each day in the summer of 1882.[10]

The Bisby Club may have been the first club to admit entire families and not just husbands and brothers, breaking a near-monopoly that men had on enjoyment in

Clubhouse, Ausable Club, built 1890. Formerly St. Hubert's Inn, reorganized as Ausable Lakes and Mountain Club in 1906, now the Ausable Club. The Adirondack Mountain Reserve held the land, while the inn and clubhouse provided rooms, cottages, and services to members and guests. The clubhouse was designed by a Philadelphia architectural firm, Wilson Brothers. Photograph by Craig Gilborn, 1998.

Colonial Fish House

Like other members of the upper class, Sir William Johnson, the king's agent to the Indians in upstate New York, had a principal house, a summer cottage called Mount Joy, and a hunting and fishing box called Fish House after a later owner. Wrote an acquaintance from Schenectady, "I long much to see your Lodge at Mountjoy, for by the description I have . . . it must be delightful & pleasant. What greater pleasure can there be than plenty of Fishing & fowling." Mount Joy was built on a knoll above a marsh of Sacandaga Creek, a tributary of the Hudson River which flooded in spring and was what Johnson called an "Extensive Meadow." Four miles distant was a "little log tenement" reached by boat. James Flexner, in his biography *Mohawk Baronet*, spoke of a rumor that Johnson would fire his rifle twice and soon be met by Susannah Wormwood, and the couple would continue in the canoe to his cabin. The sites of Mount Joy and Fish House were inundated beneath Sacandaga Reservoir, but Johnson's principal residence, Johnson Hall, is a historic site run by the state in Johnstown.

the Adirondacks. Most women, on reaching a hotel in the interior, watched as men and boys departed on camping trips miles from the hotel. Family clubs were founded by men, so, whatever their motives, they introduced wives and children to the same outdoor pleasures.

In 1893, finding itself hemmed in by a new club then being formed, the Adirondack League Club, Bisby narrowly agreed to a merger despite the opposition of nearly half its members. Bisby's reputation of being a homey club with down-to-earth members still holds to this day. The clubhouse of 1879 had twenty rooms and was believed to be one of the bigger log structures in the Adirondacks. Torn down in 1900, its replacement was considered too primitive by later standards and so was not rebuilt when it burned in 1939.

The two flagship clubs of the Adirondacks, the Adirondack League Club and the Ausable Club, still exist and are important because each, of necessity, had to acquaint itself with forest management when forestry was in its infancy. (They also may have been the first family-oriented clubs, by virtue of the Bisby Club's pre-dating A.L.C. by twelve years.)

Family clubs in the Adirondacks were an extension of the larger social phenomenon of the late nineteenth century, the golf and country club. The suburban club and its Adirondack counterpart owned tracts of land centering around a clubhouse with ancillary facilities for recreation, dining, and staff, and both were exclusionary, the approval of members being necessary before applicants could be accepted as members. The difference other than their city and woodland locations was that members owned cottages in the Adirondacks, requiring approval to sell to prospective buyers. The clubs were highly social, if insular, but they were wholesome environments for young children, given the facilities and staff available to keep them occupied.

The Putnam Camp was more like a colony than a conventional club, since all generations of men, women, and children made their own fun in simple cottages without the tennis courts, big dining room, golf course, and similar amenities only a mile or so away at the Ausable Club. Putnam inmates swam in a cold mountain stream, hiked mountain trails, discussed books around a table at tea, and sat in a circle around a roaring fire while tales were told and songs sung.

Families who banded together to form what only nominally was a club constituted the Knollwood Club on Lower Saranac Lake. A similar situation obtained at what for a few years, 1900 to 1904, was the Eagle's Nest Country Club and Golf Course. Built by William West Durant with a clubhouse, casino, and a nine-hole golf course, it actually did have a small membership until 1904, when it was sold to three men from the city by creditors of Durant's. In both instances, the buyers were Jewish families who shared common camp facilities.[11]

Families seem to have been a key to clubs that survived bad economic times, unlike exclusively male clubs, which seemed to have far shorter lives. The Adirondack League Club, the biggest of the membership clubs, was incorporated in 1890 on 91,000 acres of land purchased by Mark M. Pomeroy in northern Herkimer County. The club adopted an ethic of good resource management from the start. A forester,

Mountain Lodge, Adirondack League Club, Little Moose Lake, Augustus D. Shepard, architect, H. M. Beach, photographer, c. 1914. This lodge replaced the clubhouse designed by club member William S. Wicks, which burned in 1913. The Adirondack Museum (P9401).

Bernhard E. Fernow, was made a charter member. Fernow, a German and an early practitioner of the new profession of forestry in Europe, came to America in 1876 where he became the first forester to head the Division of Forestry in the Department of Agriculture. A.L.C., according to Philip Terrie, wanted a sustained yield from its forests, and it looked to the government-managed forests in Europe for guidance. Fernow inspected the club's holdings the year they were purchased; his detailed proposal was applauded that winter by the American Forest Association, since it marked "the first attempt at permanent forest management in this country on any large scale."[12] Club directors were determined to avoid the "barren waste" left behind by lumbermen in American forests.

By 1920, the club's holdings were 104,000 acres, which Alfred L. Donaldson, in his 1921 history of the Adirondacks, said was the "largest contiguous area of absolutely virgin forest left in the Adirondacks, making it the "largest proprietary sporting club" in the Adirondack Park.[13] The club variously bought, leased, and sold land, reaching

Dining room, Mountain Lodge, c. 1914, H. M. Beach, photographer. An economy move years later reduced the dining room to its present size. The Adirondack Museum (P1900).

a maximum of about 191,000 acres in 1897. It also disposed of lands, so by its centennial in 1990 it had 53,000 acres, less than before but more than any club in the Adirondacks. It sold land to New York State—14,000 acres in 1897 and 22,000 acres in 1900; this produced a double benefit, first because club lands now had a Forest Preserve buffer and second because the club no longer was liable for the taxes on its former lands.

To be a member, one had to buy at least one share of stock costing $1,000 in 1890, or between $10,000 and $14,000 in 1990 dollars.[14] By 1897, a share cost $1,500. The club's aggregate wealth was represented by a pool of 500 shares, each of which gave the holder an undivided interest in the club and its lands, and a deed to a five-acre lot with two hundred feet of waterfront on which to build a camp. By about 1921, A.L.C. had approximately eighty camps on sites on the three lakes with lodges on them—Little Moose Lake, Honnedaga Lake, and Bisby Lake. Members without cottages stayed in the clubhouse on each of these lakes. Mountain Lodge on Little Moose, was—and is—the biggest and most hotel-like of the three club lodges.

Boathouse, Adirondack League Club, Little Moose Lake. Still standing, the boathouse was designed by Augustus D. Shepard. Club members are shown at a regatta in this photograph by H. M. Beach. The Adirondack Museum (P 2166).

In the high peak area, about ninety miles east of Old Forge, was the Ausable Club, which took its name from the river that drained out of what were the club's jewels, Upper and Lower Ausable Lakes, to which guides and sportsmen had been coming for years, to be followed in the 1890s by families who held memberships. The club building and Lower Ausable Lake were linked by the road that gave Edith Pilcher the title for her centennial club history, *Up the Lake Road.* Land-owning Adirondack Mountain Reserve and the facilities-owning Ausable Club had overlapping boards and interests; A.M.R., formed in 1887, however, was nineteen years older than the A.C., which was preceded by the Beede House and then, in 1890, its replacement, St. Huberts Inn, a hotel whose stockholders included A.M.R. directors. The two corporate bodies later merged and are considered equivalent bodies today.[15]

Cabins used by Keene Valley guides were on Upper Ausable Lake when the property was purchased in 1887; however, the A.C./A.M.R. allowed the guides continued use of the cabins, and some shareholders now leased sites maintained by a favorite guide, using his cabin for successive years. For their part, guides were now subject to club rules regarding hunting and fishing. In 1987, there were seven camps with guides performing traditional chores. Pilcher's book also lists guides who variously "guided or worked" at the Ausable Lakes from the 1830s to the present time.[16]

The cabins were simple—single-story log cabins with roofed porches that followed no plan except that expected of shelter. The attraction was Upper Ausable Lake, which, with its companion, Lower Ausable Lake, are the most hauntingly beautiful of lakes in the Adirondacks, glacially deep with still, dark surfaces reflecting rock walls that rear out of the water and vanish into the mist on overcast days. A boathouse with dozens of traditional guideboats and canoes is on the lower lake.

There was a fundamental difference in the motivation underlying the formation of the Ausable Club in 1887 and the Adirondack League Club in 1890. The mission of the former was a rescue: to save the forest from being cut and the lakes imperiled. William G. Neilson and two other men obtained an option to buy 25,000 acres, or nearly all of the township, in September, 1886, and the property was purchased in December. A stock-holding company of twenty-nine individuals, some from Philadelphia, was formed under the name "The Adirondack Mountain Reserve." Their descendants were stockholders still in 1987, when A.M.R. celebrated its 100th anniversary.

The Adirondack League Club generated money for maintaining the club by selective cutting. The club in Keene Valley did the same, but it was less aggressive, owning a maximum of 45,000 acres by 1910, with reductions to follow, to 16,000 acres by 1933, and about 7,000 acres by 1978. The Adirondack Mountain Reserve allowed cutting when it was in need of money, in the 1890s and again between 1901 and 1918. Between 1921 and 1932, it gave up 18,215 acres in five sales to New York State. The most recent sale occurred in 1978 when A.M.R. turned over 9,100 acres of mountain summits and ridges to the state for $734,952.[17]

Sacred to A.M.R. and the A.C. was preserving the Ausable Lakes and their watershed; doing this and keeping the club financially solvent led to differences on how

Food Fare

The following list, which was largely compiled by Nancy Martin from written sources for the period 1850–1915, shows the foods available to visitors and residents. Actual diets would have varied: for example, the potato was the only vegetable in many homes for most of the year. The staple of sporting parties waiting to catch a deer or trout was salt pork, baked beans, and bread or biscuits. Kate Field said that guides, "accustomed to the roughest food," would bring food of poor quality given the chance. She advised campers to plan their menu and ship the food ahead by wrapping it in India rubber bags, packing it in a crate, and shipping it for the guide to hold until their arrival.

Meats and Fish

venison
trout, bass
salt codfish
pork, salt pork
ham
dried beef
moose
rabbit
"pidgeon," partridge
canned or potted meat,
    veal loaf
canned boneless chicken
corned beef hash
canned sauce

Grain Products

pancakes, "slapjacks,"
    flapjacks
bread
sea biscuits
crackers
rice
johnny cake
corncake
graham muffins

Boston crackers
oatmeal, cornmeal
groats
flour

Vegetables and Fruits

onions
Indian corn
canned fruits
canned vegetables
beans, pole beans
carrots
dried apples, peaches,
    prunes
lemons
pickles
potatoes
berries: strawberry,
    gooseberry, blueberry,
    huckleberry, wintergreen

Dairy Products

butter
eggs
cheese
canned condensed milk

Condiments

molasses
sugar, brown sugar, loaf
    sugar, maple sugar, syrup
arrowroot
pepper
salt
currant jelly (for venison)
tomato sauce
yeast

Beverages

cocoa
coffee
tea
lemonade
brandy
champagne
ale

Also

Jerusalem artichokes
celery lettuce
egg plant
pumpkin
asparagus

this might be accomplished. For example, club members were divided between 1958 and 1960 by a lumber contract that had been let on Bartlett Ridge, only a half-mile from the Upper Ausable Lake. According to Edith Pilcher, the matter was resolved when shareholders who had leaseholds on campsites at the lake contributed money equivalent to the amount foregone by the club.

Like other owners of large tracts of land, A.M.R. was compelled to sell timber to pay its taxes: assessments on its lands steadily went up even though steep slopes made much of the land unsuitable for logging or building vacation homes. Requests for relief were denied by local elected officials intent on keeping as much of the tax burden off full-time residents as they could, shifting it to a category of land owner who seldom chose to register and vote in local elections, the "nonresident taxpayer," so-called.

Besides selective logging and sales of land, Adirondack clubs raised money by initiation fees, selling shares, annual dues, and special assessments. The last was for new construction and for capital repairs to roads, bridges, and club buildings damaged by wind and runoffs in spring. When roads were measured in miles, as they were at the clubs and many camps, outlays for road maintenance alone was high.

The strength of the family clubs derived from their generally good management, starting with their being corporations that were governed according to parliamentary rules and could be held accountable. The clubs dispersed responsibility among their members, and this was no small advantage given the traumas of the twentieth century—two world wars, a decade-long worldwide economic depression, and interludes of inflation. The clubs sold land or trees for lumber, and their better-off members advanced loans. The boards were composed of leaders in business and the professions, so there was always someone to put the board or its president back on track. One exception to the durability of the family clubs was the Lake Placid Club, which may have failed because its board may not have developed a mature institutional foundation before the death of its founder, Melvil Dewey.

Decisions about whether to sell land or timber raised issues about club policy and long-term strategies, such as the extent to which the management plan could be modified without harm to agreed-upon goals. Storms and infestations nullified long-term plans and sent boards and consultants back to square one. The beech blight of the 1970s and after changed harvesting plans that had been projected well into the twenty-first century.

Many of the decisions required of club members dealt with setting limits: on boats and cars, for example, a classic instance of the nose-of-the-camel-under-the-tent for some members, for whom one concession led to another until the whole beast was in the tent.[18] Should power boats be allowed on the lake and, if so, should a limit be set on horsepower? The automobile divided members over where roads should be cut to make it easier to reach an interior pond or simply to get to one's roadless camp on the opposite shore. The Adirondack League Club embodies a range of compromises: powerboats are allowed on Honnedaga Lake but not on Little Moose Lake or Bisby Lake, and lawn mowers and chainsaws must be run at certain hours between July Fourth and Labor Day.

The clubs were pioneers and so naturally made errors. A.L.C., for example, selectively managed in favor of deer and trout at the expense of their predators, the wolf and the panther, as well as fish-eating birds—osprey, eagle, and cormorant. Even the otter was targeted. This management strategy is now seen to be detrimental even to deer and trout breeding populations.

The Lake Placid Club

The fall of the Lake Placid Club is noteworthy because during its heyday, down to the years immediately following the Second World War, it appeared sure to remain one of the largest family clubs in America. Its founder was Melvil Dewey (1851–1931), inventor of the Dewey Decimal System, director of two research libraries and advocate for simplified spelling. He was a remarkable man who sullied his reputation and discredited that of the club by racist dogma that the club adopted as policy to the time of his death.[19]

It is a measure of his energy that Dewey was proprietor of two clubs, the Riversea Club in Old Saybrook, Connecticut, and the Lake Placid Club, while he was serving as state librarian in Albany. In 1905, he resigned from the state post when Jewish leaders in New York City complained it was disgraceful that the position was occupied by someone who disqualified Jews from membership in an organization on grounds of "physical, moral, social, or race objection."[20] Dewey denied that he was prejudiced, and he seems to have had the support of the regents for a time. But in his history of the Adirondacks, written as a retired journalist and columnist, William Chapman White claimed the club, which was then, in 1954, still in business, "never changed its racial restrictions on members or their guests."

Dewey, who is called the father of modern library science, invented a system of classifying books that is still used at libraries in the United States and abroad. The licensing of the system, which is updated, supported the programs of the educational foundation established by Dewey when he was alive. The foundation, which has an office in Lake Placid, gave most of the books from the club library to the Town of Long Lake in 1993, along with a small grant to start the library, the first in that small mountain hamlet.

More quixotic were Dewey's efforts to rationalize spelling in English, so that words were spelled the way they sounded. Accordingly, he spelled his given name Melvil instead of Melville and wrote "Loj" for lodge for the sleeping and dining facility at the trail head on Heart Lake that is run by the Adirondack Mountain Club. Hundreds of strangers have tried to puzzle out "Loj" for "Lodge."

The Lake Placid Club was formed in 1891 when Dewey and his wife, seeking relief from a cold and hay fever, bought five acres on Mirror Lake, a small lake adjoining the far larger Lake Placid less than a mile to the north. Dewey established the Placid Hotel Company and began selling shares in the company. Early on, when it was losing money, a member said by T. Morris Longstreth to be one of Dewey's "originations," bailed out the company by giving Dewey a sum that was "more than twenty times what the original Club cost."[21] The club grew and expanded by loans or purchases of shares by Dewey's originations, that is, men in business cultivated by Dewey.

The heart of the club was Dewey himself. At its height, between 1905 and 1930, the club was as much a success as Paul Smith's Hotel to the west. Dewey would also open Lake Placid South, an extension of the club in Florida where he preferred to winter in his old age. Longstreth reported that the club had grown from eighty in 1891 to 1,263 members in 1919, when it had 749 employees, each of whom had pledged neither to drink or curse. The club leased lands with trails for its guests, and its supply of fresh meat, dairy products, and vegetables came from more than thirty farms in the area, each closely inspected for cleanliness by hotel employees.

Longstreth revealed the club's dependence on Melvil Dewey, averring that while L.P.C. was a hotel, it also was a vessel in which the "eternal verities" were nurtured. Dewey, he said, had a "dream" for a club that would be a haven for "true Americans," identified by fear of God, bravery, frugality, and honesty. Besides being patriots, club members were clean and high-thinking. The club was an Old Testament city on the hill, a haven where the elect might separate themselves from those whose lot in life revealed that God took no pleasure in them.

But Longstreth went on, continuing when he might better have stopped: the club was more than a "refuge for hay-fever victims, more than an eating-resort for indigent intellectuals"; it was a place "to see things squarely." These remarks dismissed tuberculosis patients, artists, and teachers; excluded were creative minds in science and the arts who occupied the camps and hotels of nearby Keene Valley and of Lake Placid itself, where Camp Joyland, built in 1904 for Victor Hubert, would be the composer's summer home for twenty-five years.

The club had an enormous influence on the village. The 1932 Winter Olympics came to Lake Placid because the community's reputation was known to the world through its Lake Placid Club, and it would not likely have been chosen for the 1980 Olympics except for its having hosted the event nearly fifty years earlier.[22] But behind a veneer of rectitude, the club was undermined by a smouldering legacy of prejudice that seemingly would not, as it did elsewhere, dissipate and be selectively forgotten. By the time of the club's dissolution in the early 1980s, its rooms and cottages were vastly underutilized.

Clubs were transparently exclusionary notwithstanding the framing of the question (as is still done today) as one of personal choice or preference. Jews were excluded from the club, but so also were recovering patients on outings from Saranac Lake. Dewey knew what he was doing, which was to lure wealthy or well-to-do people who wanted to be insulated from undesirables and conditions they read about in daily newspapers. They wanted to associate with people like themselves, of good character and steady habits, and they were gratified that Dr. Dewey and the club were so attentive to their needs. For example, parents about to travel could leave their "young daughters at the Club for all summer in entire confidence that no unhomelike taint will touch them," reported Longstreth. That they should not want their

Firedril *(simplified spelling),*
Lakeside Lodge, Lake Placid
Club, Lake Placid, N.Y.
William G. Distin, architect,
c. 1924. Monthly drills were
required by Melvil Dewey,
who also had watchmen
around the clock and fire hy-
drants on the club's extensive
grounds. The building shown
here was razed following suc-
cessive arsonist fires in 1991
and 1992. The Adirondack
Museum Library.

daughters or themselves to be exposed to tuberculosis by unwittingly coming in contact with someone with the disease was a common sense matter of self-interest, to those in agreement with Dewey. The irony was that tuberculosis came to appear more of a menace precisely because its victims were now concentrated in Saranac Lake, less than fifteen miles from Lake Placid. Shunning people with contageous diseases seemed reasonable.

Despite its early success, the hotel's premise was untenable in a world where adaptability would increasingly be needed in a time of change. The club, destined to fail once it no longer had Dewey's vision and energy to guide it, could not change with him and it would not change without him. Other clubs survived war shortages and economic depression, so an untenable, inflexible ideology hobbled those governing the club.

Defects aside, Dewey was innovative. He opened the club in the winter of 1904, not altogether original given the Winter Carnivals that were held in neighboring Saranac Lake, but a daring measure nonetheless, since the clubhouse and cottages—forty of them—had to be heated. Six attended the first Christmas dinner, but more guests began coming once the novelty of a winter holiday caught on, in which an "all-winter program" was introduced that was just as elaborate as the summer program.

Another aspect of Dewey's character was his courtship of businessmen, who no doubt were impressed that education and vision could be met in so practical a man at the same time. He was a fund raiser ahead of his time—forerunner of modern college and university presidents who seek alliances with business and industry. The library at the club offered more than the trifling fare of reading rooms at other clubs. It was as professional as any library at the time, with amply stocked shelves of fiction and nonfiction and presided over by a trained librarian who checked books out and ordered new ones.

The club was a health center, emphasizing exercise and nutritious food produced and prepared under clean conditions. Experts from Cornell inspected local food sources and found them unsanitary, upon which Dewey began raising the hotel's own food. Its herd of cows grew to five hundred, and its farms and those that supplied it were said to number thirty-six. The club controlled some 7,100 acres of land, much or most of it leased, and it had three golf courses—two nine-hole courses and an eighteen-hole course—plus forty tennis courts.

The clubhouse, designed by William Distin, was a large rambling wood structure of doubtful architectural merit, except for two attached structures, an auditorium and memorial chapel, the latter with six stained-glass Tiffany windows. Religious services and other programs for members and guests were held in the auditorium and chapel, which were saved, but barely, when a large part of the clubhouse was torn down following a fire—the eighth and most destructive arson episode in eleven months—on October 1, 1992.

Hunting camp, Moose River Plain. The building was destroyed in 1973 because leased land under it had been bought by the state for the Forest Preserve. Photograph by Craig Gilborn, 1973.

Modern Leasehold Clubs

The male sporting clubs of the nineteenth century continue today in clubs that lease land for hunting and fishing. They are perhaps the last all-male bastions of heterosexual males in America. Slovenly conditions rumored to prevail at deer camp may be an intuitive device for keeping women and do-gooders from intruding with brooms and moral lessons.

The clubs vary but are egalitarian within the membership itself, although some clubs are choosier than others about who can be a member. Members come from towns and cities, and they are made up of shop owners and businessmen, school teachers, and blue-collar workers and artisans for whom a week or two in "deer camp" may be their sole indulgence for the year. Men still prefer the company of men during hunting season. When she stopped to say hello in an aisle at the supermarket, the wife of an electrician replied that her husband was looking forward to hunting camp in a couple of weeks. Asked if she had ever been at the camp in all the years her husband and his friends had been going there, she looked at the author as though the question was preposterous, smiled, and said no.

The Gooley Club traces its origins to 1866, when Harve Bonnie of Pittsfield, Massachusetts, built a camp on Third Lake, half-way between Indian Lake and Newcomb, N.Y.[23] About 1875 he hired Mike and Olive Gooley to help him run it as a sporting camp, and in 1893 Bonnie sold it to Arvin Hutchins. Mr. and Mrs. Gooley purchased a farm in the same locality, at what today is called the "Outer Gooley Club Camp," as distinguished from the "Inner Camp" on the Essex County Chain of Lakes, which was three to four miles distant. George Finch bought the camps, which are separated by a narrow band of state land, but they continued to be used by individuals and groups for hunting and fishing. The present club was incorporated as the Gooley Club, Inc., in 1946, and it leases land from Finch Pruyn Company, which manufactures high-quality papers at its mill in Glens Falls, N.Y.

Kitchen area, hunting camp, Moose River Plain. Photograph by Craig Gilborn, 1973.

Ragged Mountain Camp, Blue Ridge, N.Y. This camp fits the ideal of a hunting camp, neither too refined nor too crude. Its hewn log walls are protected under a wrap-around porch. Photograph by Craig Gilborn, 1998.

The company owns many thousands of acres of forest land in the Adirondacks which it leases to clubs and individuals. Like other forest and paper products companies in the Adirondacks, income from leasing helps Finch Pruyn pay taxes on its lands. In 1998, it held about 160 recreational leases on its lands. Richard Nason, who managed the leasing program until his retirement, said that about eighty-six of these were to groups or clubs of between three and three hundred members, with the remaining seventy-four or so being agreements with individuals.[24]

A second club that leases from Finch Pruyn is the Blue Mountain Club. Located between Blue Mountain Lake and Long Lake, the club leases about 3,500 acres and three ponds and has a membership of about ninety. A flier for the club in 1997 said that all were welcome to join and membership was $250 for a year. A permanent campsite, it said, cost $150, and members must pay $25 for each weekend guest in hunting season. Members can build simple cabins so long as they do not have more than 500 square feet of floor space, the equivalent of a room measuring 22 by 22 feet. Members get considerable benefits for little money compared to the headaches of those who own land and have upkeep and taxes to pay. Leaseholders have access to forest and lakes, no encounters with public campers, no tax on land, and only a small tax on the value of the cabin or trailer. Club members are independent but helpful and generally congenial, according to Don Pratt of Long Lake. Adirondackers like Mr. Pratt make up part of the membership of these clubs; he enjoys the woods as much as anyone else, even though, to look at his home town, he can never be said to be truly out of the woods.

While the leases are still mostly with men and men's groups, Richard Nason sees that the makeup of some clubs is changing, shifting from men interested principally in hunting and fishing to families and even a few women (other than wives), one of whom, an engineer near Rochester, N.Y., was building her own cabin. The newcomers are far less intent on hunting and fishing, preferring non-consuming outdoor activities such as hiking and biking, or even bird-watching.

"Hide-Away Hanging Hooch," c. 1997. Suspended by cables, this treehouse does no damage, says Rich Entwistle. It sleeps two below and two in a loft, has a fold-up table for four, two-burner stove, counter, corner sink, woodstove, and outside deck. A pulley is for hoisting water, provisions, and the family pet; people use a ladder. Courtesy Rich Entwistle.

Like others astride the cusp of social change, these people have uncertain staying power, most being Baby Boomers. Will they be as loyal—keep their memberships—as older members have been in tough times? Mr. Nason, who has a lease himself at one of the tracts despite a job that requires inspections of his employer's 166,000 acres of forest land, says he doesn't yet know, but the answer to the question will affect company policy with regard to its land in the future. The open-space character of the Adirondacks is due in part to companies like Finch Pruyn, which have leasing as one component of a larger forest management program. Without this income, the companies, facing tax liabilities every year on lands that may wait twenty to thirty years until the next cutting, might get out of the paper business into the business of selling lots for vacation homes.

The Gooley Club traces its start from a hunting camp of 1866 on Third Lake in a remote southwestern corner of Essex County. The buildings in this recent photograph are on a tract leased from Finch Pruyn Company, Glens Falls, N.Y. Courtesy Bruce W. Kirkpatrick.

These camps are never really completed, for one
of the fascinating features of the camp is that it is
bound by no rules of time or architecture.

—Seneca Ray Stoddard, 1888

CHAPTER 7

Transitional Camps and Tents

TRANSITIONAL CAMPS were rooted in the region, retaining their regional
character while their city owners tried to pretty them up by decorating walls
and mantels with pictures, family photos, parasols, and the like. The owners readily adopted rustic ornamentation because it was available around the camps,
and camp builders were familiar with it from their own work in the woods. Rustic
ornamentation and furniture were not new to those from the city, since the movement to create park-like cemeteries and form urban parks between 1830 and 1870 had
fostered a sizable production of park buildings and furniture from wood materials
but also in other materials which replicated tree stumps, climbing vines, and lilies by
casting them from iron or cement.

These accessories to parks and cemeteries also made their way to suburban and
country homes and estates where gardens and landscaping were now held to be almost as important as the house itself. City people came to the Adirondacks in the
1870s with a certain receptivity for what they would find there, and they found
trees—a veritable inland sea of forest—as well as men whose culture had been shaped
by trees and the forest. "Trees are closets from which good woodsmen take whatever
they may need," a quotation from the *St. Lawrence Plaindealer* for 1881, is a nutshell
assessment of the men who were waiting, figuratively speaking, on docks, and railroad station platforms when city people disembarked in search of property and a
camp in the Adirondacks.[1]

The passage that opens this chapter is by a photographer whose travels very well
may have made him better qualified to speak about changes in the Adirondacks than
any person in the nineteenth century. It contains two truths, one of which is a tru-
ism, which is that it covers all camps, since they, like most buildings, are altered in
time. But this does not capture the sense of what Stoddard meant in writing about
camps on Raquette Lake. Photographs of the 1870s suggest that he visited the lake
several times in the decade, which allowed him to discern the remarkable transfor-
mations taking place there. This is the second, more restrictive, truth: that the
camps—particularly Camp Pine Knot—seemed headed in a fresh direction, the result of which was tantalizingly suggested by what already was at hand.

*"Blagden Cottage, Saranac
Inn, Adirondacks, N.Y.,"
postcard, c. 1900. The con-
cealment of logs behind
wrap-around railed porches,
log columns, and peekaboo
vines gentrified the plain log
cabin. President Grover
Cleveland stayed here. The
Adirondack Museum
(64.214.104).*

Transitional camps were a nineteenth-century phenomenon for the most part,
combining the needs of city people who purchased a small tract on the water in
September and wanted a building or two on it by early summer. They were accommodated, of course, by workmen willing to begin construction into early winter, take
a furlough when the snow and cold got too deep, and resume work in spring, perhaps after mud season or the break-up of ice on the lake, so material could be floated
on boats to the site. There were dozens of variations to the problem of how camps
got built, aggravated by short building seasons and long winters; but these earliest
efforts are perhaps the most interesting because they involved collaboration and ex-
perimentation among the two principal parties, the owners and the builders, neither
of whom could afford to enter into the relationship with too many preconceptions:
they needed one another.

Brandreth Park

Original buildings at Brandreth Park still stand and are as follows: Camp Good
Enough, 1874; Trophy Lodge (Camp Comfort), 1885; Camp As You Like It (Camp
Misrule), 1887. The dining room wing of the last was adapted from a cabin built
about 1850.

Brandreth Park, the longest continuously family-owned preserve in the
Adirondacks, was purchased in 1851 by Benjamin Brandreth, who bought some

24,000 acres at a tax sale for 15 cents an acre.[2] In 1955, 13,000 acres were deeded to Syracuse University for the use of its Forestry School by the family, who later, in 1972, repurchased it. Later, approximately 15,000 acres were sold to International Paper Co., leaving the Brandreth Park Association as owner of about 14,000 acres, along with the right to hunt and fish on its former lands. Today there are thirty camps on the north shore of Brandreth Lake with some seventy-five owners who have an interest in Brandreth Park. Annual meetings each summer are family reunions as much as they are serious occasions to examine policy and management. Brandreth's architectural importance is its grouping of three separate camps, side by side and facing the lake, all dating from the last quarter of the nineteenth century and remarkably unspoiled today. Benjamin Brandreth arrived from England in 1835 and settled in Sing Sing, N.Y., now Ossining, where he built a factory that manufactured a laxative pill invented by his father. He also owned real estate in New York City some twenty miles from Ossining, lower down on the Hudson River, where he owned Brandreth House in the mercantile district. His intent, in part at least, was to grow hops and brew beer from the fine quality water on the property; a hundred acres was cleared for hops, though nothing came of the project.

Matthew Beech (or Beach), a guide who likely was a squatter, had a small house on what a map of 1853 calls "Beeches Lake," later renamed Brandreth Lake.[3] That year a college student reported that Dr. Brandreth had an "excellent log house" containing "two apartments" (rooms) and a stove.[4] Next to it was a "bark barn or shed for the horses" and the original "old shanty" which was "yet in good order." This shanty may have been Beech's; if so, it still exists, though much changed.

This location was remote even for the Adirondacks, and reaching it from Ossining, N.Y., took two to three days, which may be why expansion did not occur until 1871, when the Adirondack Railroad opened service to North Creek, N.Y., linking the region to New York City and towns and cities in between. Time was further

Original buildings on the north shore of Brandreth Lake. Brandreth Park, 1851 and later. Photograph 1885–1900. The Adirondack Museum, gift of Mrs. Kathleen Houck and Mrs. Sarah Trube (P852).

reduced after 1892, when Dr. William Seward Webb's railroad from Remsen turned a two-day trip into one that could be completed overnight, in about eighteen hours. The family bought an additional 6,000 acres to guarantee themselves a station stop. They disembarked at Brandreth Station where they were met by an employee who took them in a horse-drawn wagon—later replaced by "Putt-Putt," a Model T Ford station wagon—which carried them eight miles to their camps on the lake.

Reuben Cary, the caretaker, made a set of chairs in 1875 at Brandreth Park. In a letter of December 28, 1874, Dr. Brandreth asked Cary to cut his order by half, to twenty-four chairs. He was enclosing, he said, a check and a bank note totaling $150. Business was slow—"83 first class stores" were available for rent near his office on Canal and Broadway, leading him to ask what work Cary was doing, what he had ordered, the extent of the bills, and when the jobs would be done. The $150 presumably covered the cost of the chairs and perhaps other expenses as well.[5] One of Cary's chairs is in the collection at the Adirondack Museum.

At Benjamin's death, in 1880, title to the park was held by his wife Virginia by reason of her being buyer of record at tax sales in 1866 and again in 1871.[6] That year, on December 8, Gen. Edwin A. McAlpin, perhaps relishing his future at Brandreth by virtue of his marriage to a daughter, wrote Reuben Cary, the caretaker, saying that business was poor in the city and that he wished he could get away for a few days. If he came, he asked, would he have "any sport?"[7]

What had been a dormitory for Benjamin Brandreth's family starting in 1874 became the personal camp for one of his children, Franklin, in the 1880s. Known as Camp Good Enough, it still looks like a dormitory or boarding house, similar in configuration to inns and taverns from colonial times. A porch a step off the ground in front was short on looks but good in rainy weather and for watching the lake. The facade was plain—a story and three-quarters high with a simple gable roof and three dormer windows breaking the eaves. Painted in white with dark red trim in early photographs, it appears to be frame but in fact has walls of hewn logs faced with siding. Good Enough's origin in the Adirondacks was displayed inside, in the thick round timbers that served as rafters and floor joists on the first floor.

Next door was Camp Comfort, built in 1885 by Edwin and Annie McAlpin, a daughter of Benjamin Brandreth. In 1943, the McAlpin interest in the camp was bought out and by a family member who replaced Edwin's mounts with trophies of his own, renaming the cottage Trophy Lodge. The third camp, named Camp Misrule and later renamed Camp As You Like It, built about 1887 for Ralph Brandreth, incorporates the Beech cabin which was converted into a dining room about 1900.

The three camps were of log construction and unexceptional on the outside. They would have been familiar to local residents of Long Lake and Raquette Lake who built them. Ralph, a classmate of William Howard Taft at Yale, had a bed made specially for Taft's corpulent body at As You Like It.

Trophy Lodge (Camp Comfort) is the likeliest to have been designed by an architect, although this is not certain. It presented three gable ends to the lake, one for the main building and two for the gables of roofs extended over the porch in front. Not special outside the region, gable ends in this combination may have been new to the Adirondacks. Log ends were mitered, and formed corners that were neat and plumb. It is the one-story wing attached to the main building that suggests the hand and eye

Camp Good Enough, Brandreth Park, built 1874. Lodging for several families before each got its own cottage. Good Enough, owned by Franklin Brandreth, was a century old when this photograph was taken. Photograph by Craig Gilborn, 1974.

Dining room, Camp As You Like It. This was originally the cabin home of a guide in the 1850s when the lake was called Beach's or Beech's Lake. Renovated with cedar bark walls, a fine stone fireplace, and barrel ceiling years later, it appears in an earlier guise elsewhere (p. 26). Photograph by Craig Gilborn, 1976.

Trophy Lodge, Brandreth Park, 1885. An architect may have helped compose the front of the plain log house built for the McAlpin family. A clerestory window above the picture window of the wing to the left admitted extra light to the living room. The Adirondack Museum, gift of David McAlpin (P28639).

of an architect. It was carefully composed outside with double columns at the corners of the porch and a gable in front that admitted daylight through a picture window and a dormer window triangular in shape, like the gable itself. Lifting eaves and punching openings in walls for light in a harmonious composition is what architects are trained to do.

The boathouse was open on three sides with a curtain on the fourth, perhaps to conceal bathers. It had a hipped roof of fine proportions which kicked or broke out over the supporting posts, again a suggestion of an architect's hand or plan.

An ethic of restraint has left the character of Brandreth Park unspoiled. Telephone service was approved but not electrical power from the outside, principally because

of the cost of running a power line from the north shore of Raquette Lake. A generator provides limited electrical power, and propane fuels stoves, refrigerators, hot water, and lighting. Some camps have oil lamps and lanterns for emergencies. Wood stoves are used for heating the camps.

Discontinuation of train service in 1965 left the automobile as the sole mode for reaching the camp on Brandreth Lake, which meant that the association of owners had to see to the repair of about six miles of dirt road to North Point on Raquette Lake.

Camp Pine Knot

Original buildings are the Swiss Chalet, Durant Cottage, and various other log cottages and service buildings of about 1877 to 1900.

Camp Pine Knot, admired from almost its inception, in 1877, was seen to have accomplished something novel, namely that it reduced "camping . . . to a fine art." The writer, possibly W. A. Rogers, who made the drawings for the woodcut illustrations, asked if "camping out . . . combined with the comforts and luxuries of city life" did not rob the experience "of some of those features which have always supposed to lend a charm to a life in the wilderness."[8] By 1880, Pine Knot had become a model of the decorous camp in the Adirondacks. Its chief author was William West

"A Temporary Residence in Sable Island Cove," c. 1915.

Mooring offshore, houseboats offered the pleasures of the water without the penalty of taxation. Floating houses represented a potential intrusion more than a real one, like the party boats which were becoming prevalent on Adirondack lakes in the late 1980s. Photograph is from an undated promotional booklet for Saranac Lake, N.Y.

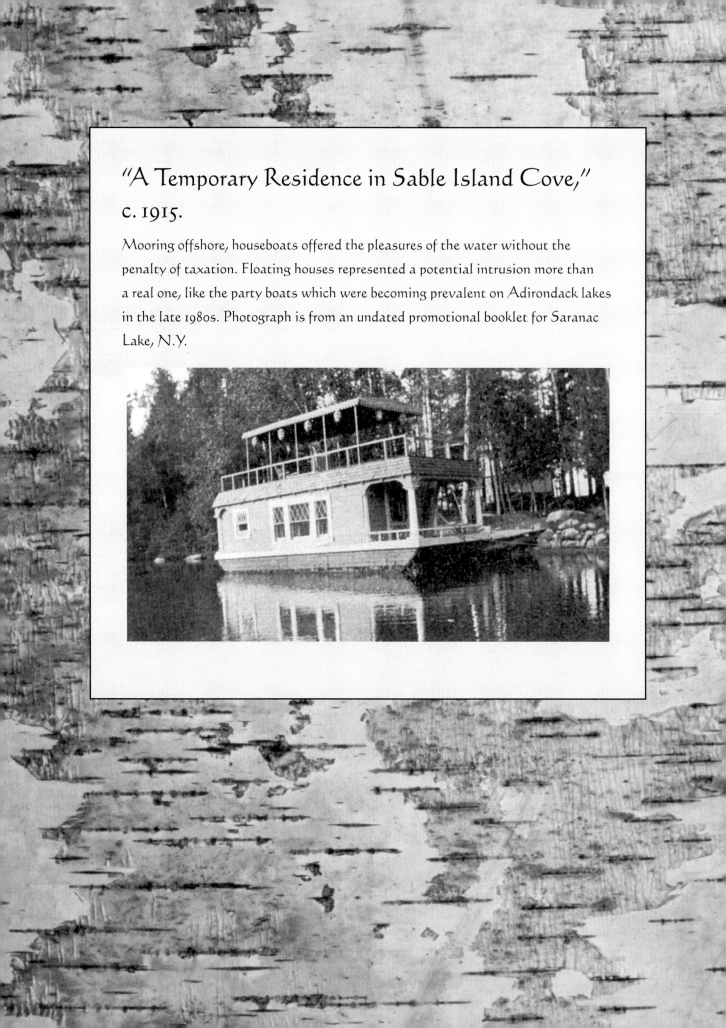

Mrs. T. C. Durant's cabin, built c. 1876. W. W. Durant outside his mother's cabin at Camp Pine Knot, c. 1889. The cabin burned in 1983. It was replaced by a replica by Cortland College, which has used the camp since 1948 for teaching outdoor recreation to students and teachers. The Adirondack Museum (P20142).

Swiss Cottage, Camp Pine Knot, c. 1883. The first of the decorous or great camps, Camp Pine Knot evolved over a twenty-five-year period, its rustic charms discernable by the early 1880s, when Edward Bierstadt took this photograph during his picture-taking tour through the region. The camp was notable for its rustic ambience and good service, orchestrated by William West Durant, whose tastes had been honed by travel abroad. The cottage still stands. The Adirondack Museum Library.

Durant, an amateur architect whose talents were that of an impresario, orchestrating projects with people having at least one of three things—money, creativity, or practical abilities. His genius was in taming forest and lake country without subduing or destroying it.

Pine Knot's rustic evocation was more than the sum of its parts: regarded separately, the buildings merited little attention. But collectively they marked a fresh approach to living in the woods. Durant, who said his visit to Raquette Lake in 1876 was his first exposure to log cabins and shanties, is the link between the builders of vernacular shelters and architect-designed camps of the 1890s and after.

Repose in the woods was a charming notion to people of cultivation: the inimitability of the Adirondack camp was that it was indigenous yet amenable to endless

variant effects by rustic carpenters having a knack for handling rustic materials. Seneca Ray Stoddard perceived an emerging rustic style after the arrival of the Durant family camps. In 1871, when he paid his first visit to Raquette Lake, there were no stylish buildings, just a handful of log cabins and shanties. By 1881, Stoddard could say that Pine Knot was the "most artistic" of camps on Raquette Lake; he later would say it was "unquestionably the most picturesque and *recherché* affair of its kind in the woods."[9]

Pine Knot became "the show place of the woods," according to Alfred L. Donaldson in 1921. People took "a circuitous route in order to gain a glimpse of it," and it became, Donaldson wrote, "the prototype of the modern Camp Beautiful." Echoing Stoddard's earlier praise, he said that before Pine Knot was built "there was nothing like it; since then, despite infinite variations, there has been nothing essentially different from it."

Pine Knot grew in increments for twenty-five years. Even after it was sold to Collis P. Huntington, in 1895, Durant continued to watch over the camp, perhaps supervising the addition of recreation and bedroom buildings there. Durant's three other camps, by contrast, were conceived *en suite* and built and furnished within one to two years, each a speculative project which Durant had to sell to cover his growing indebtedness to Huntington and others. Huntington died at Pine Knot in 1900 at the age of seventy-nine. The camp remained untouched, except for a caretaker, for the next forty-eight years, so that in 1948 it appeared much as it had at the time of Huntington's death.

Twin Towered Camps

These are: Camp Cedars, 1880, Forked Lake (not standing); Camp Fairview, c. 1879–1885, Osprey Island, Raquette Lake (not standing); Echo Camp, c. 1883, Raquette Lake (altered); Berkeley Lodge, 1896, Second Lake (altered) without the dining room and office building.

Better than the Swiss chalet at Pine Knot in embodying the idea of the villa in the woods are the twin-towered camps that proclaimed the gentrification of New York's upstate wilderness, their distinctive profile distancing them from the everyday log cabin. The towers and the cabin situated between them were easily put up by any person familiar with log construction.

Of stacked logs, these lodges presented a balanced composition to people from the water. Each was composed of a one-story central log cabin flanked at each corner of a gable end by two-story log towers. The design source for these lodges is unknown, though it derived from the Renaissance-inspired villas of Italy, in which a central

Camp Cedars, Forked Lake. A twin-tower camp built for Frederick Clark Durant c. 1880. Edward Bierstadt photograph, c. 1883. The camp was razed following the Blowdown of 1950. Saved was Sunset Cottage (p. 132). The Adirondack Museum (P6791).

Camp Fairview, Osprey Island, Raquette Lake, built for Charles W. Durant, Jr., 1880–83. The twin-tower camp was one of three on Raquette Lake; it was destroyed by fire in 1938 or 1939. The Adirondack Museum (P 48486).

mass is symmetrically framed by a wing or dependencies. The pediments of the central cabins were allusively Classical, another Renaissance feature.

The chalet at Pine Knot, despite its style and somewhat larger size, was first among equals—modest in its claims on the lake and to the other buildings around it. Such reticence cannot be found for the towered lodges, which asserted themselves both by their distinctive facade and by their placement at the front of a file of lesser buildings, like the drum major at the head of a parade.

The first two of these camps were built by Frederick and Charles Durant, cousins of William West Durant, who was chiefly responsible for Pine Knot. They no longer stand, but a third towered camp, which was built for Phineas C. Lounsbury about 1880, on the adjoining lot next to Pine Knot, is extant, although much altered after the Second World War when it became a summer camp for girls.

The towered camps, frontal and assertive, were close to the "villas" prophesied by the clergyman and Yale president, Timothy Dwight, nearly seventy-five years earlier.[10] Though stylish, they were still native in terms of material and construction methods, as anyone can tell by examining photographs of these three camps and comparing them with two other towered camps that were architect-designed.

Six towered camps are known to have been built between 1879 and 1896: three on Raquette Lake and one apiece on Forked Lake, Second Lake, and Fourth Lake. John Ellis, an acquaintance of Frederick and Charles Durant, mentioned their camps in his diary entry for September 17, 1880: he described Fred's Camp Cedars as a "Log house flanked by two towers, 2 storys," and rowed down to Raquette Lake where he

ABOVE: *Echo Camp, Long Point, Raquette Lake, built c. 1880 for Phineas C. Lounsbury, a banker and future Governor of Connecticut. Edward Bierstadt photograph, c. 1883. This twin-tower camp stands, but it was altered when it became a camp for girls after the Second World War. The Adirondack Museum (P7388).*

LEFT: *Berkeley Lodge, Second Lake, Old Forge, N.Y., 1896. Designed by Charles Cronk, Herkimer, N.Y., for President Benjamin Harrison, shown on the steps in this photograph from a report of 1902. The twin-tower lodge still stands, but the dining wing with Harrison's office, seen on the right, was removed years later. The Adirondack Museum (P25616).*

saw "Charley Durant's new camp now building" on Osprey Island.[11] Echo Camp was built about the same time, 1880, for the Lounsbury family of Connecticut.[12]

One of the towered camps is known to have been designed by an architect. Berkeley Lodge, which still stands on Second Lake, on the Fulton Chain of eight connected lakes, was built in 1896 for former President Benjamin Harrison from a design by Charles E. Cronk of Herkimer, N.Y. Berkeley Lodge belonged to the generation of camp design for which the so-called transitional camps of this chapter were forerunners. The great sophistication of Cronk's lodge is apparent by comparing it to the earlier towered lodges: Berkeley's elements are integrated, proportionate, and yet varied. The two towers and their roofs, for example, are octagonal, and two levels or floors are indicated by logs on the first floor and shingles on the walls of the level above. The merging of the porch into the recessed space between the towers is especially revealing of what builders do only after they have been shown the way by an architect. Bedrooms at Berkeley were reached from inside, in contrast to Camp Cedars and Camp Fairview, where one had to climb outside stairs to reach the bedroom at the top of each tower.

The Durant camps were several expressions of the same point, which was that travelers and prospective camp owners could be sure that Raquette Lake and vicinity were safe for vacationing families in the woods. The camps were photogenic to show that a life both simple yet elegant was to be found in the Adirondacks.

The North Woods Club

The Clubhouse was built in 1920 and the cottages date from the 1890s. The Brush Cottage, perhaps the most self-consciously architectural of camps, was built in 1894 for Charles Brush, a civil engineer in New Jersey.

The North Woods Club was established in 1886 on what originally had been a farm cleared in 1854 by Rev. Thomas Baker, who was said to have been a disciple of the abolitionist John Brown. Aided by his wife and a handyman, Baker cut hemlock bark for tanning, "lumbered in winter, farmed the cleared land in summer, and took

Sunset Cottage, Camp Cedars, Forked Lake, 1880s. This one-room cottage, on land acquired for Whitney Park, was skidded across the ice following the Blowdown of 1950; it was given to the Adirondack Museum in 1995 by Marylou Whitney in memory of her late husband, Cornelius Vanderbilt Whitney. Early pictures show it to have had a wrap-around porch. Photograph by Craig Gilborn, 1976.

on boarders."[13] Among the boarders were writers and artists who were members of the Century Club in New York City, as well as business people also in search of a wilderness vacation. At first they stayed in the log house in the lower part of the clearing, but later they were put into a three-story log house that was completed in 1863, after Thomas Baker's death.

The Bakers had two daughters, Juliette and Jennie, the latter having been born at the farm in the dead of winter in 1855. Juliette, who married Wesley Rice in 1864 when she was twenty-two years old, ran the farm and boarding house with her husband. In 1870, they bought a house closer to Minerva where they stayed in winter, returning in late spring to run the farm and care for boarders. Moving the household, including animals, was quoted from Juliette's diary by Leila Fosburgh Wilson, from whose history of the club this information has been drawn. Juliette, whose journal and correspondence reveal a resourceful, hard-working woman, refers to herself "driving the horses taking out a load of hay" on which were "2 hen turkeys, a cat and 2 dogs." Wesley followed "driving cattle, colts, sheep, and calves." As Wilson noted, there was no bridge over the Boreas River, but there must have been a crossing for this menagerie.[14]

Rice died of pneumonia in 1873, but Juliette and her mother continued returning to Baker's Tract until about 1878. The second daughter, Jennie, married Robert Bibby, a blacksmith, in 1875, and the couple bought out her mother's interest in 1878, made repairs to the buildings, and ran the farm and the boarding house. In 1887, the couple sold their interest—buildings and perhaps 250 acres of land—to former guests who wanted it for a private club.

A continuity at the club is indifference to fashion and landscaping: cottages are arranged according to no discernible plan, and they are surrounded by a meadow where deer now graze. The present clubhouse was built in 1920 to replace the three-

Clubhouse, North Woods Club, Minerva, N.Y., built 1920. This replaced the 1863 log boarding house that had been a clubhouse for members since 1886 (see p. 102). Assembly rooms are on the ground floor and apartments are upstairs for members and guests without cottages. Photograph by Craig Gilborn, 1998.

Dining room, clubhouse. The kitchen can be seen through the door. Photograph by Craig Gilborn, 1998.

Brush Cottage, North Woods Club, 1894–95. Charles Brush, a civil engineer from New Jersey, built a stylish summer cottage that took in a panoramic view of distant mountains to the north and west from any of three porches. As seen in pictures that follow, the cottage stands. The Adirondack Museum Library.

story log house of 1863 which burned; though relatively new, it retains the configuration and feel of the log house it replaced. At one end is the kitchen and dining room, over which are rooms formerly used for summer help but used now as storage. Attached to the dining room by a breezeway is the Clubhouse, a simple building with a continuous porch a step off the grass in front and affording views of the high peaks to the north and Blue Mountain to the west. Inside are several rooms for meetings and playing games, while upstairs are rooms for members and their guests. Members eat in their own cottages but are expected to take a minimum number of meals in the dining room.

Club life was simple if not primitive, as much from the club's changing financial situation as by choice. Leila Fosburgh Wilson, who in 1998 greeted the author at the Brush Cottage that she owned, had both lived and researched much of the club's history. Running water was introduced in 1906. A water supply meant water closets for men and women, and a third

Studio, Brush Cottage. A large window was installed by the late James Fosburgh so the room could be used as a painting studio. Photograph by Craig Gilborn, 1974.

Kitchen, Brush Cottage, North Woods Club. Cottages have generators for electricity, so old iceboxes like this one may be used for keeping dry food from mice. The wood-stove and a pair of silver candlesticks on the table reveal the self-reliance of the occupants. Photograph by Craig Gilborn, 1998.

for employees, all distant, apparently, from the clubhouse and cottages. That year, in 1911, a tub and sink were installed in the clubhouse and fees of 50 cents for a bath and 25 cents for a shower were introduced. The clubhouse, it should be mentioned, was the same three-story log building that had been built in 1863 for sportsmen. The arrangements, Mrs. Wilson said in her brief but entertaining history, were not favorable for attracting new members, which the club needed.[15]

Tent, 1880

The following excerpt was written by Bradford Sherwood, a student at Hamilton College who camped on Raquette Lake in the summers of 1881 and 1882. He seems to have been in poor health, but returned to school much improved. He had a platform tent which he shared with his mother between July 16 and September 6, when she returned to Jamesville, N.Y., to be replaced by his father about September 29. His father would not buy land on the lake, but he agreed to let his son build the log cabin described in a second excerpt in this book. The following has been abridged. The boy mentioned below, who helped Bradford and Mrs. Sherwood set up the camp, must have been a resident.

"The boy made a narrow bedstead before he left and we stuffed some coarse cloth on it for a bottom. We had blankets and carpets enough to keep us warm if we kept our clothes on, which we did. We had an old tin pail without a handle which we used for a stove. We had gone from July 16 to August 7 in the tent [before] supplies came from home along with our little parlor stove. A red-letter day in our camp [as] our stove was on the dock, at Bennett's. A guide brought it over and I immediately went to setting it up. Mother baked potatoes and biscuits for dinner. The stove added a great deal to our comfort and in a few days we had our camp in fine shape with a cupboard made from one box that had a door on it and another set up with shelves for tinware. We had one chair and a cot on which we could sit at the table. When the tent flaps were closed, and the floor had been made tight with a little fire in the stove, and our kerosene lamp was burning on the table, we felt very cozy indeed."

Indoor plumbing with septic tanks for each cottage was a requirement in the 1920s, a period described by Mrs. Wilson as "a great leap forward." Before this time, cottages had a cold-water spigot at the kitchen sink which drained into a hole in the floor. Cold as well as hot water had to be "brought around the house in those ubiquitous pitchers," to bathing tubs. One cottage, for the Fricks, concealed a tub for bathing under a kitchen table with a hinged top. Chamberpots were in use everywhere, some concealed in wooden stands that now serve as end tables, and most houses had "two outhouses, usually connected to the woodshed." Outhouse "pans" were cleaned by a man in a horse-drawn wagon that circled the clearing each day. Blocks of ice were also delivered to iceboxes.

An electric generator was installed for the first time in 1928, in the Cluett house, and the Clubhouse followed suit in 1932. Serious farming at the club was abandoned in the 1930s, but a sawmill provided logs and lumber for buildings and their repair until about 1950. The North Woods Club has managed its forests, deriving needed income from cutting of timber for road repairs and other infrastructure, much of which is under the supervision of a caretaker who usually has lived on the property with his family.

The Putnam Camp

At St. Hubert's, Keene Valley, N.Y., this is an enclave of about ten buildings dating from the last quarter of the nineteenth century.

Painters were among the first outsiders to seek Keene Valley when word got out about its beautiful scenery, a combination of mountain prospects, valley views, and

Putnam Camp, Keene Valley, St. Hubert's, N.Y. The camp was a summer boarding house operated by Smith Beede, a farmer with land more scenic than arable, to judge by the boulders in this photograph, taken after 1875–77, when the property was purchased by three physicians and a psychologist (William James) from Cambridge and Boston. More like a colony than a club, Putnam Camp was functional, offering no frills, in which respect it had changed little when the author visited it in 1998. The Adirondack Museum (P14301).

Bowditch Cottage, Putnam Camp. Named for Dr. Henry Bowditch, dean of the medical faculty at Harvard and one of the four original buyers. The Adirondack Museum (P 11545).

swift flowing streams with pools for swimming and bathing. Asher B. Durand, who two decades earlier had sketched in the Schroon Lake region to the south with Thomas Cole, came to Keene Valley in 1858 with two other artists, John Kensett and John Casilear. Other creative spirits, many from Cambridge and Boston, followed and would comprise an informal colony of artists, writers, and college professors whose regard for the life of the mind and spirit lingers in the valley to this day.[16]

Residents in the valley were farmers. For the newcomers, they opened their homes and took them in as boarders for weeks at a time. Smith Beede did so well at this that in 1875 he sold a small parcel of land to four men, the brothers James and Charles Putnam, Henry Bowditch, and William James, and erected a hotel a mile to the north. James was an eminent Harvard philosopher, and the others were medical doctors. The four returned the following year and bought Beede's farm house and additional land, agreeing to the farmer's demand that they would not open a competing hotel.

More lands were added to what was known as the Putnam Camp; in 1901, when it joined an association of preserve owners, it was listed as a preserve of 3,540 acres of mountain land, much more than it had in 1998. (It may have leased some of the land.) Its members, largely from the Boston area, were convinced of the importance of nature and its rediscovery and preservation. Theirs was the same mettle that led another Yankee and Harvard graduate, Henry David Thoreau, to build a one-room house on a wooded slope above Walden Pond and live in it for twenty-five months, recording his observations in a journal later distilled into that American classic of 1854, *Walden, Or Life in the Woods.* The Putnam colony were secular humanists, nominally Christian but inquisitive and open-minded with a reverence for nature and egalitarian in matters of gender, age, and personal expression.

The Beede farm became Putnam Camp. Buildings were plain and weathered, then as today, rustic sermons that content and not wrapping is what should be valued. Among the distinguished men and women guests at Putnam Camp was Sigmund Freud, who said it was "by far the most amazing" of all he had experienced in America.[17] He was living in a cabin with three rooms called "Chatterbox." Everything in the camp "is left very rough and primitive but it comes off."

College students have worked summers at Putnam Camp in the kitchen, in the dining room, and on the grounds. This young man was making pies for dinner in a photograph taken in July 1998. Photograph by Craig Gilborn.

Walls on two sides of this community room are hinged and can be propped open on warm days. The literary gathering (previous page) met in this room. Photograph by Craig Gilborn, 1998.

The flavor of Putnam Camp in its early years was captured in a paper read by Ellen Putnam McIver in 1940 at the Keene Valley Historical Society. In the segment that follows, the Stoop, which still stands, is a two-story cottage with a dining room and kitchen attached at the rear.

> Dinner, at seven, was of the regular sort, with everyone fresh from [bathing in] the brook after a long afternoon walk or all-day climb, and often clothed in peasant costume from one country or another. After coffee, strong and delicious, made by Miss Annie in the "Stoop," the evenings were usually spent in talking, singing and telling stories around the campfire, comfortably seated on a semicircle of low seats covered with blankets. Everyone had his own particular song or story which he was frequently called upon to produce. We never tired of seeing Dr. Bowditch as the organ-grinder, standing on one leg with the other held up as a hand-organ, grinding out his tunes and passing his hat round afterward.[18]

Today the Putnam Camp is run by a not-for-profit corporation which owns about 200 acres and has about 240 members. Students from New England colleges have traditionally found employment each summer, to work in the kitchen and on the grounds. It looks much as it did a century ago except that trees have grown up on the perimeter of the clearing so the camp has lost many of the mountain views it had in its early years as a farm and then as a colony of like-minded friends.

Adirondack Lodge

This hotel was built in 1879–80 on Heart Lake, formerly Clear Lake, North Elba, N.Y. It burned in 1903.

Claimed to be the largest all-log structure in the region when it was built, the Adirondack Lodge was strategically located at the northern end of the thirteen-mile pass through the High Peak district. Hikers took this route on their way to the summit of Mt. Marcy, the highest point in the state, and they could follow the trail to Tahawus, where an iron works and company village were located. On the way they passed by the high narrow rock face of Indian Pass, an attraction for hikers then as today.

The main building was three stories high, eighty-five feet across the front, and thirty-six feet deep, with a wing in the rear and an observation tower—its chief feature—in front. Spruce logs two feet in diameter were used on the lower courses, and the observation platform was seventy feet off the ground. Raised porches or piazzas enclosed the building below and supported the deck of a porch with rustic railing on the second floor.[19]

Except for its log construction, the lodge was a forest version of serviceable public architecture of a century earlier, both in scale and in the symmetry and projecting pavilion of its facade, of which Independence Hall in Philadelphia is an example. An architectural fillip was evident in the columns that held up the porch roof and the promenade deck above it: each of the fifteen columns was tapered and had a rustic capital at the top formed just below the part of the trunk where it flares to send roots

Adirondack Lodge, Heart Lake, built 1880. Seneca Ray Stoddard took this picture in 1888. An observation tower six stories high was a feature of this large log hotel. The hotel was destroyed in a forest fire in 1903. The Adirondack Museum (P1696).

into the earth. A theory about the origins of Greek and Roman temples held that people in earliest times inverted tree trunks so root ends supported logs or timbers or logs laid across their tops. Whether true or not, the columns at the Adirondack Lodge may be fairly said to have constituted an "Adirondack" order of column and capital.

The lodge was built by Henry Van Hoevenburg, an inventor with patents in telegraphy, who, in 1878, purchased 640 acres of land that included a lake and mountain. His fiancée helped him pick the site while they were on Mt. Marcy, but within a year she died, leaving him to go ahead with the hotel on his own. The hotel opened in 1880 and became a popular destination, since it was comfortable and was one of the first hotels with private baths in the Adirondacks, and it had trails radiating from it with every degree of difficulty. Litigation involving Van Hoevenburg patents lost him ownership of the lodge in 1895, but he was reinstated as manager in 1900, when it was purchased by Melvil Dewey, a good friend of his and the genius behind the Lake Placid Club.

The hotel and surrounding forest were burned in the conflagrations that destroyed thousands of acres of trees in the spring of 1903. "Van," as he was known, watched from the observation tower as the fire approached from two directions. He had workmen put his large telescope in a boat and push it away from shore, throw the table silver into shallow water, and let the horses loose from the stable. One route of

FAR LEFT: *The log columns of the Adirondack Lodge evoke the theory that the Classical column originated in the trunks of trees in ancient times.*

LEFT: *Design for column in the form of a tree trunk by the French architect Philibert DeLorme (?1515–1570).*

escape remained—the trail to Indian Pass—and the others headed for it while one, Frank Williams, returned for Van Hoevenburg, who insisted on remaining with the hotel. The two barely escaped when Williams sat down and said he would not leave without Van Hoevenburg.[20]

In 1911, the Adirondack Camp and Trail Club was formed with Van Hoevenberg for its first president. Today, the Adirondack Mountain Club, the successor organization, operates a small hotel on the site. Phonetically spelled "Loj" in deference to Dewey, who advocated simplified spelling, the lodge is less stylishly rustic, but it is a place where hikers and vacationers alike can spend a few nights, venturing onto trails, swimming in Heart Lake, and dining in the restaurant.

Castle Rustico

No longer standing, this hotel with theater was built in 1886 on Lake Placid.

"A very pretty rustic house has been built on [Lake Placid], known playfully as 'Castello Rustico,'" wrote Joseph W. Stickler, a physician whose severe bronchitis had been relieved in the Adirondacks. Castle Rustico, he said, was "plain and rustic" and would "hardly do for invalids."[21] Located on the west bank of Lake Placid, it was preceded by a log cabin erected in the 1870s by William Fox Leggett and his wife, both actors. Later the Leggetts enlarged or replaced the cabin, a combination hotel-and-theater, where they declaimed passages from Shakespeare plays before summer guests.

The stage at the hotel may have been on the top floor, since a photograph shows few windows on what would have been the fourth story of the building. The building did push the limit of how high a wall of stacked logs could go. Four stories high, it spanned distances of forty or so feet, set perilously on stone footings three to five feet off grade at the front. The central pavilion with gable that projected in front may have extended into the structure, forming interior walls from front to back, helping to stabilize the building.

The pavilion was off center; this may have been dictated by organization of rooms inside, though it may have been that Mr. Leggett or his builder found the area's forest yielded trees of the length and quality sufficient for one end but not both. Logs in continuous, tapered lengths extended two to three feet beyond corners; joists supporting the floors inside could be seen on the outside between the logs under the windows. Openings were cut in solid walls for windows and doors, a technique used by loggers when throwing up a new bunk house in the woods. Castle Rustico showed similar evidence of haste and improvisation.

Leggett was one of a number of artists and literary figures who gravitated to Lake Placid starting in the 1870s, where he was called "Edwin Booth Leggett" on account of his colorful attire and dramatic manner.[22] For all his theatricality, he had a practical side: he was said to have furnished the camp "with what he could make himself," so he may have helped build Castle Rustico, which was thought to be the largest log building in the region, a claim also made for the Adirondack Lodge, which had been built in 1879 and was not more than a dozen miles from Lake Placid.

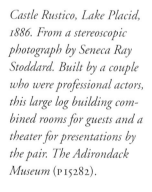

Castle Rustico, Lake Placid, 1886. From a stereoscopic photograph by Seneca Ray Stoddard. Built by a couple who were professional actors, this large log building combined rooms for guests and a theater for presentations by the pair. The Adirondack Museum (P 15282).

Tents and Tent Life

"Tent life," a nineteenth-century term and phenomenon, is placed in this chapter on transitional camps because tents were universally used in the nineteenth century by blue collar workers, soldiers, sportsmen, and groups at religious camp meetings, and in secular recreational activities, such as outings of the American Canoe Association.

Tent life took two forms in the Adirondacks, the first being portable shelter for sportsmen and guides on the move, and the second being fixed tent platforms at permanent camps or the semi-permanent camps of guides. One practice, which still continues, saw one or two hunters lug a wall tent to a remote location, setting up cots and staying in it for periods of weeks, or leaving it for work and returning on weekends. The author has come across these tents in clearings in fall. Both Boy and Girl Scout camps rely on tents, six to a tent.

Tents were a traditional part of life in many parts of the world—homes for nomadic peoples, protecting them from sun, rain and wind. Tent materials were woven fabrics and grass or reed mats, as well as bark and perhaps even animal skins. Waterproofed canvas, a modern improvement rather than a new invention, got a tremendous boost in the early nineteenth century by the back-to-nature movement

Pup tent. Two-man tents like this one could be folded flat and carried in the bottom of a guideboat or canoe. The chest kept ammunition, matches, and valuables dry. The Adirondack Museum (P38433).

Platform tent. Adirondack Mountain Reserve, 1886, George Bacon Wood, photographer. Pith helmet by his side, Col. H. Selden Loring chats with visitors outside two tents set up on a platform near one of the Ausable Lakes. A fern has been planted in a hollow log under a rustic frame in which a Japanese lantern is suspended. The Adirondack Museum (P20916).

Platform tent. Youths and young adults posed in front of a platform tent at Seven Pines Camp, Lake Eaton, Long Lake, N.Y., c. 1900. The Adirondack Museum (P38444).

and then by the Civil War, during which the tent was the primary mode of shelter for the armies of the North and South. Paintings and photographs reveal the prevalence of tents at training camps for the military at this time, and prolonged living in them by soldiers and officers must have had an impact on recreational camping after the war.

Photographs show two-man wall tents as part of what often was called an "open camp." Other shelters in open camps were lean-tos and dining areas consisting of a long table with benches under the shelter of a brush or bark roof for shade or fending off rain. Explorers and surveying parties in Eastern forests and on the plains west of the Mississippi River carried tents with them, and raftsmen poled flatboats down rivers with canvas stretched over poles to protect them from sun and rain. What were called "tent cities" grew up almost overnight on sites near gold and silver fields in California, Colorado, and Nevada. So-called "camp meetings" of hundreds of men, women, and children gathered in and around 50-foot long "society" tents starting in the second quarter of the nineteenth century.[23] Hundreds of people camped together at Lake George in 1869, according to B. F. DeCosta, who noted "a great throng" from towns and cities who "rough it in the rude shanty [and] sleep under white tents that dot the wide expanse of living green."[24]

Lady Amelia Murray was a member of a genteel party that traversed the Adirondacks with several guides in 1855, among them Governor Seymour of New York and Martin Moody whose father had settled in Saranac Lake in 1819. Traveling mainly by boat, they were once forced by black clouds to head for shore where the guides quickly pitched a tent. Lady Amelia and her companions ducked into the tent as it started to pour, only to discover that it leaked. In her journal, she observed that

Camp in a military context meant a place where men waited for orders to move. This chromolithograph shows a Confederate encampment at Corinth, Miss., of the 3rd Kentucky Infantry on May 11, 1862. Boughs laid over a sapling frame protected officers and men from sun—a field shelter, along with tents, that was common in the Adirondacks. The Valentine Museum, Richmond, Virginia.

Logging raft, Adirondacks. The raft was poled and boats tied to it; men kept their duffel under canvas and tied the raft at campsites, where they ate and rested as they drove logs to mills downriver. The Adirondack Museum (P9384).

the guides had "stowed themselves under one of the boats" and appeared to be better protected than they were.[25] Murray, age sixty and Maid of Honor to Queen Victoria, was traveling with Horatio Seymour and his young niece and one or two other "gentlemen" who may have been his relatives.

Lady Amelia was a good sport. During a wet spell, she prepared a "comforting warm mess" for "cold and tired hunters," meaning the guides. It was a concoction of arrowroot, Malaga wine, lemon, molasses, and biscuits, all heated in an iron kettle over the campfire.

Once, when rain confined them to the tent, she noted the "wild, careless, picturesque appearance" of the contents. The variety of items carried on the trip, which she inventoried, is impressive:

> Pans of tea, and plates of tin, air-cushions, and variously coloured plaids and felts scattered around; sketch-books and presses, books and maps; a large tin case, containing our store of grocery, a huge basket of biscuits, a hammer ensconced among bunches of berries; tallow candles, under protection from the damp: towels, hats, bonnets, and other articles of attire impartially scattered; accidentally bestowed touches of scarlet and blue upon the interior, lit up as it was by the warm glow of a blazing fire—this would have formed a picture for Gerard Douw.

Gerard Douw was a seventeenth-century Dutch painter known for his still-life paintings. The "presses" she mentioned may have been for flattening plant specimens, or storing sketches and for watercolors.

Guides maintained semi-permanent camps, which they ran as primitive hotels, in which tents were combined with rustic shelters like those illustrated in previous chapters. These camps were fugitive because they occupied waterfront sites owned by someone other than the builder. Chauncey Hathorn variously lived on three lakes—Tirrel Pond, Blue Mountain Lake, and Raquette Lake—and took guests at two of these sites. The 1875 guidebook of Edwin R. Wallace said that Chauncey Hathorn's camp on Blue Mountain Lake was "a series of tent and bark, board and log shanties, with floors, stoves, windows, etc., and a dining room for general use—simply a rustic canopy supported by 'pillars' but not enclosed."[26] Hathorn moved from Blue Mountain Lake to Golden Beach on Raquette Lake in 1877, perhaps because he had been ejected from a site he did not own. He did not own the new site, which belonged to Dr. Thomas Clark Durant and later his son, William, who seem to have allowed Hathorn to use it until he drowned accidentally in 1891.[27]

Henry Radford, who assisted Adirondack guides in forming the Adirondack Guides Association, said that guides "sometimes" supplied a tent. One of the city men who was a member of the Philosophers' Camp in 1858 brought his own tent which the guides set up on Follensby Pond.[28] Tents took valuable space in guideboats and canoes, and they often were musty smelling due to damp and mildew. When artist Jervis McEntee wrote, "we pitched our tent for the first time," in 1851, it may have implied that he and his companion used it only when a better shelter was not available.[29]

However, a traveler who stayed at Wilbur's Raquette Lake House at about the same time said that he "slept sound enough on Wilbur's straw bed" but missed "the spruce and fir balsam boughs of the tent."[30] The same author, who made his trip

Tent and bark shanty. Stillwater on the Beaver River, c. 1902. Peeling bark for shanties and lean-tos had destroyed stands of spruce and scarred campsites and waterfronts. The annual report of a state commission for 1902–3, in which this photograph was published, showed the discredited bark shanty and its alternative, the canvas tent. The Adirondack Museum Library.

Tent Life in the Adirondacks. *F. J. Severance, photographer, c. 1890–1900. A split-level platform, the lower deck for sitting and the upper for the wall tent. Wall tents could be as comfortable as frame cottages; both were found at permanent camps on waterfront sites starting about 1875. The Adirondack Museum (P9497).*

about 1859, came upon a party of seven or eight that included the widow of A. J. Downing at an "encampment" on Raquette Lake—"How jaunty they look in their short Balmorals and hob-nailed shoes!," he wrote, referring to figured skirts. Balmoral was Queen Victoria's country retreat in Scotland.

The platform tent kept occupants off the ground, which was hard, lumpy, and often damp. They were features of "day camps" which soon evolved into permanent camps on Upper St. Regis Lake, used in summer and stored in a shack for winter, leaving the platform and its steps and footings exposed to winter snows. The St. Regis tents had two rooms: one entered from a porch in front into a combination living-and-sleeping room; in back was a dressing room. A flap, or fly, served as a door and could be drawn shut and secured from inside. There was precedent for the St. Regis tents of the 1880s in camp meeting tents that were preferred because they afforded far greater privacy than communal tents. An account of 1854 said that these were family tents that had parlor and kitchen in front and a compartment in back for sleeping.[31] St. Regis campers departed from this arrangement, probably because they did not take their meals in their personal tents but instead moved to a dining room where the household gathered, the meal being prepared in an adjoining kitchen tent or building.

Tents were shelters in their own right; although, as matters turned out, they were interim shelters for cabins and cottages that followed. Initially they were viewed as medicine for healing the body and spirit from the harmful effects of city life, and the notion that comforts should be transplanted from town to the Adirondacks would have struck patricians as foolish and counterproductive in the extreme. The straight-thinking and disciplined men and women who occupied tents on Upper St. Regis Lake believed a measure of discomfort was salutary to health and a positive outlook. That they stayed at Paul Smith's, which lacked little in the way of good food, comfort, and recreational opportunities, was true, but then that was why they camped at distant sites in tents and tiny cabins. That a guide was in shouting distance and the hotel was in easy reach did not mitigate the symbolism of camping out.

Birch Island Camp had fifteen tents by about 1883—five measuring 14 by 14 feet, six 9 by 9 feet, three 7 by 7 feet, plus a dining tent. Men who were guides and carpenters set the tents up, along with Stokes family members and staff pitching in, all supervised by Mrs. Anson Phelps Stokes, a spirited and talented lady who was then mother of seven children. Behind each platform tent was a frame cabin that was used as storage for furniture and the canvas tent and awning. Mildred Stokes Hooker, who was a small girl at the time, gave a practical reason for the change from canvas tent to cabin: "When the tents wore out it was a natural transition . . . by putting cabins instead of tents in front."[32]

Camp owners eventually replaced tents with framed cabins that exactly resembled canvas tents in configuration and striping. Wood cabins that replicate the configuration and stripes of canvas tents had counterparts at ocean resorts in New Jersey and

Bedroom cottage, Birch Island, Upper St. Regis Lake. A wood cottage painted to look like the tents it replaced. Photograph by Craig Gilborn, 1976.

Birch Island Camp

Upper St. Regis Lake, 1881 and after

The family of Anson Phelps Stokes stayed at Paul Smith's hotel but had a "rough camp" on Birch Island a couple of miles distant. Tents on platforms evolved into a developed enclave of many buildings and features. Life at the camp in 1880–1900 was recalled many years after by a Stokes daughter, in *Camp Chronicles,* later published by the Adirondack Museum. For pictures of Birch Island Camp elsewhere, see pp. 151 and 179.

Waterfront, 1880s. Fanciful rustic work and canvas marked the early years at the camp. The Adirondack Museum (P20160).

The Main Cottage, 1890s and after. Photograph by Craig Gilborn, 1976.

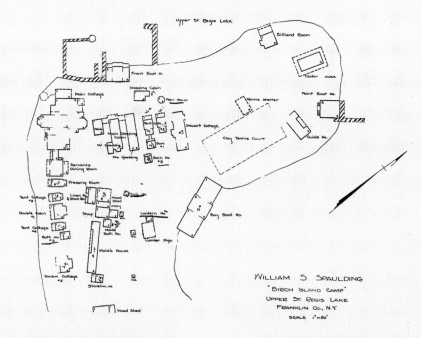

"Birch Island Camp," ground plan, 1934, used for insurance purposes. William S. Spaulding was owner. The Adirondack Museum Library.

Massachusetts, and in the Thousand Islands region of the St. Lawrence River.[33] The change from canvas tent to log or frame cabin was perhaps inevitable once Adirondack summers became more like a marriage than a honeymoon.

Marc Cook, in *The Wilderness Cure,* describes a tent that had most of the things found at home or in a hotel room:

> The board floor is partly covered with rugs, while the open stove rests on a stone fire-place. The furniture of the tent, albeit most home-made, is comfortable and designed for use. There is a bed, quite as inviting as one finds in his own room. A writing-table, a set of shelves, a bookcase, a washstand, two easy chairs and a trunk, transformed into an ottoman, complete the equipments.[34]

Next to Cook's tent was a bark shanty that was his dining room.

"Let there be tents," invoked Kate Field, in 1870, whose voice was early among those calling for the elimination of bark for lean-tos, shanties, and camp decoration. "To peel a tree," she said, "is to kill it."[35] This message, repeated many times in years to come, was taken to heart by the state after 1885 when it began buying lands for the Adirondack Forest Preserve and began educating the public. One vehicle was a photograph in which the discredited bark shanty and recommended tent are shown side by side. A. Judd Northrup was a convert to tents. Bark, he said, was "indispensable" a couple of decades earlier, in the 1880s, but conditions had changed.[36] Campers should leave bark on the tree and use "light, waterproofed tents" instead.

Discerning writers commented on the singularity of tents in the Adirondacks. One, in 1872, encountered half a dozen or more tents on an island in Raquette Lake. There they stood, he said, "basking in the sun, backed by the thick foliage of the

A.C.A. Camp, *1887.* Wigwams of Squawland. *Seneca Ray Stoddard, photographer. Festively patterned and draped tents are shown at an outing of the American Canoe Association on Lake Champlain. The Adirondack Museum* (P10829).

woodland," their appearance "picturesque in the extreme."[37] St. Regis Lake was where tents were displayed to best advantage. An anonymous journalist who had visited the lake in 1884–1885 thought "the man of taste" would find the canvas tent in front and log cabin in back to be charming. The effect of "snow-white canvas" stretched over "creamy white" frames of freshly peeled spruce poles made for an impression "purer" than anything the writer had seen.[38]

Harold K. Hochschild's "summer quarters" for about fourteen years was a wall tent, one of two on platforms at Eagle Nest Park, his parents' camp on Eagle Lake in the central Adirondacks. He used it, he said, from his early teens through college and a stint in China for the family-owned company business, until he was twenty-eight years old.[39]

Workmen at construction sites stayed in any shelter that was available until the camp or project was finished. At Eagle Nest they lived in tents, temporary cabins, and a cottage already built. Stone masons at Litchfield Park in 1912–1913 built a temporary stone dormitory next to the stone castle they were building, said Pieter Litchfield, pointing to an early snapshot. Recruits in the Civilian Conservation Corps camps of the Depression era occupied tents and barracks in the Adirondacks, as elsewhere, and tents were designed specifically to be carried and opened up next to cars.

In 1916, the state authorized issuance of permits to camp sites on Forest Preserve land. Platforms for tents were allowed, a clear contravention of state law prohibiting structures not intended for administrative purposes. Leasing camp sites was especially popular on the Saranac Lakes. But, in 1972, the state revoked the practice, since the sites were not temporary—permits tended to stay among family and friends—and they were not unobtrusive. Some sites evolved into clusters of platforms with tents containing gas stoves, lights, ice-boxes, and at least one battery-powered television set, according to a Department of Environmental Conservation employee, in a 1998 interview with the author. D.E.C. staff, he said, still find trash at the camp sites despite their having been cleaned out for more than twenty-five years.[40]

Survivors of Early Times

Any camp or club built before the Depression of the 1930s is likely to contain remnants of a past way of life. Some snooping is required, to find places frequented seldom or not at all—cellars, attics, sheds, small buildings tucked away in a corner of the camp or farther back in the woods, as with a spring house, for example. Evidence is *inside* and *outside,* the former in family parts of the camp and the latter in the remainder of the camp, domains which overlapped in the dining room and kitchen area.

What was to be done with an automobile that had perhaps never had a tire on a paved road? You store it in a barn at Brandreth Park. Dating from the 1920s, "Putt-Putt," as it was called, a Model-T Ford with canvas top and wooden sides, was never operated off the preserve after it was delivered, new, by rail at Brandreth Station. At the Kildare Club is the open car that was used to carry people on miles of club roads.

It made taxi runs to the flag stop at Kildare Station and, when rail service ceased there in 1937, to the depot at Tupper Lake Junction.

The contents of camps may need explaining by oldsters, as when Leila Fosburgh Wilson revealed in her centennial history of the North Woods Club that side tables had formerly been used to conceal chamberpots at her camp. Also at her cottage, on a second floor porch beneath the overhang of the roof, is a bathtub on wheels with a handle. She spoke not from personal experience, she said, but it was likely that the tub had been rolled on the boardwalks that once connected some of the cottages.[41]

Children, naïve as they are, easily passed from one domain to the other, blissfully indifferent to the unwritten rule about intruding on employees' turf. Lewis Spence recalled that he followed Oscar, the caretaker, on his chores at "Camp Woodwil," built on Upper Saranac Lake about 1927. Young Lewis also watched Oscar's wife, Julia, while she worked in the kitchen.[42]

Buildings that survive from a time when food and repairs were done on the grounds can be found at these camps, although they may now serve different functions or may simply be abandoned, as happened to smoke houses, ice houses, and buildings for water pumps and electrical generators. The most unchanged of early buildings is the workshop with its bench and tools, a woodstove, and a couple of chairs. These workshops were a combination of work-place, office, and clubhouse for the caretaker and other men at the camp, a refuge that was warm in winter and cool

Bathtub on wheels, North Woods Club. Ostensibly this tub was wheeled from room to room or on boardwalks connecting one cottage to another. Photograph by Craig Gilborn, 1998.

ABOVE: *At rest. The room is a kitchen, but given this familiar sitting pose—one foot on the floor, the other propped on the woodstove—it could as well be a workshop in any multibuilding camp. The Adirondack Museum (P20854).*

RIGHT: *Guide house, Kildare Club, Jordan Lake, early twentieth century. The house accommodated two year-round families and a couple of men in summer. Photograph by Craig Gilborn, 1998.*

in summer when under a loft. The snugness of these workshops remains at the Putnam Camp, Kildare Club, and the Kirkham Camp, enough to point to their role in preserving the continuity of the camp as a whole.

Another traditional building at camp are guide houses, properly referred in the singular, as in the 1895 inventory for Camp Pine Knot, "Guide House: Kitchen Building," which had two bedrooms, dining room, and kitchen.[43] The Guide House at the Kildare Club was for the caretaker and his wife, as well as one other couple and single men in seasonal jobs. The term, which is still used at camps after their guides disappeared, is a reminder of the much-admired Adirondack guide, who, like his guideboat, embodied the spirit of the Adirondacks and may have built much of the camp himself. Guides are still in the Adirondacks; as before, they hire out their services, but they are likely to live in their own homes and commute to work.

CHAPTER 8

Decorous Adirondack Camps

WHAT MADE the Adirondack camp inimitable and therefore delightful was that it was indigenous and yet susceptible to variations at the hands of local workmen with a knack for handling rustic materials—twig, limb, trunk, root, and bark.[1] Families for whom a summer vacation could last three or four months, from late May to September or even October, made suggestions to one of the workmen who perhaps had divided his time between carpentry and other duties at the camp. Life in the woods was utterly unlike life anywhere else, at work and home, so that memories of summers in the Adirondacks—of the dalliance of a couple on a nest of boughs in a lean-to at the edge of a lake—were remembered vividly and usually with satisfaction for the rest of one's life.

Seneca Ray Stoddard, a photographer and publisher of annual guidebooks to the region, who knew the region's attractions better than any individual alive during in the period 1871–1915, recommended Camp Pine Knot and the other camps on Raquette Lake, calling them "works of art" because they were "in keeping with their native environment." They were, he said, "filled with dainty bric-a-brac," but his punctuation reveals that he meant that function and not ornamentation was the source of their artistry. He perceived that rustic artistry was being pushed in new and intriguing directions on Raquette Lake by 1888.[2]

The decorous camp was the mediator between the individual and nature: this appealed to cultivated people fascinated by nature's many guises, as in gardens, rural cemeteries, city parks, or as totally independent of the hand and mind of humans, in the forests, waters, and mountains of untamed places like the Adirondacks. The decorous camp was an attempt to find a balance between the polarities, the primitive hut and the prodigy country house.

The Country Estate and Villa

A house away from town has been desired from early times, perhaps from the moment households were safe from harm outside protective city walls. "Villa," an Italian

OPPOSITE: *We take the best of cities to nature, according to Emerson. An illustration of fashionable Parisians dining in the branches of a tree is a glimmering of the implications. The engraving appeared in the* Illustrated London News *on October 19, 1872.*

Decorous cottage at Camp Woodmere, Upper St. Regis Lake, built in 1923. This family cottage was designed by John Sinclair for Mr. and Mrs. Robert Garrett of Philadelphia. Photograph by Craig Gilborn, 1976.

word with Latin origins, was synonymous in Europe and North America with a country home that could be big or small but was ornamental; like "camp" and "cottage," villa did not differentiate by size.

Well-to-do Romans sought hillside villas overlooking the Mediterranean, where summer breezes made the heat more bearable. Merchants and princes in the Italian Renaissance built villas on what were productive farms outside Venice and other cities; wheat and other crops, sold in cities and abroad, created personal fortunes enabling grander villas to be erected. Likewise in England farms generated wealth for the so-called "landed" aristocracy and gentry, principally from crops and leases, though Scotland and Wales were wilder and more suited to estates and lodges for hunting and fishing. A country estate was a badge of high social status, and it was to England's landed class that Americans looked when they began searching for ways to spend the immense fortunes amassed in the last half of the nineteenth century, starting with purchases of city lots, suburban tracts, country farms, and woodland preserves. They found architects who designed city palaces, country mansions, and hunting camps for them, principally after the Civil War and before the Great Depression of 1929.

Anyone desiring to climb the social ladder in England needed at least two residences, one in town and a second or third in the country. In the comedy *The Importance of Being Earnest,* a play in which Oscar Wilde wickedly exposed the inanities of life among England's upper class, the protagonist Jack says that he owns "a country home with some land" but cannot depend on it for "real income." As far as he can make out, he says to the mother of his fiancée, poachers were the only ones who got anything from it.

Country estates were eminently practical for anyone in public life: they were havens in the Middle Ages for families on the side of a defeated or discredited faction, including communion in the wrong church. One might be physically safe in the country, since estates were largely self-sustaining; but prolonged retirement became house arrest—banishment—pending a change of heart at court or by the powers that be. Estates were refuges during outbreaks of diseases like yellow fever and typhoid that swept cities and afflicted rich as well as poor. Families in eighteenth-century Philadelphia summered at small farms in the country that now are part of the inner city; they sought the cooler air and quiet, but they also felt safer from flare-ups of illness that broke out in warm weather.

The Adirondacks similarly offered a haven from New York City and other cities visited by disease, notably tuberculosis in the nineteenth and early twentieth centuries and polio epidemics in the 1930s and 1940s. The region briefly served as a summer home for refugee children from the war in Europe, at Tarnedge and also at the North Woods Club. Heloise Durant Rose, sister of William West Durant, claimed that her brother William had closeted himself in the Adirondacks to avoid being served with papers in New York City, where he had an office and an apartment at the old Waldorf Astoria hotel.[3]

Ownership of a camp and a tract of land in the Adirondacks satisfied middle- and upper-class men against a future contingency. Ned Buntline lived in a cabin on Eagle Lake for four to five years, starting in 1857, because, while successful as a writer of dime novels, he had a talent for getting into trouble. He spent a year in prison in 1849–1850 for inciting an anti-foreigner riot in Astor Place, and he was indicted during a lecture tour in 1852 for causing an election riot in St. Louis; he jumped bail and returned to New York City where he helped reorganize the Know-Nothing Party.[4] His stay in the Adirondacks may have been intended to keep him out of saloons and crowds. For personal and creative reasons, men and women have lived in Adirondack camps for periods of months, fulfilling a vow to test their fortitude and take time to write. Hugh Fosburgh's *A Clearing in the Wilderness,* which traced history and seasonal changes at Baker's Clearing over the course of a year, was written in residence at the family's cottage at the North Woods Club. Fosburgh did not identify it as a club, probably because "club" implied greater comfort and conviviality than really existed, since he and a caretaker were fifteen miles from the nearest town, Minerva, N.Y., at the end of a snow-covered forest road. More recently, Anne LaBastille, author of *Woodswoman,* earned admirers for her writings about her life and experiences at a cabin on an Adirondack lake. An ecologist with a doctorate, she travels widely but makes sure she has time for her cabin, where she does much of her writing.[5]

It would be an error to ascribe "getting away from it all" as removing oneself from the company of other people, since camp more often than not was social and interactive. True, the "getting away" phrase has been construed to imply a momentary retreat that was more contemplative than social, but the reality was that camp life could be frenetically active, especially when children were in the picture. A startling statement by the late John Brinkerhoff Jackson illumines the character of the modern experience of wilderness: it is not, wrote this historian of the landscape, solitary or contemplative, and "it is less concerned with awareness of the environment as a distinct phenomenon than it is with the cultivation of awareness."[6]

At camp a person might feel more free than ever before, but he or she still adhered to meal schedules and was expected to extend courtesies to others. Campers, then, did not have a life of their own, at least not while the camp was occupied and most especially when it was full. A cabin of one's own was a prize, for it conferred privacy and even allowed a measure of independence from the dining room with its timetable and complaining cook. Tea and biscuits or cookies saved from the dining hall and squirreled away sufficed for a mid-morning or afternoon snack. Water was heated on the wood stove and packaged delicacies brought out from a closet or drawer, perhaps to be shared with a friend. Absences by one or two campers invited attention and eventually speculation by others in the group. The social constraints of home were more intense in camp because life was focused there.

The raison d'àtre for going to camp was largely shaped by the city, which, even though pilloried for clamor, contagion, and artifice, was the incubator within which ideas about nature and wilderness grew. Ralph Waldo Emerson, who camped on Follensby Pond with nine other intellects from Boston and Cambridge in 1858, expressed the idea that nature cannot be understood except from the perspective of the city-bred mind: "We flee from cities, but we bring/The best of cities with us," he wrote in his blank verse poem, "The Adirondacks."[7] Appreciation of nature, Emerson suggests, is conditioned by the city.

The Decorous Camp of Harvey Ellis

Harvey Ellis (1852–1904) chose the term "decorous shelter" to describe the sensible compromise represented in his design for an Adirondack camp.[8] The specifics of his camp and its plan are less important than his rationalization for a cottage that was expressive of its woodland surroundings yet served the social and personal needs of its occupants: his was a generic vacation cottage at the start of the new century.

He opens by saying that any "decorous shelter" must combine two things—the "privacy and the many domestic comforts which our civilization has changed from luxuries to necessities," as well as the openness and freedom of the tent and accessibility to the outdoors. It must be immune from outdoor pests, like flies and mosquitoes, and offer occupants opportunity to withdraw "absolutely from the outer world." The lodge or camp should not be expensive, and it should be built of material from and near the site; if this is done, the camp will be—as "it should be," both "honest and sincere, frankly direct in its purpose and methods." Discerning morality in handmade, regionally oriented products was the mission of the *Craftsman*

magazine for which he was writing; the magazine was perhaps the most influential vehicle for popularizing ideas about the Arts and Crafts movement in America, although historians of art and architecture generally have viewed it as exploiting intellectual soil cultivated in Britain and America long before it began publication in 1901.[9]

Introducing amenities and good manners to the woods was defended on grounds that while people of cultivation would benefit from what for Teddy Roosevelt was the rigorous outdoor life, they needed more than life's bare necessities: a shanty might suffice for a reclusive bachelor, or an impoverished pioneer family, but persons of sense and sensibility needed a measure of comfort if only to take stock of the beauties of nature around them. The answer was the decorous camp—neither hovel nor palace, but a safe and dry place whose proximity to nature would nourish its occupants.

When children and elders began coming to the Adirondacks, shanties and cabins built for men were unacceptable; the new arrivals required supervision and warm beds, considerations that shifted the Adirondack experience from camping and tramping to a life oriented less to roving than settling down in one place. Creeping civilization in the wilds was held to be regrettable but inevitable.

Families altered how the Adirondacks were experienced. For one thing, families did not move well; the shift from home to camp and back again was undertaken after an effort that resembled mobilizing an army unit. The result was that families got attached to their camp for practical as well as emotional reasons, so they took a proprietary view of the mountains in the distance, pointing and naming each to visitors

Tip Top, Schroon Lake, N.Y. A nineteenth-century farmhouse that was altered and enlarged into a country home in the twentieth century. Photograph by Craig Gilborn, 1998.

on the porch. In time, a family's knowledge of the Adirondacks was limited to the locality—to local people, favorite views, and summer neighbors—and to little beyond it. This provincialism fostered loyalties and garnered help to communities in times of need.

Harvey Ellis's decorous camp was a family camp. He likened the living room, which he called the "Great Hall," to a parade ground where at the end of the day the head of the family—the "commander"—would review those assembled and then retire to his "headquarters," or bedroom, on the floor above, exiting by way of a stairway off the corridor to the dining room. Adjoining the stairs was an L-shaped nook—called the "Ingle"—consisting of a fireplace facing the living room and built-in seat to the right, and sharing a stone hearth. The living room was nearly fifty feet long and sixteen feet deep. A terrace rather than a porch extended across the front, a departure from the majority of Adirondack camps. At the top of the stairway was a "Family Room" off of which were doors to five bedrooms, a bath, and two porches.

Rules and roles imposed at home were more or less put aside in camp: informality and the unexpected were tolerated, and people were permitted to lower their guard. For children, this may have been their introduction to parental or adult behavior unseen before. There was, then, an emotional component to the family camp. Its pleasures and ease were ephemeral, and knowledge of this was bittersweet for adults and even for children, for whom the last few days were countdowns of "lasts"—the last swim, the last trip for ice cream, the last meal, the last glimpse of the lake from the car as they returned home.

Ellis would eliminate all extraneous ornamentation from the camp: anything "savoring of the 'artistic' shall be vigorously thrust aside." Balconies are tolerable on the second floor for the seclusion they afford in the bedroom. Floors are of pine, and the interior walls of the living room, and the ceiling between the beams, are of "mortar board." The fireplace is of local stone, "boulders preferred," and these are split and laid with their flat sides out. The fireplace is "extremely primitive" but "eminently practical." Therefore, he says, do not conceal the mortar between the stones, and consider putting in a ledge or recess for displaying a "few household gods."

Color is an important element in Ellis's decorous camp. Rag rugs and hangings offered accents of color. Ellis preferred stain to paint since staining showed the graining of the wood. A choice of effects was available. A dark olive brown stain could be used on the woodwork—beams, casings, and doors—while "rose" instead of "tawny yellows" might be used in the dining room, while bedrooms might be "a dull grayish blue" for an air of coolness. The kitchen, pantry, and similar rooms should have walls and ceilings of spruce boards stained a "strong grass-green." Furniture, he said, should be "of the simplest," each piece having its own function, since "this is no museum, but a camp in which to live."

Except for its log construction, Ellis's Adirondack camp might have been found in any residential area of upstate New York, differing more in detail and in furnishings than in form from hundreds of houses in Rochester where Ellis was born. He retained the conventional division of public and private rooms, placing them on separate

floors, although he did have a play room on the second floor. He did this because bedrooms and living rooms do not belong on the same floor, but also for economy, since "the same roof which covers one story will cover two equally well."

Like the magazine for which he was writing, Ellis was addressing middle class readers who no doubt felt comfortable with a camp not too dissimilar to what they already knew of their homes in town. His *decorous* camp of 1903 would have seemed a novelty two to three decades earlier, when architects found little in the way of commissions in the Adirondacks. All architect-designed Adirondack camps retained something of Ellis's generic ideas for a camp. The ideas were not his but belonged to the Arts and Crafts movement of which he was a part. Decorous Adirondack camps had some common structural features.

Cottage, North Woods Club, built c. 1900. Still standing, this log cottage is reminiscent of Dutch colonial houses in New York. Here the porch is not covered by an extension of the roof, as in the illustration on page 8 (Moodie Cottage). The Adirondack Museum Library.

The Decorous Durant Cottage of c. 1889

The Durant Cottage at Camp Pine Knot, built about 1889, was small but tightly composed outside and well organized inside. Despite its familiar appearance, it was as fashionable as any building on Raquette Lake at the time. It was structurally complex, notwithstanding its few rooms—a sitting room with bed, a bedroom, and a bathroom with a small "stove room" behind it for heating water. Pine boards beveled at the edges resembled the facing of hewn logs on the walls, a type of wall paneling Durant would use Camp Uncas, Sagamore Lodge, and at his camp on Arbutus Lake.

Exposed in the roof were peeled pole rafters and trusses and a covering of birch bark, and a stone fireplace had a rustic overmantel and chimney encased in birch bark.

The cottage in conception and detailing constituted an essay reserved yet suited to its Adirondack setting, revealing Durant's talent as a designer or in orchestrating the design and work of others. The cottage was intended for himself and his wife, but his real aim may have been to put it at the disposal of Collis P. Huntington, his friend and chief financial backer, who rented or used Camp Pine Knot starting about 1890 and purchased it in 1895. Interiors at Pine Knot and other camps were brightened by textiles or fabrics, as well as by grass matting on the floor. Throw rugs and oriental carpets were placed on floors, and slip covers and throw pillows were used on chairs and settees or couches. Bright red curtains were used in windows at Pine Knot.

What Architects Brought to the Decorous Camp

MORE DAYLIGHT

Architects addressed a number of issues when they began designing Adirondack camps in the last two decades of the nineteenth century. One of these was admitting more light into rooms, especially the main room where as much as half of the ambient light might be cut off by the porch. Reading in these rooms could be difficult on cloudy days, and a gloomy interior was oppressive. One solution was to open the living room to the rafters and introduce windows—clerestory or dormer—above the porch roof. To these the architect might add a polygonal cupola with windows in its side, creating a shaft down which light spilled to the floor below, perhaps onto a dining area and table.

Living room, Camp Wild Air, built c. 1895, burned in 1916. William R. Mead of McKim, Mead and White designed the replacement, which still stands with later alterations. Mead could have been the architect of the earlier building (see p. xxx). Note the exposed logs, the use of wall fabrics, and treatment of the fireplace nook and its hidden skylight. The Adirondack Museum, gift of Whitelaw Reid (P11413).

Getting daylight into a living room with a floor overhead always posed a problem. A skylight over the hearth of the fireplace, or a concealed dormer window where the chimney went through the roof, were tried. Bay windows, often fitted with cushioned window seats, were another device for bringing light into camp interiors. The designs of Augustus D. Shepard in the 1920s dealt with the problem by eliminating the porch and introducing French doors that opened onto a terrace or patio.

More Space

Architects also addressed the problem of creating larger living rooms unobstructed by posts or columns. Roof trusses were used in rooms open to the roof. Large log beams were used in camps with two or more floors; even so, these rooms were restricted in size and had low ceilings. Larger spans were possible but required posts or columns to prevent beams from sagging toward the middle. Steel beams in the ceiling and steel posts in the wall, perhaps concealed by being encased in hollowed logs or boxed-in, allowed ceilings to go higher and exterior walls to become more window than wall.

Public-Privacy Divisions and Camp Layout

The decorous camp must allow the individual the choice of joining the group or being apart from it, as Ellis said. Middle- and upper- class homes did the same, so this was not a concern exclusive to the camp. However, camp by definition was *com-*

Living room, Crane Point Lodge, Blue Mountain Lake, N.Y. Photograph c. 1920. An exterior view is on page 68. Lumberjacks built the first lodge, which may explain the contrast of this room with one designed by an architect, in the preceding illustration. The Adirondack Museum, gift of George Kirkham (P20334).

The Telephone Comes to Camp

Lewis Spence spent his eleventh to fourteenth summers as a companion for his grandfather, John Robertson Dunlap, who had been widowed and was a Kentucky gentleman of decided opinions. In a memoir of the early 1930s, which he wrote years later, Mr. Spence said that, having no one his age to play with, he shadowed Oscar the handyman around the grounds and closely observed his wife, Julia, in the kitchen. The passage is used with permission of Mrs. Lewis Spence.

"The telephone was used almost exclusively by the cook, Julia, to order groceries and other victuals from the market in Saranac Lake. As for Grandfather, I don't believe he ever really understood the function of a telephone, as whenever he used it, he bellowed so into the mouthpiece that he might as well have stood on the veranda and shouted to whomever he wished to speak. The rare long-distance calls, from my mother at home on Long Island, or from an acquaintance of Grandfather's, were regarded in much the same light as the communications between astronauts and Mission Control in Houston. Call times were set in an exchange of letters, and the recipient of the call would be posted in the pantry a full fifteen minutes before the appointed time. All these preparations were in a way superfluous, however, as such were the burblings and squeaks on the underwater telephone cable that it was lucky if one could catch every tenth word of the person at the other end of the line."

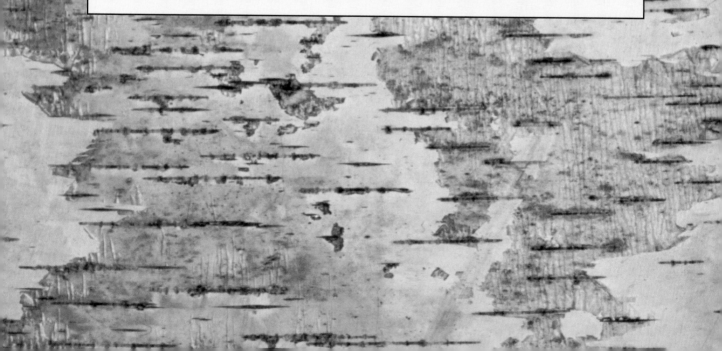

munal, which houses were not; so the layout of the camp was a special consideration when architects began addressing the allocation of private and public spaces in separate buildings, wings, and floors and even parts of one room, the main room.

Even primitive camps provided private and public spaces; as seen in the chapter on open camps, camps in the field did this by separation of shelters and buildings, a lean-to here for the client and tent there for his guide. So multi-building camps like Camp Pine Knot may have owed something to guides' camps, both the temporary camps which were flattened in the snows of a winter and in semi-permanent camps consisting of a variety of tents and log cabins on a beach which were rented to sportsmen and a few vacationers.

Permanent camps, one of the earlier of which was Camp Pine Knot, followed these precedents. And architects a decade or two later, perhaps beginning with Santanoni in 1892, would adopt the multi-building plan but begin the consolidation of buildings that seems to mark the arrival of the architect to the Adirondacks. At Santanoni this meant clustering five independent buildings but connecting them by a continuous porch and roof. Cabins at Kamp Kill Kare were placed end to end and connected by a series of verandas and steps across the front.

Camp Pine Knot by 1880 had a cluster of sleeping cottages or cabins and one or two platform tents near a cabin in the style of a Swiss chalet. The front room of the chalet was a living room, and bedrooms were in rooms to the rear and on the floor above. Camp living rooms were common rooms in which family and guests felt free to enter and leave as they wished, usually before and after meals but also when rainy weather forced activity inside. They were sometimes referred to as the "family room" or "family building."

What architects accomplished—William Coulter being the most notable example—was the consolidation of functions while presenting the camp in what appeared to be a unified or organic "envelope," a departure from the four Adirondack camps of William West Durant with their independent structures. Robertson's Santanoni and Coulter's Levi Morton Camp marked a distinct advance in the attempt to impose a visual order to the Adirondack camp predicated not on a style but what the construction site offered and the patron would accept.

Architects became adept in dealing with the privacy-public issue at camp. One plan placed family and guests at opposite ends of the main building, with the living room in between as a common meeting place. There were variations of this plan in camps that appeared to be quite different on the outside. One variant was the butterfly or suntrap plan used by Augustus D. Shepard at the Adirondack League Club and by William Distin at William Rockefeller's camp on Upper Saranac Lake and the Walter Hochschild camp on Eagle Lake a few years later. Shepard's plan at the Place Camp of 1922 had wings off a central living room building with a cathedral ceiling. The Rockefeller camp of 1933 segregated owner and guests in wings off a very large hall open to trusses in the roof and stone fireplaces at each end.

These plans were strung out because the entire camp might have a single floor, except for the central living room which was a half-story or so taller than the wings flanking it. But the architect of a camp on Fish Bladder Island, on the Vermont side of Lake Champlain, accomplished the same arrangement in a cottage that looked like any two-story camp, except it wasn't. Built about 1905, it is square in plan and enclosed by a roofed porch on three sides. Inside, however, in the center, is a large room open to the roof with a living area and dining area separated by a free-standing brick chimney with fireplaces, opposite sides, one for each area. Flanking this central room, which has a balcony with windows for additional light, are two sets of rooms that might have been wings but are not. On one side is the master bedroom and a bunk room for children; and, on the opposite side of the living room, are bedrooms off a hall for guests. This Vermont camp accomplished the same end with greater economy than did the New York camps of Shepard and Distin with their butterfly plan in buildings very different in appearance.

A second disadvantage of a two-floor camp, besides the lack of light, was that swimmers headed for the lake or coming from it traipsed through the living room or kitchen. An outside stairway like those in early photographs, attached in the rear or under the gable ends of hotels, was a solution, but not one that would be attractive. Augustus D. Shepard designed the Place Camp entirely on grade, so all bedrooms had direct access through a door to the outside placed in each room. The Vermont camp likewise allowed people to go directly to the outdoors via the section of screened porch that was allocated to most of the bedrooms.

Living and Dining Areas in Camp

Dining rooms became superfluous or expendable in the open-plan houses of the late 1800s, the space being reduced or even eliminated in favor of the living room. Several camps banished the dining room entirely, either by placing a table and chairs in a corner of the living room, or at one end, and off a pantry and kitchen. The combination living-dining area was not, according to Arts and Crafts advocates, a new idea, but a return to the Medieval hall where households, including some servants, gathered and dined communally. Spacious living rooms at Adirondack camps, oblong and rising a half-story to as much as three stories off the floor, as at the Castle at Litchfield Park, derived from the halls of manor houses in England between the twelfth and seventeenth centuries. Unlike Classical architecture, which was formal and academic, domestic buildings of the Middle Ages were appealing because they were far less concerned about a building's appearance, on the outside especially: what counted were the living spaces for its occupants inside.[10]

When incomes were ample, labor cheap, and vacations lasted two to three months, sometimes well into September, large Adirondack camps had detached dining and kitchen buildings where food was prepared and served to a dozen or more people three times daily. These dining buildings, expensive to staff and to run, fell into disuse after the Second World War, although their impracticality was likely apparent as early as the First World War, when labor was hard to find and personal indulgences were viewed as unpatriotic.

Communal dining was doomed by the drifting apart of family members. Vacations were not taken together as before; the Adirondack region was less exciting than resorts beckoning in Florida, Colorado, and Europe. Besides, when the camp was empty, or nearly so, no one wanted to eat in the dining building; it was closed and meals prepared in cottages which had been retrofitted with small kitchens. People preferred to eat where and when they wanted, and they gave fewer big "dinner parties" than before. Guests were fewer and more intimate, and the trend was to dress down, rather than force everyone to arrive in long gowns and tuxedos, as one's parents routinely did at the turn of the century. Neglected, the dining hall eventually was torn down, as happened at Camp Wild Air and at the Knollwood Club.

A few camps seem not to have had a separate dining room or dining building. The Clubhouse at Eagle Nest has a dining *area* at one end of a living room, designated by a dais a step or two above the main floor. A screened porch for breakfast and lunch on warm summer days was reached through French doors next to the long dining table. A dining porch was another excuse for eliminating or diminishing the size of a formal dining room.

At the William Rockefeller Camp, meals were served in front of one of two fireplaces at opposite ends of a large living room open to the roof. Santanoni had a similar arrangement, although the two fireplaces shared a common chimney that separated living and dining areas of one room. A former hotel renovated into a

Lodge on Crane Point, Blue Mountain Lake. J. Scholtes, architect. Built for George D. Kirkham, 1926. Alterations by Mr. and Mrs. J. Richardson Dilworth after 1967. Photograph by Craig Gilborn, 1998.

private lodge on Blue Mountain Lake has no dining room despite its generous size and many bedrooms. A dozen guests sat at a long table to the right of the fireplace, and food brought from a small kitchen was placed on a side table where guests served themselves.

The owners of the lodge, Mr. and Mrs. J. Richardson Dilworth, renovated several rooms at one end as their personal apartment. Comprised of a living room, a "cube" bedroom, walk-in storage vestibule, and a bath, the apartment is small compared to the rest of the building, especially the living room, which is cavernous because it dates from the time the lodge was run as a hotel. An accordion door in the corridor between their quarters and the living room allows their end of the lodge to be closed off from the rest of the house in winter.

The Dynamic of the Living Room

Living rooms were big less to accommodate more people than to accomplish something close to the opposite, which was to offer areas of privacy within a public space. A person could be with others, in intimate conversation with one other person, or they could be alone, albeit in the same room with others. Seasoned guests learned how to take stock of the landscape of the living room from the staircase, sizing up the scene below as ripe, uncertain, or to avoid-at-all-cost.

Main living room, Crane Point. "Carenaught" was the name of the lodge that opened and accepted paying guests after 1926, explaining this room's size. Five bedrooms and baths are on the floor above. Photograph by Craig Gilborn, 1998.

In the Clubhouse at Eagle Nest, the living room was demarcated by furniture into several concentric areas centering on the alcove where the fireplace was located, with couches and chairs arrayed in a semi-circle toward the fire. By un-written custom, perhaps a vestigial rite of the tribal fire, any and all persons were entitled to the space between the fire and the circle of furniture regardless of age. The second area, just beyond, might have tables for card or board games; and the area beyond that, the outermost area, was for singles and pairs, perhaps on a window seat big enough for one or two but certainly not three. A stodgy guest might sit near a lamp or window here, absorbed in a newspaper or book.

Private bedroom, Crane Point. Designed by William S. Short, Princeton. The room is a cube, fifteen feet on each side. Photograph by Craig Gilborn, 1998.

A one-room cottage on Blue Mountain Lake has one wall almost entirely of glass with sliding doors opening onto a terrace and lawn beyond. A bed and kitchenette are at one end, a dining table and chairs are in the center, and a couch and easy chairs are arranged in front of the fireplace at the other end of the room. Built in 1975 from

Family room, Crane Point. Located well away from the owners' apartment are quarters for children and grandchildren. Designed and built by James and Sheila Hutt in the 1980s, it has an open area for play and dining, and to the right, a kitchen. A bedroom and bath are nearby. Photograph by Craig Gilborn, 1998.

Living and dining room, clubhouse, Eagle Nest, 1904–5, with later alterations. Max Heidelberg, architect. Schuyler Kathan, stone mason for W. W. Durant, built the fireplace. On a raised floor to the right is the dining area adjoined by the pantry and kitchen. Photograph by Craig Gilborn, 1998.

a design by Katie Kirkham, this cottage was connected by a breezeway to an older house, which now is used by children and guests. George and Mary Kirkham invite friends for dinner, greeting guests by the double bed, giving refreshments in front of the fireplace, and then serving them buffet-style from the central table and letting them find a seat near the hearth or on the terrace. Precedent of a kind for this all-

One-room cottage, Blue Mountain Lake, late 1970s. Dining and living areas ahead, bed behind camera, kitchen and door to bath are to the right. An older house is about twenty feet away, across a terrace. Photograph by Craig Gilborn, 1998.

purpose room can be found in one-room cabins of the nineteenth century. The Kirkham bathroom is located along the back wall of the cottage, parallel to the glass wall facing the lake, with light from windows at the top of the wall, near the ceiling, which also has a skylight.

Porch, Lawrence Camp, Adirondack League Club, Little Moose Lake. A corner porch was architecture's solution to the porch across the front. Photograph by Craig Gilborn, 1998.

The Veranda or Porch

The porch was the defining feature of the Adirondack camp; even tents were given an awning for a porch in front. Porches were human verges, neither in the house nor out of it, but in-between. At a time when porches were unused and systematically removed in residential neighborhoods of American cities, especially in the years following the advent of television, the porch retained a central place at Adirondack camps, although, as seen, not all of Augustus D. Shepard's camps were given a porch. Porches at Harvey Ellis's decorous Adirondack camp were on the *second* floor, tucked under the overhang of the roof.

Porch memories were perhaps the most durable, since truths rather than facts were revealed there, where talk and family skeletons and generational attitudes mingled with sensations of lake and pine. A meeting place, the porch was the outdoors for elders for whom swimming had long since lost its attractions; and for boys and girls fresh from the lake, it was as close to indoors as they wanted to be. The porch was a rainy-day shelter, but it also was a shady spot on warm days and caught passing breezes. A porch hammock was an ideal spot for drifting off to sleep after lunch in the afternoon.

Sleeping cottages at the Garrett Camp on Upper St. Regis Lake each had a screened porch in front, facing the lake, and a cabin in the rear which was a changing and warming room that served for storing canvas and furniture in winter. Camps with a half-floor above the first floor—a kind of bungalow—had bedrooms with an

Sleeping porch in front, cabin in back, offspring of the platform tent. The porch is screened and has canvas curtains on the sides that un-roll. Camp Woodmere, Upper St. Regis Lake. Photograph by Craig Gilborn, 1976.

alcove beneath the overhang of the roof and enclosed by a railing or low wall. Some camps had large porches on the second floor that were conspicuous, extending as they did over a porch below. Fresh air was regarded as healthful; sleeping on porches, even in winter, was regarded as therapeutic. People were bundled, their heads covered, so only a nose and mouth were exposed to the cold.

The porch has been rendered a nullity by attrition—by a succession of technological advances—miracle medicines and air conditioning among them. In the Adirondacks it prevails, but its future is uncertain; desultory con-

Sleeping cabins separated by a boardwalk. Camp Woodmere, Upper St. Regis Lake. Photograph by Craig Gilborn, 1976.

versation on the porch now competes with television beamed from satellites; given exposures to the south and west, no camp is so remote that occupants cannot be part of the global village of passive spectators. The porch remains the best place in camp for experiencing what television cannot offer, the countryside and company of other people or, if alone, the memories of previous summers in this chair and on this lake at the same hour of day.

Sleeping porch, Adirondack
League Club. Architects put
a hollow gable on the second
floor as a sleeping porch in
summer; sometimes a regular
bedroom was placed behind
the porch. The photograph,
of a camp on Little Moose
Lake, is from Camps in the
Woods (1931) by the architect Augustus D. Shepard.

Indoor Recreation

Entertainment was a consideration in a wet climate, since people—especially children—got testy and querulous when confined by rain. Places to play were the porch,
the living room, the dining room table, and the loft over the boathouse. Large camps
often had playrooms, sometimes referred to as casinos, which were as amply
equipped as luxury hotels and country clubs. The Alfred G. Vanderbilts, newly married, added a recreation building in 1901 and a two-lane bowling alley later. Margaret
Emerson, Mr. Vanderbilt's widow and his second wife, used these facilities into the
1950s. (He went down with the *Lusitania* in 1915.) Birch Island on Upper St. Regis
Lake has a bark-covered playhouse in the form of a Greek temple. Members of the
Kildare Club have a playroom not in a separate building but in a communal all-
purpose room of the main camp building facing Jordan Lake. The Whitelaw Reid
family at Camp Wild Air, within view of Birch Island Camp, has a billiard table in
a polygonal rustic cottage built into the lake. A log lodge inspected in the 1970s by
the writer contained an indoor swimming pool about thirty feet in length. The
lodge, which may have dated from the 1920s, had seen better days and carried a For
Sale sign.

Mrs. Merriweather Post and her then-husband, Joseph E. Davies, who was
Ambassador to the U.S.S.R. in 1936–38, returned to the U.S. with measured plans for
a dacha, a traditional summer house as popular in Russia today as it has been for cen-

Recreation building, Birch Island, Upper St. Regis Lake. This playhouse, in the form of a Greek temple, is unique in the Adirondacks. Early twentieth century. The Adirondack Museum Library.

Most camps had a place for games and play, whether it be a single room or one or more buildings. The recreation building at Sagamore Lodge, built in 1901 for Alfred G. Vanderbilt, its new owner, would be joined later by a two-lane bowling alley. *Photograph, c. 1950. The Adirondack Museum* (P 6891).

Dacha, Camp Topridge, Upper St. Regis Lake, built c. 1938. An office and a place for dances and showing Hollywood films, this was a replica of the country houses beloved by Russians. Mrs. Merriweather Post and her husband, Joseph E. Davies, returned to America with the plan following his stint as ambassador, 1936–38. Photograph courtesy of Frank Kawatch.

Interior of Dacha, Camp Topridge, as it appeared after Mrs. Merriweather Post's divorce from Davies. A painting showing happy Russian peasants was a study in irony, given the rich and powerful guests who square-danced under it, the women in peasant dresses. Photograph courtesy of Frank Kawatch.

turies. A replica was constructed for Mr. Davies as an office, but then, after their divorce (Mrs. Post had four husbands), it was renovated and used for dances and showings of Hollywood films delivered by Mrs. Post's private plane from Washington to the Saranac Lake Airport and from there to her camp by limousine and boat.

The recreational riches of White Pine Camp, which was not far from Topridge, were exaggerated, but only partly, in a newspaper cartoon of 1923, in which the subtext was

"Roughing It," a newspaper cartoonist's spoof of Calvin Coolidge, a "President of Simple Habits," vacationing at White Pine Camp in 1926 (see p. 210). The Adirondack Museum (p 27647).

how far bowling, billiards, tennis, horseback riding, and other amenities had carried Americans of Calvin Coolidge's ilk from a simple rural life of basic needs to the acquired appetites of the idle rich they detested.

Bowling alley, c. 1920. White Pine Camp, Osgood Pond, Paul Smiths, N.Y. (see p. 210). Sagamore Lodge had alleys; so did Kamp Kill Kare, which also had a squash court. Photograph by Craig Gilborn, 1998.

Bedrooms

Guest rooms at most camps were plain and functional, as if to convey a message to occupants to be up and about. Owners' bedrooms, by contrast, could be as comfortably furnished as the apartment they really were—complete with fireplace, desk and easy chairs for sitting and reading, and a separate bath and dressing room with walk-in closets.

Cubicle bathroom. Childs Camp, Adirondack League Club, Little Moose Lake. A tiny sink and half-tub are in a room off a landing of the main stairway between the first and second floors. Photograph by Craig Gilborn, 1998.

Bathroom, Sagamore Lodge, 1899, Seneca Ray Stoddard, photographer. Modern for their time, these bathrooms were functioning a century later. Gas was piped to light fixtures from an acetylene gas generator. The Adirondack Museum Library, gift of Mrs. Bromley Seeley.

Simplicity prevailed at most camps with minimal space and few frills: a double bed or twin beds, a chest of drawers, mirror, and a night table and lamp, but not much else. Closets sometimes seem to have been an afterthought at camps, since some closets were created by partitioning a corner of the room. Furniture was factory made as a rule and inexpensive but serviceable.

Rustic privy. Adirondack Mountain Reserve, Keene Valley, George B. Wood, photographer, c. 1895. The screen afforded privacy. The Adirondack Museum (P20925).

Bathrooms with toilets and running water were a twentieth-century phenomenon at Adirondack camps. Sagamore Lodge had baths with piped hot and cold water, flush toilets, and a septic tank system by 1899, when it was finished. When the Prospect House opened on Blue Mountain Lake in 1882, it had an electric light in most of its 300 rooms, running water piped from a remote pond, and a steam pipe for taking the chill off rooms in cold weather. But this hotel did not yet have separate baths or toilets, these being provided in a bath-house at the rear and a giant two-story outhouse connected to the hotel so guests would not have to climb or descend stairs.[11]

Shower contraption. Water splashes into the lake from a canvas bucket; whether the bucket was lowered into the lake for refilling or supplied via the hollow log from which it is suspended is uncertain. The Adirondack Museum (P42288).

Other camps eventually followed what must have been a pioneering triumph. Even so, some camps retained wash stands and crockery basins and pitchers as reminders of an earlier era before the water closet and bathroom, when people used the outhouse by day and a chamber pot at night, emptying it the next morning. Children were instructed to use a chamber pot on occasion when a lone toilet was deemed too far to reach in the dark.

A privy or outhouse was located behind cottages that did not yet have a toilet, perhaps screened by trees or shrubs. Some cottages, such as the one-room cabin that was part of the Blue Mountain House hotel, now the Adirondack Museum, had a seat over a hole in a shed attached at the rear, reached by a door from inside. As for bathing, that could be done with a cake of soap and washcloth in the lake. Dr. Gerster's Camp Kwenogamac on Long Lake may have had a bath house of its own—perhaps an enclosure over the water with the addition of a wood stove on which to heat water. An early snapshot shows a canvas enclosure with a canvas bucket that could be filled and lifted and emptied on the soapy person inside. For the squeamish, disrobing and immersion on a moonless night would suffice.

Furniture for the Camp

Informality at the Adirondack camp made any combination of furniture acceptable, one writer asking only that owners not allow the camp to be a dumping place of furniture no longer wanted at home.[12] What was allowable, according to an emerging number of design critics, could be picked from an omnium-gatherum of assorted seats, tables and stands of wicker, along with blocky oak furniture of Craftsman or Mission origin, stained brown and often adorned with black-colored hardware and leather attached to frames by large-headed brass nails. Other furniture was of the

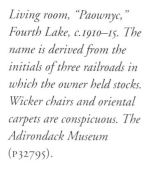

Living room, "Paownyc," Fourth Lake, c.1910–15. The name is derived from the initials of three railroads in which the owner held stocks. Wicker chairs and oriental carpets are conspicuous. The Adirondack Museum (P32795).

assembly-room variety—lathe-turned and produced in vast numbers by dozens of locally owned factories in mill towns in New England and upstate New York.[13]

William West Durant, who had entertained the Prince of Wales on his yacht *Utowana* and knew when to bend the rules, placed canvas director's chairs at the table in the dining room at Sagamore Lodge. Their canvas backs and seats imparted a jauntiness to a room otherwise dark and close. William Coulter, who had seen Sagamore by 1901, may have been following Durant's example when he introduced similar canvas chairs in one of the bedrooms at the Lewisohn Camp on Upper Saranac Lake.

Manufacturers of furniture for residential and vacation homes sold their products to department stores in larger cities as well as to regional outlets and suppliers, including boat liveries and similar small businesses in Adirondack towns. The amount of furniture must have been enormous considering the explosion of housing of all kinds before the Civil War but especially after it. The market expanded not only in the East but in resorts that were removed from the frontier by barely one or two decades, in California and the Southwest.

Harvey Ellis, from whose article "The Adirondack Camp" the term decorous camp has been coined, was perhaps the best of the designers employed by Gustav Stickley, one of four brothers who operated three furniture manaufactories that were

Dining room, Sagamore Lodge, 1899. Seneca Ray Stoddard, photographer. A club-like, masculine interior with American and British flags, wine on the sideboard, a bench with dark velvet cushions, and director's chairs around the table. The Adirondack Museum Library.

Bedroom, Adolph Lewisohn Camp, Prospect Point, Upper Saranac Lake. William L. Coulter, Lewisohn's architect, furnished the room with peeled log beds and director's chairs, which he may have seen during his visit to Sagamore Lodge in 1901 (see the preceding illustration and p. 192). This illustration is from Town and Country *magazine in 1904.*

in competition with one another. Located in towns in upstate New York and Michigan, the factories produced practical oak furniture that was heavy but durable, unadorned, and cleanly rectilinear.

Stickley furniture was suited to Adirondack interiors, where wood and stone were prevalent. Architects selected this Mission or Craftsman furniture for Adirondack camps after 1900.[14] Within months, other manufacturers, said to be "dozens" in number, were producing furniture similar to Gustav's line—his brothers among them.

Architects chose Stickley furniture because it was available in quantity, bore an Arts and Crafts movement mystique, and was compatible with other types of what was called cottage or bungalow furniture, such as wicker work and rustic hickory furniture that was made and shipped in large quantities from Indiana starting about 1899. The owner of Paownyc, a camp on Fourth Lake named from the initials of three railroads in which he was a stockholder, got furniture for his new camp from the L. & J. G. Stickley Company in Fayetteville, N.Y., about 1914. Two large camps, the Read Camp on Little Simon Pond and Camp Ziegler on Loon Lake, contained similar chairs and tables bearing a carved pine tree motif. Both camps were built a year apart, in 1906–7. Camp Ziegler, according to a two-part article in *International Studio* magazine, contained furniture that had been designed by Charles F. Rohlfs (1853–1936), an actor who turned to design about 1889 in Buffalo, N.Y.[15] The furniture at Camp Ziegler was sold to a dealer, and the main building burned to the ground some time after, a woman who later owned the property told the author. The furniture at the Read Camp is not only intact, but it also seems to be in the same

Dining room, Paownyc, Fourth Lake, 1910–15. The new camp was partly furnished with Mission-style furniture from one of several factories run by the Stickley brothers. The camp still stands. The Adirondack Museum (P 32796).

Covered sitting area, Read Camp (Three Star Camp), Little Simon Pond, Tupper Lake, N.Y. Looking down the footbridge toward the lodge. Hickory furniture from Indiana was used in large quantities at Adirondack camps and hotels at the time of this photograph, about 1906. Courtesy Peter B. Read.

spots as it was when the rooms were photographed, in about 1907. The combination living and dining room that is the main room of the Clubhouse at Eagle Nest has Craftsman style settees and tables which likely came from one of the Stickley brothers' factories before the First World War.

Living area, Camp Ziegler, Loon Lake, Chestertown, N.Y., 1907. James L. Burley, architect, with "designs by Louis J. Keimig." The camp burned in the early 1970s, but furniture attributed to Charles Rohlfs of Buffalo was said to have been removed before the fire. The furniture had a pine tree motif and was Arts and Crafts in style, appearing in International Studio *magazine in 1909. Bedrooms off the balconies on the second floor were reached by stairways flanking the fireplace.*

Hickory furniture with backs and seats of woven hickory bark was manufactured in large quantities by several companies in Indiana, the first, Old Hickory Chair Company, established about 1899 by Edmund Llewellyn Brown in Martinsville. Brown's seat factory eventually widened its line to other types of furniture—tables, beds, stands, porch swings, coat racks, and the like. Men handled the hickory rounds, fashioning them into frames, and women wove splint backs and seats with inner bark that had been stripped and soaked in water to keep it pliable.

Inexpensive and tough, hickory furniture was used inside the camp, on porches, and in boat houses. The porches and sitting areas at the Read Camp had hickory furniture by 1907, and the furniture was in good condition when the author saw it in 1998. Box cars loaded with hickory furniture were said to have been parked on a siding in Thendara, N.Y., near Old Forge, awaiting delivery to camps, hotels, and retail outlets.

ADIRONDACK RUSTIC FURNITURE

Rustic furniture could not be made in sufficient quantities after 1900, when camps were built by the dozens and perhaps even the hundreds.[16] Rustic furniture had its drawbacks: it was quirky and a dust-catcher, and of uneven quality and comfort. It also was difficult to produce in quantity and in ensembles.

The first rustic furniture, improvised and crude, consisted of seats, benches, and tables for shanties and cabins. The arrival of city people after the Civil War and the construction of camps for them was followed by better rustic furniture, some of it of excellent quality. The output was not large, which suggests that rustic furniture was more a novelty or native accent than a serious solution to furnishing any single camp. Rustic furniture was a sideline activity to the construction and finishing of cottages and boathouses, as well as ancillary camp structures such as lean-tos and summer houses.

Joseph O. A. Bryere, who came to Raquette Lake from Canada at the age of twenty, about 1880, made furniture which turned up in a number of camps—his own hotel among them—on the lake. He was variously employed by Durant families, starting perhaps with Charles Durant's Camp Fairview where he became a caretaker for a period, leaving it for Camp Stott, which had Durant connections by marriage, where Bryere and his wife worked until 1890, when he turned his attention to running his hotel, Brightside-on-Raquette. The influence of the Durant families—four counting William's in-laws, the Stotts—may have been a factor in the flowering of the rustic craft on Raquette Lake and vicinity in the last quarter of the century.

Rustic frieze (detail), early twentieth century, playroom, The Hedges (hotel), Blue Mountain Lake, N.Y. Photograph by Craig Gilborn, 1974.

Mosaic twig sideboard, c. 1880–90. Possibly made by Seth Pierce, although other men on Raquette Lake and vicinity did this kind of work. At an early camp on Bluff Point, it measures nearly seven feet from bottom to top. Photograph by Craig Gilborn, 1974.

The photographer Seneca Ray Stoddard called Bryere "an artist in rustic wood," noting in the 1892 edition of his guidebook to the region that Bryere's "services in this particular line are at a premium in the woods, and many camps hereabout show beautiful specimens of his skill." Other rustic workers on Raquette Lake and vicinity were: Joseph Asher, who was William West Durant's head ship-carpenter; Andrew Fisher, a guide and carpenter who built a mosaic-twig sideboard at Endion, a hotel and family residence on Long Lake; Frank Fortin, a carpenter to whom was credited, in an item in a 1900 issue of the *Warrensburg News,* "one of the finest pieces of rustic work that has ever been seen in this country," a picture of a hunter in the act of shooting, composed "on birch bark, twigs and moss" in natural colors and displayed at Camp Pine Knot.

Another maker was Seth Pierce, a Civil War veteran who conceivably assisted with the construction of decorative rustic cabins and even a church, called Poplar Grove Church, which a detachment of engineers built during a quiet spell in the Union army's siege of Petersburg, Va., in 1864. The patterns formed by split poles on the church tower bear an approximate resemblance to the smaller-scale mosaic work of two sideboards and a corner cupboard that have been attributed to Pierce. One of the sideboards, at the Stott Camp on Bluff Point, Raquette Lake, is so big that a door would have to be widened to move it. The other, equally splendid, is in Trophy Lodge on Brandreth Lake, a few miles north of Raquette Lake. A family picture of the 1890s shows the looming presence of the sideboard behind the assembled McAlpins and Brandreths on the porch. Pierce is also the attributed maker of the corner cupboard from Camp Cedars that is now at the Adirondack Museum. The cupboard, which adopted a quilt design of the late nineteenth century known as "Flower Basket," was a gift from Frederick Clark Durant, Jr., a son of the owner of Camp Cedars and the Prospect House hotel.

Another maker of rustic furniture was George Wilson, the gardener at Sagamore Lodge about 1910 who by 1916–17 had taken a job at the neighboring camp, Kamp Kill Kare, where he was employed by Mr. and Mrs. Francis P. Garvan, the new owners. Yet another rustic worker, who worked for the Garvans, had the name Stickney.[17]

Rustic makers on Raquette Lake seem to have had a ready market in camp owners that employed them. A few workers produced furniture on speculation, that is, for buyers unknown to them. Two of these were Lee Fountain and Elmer Patterson, who separately produced chairs, rockers, and tables between about 1915 and 1930, selling to summer tourists passing through Speculator and Lake Pleasant, N.Y.

A third rustic worker who produced furniture in quantity was Ernest Stowe, a bachelor who was one of a small army of carpenters employed in building dozens of camps on the Saranac Lakes between 1900 and 1930. Stowe's furniture was made from rounds and half-rounds of yellow birch and sheets of white birch bark tacked to case pieces or table tops of pine boards. According to the Petty brothers, who saw Stowe at work with others at the Isaac Seligman and Otto Kahn camps on the south shore of Upper Saranac Lake, Stowe turned out furniture at his cabin home at Corey's Rustic Lodge, an old hotel located near the carry between the lake and the Raquette River. Opened in 1850, it was run by Jesse Corey until 1894, when he retired and leased it to Charles Wardner.

About sixty-five pieces of fine rustic furniture, some of which had cornices, quarter-columns, and fielded paneling of high-style furniture, are attributed Ernest Stowe. Among these are three assemblages, one of which includes a dining room

Pedestal table. Tables with polygonal tops on which twigs are tacked in geometric patterns turn up at camps in the Raquette Lake region. A yellow birch supplied the base of this table, but cage-like bases fashioned from cedar were also used. Photograph by Craig Gilborn, 1981.

Dining room table and chairs by Ernest Stowe. At Corey's, on the carry to Upper Saranac Lake, Stowe made furniture at his cabin home when he was unable to work on camps. Working almost exclusively with white birch bark and yellow birch segments, he produced assemblages of rustic furniture. In 1986, this table and twelve chairs of c. 1900 sold for more than sixty thousand dollars at an auction house in New York City. Helga Photo Studio.

Bedroom, Sagamore Lodge, 1899. Seneca Ray Stoddard, photographer. W. W. Durant may have introduced furniture and fitments of whole and halved peeled logs to Adirondack camps, beginning at Camp Uncas in 1895 and soon after at Sagamore Lodge, shown here. Adirondack Museum Library.

table and twelve matching chairs which brought $45,000 at an auction in New York City in 1986 and was said to have come from a Vanderbilt estate on Long Island. Fifteen pieces by Stowe, which the writer had examined in the late 1970s and wanted for the Adirondack Museum, came to the museum years later as a surprise bequest of the owner, the late Warren W. Kay.[18]

Stowe's move to Florida in 1911 was likely prompted by the impending change of ownership of the property where he lived. Clarence Petty, who thought Stowe was from Colton, N.Y., said that Stowe later wrote and said the Petty family could have the cabin, which was skidded to their home, where it remained as recently as 1987. Stowe also gave his carpentry tools to the Petty family.

A type of log furniture that could be produced in quantities made an appearance in the 1890s. The furniture, which consisted of fat round posts and rails, appeared at Camp Uncas and Sagamore Lodge in 1895–97. The log-like character of the furniture was retained and gave an even appearance to the bedrooms where it was found, in twin beds and chests of drawers. Durant, who built Uncas and Sagamore, deserves credit for devising furniture that could be produced in multiples from a working plan. A young architect, Grosvenor Atterbury, whose name appears in the guest book at Camp Pine Knot, was hired by Durant to design Camp Uncas, suggesting that Atterbury designed this type of practical rustic furniture, which could be moved readily on casters.

The furniture turned up at later camps, at Kamp Kill Kare in 1899, the third of a rustic trio of neighboring camps; and it appears also at camps designed by William Coulter in 1897–1907. Coulter, who had gotten the job for designing a recreation building for Alfred G. Vanderbilt at Sagamore Lodge, visited Raquette Lake about this time, in 1901, when he may have taken the snapshot of the stairway in front of the Chalet that was in the scrapbook he left behind with his partner at the time of his death in 1907. He may have borrowed this stained, semi-rustic production furniture at his camps on the Saranac Lakes, though it is so plainly generic as to hardly warrant belaboring its authorship. Years later, in 1937–38, log chairs, tables, and various "fitments," or built-in furniture, were constructed at the Walter and Kathrin Hochschild camp on Eagle Lake. Some of the furniture was designed by Calvert Coggeshall of New York, but the dining room table, eighteen chairs, buffet and sideboard were designed and built by Kendall Rogers of Willsboro, N.Y. The furniture for the camp was made in Plattsburgh in 1937.[19]

Japanese and American Indian Ornamentation

Japanese artifacts appear in so many photographs of camp interiors before 1900 as to constitute a defining feature of the decorous camp, distinguishing it from unlettered cabins elsewhere on the lake. American Indian blankets, pottery, and other craft objects found a place in Adirondack camps early in the twentieth century. However, Kamp Kill Kare in 1897–99 had an Indian bedroom with Indian leather and bead work. The room was destroyed in the fire of 1915, but Kill Kare's new owners, Mr. and Mrs. Francis P. Garvan, asked the Woodruffs' designer, Charles C. Hiscoe, to design and reconstruct a bedroom similar to the one that burned. Another camp with American Indian artifacts was Camp Topridge. When Mrs. Post acquired the camp in 1924, she and her designer furnished it with Indian craft objects from which a selection was made by the Smithsonian Institution for its collections following her death in 1973.

Decorating for Mood

Making camp interiors lighter and cheerier was a development of the late 1890s and after. Camp Uncas was an example of the early interior, lair-like and muscular, and favored by the men of industry for whom the camps were designed and built. The camps were fine for the owner who had returned with his guide from a day of hunting or fishing; but these all-wood, dark interiors could be uncongenial for anyone stuck inside for a couple of days.

   The changes to come were augured by Lillie Hamilton French in her article, "Adirondack Camps," in *Harper's Bazaar* for September 1899. She applauds variety in the camp while warning against "artistic effects and cozy corners."[20] Let nature "do all the work she can," she says, an instance of which was leaving wall shingles unstained so as to weather to a natural gray. She suggested oil and varnish for the

living room floor but proposed covering walls and ceiling with bark or slabs with the bark still on. Willow chairs she would cover with "simple stuffs" and use a combination of crimson, brown, and yellow—"golden russet tones of autumn woods"—on the fabrics.

French's remarks are consistent with the interiors of William Coulter's camps at about the same time, which she may well have seen on the Saranac Lakes, in addition to those she is sure to have visited on the St. Regis Lakes nearby. Different moods should be elicited in rooms depending on their function, she said, advice that may have signaled the arrival of a feminine sensibility to the Adirondack camp. She banned pink, purple, and blue from the living room, but allowed them in the dining room, in such items as blue china, Japanese rugs, and a combination of linens or fabrics. Windows in the dining room have curtains of "sheer flowered wash materials."

French was indifferent to Harvey Ellis's stricture against covering wood grain with paint, since she would allow dining room furniture to be painted white because it helped the room become "cool, cheerful, and charming." The dining room at Stonehenge, a camp belonging to Edwin Norton on Mirror Lake, not only had white painted table and chairs, but the floor joists in the ceiling and wood trim around doors and windows were white as well. The shingle bungalow built by George J. Whelan on Raquette Lake about 1910 was a good example of this breezy, psychological approach to decorating the camp.

A FULL HOUSE.

BURDICK'S SUMMER HOUSE.
BIG MOOSE. N.Y.

We are all children and enjoy playing house;
only at sixty, we need a $10,000 lodge in a vast
wilderness, when at six, a piece of old carpet
stretched over a corner in the rail fence satisfied
all our worldly desires.

—Seneca Ray Stoddard, 1893[1]

CHAPTER 9

Other Features of the Decorous Camp

Gazebos and Follies

OWNERS INSISTED on a lean-to or two at their camps. These were log-and-lumber versions of the improvised sapling and "boughed" lean-tos of one to two generations earlier. Some lean-tos were quite large, big enough for a dozen city people to crowd into for an evening song-fest in front of a roaring fire. Children were introduced to the outdoors by sleeping in a lean-to, which usually was not far from the camp where the family was staying. In time, open camps fell into disuse but were usually tokenly repaired because they were seen as survivors of an Adirondacks of an earlier era.

Outdoor structures intended more to be seen than used offered Adirondack builders and do-it-yourself owners with opportunities to display their inventiveness. Parks and gardens were a precedent: Thomas Jefferson, in notes made in 1804, recommended temples or seats at those "spots on the walks most interesting either for prospect or the immediate scenery," an idea he could have picked up from any number of books on landscape gardening that were published in English after 1725.

A "round temple" made of "unbarked saplings and boughs" was shown to Rebecca Harding Davis by Bronson Alcott, the impractical head of the large family of which Louisa May Alcott, the novelist, was a member. "You could look at it and admire it, but nobody could go in or use it" because Bronson "had forgotten to make any door," a fitting symbol, Davis observed, "for this guild of prophets and their scheme of life," a pointed reference by this Boston lady to the woolly notions emanating from Concord.[2]

Adirondack summer houses, fashioned from lumber and logs and log slabs, and finished with twiggy brackets, could be square or oblong or be polygonal in section, six and eight sides being common. Open to catch breezes and views, they were placed on an elevated spot or at the edge of the lake or even at the end of a peninsula made for this purpose. Often table and benches were inside.

OPPOSITE: Burdick's Summer House, Big Moose, N.Y., *c. 1915. The Adirondack Museum* (P2809).

Boardwalks

Decorous camps sometimes had boardwalks that connected a few key buildings and kept shoes free of mud in wet weather. Some boardwalks were covered, as at Camp Pine Knot and Camp Kwenogamac, so heads as well as feet were kept dry. Boardwalks made the walk between buildings easier, especially in the dark, and they kept ferns and other green cover such as myrtle from being trampled by errant feet. Some walks had lanterns and electric lights to point the way at night. At the Read

Camp, the covered boardwalk connecting lodge and dining building was partially a bridge over a stony declivity on the shore of Little Simon Pond. William Coulter improved the boardwalk by turning the boardwalk into enclosed passageways with windows above the rail at the camp he designed for Adolph Lewisohn in 1904.

Boardwalks were scrapped at many camps because, resting on the ground and shaded in summer, and buried under winter snows and spring thaws, they quickly rotted and needed frequent repair. Why come to the Adirondacks if not for the experience of getting feet and head wet on occasion? That question enlivened more than one discussion at mealtime, since one's response to it was a litmus test where one fell on a scale between austerity and sybaritic ease in the woods.

Boardwalks became unnecessary when separate log buildings were joined end to end, as at the original Kamp Kill Kare of 1897–99. The veranda that connected the several buildings across the front at Kill Kare was a boardwalk of a kind; it also served to integrate the elements of the lodge, which was a series of cabins connected at their gable ends, a stratagem by which the lodge followed the downward slope of the site.

On the Waterfront

The boathouses of William West Durant were modest and unprepossessing, probably because his camps of 1895–1900—Uncas, Sagamore, and Arbutus—each had its own lake and needed no large boat or showy boathouse. The big boathouse made its appearance on the Saranac Lakes about 1900, and came to assert, along with the speedboats and launches they housed, a hegemony over lakes that formerly had been crossed in sedate silence in guideboats and canoes. Because they covered lakes in minutes rather than hours, speedboats and runabouts made bigger lakes like Raquette, the Saranacs, and Lake George especially desirable. Clubs and associations of owners of lakefront property debated restricting and even banishing powerboats altogether.

Corner of boathouse, Edmond Guggenheim Camp, Lower Saranac Lake. William G. Distin, architect. "G-3" identified a speedboat. Photograph by Craig Gilborn, 1998.

In 1900, a member of the Adirondack League Club had to get permission to operate a power boat on Honnedaga Lake; it was not until 1913 that a "high-speed" runabout—Herbert Parker's *Gypsy*, which was capable of doing twenty-five miles an hour—was allowed on the lake.[3]

Speed boats required the attention of a mechanic, and they had to be suitably sheltered, in which regard they resembled fast and expensive automobiles of the day. Boathouses after 1900 became the most conspicuous feature on a lake, sometimes being more spectacular than any other building at the camp, as at the Knollwood Club. William Coulter was perhaps the first architect to design out-sized boathouses.

Augustus D. Shepard gave the name "boathouse camp" to a type of camp with a site that required that the main cottage be built over the water.[4] These camps had living quarters built against the bank and over the lake, under which were built a dock, slips, and boathouse. One of the earliest of these was Camp Ohfora, which was designed by William Winthrop Kent and built on Honnedaga Lake for R. dePeyster Tytus in 1892. Ohfora had slip and docks under the house, which was built into the hill in back and supported in front by posts and braces over the water. Architecturally, Ohfora was a log-and-shingle version of the English country house of the nineteenth century with its distinctive blanket roof that alluded to thatched roofs in Britain. Enlargement at the camp altered its original charm. Another boathouse camp was the Ziegler Camp on Loon Lake, designed about 1907 by James L. Burley.[5]

Boathouse camp, formerly called "Ohfora," Adirondack League Club, Honnedaga Lake. Designed by William Winthrop Kent and built in 1892, with subsequent alterations, as they appear here. Photograph by Craig Gilborn, 1975.

Boathouse, Camp Topridge, Upper St. Regis Lake. Built by Ben Muncil, a local contractor, who also designed it, for Mrs. Merriweather Post in the late 1920s. An apartment above the boat slips has a porch over the water. Richard Linke, photographer, 1973. The Adirondack Museum (P42510).

A late boathouse was designed by William Distin for Walter and Kathrin Hochschild. On Eagle Lake and built in 1937, it was nearly as big as a house and contained two mahogany speedboats and several smaller boats. Upstairs was a large open room with fireplace and railed decks outside, which was used by Mrs. Hochschild as a studio.[6]

The most original rustic structure in the Adirondacks, from a design standpoint, may be the boathouse at Camp Topridge. Built in the 1920s from cedar columns with the bark on and applied sheets of cedar bark, it was designed by Ben Muncil who was contractor for many camps in the Saranac area. He is said to have looked at the plans submitted by Mrs. Post's architect and commented that he did not think it was appropriate for the Adirondacks. She asked that he give her his plan and he complied.[7]

Conspicuous boathouses were resented because they asserted a claim to more of the lake than others on the lake thought fair. Criticism focused more on visibility than on size: a boathouse could be seen from neighboring camps and from boats, and it often was visible from mountains around the lake. The lake belonged to everyone, a view that prevails today, when planning boards, mindful of storage lofts surreptitiously transformed into apartments, scrutinize building applications, boathouses especially.

Staff and Service Buildings

The monthly cost of staffing Sagamore Lodge in 1900 "without entertaining" was estimated by William West Durant as follows:

Caretaker and wife, including board	$100
1 teamster, including board	60
2 laborers, including board	100
2 horses	30
2 cows	30
Taxes	75
Incidentals	45–55

The annual total of $5,400 did not include household staff that would likely have been needed when the owners were in residence in the summer.[8]

Employees at camp ate at a kitchen table or in a room reserved for them next to the kitchen. Children of camp owners sometimes ate there or, at larger camps, in a dining room of their own, where they might be fed by a nurse or eat with a governess. Staff did not eat with employers, except for personal secretaries or tutors who were in such close proximity to the family as to be in a position of confidence. Margaret Molineaux was a companion and possibly a cousin of Mrs. Thomas Clark Durant. Her job, she said, was that of an "amanuensis," a kind of recording secretary. She was indispensable to Mrs. Durant, who, more years than not, saw little of her husband. She was present during spats between family members, which was why she was called as a witness in the suit brought by Mrs. Durant's daughter against her brother.[9]

Near the kitchen, perhaps connected to it by a walk or breezeway, was the ice house and cooler for perishables. A woodshed also was nearby. Often there was a residence for the caretaker and his wife. Women or girls sometimes had rooms over the laundry building or kitchen, or in a wing behind the kitchen. A workshop, barn, carriage or wagon shed, and car garage were other structures found in the service area of most Adirondack camps, the majority of them not as extensive as this inventory might suggest, since most were confined to a few acres or a little more. Other buildings were wood or brick enclosures for pumps and generators, preferably far enough away so the noise was not a continuous annoyance, as it was said to be at some camps.

The caretaker and his wife had a residence, and their children, if they had any, had to be schooled in the camp, as was done for the four children of Richard Collins at Sagamore Lodge; otherwise, an arrangement had to be made which included resigning and moving nearer to town. His wife usually was the cook at the main house, although the caretaker often did that job as well, his years as a guide standing him well in the kitchen. At the Kildare Club the caretaker and his wife shared a large cottage with one other couple, year-round residents like them. Basil Cheney recalled that the

Pine Tree Point
Upper St. Regis Lake

Japanese artisans from the Pan American Exposition of 1901 in Buffalo remodeled buildings at an existing camp and added new ones in a Japanese style. Servants were mortified when they were told by the Frederick Vanderbilts to dress in Japanese costume while waiting on guests. Photographs by Craig Gilborn, 1976.

Japanese cottage.

Japanese cottage interior.

Pagoda.

Spiral staircase inside pagoda.

house was large enough for single men in summer—a guide and gardener. Women and girl employees had rooms over the kitchen in a wing of the main building.

Basil Cheney, seventy years old when interviewed at Kildare in 1998, started as a "chore boy" at what really is not a club but a camp for families of original owners who bought the preserve in 1898, from what briefly had been a membership club. Mr. Cheney, whose family was from Nicholville, Parishville, and Potsdam, all North Country towns, came to Kildare in 1942, at the age of fourteen. He worked for the caretaker (a job he later held), who had him supply wood to fireplaces and stoves. One wing of the camp was heated by a furnace so the camp could be occupied—as it is—as late as Thanksgiving and in spring. As chore boy, Mr. Cheney fed wood to the furnace on chilly days, and since the cooking stove in the kitchen burned coal, he tended that as well.[10]

Before 1948, when an electrical generator was installed, Kildare's lighting was from a gas generator buried in the ground. Gas was produced by mixing carbide "gravel" with fresh water in the tank, from which gas was distributed by a system of pipes to lamps around the camp. The gas was explosive—which is why the generating tank was buried eight feet underground and away from the buildings. Cheney made rounds of the camp regularly to clean the lamps and valves. At busy times, when the camp was near capacity, the tank had to be replenished every other day, a job for the superintendent himself. This involved introducing fresh water in the tank and filling

Large kitchen, clubhouse, Eagle Nest, built 1904, later modernized. Photograph by Craig Gilborn, 1998.

a hopper above with 200 lbs. of carbide; the demand for gas reduced pressure in the tank, causing the hopper to dump additional carbide into the water. The young Cheney also carried ice.

Kildare's generator, which runs around the clock, can be faintly heard from the main building and cottages on Jordan Lake. Litchfield Park likewise supplies its own electricity, and guests may find themselves followed by their host, Pieter Litchfield, in the family's Castle, turning off lights and apologizing that the generator in a building a quarter of a mile distant mustn't be overburdened. Brandreth Park could have gotten outside electricity years ago, but did not, to the regret of some in that extended family. The Read Camp did get outside power by agreement with the village of Tupper Lake, which gets its water from Little Simon Pond on the Read family preserve.

Camp owners often arrived at camp with servants from home—a nurse for small children, a cook or maid. Mrs. Garvan brought five servants with her: a butler, a personal maid, a personal assistant, a chauffeur, and one chef or cook, as recalled by Dana Winslow, who spent summers at Kamp Kill Kare as a boy and youth, from the late 1940s to the early seventies.[11] There were four cooks and two assistant cooks at

Kill Kare: a cook for the children's cottage, a cook and an assistant for the men's camp, and, at the Main House, an executive chef, a *sous chef,* and an assistant cook.

Help were segregated by sex—men in houses known as guide houses, and women, who often came from the locality, in rooms above a kitchen or laundry. Menial help sometimes were put in an attic of the main building, where sleep might be difficult due to hot and stuffy quarters in summer.

Bigger cottages and camps had ice houses for storing blocks of ice cut from the lake in the dead of winter. The blocks were stacked with sawdust from pine or another soft wood to keep them separated; at Kildare, however, snow was used. The ice house had a large area in back for the ice, and in front were two coolers separated by an aisle, one for meats and fish and the other for vegetables and dairy products. Single-family camps with a lone icebox had a block or two of ice delivered by wagon or truck every second or third day. Under the kitchen at Kildare was a root cellar for storing potatoes, vegetables, and apples in winter.

Gas and electric refrigerator-freezers eliminated the need for the ice house, the stocking of which had been a winter ritual for every caretaker. Kildare's ice house was razed between 1948 and 1950, thought Mr. Cheney. Adirondack ice was still being shipped by rail, for it was needed for the delivery of milk and dairy products to homes and grocery stores into the 1960s. Water for drinking and ice preferably came from a remote source—a spring or pond—rather than lakes where there was a lot of summer activity. Finding a source of pure water was not always feasible, even today, in which case campers sometimes carried in their drinking and cooking water. The Prospect House got its water and perhaps its ice as well from Crystal Pond, while water for bathing and cleaning was pumped by windmill from Blue Mountain Lake into an elevated storage tank, from which it flowed by gravity into rooms, bathhouses for men and women, and water closets located at one end of the hotel's three floors.[12]

Septic system for the modern camp. From Augustus D. Shepard, Camps in the Woods, *1931. Settling tank overflowed into holding tank, and this effluent was pumped to a distant disposal bed, away from camp and lake.*

The Gardner Camp was on a bluff about a hundred feet above Blue Mountain Lake, so water was pumped to a holding tank in a tower incorporated in the design of the camp by a wood-fired heat pump at the base of the bluff. The pump was not fast, but by tending the fire in its boiler and by dint of the pump chugging and lifting one pint after another up the hill, the tank amply supplied the needs of the five or so people who filled the camp to capacity in 1900.

Running water and flush toilets were introduced to camps between 1895 and 1915. This solved a couple of problems but created others, for the infusions of gallons of waste water instead of a quart or two greatly added to the old problem of pollution by spreading it faster and farther. Settling tanks were used, the overflows draining into a leach field with the semi-solid remainder in the tank periodically pumped and hauled to be dumped at a remote spot. William West Durant had bathrooms and settling tanks at Uncas, Sagamore, and Arbutus, all dating from 1895–1900 and as modern as any waste system in the Adirondacks. They may still have been in use a century later.

A succession of outbreaks of typhoid fever in 1900, 1903, 1906–9, 1910, and 1916, variously at the Prospect House on Blue Mountain Lake, Eagle Nest on Eagle Lake, and Kamp Kill Kare led to greater care in matters of hygiene and hygienic practices in the central Adirondack region. The outbreaks at Eagle Nest, in which there were about twenty-five cases over four years, were followed by a scientific investigation that traced the carrier of the infection to one Harry Williams, who had settled at Blue Mountain Lake in 1900 and was employed at Eagle Nest as night watchman. The report, which was reprinted by Harold K. Hochschild in *Township 34,* points up the rigor applied to matters of public health at this time.[13] For example, testing showed that ice from Eagle Lake and drinking water from a spring three-quarters of a mile from the camp were not contaminated. Once identified, Mr. Williams, a Welshman who "scorned the theory" about typhoid infection, eventually accepted a small farm in Forestport, N.Y., and a monthly pension to go with it, on condition that he leave. Citizens in Forestport were warned of his condition, and no cases were known to have occurred in Harry's life there.[14]

There was yet another outbreak—perhaps the last one—at Kamp Kill Kare in 1916, involving, apparently, a different carrier. It explains several things, such as why the old septic system was removed and a new one installed, and why a "Dr. Kabel," who owned a camp on Raquette Lake, gave a talk at the hotel in town in which he laid "out for all and sundry . . . the dirty condition of the place," meaning the town in general and Dillon's hotel in particular. Reporting to the owner of Kill Kare, where the fever had broken out the year before, was Charles Hiscoe, decorator at the camp during its initial reconstruction, in 1915–17. It explains why Hiscoe reported that a painter working for him had "stuck up signs everywhere" which read, in effect, "If you spit on the floor at home, do so here by all means." The sarcasm of the signs ostensibly was aimed at those men habituated to spitting, in this instance, in Mr. Garvan's buildings then under construction; but it may really have been a joke by the workmen—some Irish—at the expense of a visitor with an English accent.

Other Infrastructure

When his father was ill following an operation in 1883, William West Durant had a telegraph installed in the family's home in North Creek, putting him in communication with Saratoga Springs and points south. Eventually he would have telegraph service to Camp Pine Knot and to Blue Mountain Lake, where he had a telegraph office. Other technological advances came to the region in rapid succession, just when and in what sequence remains to be seen, although the transformation was under way by the late 1890s, when Durant and William Coulter separately were supervising the construction of camps that were as modern below ground as they were above.

Durant, who possessed hands-on mechanical skills, had an engineer's pride in what friends and guests could not see but which enhanced the quality of their experience at his camps. In a letter of May 1, 1900, to Seneca Ray Stoddard, he said of Sagamore, "It has cost me a great deal more than any of the other camps I have built, and is more elaborate . . . in the way of gas and water works, furnace as well as by fireplaces, system of draining, roads and stocking the lake with fish—than anything I before attempted."[15]

Another individual who dealt with the complex logistics of building the equivalent of small villages in the woods was William Coulter who had the advantage over Durant of spending other people's money. An architect, he knew what these extensive properties required, since he likely designed country estates at the firm that employed him in New York City in the early 1890s. His camps on Saranac Lake, dating from 1897, were wired for electricity with lights on paths and coolers big enough to hold provisions for family and staff for an entire summer.

Adirondack camps were vulnerable in the roads that carried people to the clearings where camps and farms were found. Some camps were "roadless," being on an island or reached from a landing on a distant shore. As rail passenger service ceased sporadically between 1937 and 1965, new roads had to be cut or old ones improved for motor traffic.

Brandreth lost train service in 1965, leaving camp owners only with cars to get them to Brandreth Lake. The road from North Point, on Raquette Lake, becomes a mire in spring and following spells of rainy weather. Indeed, roads to all camps are plagued by holes, washouts, and blockage from trees and limbs too big to be pulled out of the way. The Brandreth road was put in sufficient condition to lessen fears of breaking an axle or oil pan in the nine-mile trip to the camp. Eventually, the International Paper Company maintained part of the road when it acquired a tract of land from the Brandreth Park Association.

The Kildare Club may have the longest stretch of road of any developed camp in the Adirondacks—about thirteen miles of unpaved road, much of it single lane, between the highway in Tupper Lake Junction and Jordan Lake. Other destinations reached by long, lonely roads are Bisby Lake and Lake Honnedaga, arduous for Adirondack League Club members traveling to these remote lakes. Even after driving for hours just to get to Alder Creek, N.Y., or Forestport, N.Y., one still has an-

White Pine Camp
Osgood Pond, Paul Smiths, N.Y., 1907–1913

William G. Massarene and Addison Mizner, architects. Ben Muncil, builder. The cottages, patterned after houses Massarene said he'd seen in Italy, anticipated shed-style houses of the 1960s and after. Mizner, who finished the camp when Massarene was fired, added an L-shaped service building that he said was inspired by mining towns in the West. President and Mrs. Coolidge stayed at the camp in 1926, transacting the nation's business in the "Summer White House," putting the Adirondacks in the national limelight for the first time. The camp was being restored but open to the public at the time the pictures were taken. See also page 181. Photographs by Craig Gilborn, 1998.

Interior, with clerestory window and picturesque fireplace.

Cottage, c. 1907. Waney-edged siding, also called brainstorm siding, is said to have been introduced to the Adirondacks by Ben Muncil, a local man who built many camps in the vicinity of Saranac Lake.

Service building, c. 1910.

Summer pavilion on island.

Summer pavilion. Footbridge and boathouse in the distance.

other hour of driving time before reaching Honnedaga Lake, some twenty-five miles distant.[16]

Road repair and maintenance were the responsibility of the caretaker or superintendent, for whom it was a year-round job. Ditches and culverts had to be dug and kept clean of debris since a sudden rainstorm—a gully washer—could plug a culvert or ditch and in a few minutes do enough damage to take days to repair. A thaw presented a different problem, and not just from puddles or erosion caused by runoff. Although the road surface was soft, the portion beneath it might still be frozen solid; vehicles turned the surface into a slithery mire that could send them into the ditch, and the ruts thus formed would turn rock-hard at the next freeze, transforming the road into an obstacle course.

Bridges constituted a category of problem all their own, since a civil engineer might be needed when steel and stone or cement abutments were called for. Camps and clubs graded their roads while traffic could be expected on them, usually between May and November, and of course they had to be kept plowed in winter. Sagamore Lodge can be open only as long as the public can get to it on two bridges across two streams. When one bridge badly needed to be repaired, the state, which owned the bridge, responded slowly to pleas from Sagamore's executive director and her board. The lodge paid for the repairs itself, although it was later reimbursed by the Department of Transportation.[17]

Camp in Winter

Winter visits to camp were infrequent but not unheard of. During the holiday period between Christmas and January of 1892–93, a party that included William West Durant, his wife, and some in her family stayed at Camp Pine Knot and held a party for Raquette Lake residents. On the third of January, they rode in horse-drawn sleighs to Mohegan Lake where they walked on snow shoes and picnicked in the "snowy forest." William also picked out a site for Camp Uncas.[18]

Small log cabins were eminently practical as winter housing; they quickly warmed to a wood stove and were snug and could be occupied for as long as food held out. Resistance to a winter excursion was dissolving, though it never displaced the primacy of the summer vacation. Most summer cabins and cottages were not tightly built and could not be heated or kept warm, no matter how big the fire in a fireplace or woodstove. For all their accents of Swiss and Medieval construction, the two cottages built for the Reverend Archibald Bull, now part of the Adirondack Museum, are so barn-like and drafty as to be habitable for, at most, the four months between June 1 and October 1.

Lieutenant Governor Timothy Woodruff opened Kamp Kill Kare for a couple of winter days and nights in 1899, as reported in an Albany newspaper in an effusive account by James Whipple, a lawyer and Clerk of the Senate who may have been a crony of Woodruff's. An excerpt from the story appears on page 282. Kill Kare was equipped for winter occupancy, which is not to say that all its buildings were heated:

camp owners and architects came to expect that at least one or two cottages would be winterized, perhaps a wing of the main building, as at the Kildare Club. The Adirondack League Club had a "Winter Cottage," an ample but plain structure, which members could use during winter visits to Little Moose Lake.

Winter readiness dictated a house tight against cold blasts and insulated from bitter cold, even if that only meant the thickness of a log or dead air between outer and inner walls. Designated rooms had to be small enough to hold the heat, and there had to be a foundation around the base of the house instead of footings, preferably with a partial basement or cellar, as a barrier to cold and damp creeping through the floor boards.

In time, large camps were heated by basement furnaces which burned every kind of fuel—firewood, coal, oil, and (more recently) propane gas. The Castle at Litchfield Park still burns about sixty tons of rice coal a year. The coal reached Tupper Lake by rail until the 1960s, when the train stopped running, at which point it came by truck from suppliers as distant as Pennsylvania. The lodge at Crane Point on Blue Mountain Lake is heated by propane gas, a costly fuel given the lodge's size. The owner, admitting the extravagance, hastily adds that the thermostats are set at 45 degrees F. and that the lodge is checked each day by a caretaker from town.

Most daring of efforts to stimulate interest in winter recreation was undertaken by the Lake Placid Club, which early in the twentieth century heated the main building and winterized a large number of cottages for members and guests. The club offered a program of winter activities that was hardly inferior to the already elaborate summer schedule for which it was famous.

Camp Farms

Most camps before 1920 had working farms attached to them. Farms were not, as believed by some, indulgences of the rich, but were necessary to sustain preserves distant from outside sources of support—from other farms, general stores, and purveyors in distant cities and towns. Vegetables were grown and horses used for pulling plows, mowing hay, and hauling people and freight. Livestock were kept for milk, eggs, and meat: cows, chickens, sheep, and pigs—a "piggery" was at Camp Cedars. From all accounts, everyone in camp, upwards of forty men, women, and children, were amply fed.

Men worked full-time at farming, and some tended flower beds and cutting gardens. Some camps had high fences around their vegetable and flower gardens, to keep deer out. Grain and corn were fed to deer by some camp owners, a practice that turned deer into pests. A few camps—Kamp Kill Kare and Tarnedge on Bear Pond were two—had greenhouses for starting seedlings for late spring planting. Food was needed for summer, when the camp was fullest, but a supply had to be set aside and canned or placed in a root cellar or cool basement for the winter and spring to come.

Early farms at Adirondack camps included Brandreth Park (1870s), Camp Pine Knot (late 1870s), North Woods Club at the former Baker Farm (1860s and later),

Santanoni, Nehasane, and Sagamore Lodge (1890s and later). Buildings for these were one or two barns for cows and horses, a wagon or carriage house, a shed for pigs and fold for sheep, chicken houses, gardens for vegetables and flowers, and other out-buildings, such as root cellars, and a sugaring shed for boiling maple sap into syrup.

In late spring, camps with farms saw employees readying cottages and gardens for the owner, who might make a preliminary visit in May to direct preparations, such as airing out bedding stored in trunks or on shelves in a tin room. The caretaker and his wife, who often had a year-round house on the grounds, usually shared responsibility for managing and supervising what was a woodland community of five to fifteen or more.

Wives came with caretakers at Ragged Lake; a couple at any camp was such an advantage that most owners looked for married candidates with wives willing to

Cultivated fields, possibly Santanoni, Newcomb, N.Y., 1911. Mr. Pruyn's farm at Santanoni produced surplus food, a rarity in a region believed to be too mountainous, cold, and sun-deprived for commercial farming. The Adirondack Museum, gift of Susan and Thomas King (P63039).

cook and clean. On the face of it, the caretaker and his family got a good deal: a house and equipment for repair, plowing snow, etc., the expense of which was paid not by them but by others. The disadvantages may have been less the long hours of work than the isolation from other people. The automobile and bus transportation changed these arrangements beginning in the 1930s, as caretakers could commute to camp in their own cars, and their wives were in a better position to negotiate the terms of their employment.

Farming became less necessary as provisioners in distant cities delivered food and other items by a system of transportation that grew up rapidly and was both efficient and reliable, an aspect of the region's history that bears closer examination. Passenger and freight rail service in the diagonal roughly between Utica in the southwest and Plattsburgh and Ogdensburg in the northeast and north, after 1892, cut a swath through the forest, transforming wilderness that was relatively valueless into a potentially promising commodity. Camps and preserves along this diagonal corridor—Brandreth Park, Dr. Webb's Nehasane, Tarnedge, Litchfield Park, the Kildare Club—had access to suppliers in Utica, N.Y., once or twice every day. To suddenly have cities and towns an hour or two away from camp, or a remote mountain village, must have had a tremendous psychological effect and practical consequences, turning a once-in-a-lifetime visit to Albany or New York into a daily possibility.

The delivery truck, automobile, and expanding networks of roads and track eroded the need for farms productive enough to render camps of which they were a part largely independent of outside sources. Little by little, farms slipped into decline; the Depression years in the 1930s and labor shortages in the 1940s may have been the end of serious farming, although this remains to be seen.

Camp Santanoni had a commercial farm in the first quarter of the twentieth century, meeting its own needs as well as providing a surplus of milk and food products to hotels in Newcomb and to the household and friends of the Pruyn family in Albany. An expensive operation, it declined as Mr. Pruyn lost his health and involvement, as well as his money, to advancing old age.[19]

Momentarily, at the start of the Second World War, readiness held that the Adirondacks might become a refuge for children and a source of food in the event of an invasion by the Germans. The perception of camp farms as playthings of the rich took hold among post-war generations accustomed to supermarkets for food and ignorant of food logistics.

At some camps there were extravagances. A small fortune was spent in about 1920 on a cow barn and a stable at Kamp Kill Kare that seem to have been little used. But this was an exception, since almost every large camp and preserve established before 1900 had its own farm. Mr. Stokes, who built the camp on Birch Island in Upper St. Regis Lake, also bought a tract on the mainland for a farm to supply his camp with fresh meat, vegetables, and milk.[20] Pieter Litchfield remembers as a boy in the 1960s searching for a stray cow at Litchfield Park, the last of the herd that was formerly at the preserve.[21]

At Eagle Nest in 1910, vegetables were produced in a garden, and milk came from five cows pastured on the premises. However, much food was shipped from New York City: groceries, meats, fruits, butter, and eggs—a commentary on the efficiency of transportation between the city and the Adirondacks, since fish and shellfish arrived "regularly" at the clubhouse kitchen in summer. It also indicates the importance of ice to refrigeration. Perhaps kitchen and upstairs help got a share of this city food. It was a different matter for residents of the Guide House, most of whom were men: they had "no garden and used no fresh vegetables or fresh fruits," and depended instead "entirely upon canned goods to the great complaint of its boarders." All their supplies came from stores in the village on Blue Mountain Lake.[22]

An Adirondack camp does not mean a canvas tent
or a bark wigwam, but a permanent summer home
where fortunate owners assemble for several weeks
each year and live in perfect comfort and luxury,
even though in the heart of the woods.

—1903

CHAPTER 10

Trophy Camps and Their Early Designers

T ROPHY CAMPS were large decorous camps which seem always to have been designed in part or in their entirety by an architect.[1] Architects are conspicuous by their absence in the Adirondacks before the 1890s; they designed hotels, churches, and houses before about 1892, when Robert H. Robertson designed two camp compounds that may be said to have been the first of the region's planned trophy camps, as opposed to the Durant camps and the enclave at Brandreth Park which were earlier and may have had one or two buildings designed by an architect, though no name other than that of William West Durant has turned up. These early camps seem better categorized as *transitional camps,* discussed in chapter 7.

OPPOSITE*: Sitting room, Adolph Lewisohn Camp. A gallery above looks down on this room. The Adirondack Museum* (P38256).

Earliest Architects

Among the pre-1890 architects was Henry Searle (1809–1892), said by Seneca Ray Stoddard to be the architect of Horicon Pavilion, a destination primarily for day-trippers, since it had a large dining room and only about twenty bedrooms. It was a rustic confection on the east bank of Lake George, built in 1879 by Cyrus Butler, a businessman and developer with an interest in the arts.

Summer churches were designed by architects between 1877 and 1885. The earliest documented log church by an architect was St. John's-in-the-Wilderness which was built for guests at Paul Smith's Hotel in 1877. The name of the architect is not known but likely was an acquaintance of one or more of the guests who raised money for the church's construction and support. It burned in 1927, which is unfortunate, since it seems to have been high church Episcopalian with black walnut wainscoting to the chair rail and stone-colored plaster above that, and an arched ceiling tinted blue. It had a capacity for only forty and sometimes lacked space, but it was consecrated by Bishop Doane of Albany, and the best people attended it in summer.

Two other log churches were built in 1885: the Church of the Ascension at Saranac Inn, N.Y., after a design by David Jardine (1840–1892); and the Church of the

Log church (Episcopal), Blue Mountain Lake, 1885. Manley N. Cutter, architect. Camp owners and hotel regulars helped build and support churches and chapels near their summer homes. Photograph by Craig Gilborn, 1975.

Transfiguration on Blue Mountain Lake. The latter, designed by Manley Cutter (fl.1885–1905), still stands, its beach a favorite spot for swimmers in summer, except during Sunday morning services. It was constructed by Thomas Wallace, a local builder, on a small plot of land donated by one of the owners of the hotel across the road.[2]

Brook Knoll Lodge in Keene Valley, N.Y., was designed by an architect. Built in 1875, it was one of the first of what Seneca Ray Stoddard called "city men's homes" which were then, by 1880, being erected in this loveliest of mountain valleys. Like other houses in the valley, it sat upright like the mountains seen from its windows and porches, a posture that made it more manse than camp, drawing attention for miles around because its site was on a rock knoll above the valley. Of log construction, it had, Stoddard wrote, "shaggy cedar logs" which were "gabled, balconied and dormer windowed." Inside were "native and foreign woods" and "elegant and chaste furnishings and many an article of *vertu*." It had "neither plaster nor paint in its composition," Stoddard said, implying that this was not a house for town.[3] The builder was George Egglefield, a contractor who owned a hotel in town, according to Adrian

Edmonds. John Matthews, for whom the house was built, held patents to soda dispensing equipment which he manufactured in New York City, which suggests an architect in the city.

Brook Knoll remains much as it was, except for the stone steps in front and partitions which were removed by an owner to enlarge both floors. The front door opens into an anteroom in the base of the tower, and a second door opens into an open room large enough for public receptions or dances; overhead is a timber beam ceiling, ahead is a fireplace, and to the right is a wide staircase leading to the principal living areas upstairs. The layout is decidedly unconventional, with the living room and dining room in front, the latter in the tower, behind the three-part window. Kitchen and bedrooms are in back, and a stairway leads to more bedrooms on the third floor, where there also is passageway to the chamber in the mansard tower with four windows. Like other nineteenth-century vacation homes, Brook Knoll had no furnace and would not have been habitable in winter.

Brook Knoll Lodge, Keene Valley, *built 1875. Seneca Ray Stoddard, photographer, 1880. A city man's home, one of the first, according to Stoddard. Still standing, it was more manse than camp, although it was of log construction. The Adirondack Museum* (P15185).

Railroads Made Trophy Camps Possible

Railroads made large preserves and camps and clubs feasible, beginning with rail service to North Creek, N.Y., in 1871, by the Adirondack Railroad, which was purchased by the Delaware and Hudson Railroad in 1889. The D & H already had rail service between Albany and Plattsburgh. These routes invited vacationers and development on the eastern edge of the region, with corridors to North Creek and stage service to the Lake Placid–Saranac Lake region from Plattsburgh. But two-thirds or more of the region was inaccessible to most travelers and prospective buyers.

What tipped the balance was the Mohawk and Malone Railroad which started service in 1892, opening a diagonal southwest to northeast corridor between Utica and Malone, N.Y. People in New York now could board in early evening and be in the Adirondacks by eight the next morning. Much of the forest land along the right-of-way had been bought by a few wealthy men, including its builder, Dr. William Seward Webb; lakefront properties, however, were ample near towns like Tupper Lake, Saranac Lake, and Lake Placid, which soon were served by spur lines off the main trunk.

People followed behind the new railroad, not permanent settlers so much as summer visitors and buyers of land for private clubs or vacation camps not too distant from a town or general store. The newcomers were in business or a profession, many were educated, and a few—the ones for whom the Trophy Camps were built—were millionaires who conceivably never saw the camp or its site until their first night in camp. Architects materialized where none had been found before, most traveling up from New York, the busiest center of architectural activity in the East, and also the home of the majority of the men and women for whom the architects worked.

William West Durant (1850–1934)

William West Durant accepted credit for his camps, but he never, so far as the writer knows, said he had been the architect of any one of them. Given the multiple buildings that make up his four camps, as well as the three camps of his cousins, Frederick, Charles, and Howard, and a fourth belonging to his father-in-law's family on Bluff Point, an architect, or architects, seems likely. The design for a cabinet and desk at Camp Uncas points up the uncertainty of authorship for the Durant camps: Grosvenor Atterbury's name has "W. W. Durant" penciled over it. William may have put it there, though Anne Cotton Durant, his second wife, may have added it after

Elevation of "Proposed Cottage," ink on coated linen, 1901. "Designed by W. W. Durant" is partial evidence for Durant's claim that he designed his camps, notwithstanding the work done for him by Grosvenor Atterbury at Camp Uncas. The Adirondack Museum Library, gift of Mrs. W. W. (Anne Cotton) Durant.

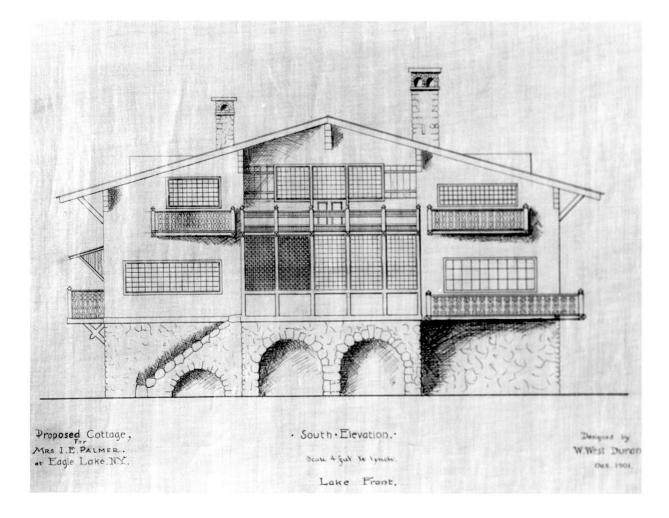

Proposed Cottage, for Mrs I.E. Palmer. at Eagle Lake. N.Y.

· South · Elevation. ·

Scale 4 feet to 1 inch.

Lake Front.

Designed by W. West Durant. Oct. 1901.

his death. (See chap. 7 for Camp Pine Knot and appendix B for a list of buildings and projects variously ascribed to William West Durant or members of the Durant family. The author's book *Durant: The Fortunes and Camps of a Family in the Adirondacks* gives a fuller treatment to the Durant camps.)

Deception was never William's intent; instead, he recognized that his camps would not have been the same without him, his role being that of today's "artistic director," except for his being an eminently practical man, supervising the construction

Bedroom, chalet, Sagamore Lodge, 1899. Personal items on desk and bureau point to this being W. W. Durant's room. An etching of Alvah Dunning, a colorful Raquette Lake figure, is above the window. The Adirondack Museum Library.

Manor House, Camp Uncas, Mohegan Lake, built 1893–95. Grosvenor Atterbury, architect, with W. W. Durant. Stone foundation, whole log walls on first floor, and framing on the second floor. Photograph, c. 1896. The Adirondack Museum (P38242).

and finishing of camps, their furnishing, as well as hiring and training domestic staff and superintending the camps if the new owners desired it. Like his father, who was a far more formidable personality than he was, William West Durant delegated little to the men and women who worked for him. He may have exceeded his father in his

Living room, Manor House, Camp Uncas. Photograph, undated. Durant was finicky about his fireplaces. Compare this splendid example with the sketch in the next illustration. The Adirondack Museum (P25627).

Durant's friend Arpad Gerster credited Atterbury in a sketch of a fireplace at Camp Uncas. The Adirondack Museum, gift of Dr. John W. Gerster (83.26. Book no. 23).

experience of first-class hotels and service, since from the age of twelve to twenty-two, he had traveled through Europe and had received a gentleman's education, having attended Twickenham School in England and having had a tutor. In 1873, when Dr. Durant summoned the family to meet in London, William came from Ethiopia or

Tarnedge
Bear Pond, 1912–1913

This half-timbered, Swiss style lodge was designed by Neil Smith for Mrs. Charles M. Daniels, daughter of a railroad and lumber company executive in Buffalo, N.Y. It was on a 5,558 acre preserve about a mile from the railroad station in Sabattis (Long Lake North), N.Y., which meant that construction materials and workmen were easily transported to the site. The camp, which was constructed by seventy men in ten months, had a nine-hole golf course, tennis court, greenhouse and gardens, boathouse, a children's playhouse half the size of a real house, and a farm with barn and ten cows. Interior rooms were white, which led architect Neil Smith to call them "the immaculate conception." Refugee children were housed here for a brief time after the Second World War, and a Saratoga Springs business-man tried running it as a hotel. In 1957, it was sold along with some 1,300 acres to the Watchung (N.J.) Area Council of the Boy Scouts of America. The barn and a few cottages remain, but the lodge, which had five floors above ground and a full basement below, and followed the butterfly plan, was razed due to water damage from a pipe that broke in the caretaker's absence.

Main building, Tarnedge ("Beside the Lake"), 1912–13. Photograph, c. [?] 1950. Blueprints are in the Adirondack Museum Library. Adirondack Museum (P31139).

Children's playhouse. Still standing in 1998, it had a working furnace in the basement. Photograph by Craig Gilborn, 1998.

the Sudan where he had been hunting "wild beasts." He presented a lion cub as a gift to his father, to be shipped from a German port and given to the zoo in Central Park, together with a cash gift sufficient for feeding it at 50 cents a day.

William was a stranger to the Adirondacks when he first saw the region in the summer of 1876. Camp Pine Knot, which grew incrementally under William's direction starting in 1877, was a conscious effort to draw attention to Raquette Lake and vicinity, where picturesque camps would be erected for other Durant family members between 1879 and 1883.[4] Pine Knot became the showplace for how people bred to the city could live in a rustic cottage and be beguiled by the lake and forest around it.

Not an architect, William was knowledgeable about camp layout and infrastructure; he knew what he wanted and likely was capable of designing smaller cottages on his own, perhaps from illustrations in magazines or books. We now know, from designs recently acquired by the Adirondack Museum Library, that Grosvenor Atterbury (1869–1956), who was a guest at Durant's Camp Pine Knot in 1893 and 1896, designed the buildings at Camp Uncas in 1894–95. In 1895 he designed a fireplace for Camp Hoff on Lower St. Regis Lake. One "C. L. Atterbury" was a member of the Adirondack Club (later the Tahawus Club) in 1878, so the architect, who went on to design estates on Long Island, may have had a connection to the Adirondacks through older members of his family.

Robert H. Robertson (1849–1919)

A remark by William Frederick Dix in "Summer Life in Luxurious Adirondack Camps" is hearsay evidence for 1890 as the approximate moment at which architect-designed camps began making their appearance; writing in *The Independent* for July 2, 1903, Dix, who was editor of *Town and Country* magazine, and whose comment appears as the epigraph at the start of this chapter, observed that "only within a decade or so has the cottage idea flourished" in the Adirondacks.

Going back ten years from 1903 gives the approximate date for the construction of two trophy camps by Robert H. Robertson, Nehasane and Santanoni, the first trophy camps by a trained architect in the Adirondacks.

Born in Philadelphia, Robertson graduated from Rutgers and was apprenticed in the office of Henry Sims in his birthplace. He entered the New York office of William A. Potter, designing country estates for wealthy clientele who lived and worked in Manhattan. In her profile of Robertson, Mary Hotaling, quoting Sarah Landau, says Robertson designed large country and town houses, institutional buildings, railroad stations, banks, and skyscrapers.[5] His work in the Adirondacks seems to have been limited to Nehasane and Santanoni, the design and construction taking place at about the same time, in 1891–93.

Forest Lodge, the principal building at Nehasane, was a Shingle style house, two stories high with a prominent blanket roof, multiple dormers for rooms on the second floor, and a deep porch in front. It was a type of fashionable house, not formal

Forest Lodge, 1892, Lake Lila, Nehasane Park. T. E. Marr, Boston, photographer, 1902. Robert H. Robertson designed a house and farm buildings for Dr. and Mrs. William Seward Webb in Shelburne, Vt. Five or so years later, he did the same for the Webbs at what became their Adirondack home. The lodge, shown here, was a smaller and less elaborate version of the Webbs' house in Vermont. The Adirondack Museum, gift of J. Watson Webb (P23738).

but self-possessed and gracious. Robertson had designed a similar but more elaborately detailed house for the Webbs in 1887–88 at their estate and farm on Lake Champlain in Shelburne, Vt. He also designed the farm buildings at Shelburne, of which the Breeding Barn is the most interesting, since it remains one of the largest open spanned interiors of any wood structure in the world—418 feet long, 108 feet wide and rising several stories above the exercise ring.

Nehasane, which in Indian meant "beaver-crossing-river-on-log," was perhaps eighty-five miles to the west of Shelburne as the crow flies but half again farther by rail. The Webb family took a private parlor car from a station at Shelburne Farms to the junction at Malone, N.Y., where it turned south on the railroad built by Dr. Webb in 1892, stopping at a station near Forest Lodge that could be used only by those with a pass signed by Dr. Webb.

Robertson had Adirondack connections apart from his two camps. His family shared ownership of the village and iron works at McIntyre, N.Y., which dated from the 1820s and had ceased operations by about 1853. He was a member of the Tahawus Club, and his Adirondack clients, the Webb and Pruyn families, were friends. Robertson had been a classmate at Rutgers of Robert C. Pruyn, a bank president in Albany; he designed Pruyn's Camp Santanoni, and would die while staying at the

Webb camp in June 1919. He was an amateur watercolorist and may have been the "Robertson" who allegedly, according to a traveler's account of about 1870 (lost by the writer), decorated the birch bark shanty of Mitchell Sabattis's on Long Lake.[6]

Forest Lodge at Nehasane Park introduced the country house to the Adirondacks, perhaps for the first time. Presenting a serene facade to Lake Lila, it had a blanket roof penetrated by large roof dormers that extended as a roof over the veranda across the front and sides. Clipped lawn—never common at camps—ran from the veranda to the water's edge. The lodge was meant to be seen as an entity, sculptural and riding lightly on the greensward, its massing and parts serenely balanced so as to satisfy the desire for harmony.

The lodge was in the Shingle style, or what an historian, Roger Hale Newton in a 1941 article called the "Free Classic Style," a term that seems as suitable but has not been adopted by architectural historians. Newton, who used both terms in his article, characterized the style by its use of local materials, simplified forms reminiscent of country buildings in New England, and sensitivity to the fit of building to site.[7]

In addition to the lodge, which held twenty-five people, twelve cabins were on the lake: a sitting-room cabin, a dining room cabin with a kitchen in back, a cabin with separate toilets for men and women, and nine other bedroom cabins.[8] Later members of the Webb family may have gravitated to the cabins, leaving the lodge to employees. Lloyd Page, who was superintendent for many years and occupied a cottage on the property, told J. Watson Webb, grandson of Dr. Webb, that there were eighty-seven buildings on the property, the roofs of which had to be kept shoveled off in winter. A telegraph at Nehasane kept Dr. Webb in touch with his residence and office in Shelburne, Vermont.[9] Nearby was a farm with barns and stables, and a variety of children's playhouses and log cabins were located in the woods and on an island in Lake Lila, with additional buildings on lakes elsewhere on the preserve.

The interior of the lodge, which the writer saw one cold January day in 1976 with a curator from the Adirondack Museum, had many rooms but little architectural character, except for the living room which had a massive fireplace and chimney of stone that rose through a raftered cathedral ceiling. The other rooms, including the dining room, had walls and ceilings of beaded boards which had been painted white, probably as a measure to brighten interiors shaded by the porch roof across the front.

Nehasane Park, which was listed as having 34,200 acres in 1901, grew to a maximum of about 44,000 acres. It was divided in 1978 when descendants of Dr. Webb sold 14,644 acres to the state, including Lake Lila, for a reported $1.5 million. They kept nearly 18,000 acres and three lakes, Nehasane Lake, Gull Lake, and Rock Lake. Cottages on these lakes are modest and can be reached by car at the end of a dirt road that gets narrower twelve or so miles from the nearest paved road. The lodge was torn down by the state in the early 1980s, in accordance with Forest Preserve law and policy.

Santanoni was a radical departure from Nehasane's Forest Lodge, a dramatically different building more suited to a steep slope to the water. The *Report of the Forest Commission* for 1893 called Santanoni Camp the "largest and finest" residence in the

Adirondacks.[10] It was built for Mr. Robert C. Pruyn (1847–1934), whose father was appointed by Lincoln to be the first ambassador to Japan. By the time of his death, Mr. Pruyn had amassed a preserve of 12,900 acres on the southern edge of the high peaks visible to the north. The lodge was what a writer in 1907 called a "veranda house," in which the veranda and its roof was the unifying feature, enclosing the cabins.[11] At camp, the article explained, staying indoors was unnatural: "There is so much rain in the Adirondacks and life indoors is so unnatural, that provision against confinement was made by adding 5,000 square feet of piazzas," which had 265 feet of frontage toward the lake.[12] The veranda, because it facilitated outdoor living, was fully as important as the cabins. Men from Newcomb and more distant villages made up the work force at Santanoni.

Santanoni's lodge was comprised of four log bedroom cabins and a fifth log cabin with a family room for living and dining, set within the porch-and-roof matrix. A covered walkway connected this main structure to the kitchen and service building in the rear. The main cabin had an open living and dining room divided by a central stone chimney with fireplaces on opposite sides. Two bedrooms were upstairs. The

Sleeping cottage, Santanoni. One of four, two on each side of the family building, which had a living and dining room below and bedrooms on the floor above. Photograph by Craig Gilborn, 1975.

Lodge, a rear view, c. 1893. The service building is ahead, the covered passageway from kitchen to dining room is right center, and chimneys of two sleeping cottage can be seen left and right of the Family Building chimney. Facing the lake is the continuous porch and roof that enclosed the buildings in front, making the assemblage a variant of what a writer later called a "Veranda Camp." The Adirondack Museum, gift of Susan and Thomas King (P62928).

larger complex included two buildings on Newcomb Lake, a boathouse, and a studio. The service building behind the lodge contained seven bedrooms for staff. Nearby was a cottage for the caretaker, as well as a workshop, ice house, and various other buildings.

The camp, which cannot be seen or comprehended at a glance, was experienced as an extension of nature, an organic whole that was part of the continuum of space and foliage around it. Thus the symmetrical disposition of the six cabins, shown by Paul Malo in his reconstruction of the camp, comes as a surprise.[13] Photographing the lodge as a whole has never been done, despite pictures taken by amateurs and professional

Dining area, Santanoni, c. 1900. Oak furniture, possibly from a factory in Michigan. The Adirondack Museum, gift of Susan and Thomas King (P64399).

photographers between 1892 and the early 1930s, because of trees and an elevated position.

Santanoni had two other compounds besides this one. One, five miles from the camp, was the gatehouse complex, reached by a driveway from the main road in Newcomb, between Long Lake and Minerva, N.Y. The Gatehouse, as it was called, had been designed by Chester Holmes Aldrich of the New York firm of Delano and Aldrich and was built in 1905. Other buildings nearby were a bridge, the caretaker's house, wagon shed, and barns.

The second compound, the farm, was located a mile from the Gatehouse. It was perhaps the most ambitious and successful farm operation in the Adirondacks, except for the assemblage of dairies and garden farms that supplied food to the Lake Placid Club. Whether Robertson designed the attached barns at the farm remains to be seen, though he had designed far bigger barns in a similar Shingle style at Shelburne Farms. A site plan prepared by Wesley Haynes gives the following buildings at Santanoni's farm:

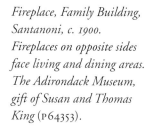

Fireplace, Family Building, Santanoni, c. 1900. Fireplaces on opposite sides face living and dining areas. The Adirondack Museum, gift of Susan and Thomas King (P64353).

Barn; cottages for herdsman and gardener; a new cottage for the farm manager; creamery; smokehouse; icehouse; blacksmith shop and tool house; sheep fold; four coops and runs for chickens, hens, ducks and turkeys; spring house; piggery; slaughter house; potting shed; several sheds and other unidentified structures, possibly a kennel and a root cellar.[14]

The farm met the camp's needs, but it produced a surplus as well, sold to hotels and other outlets in Newcomb and sent from North Creek by railroad to the Pruyn family and their friends in Albany. The region's reputation for soils too poor for commercial farming, as expressed in the epigraph at the start of chapter 7, may require qualification. Mr. Pruyn does seem to have sunk a good deal of money for his to flourish as it did. Wool from sheep on the farm was also produced.

Gatehouse, Santanoni, 1905. Chester Holmes Aldrich, architect. The gatehouse is about five miles from Newcomb Lake and the lodge. Standing but altered. The Adirondack Museum, gift of Susan and Thomas King (P64507).

Breaking the history of the farm into three phases, Haynes sees the second, 1902–8, as a high point, since that was when Edward Bernett, an agricultural planner who modernized and designed farms for wealthy estate-owners, devised a plan reflecting Mr. Pruyn's desire for a model farm, when about two hundred acres were under cultivation. Health and the financial Depression of 1929 caused Mr. Pruyn to cut back on the farm and eventually to sell the livestock. He died in 1934. The caretaker at Santanoni for forty-eight years was Arthur Tummins.

Barns, Santanoni Farm, photograph of c. 1925. It is not certain that Robertson designed these barns. Mr. Pruyn stands with a girl and boy. The Adirondack Museum, gift of Susan and Thomas King (P64202).

In 1953, the estate and preserve were purchased from the Pruyn estate by two brothers, Crandall and Myron Melvin, for $79,100. Their families enjoyed the camp on a simpler scale than before. Tragedy struck in 1971, when an eight-year-old grandchild, Douglas Legg, wandered off and was lost. Despite weeks of searching by volunteers, who combed the woods around the camp, his body was never found. Heartbroken, the Melvins put the property up for sale. An agreement was reached for the purchase of the preserve by the owners, the state, and intermediary groups headed by the Adirondack Conservancy. A contribution of money from Harold K. Hochschild helped as a match for Federal dollars from a park acquisition program. Santanoni was acquired and became part of the New York State Forest Preserve in 1971.

The furnishings in the camp were dispersed, an unfortunate oversight considering the valiant efforts thirty years later that allow the public to see the camp. At the time, as discussed elsewhere on these pages, such camps were generally regarded as anachronisms, and their furnishings got little of the admiring attention that they and the camps would receive less than five years after the sale.[15]

One other veranda camp would be designed besides Santanoni. By William L. Coulter on Eagle Island on Upper Saranac Lake, it was perhaps Coulter's finest contribution in the Adirondacks.

William L. Coulter (c. 1864–1907)

William L. Coulter was likely the region's first resident architect. His training and practice before his arrival in Saranac Lake about 1896 were in New York, and he was referred to as a "New York architect" in a newspaper story even though he had been

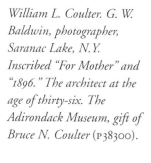

William L. Coulter. G. W. Baldwin, photographer, Saranac Lake, N.Y. Inscribed "For Mother" and "1896." The architect at the age of thirty-six. The Adirondack Museum, gift of Bruce N. Coulter (P38300).

working in Saranac Lake, N.Y, for three to four years. His arrival in the Adirondacks had to do with his tuberculosis, and his architectural firm, Renwick, Aspinwall and Renwick, which wanted him to assist James Aspinwall, cousin of Dr. Edward Livingston Trudeau, in an expansion of Trudeau's Adirondack Cottage Sanatorium. The village had become a center for the treatment and study of tuberculosis, thanks to Dr. Trudeau. Coulter, whose pictures show the hollowness of cheek and eye ascribed to victims of the disease, was among dozens of talented people who continued their life's work in the village, assured of treatment when it was

Camp Inman
Inman (Dog) Island, after 1890, Raquette Lake

Arguably the most exotic of Adirondack camps, this was on a four-acre island and consisted of thirty-five structures that were rustic but allusive of Japan and of American Indian culture all the same. Orchestrator was Horace Inman, who invented the first paper box machine, manufacturing it in Amsterdam, N.Y. He combined business with pleasure, visiting company offices in London and Germany, and traveling to Asia from which he returned with souvenirs for his camp. He kept peacocks on the island and had a Japanese fountain with cascading water and a pool of trout for the table, fed by a steam pump that supplied the island with water from Raquette Lake. A Japanese teahouse and floating garden enclosed by logs were on the lake. He learned blacksmithing from his father, and made wrought iron hardware and chandeliers at a forge on the island. Mr. Inman died in 1910 at the age of seventy-three. The storm of July 1996 necessitated the removal of nearly all of Inman's handiwork by his great grandchildren.

Interior, main house (Wigwam), c. 1900. Letters in Horace Inman's name substituted for numerals on the mantel clock. The Adirondack Museum, gift of Harry A. Inman (P7198).

Ace of Clubs Cottage, c. 1900. The Adirondack Museum (P9182).

Casino, photograph before 1930. Harry A. Inman, grandson of the builder, helped dismantle this Quonset-like building when he was a boy. It had a parquet dance floor; below were dock and slips for boats. The Adirondack Museum (P19433).

Defunct Japanese fountain. Photograph by Craig Gilborn, 1975.

needed. (See appendix B for a list of projects credited to the Coulter office and to the Coulter and Westhoff partnership.)

Coulter had but ten to eleven years remaining to him, dying at the age of forty-seven, in 1907, and he was in full-stride with two to three dozen commissions completed since 1896–97. He worked alone until 1902 when he took in a seasoned architect, Max Westhoff, who soon became his partner.[16] There were one and sometimes two draftsmen in the office, one of whom, William G. Distin, later took over the firm. Distin designed the last of the trophy camps, Minnowbrook, in 1948.

Coulter was born in Norwich, Ct., to William and Hannah Coulter, who would survive him. At sixteen, he entered an architect's office in New York, working as a draftsman by day and taking courses at Cooper Institute at night. It is doubtful that he graduated with an architectural degree, but he arrived in Saranac Lake with fifteen years experience in a respected firm that had designed buildings around the nation. Mary Hotaling, who wrote her graduate thesis on Coulter, followed by articles, said that Coulter went to Montana to rest at a ranch but also to try to win the commission to design the State Capitol for his firm back in New York.[17]

Recuperating and working seem to be contradictory, but it is consistent with Coulter's capacity for work. The number of *camp* buildings or commissions bearing

Cottage, Knollwood Club, Lower Saranac Lake. William L. Coulter, architect. One of six duplicate cottages built c. 1899 for six families. Cottages and boathouse are largely intact today. The Adirondack Museum (P38245).

Living room, cottage. Knollwood Club. The Adirondack Museum (p38246).

his name in ten years was comparable to the camps that William Distin, his student and successor, produced in a career longer by five times. Coulter left the Renwick firm soon after his arrival in Saranac Lake. The separation was amicable, according to Hotaling, although the reason is unclear. Certainly Coulter saw opportunities in the village and lake country around it, in residential and vacation homes to be designed and built.

By 1899, he was at work on three projects. Two were on Upper Saranac Lake: Moss Ledge for Isabel Ballantine, and Camp Pinebrook for Levi P. Morton, a banker who was a congressman, vice president of the United States, and lieutenant governor of New York. The third project was on Lower Saranac Lake. Called Knollwood Club, it was built for six New Yorkers—Elias Asiel, George Blumenthal, Daniel Guggenheim, Louis Marshall, Max Nathan, and Abram Stein. The six cottages were identical, ostensibly to prevent the owners from competing with one another. Occupants of the cottages and their guests shared a boathouse and a combination building which had a dining room and kitchen on the first floor and a recreation room and guest rooms on the second floor.

Coulter's Adirondack practice started at the moment that educated and wealthy Jews in New York City began looking for summer places for themselves and their

Knollwood Club. Later demolished, this large building contained a dining room and kitchen, a billiard room, and guest rooms. The Adirondack Museum (P38247).

Billiard room, Knollwood Club, c. 1900. The Adirondack Museum (P38249).

families; perhaps half of his camp commissions came from Jewish clients. His acquaintance may have dated from his years in the Renwick office in the city.

He worked without a partner for three to five years, although it did not seem to limit his output. His frantic pace is suggested by a story datelined July 21, 1900, from an unidentified newspaper. In it, Coulter is credited for much of the boom in camp construction over the prior three years.[18] Coulter had "drawn plans for more than $600,000 worth of work which kept an "army of workmen" busy and contractors searching "in vain" for more carpenters.

The story points up the influence of New York City on the region. Enormous numbers of people were flocking to the Adirondacks at the turn of the century. A standard for newspapers were stories in summer about luminaries from the city who were away on vacations in the Adirondacks. "The beauty, wealth and refinement of New York and Brooklyn is for the time being located in the Adirondack wilderness," noted the July 21, 1894, issue of *The Brooklyn Daily Eagle,* for readers stuck in town. The size of the migration is suggested by a page of the *New York Daily Tribune* for August 24, 1902, which was entirely filled with names of vacationers in small type.

Floyd-Jones Camp, Lower Saranac Lake. Coulter and Westhoff, architects. Built c. 1905, this camp had log walls on the first floor, wall and roof dormers on second floor, and a polygonal screened corner porch. The Adirondack Museum (p38226).

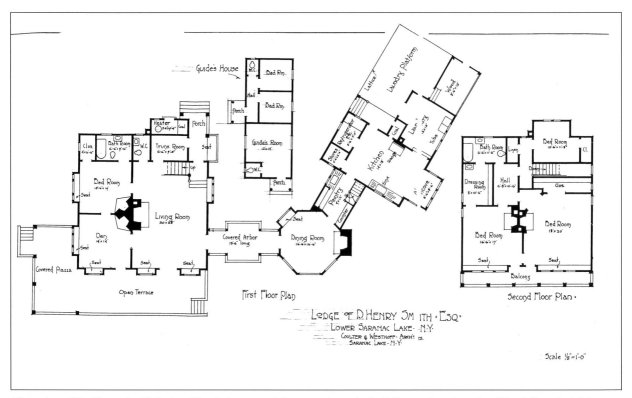

Floor plan of D. Henry Smith Lodge. The dining room is between the main building and service wing. The Adirondack Museum Library, courtesy Wareham DeLair, Architects, Saranac Lake, N.Y.

Dining room (octagonal), Henry Smith Camp, Lower Saranac Lake. William L. Coulter and Max Westhoff, architects. Moss was placed between stones in this picture of c. 1905. The Adirondack Museum (P38254).

By 1902, Coulter had designed perhaps eighteen projects on his own, the majority residences in the neighboring villages of Saranac Lake and Lake Placid, as well as camps on the Saranacs. [19] He tried to be the contractor for buildings he designed, according to his son, Bruce Coulter, on a visit to the Adirondack Museum. His father found he was not up to it. Coulter turned all or most of his work over to Branch and Callanan, a building and supply company in the village. The company was contractor at the Knollwood Club in 1899–1900, and at Eagle Nest Park in Blue Mountain Lake, N.Y., shortly before and after the Second World War.

Coulter hired the son of William L. Distin (1864–1930), a friend and photographer in town. The son, William G. Distin, may already have been working in Coulter's office before his graduation from Saranac Lake High School. In any event, Distin would be at Coulter's side for seven years and possibly one or two more, matriculating at Columbia University the year of Coulter's death, 1907. He graduated three years later with a degree in architecture.

In 1902, Coulter hired Max Westhoff, an architect who had attended Pratt and had been in the New York firm of Eidlitz and McKenzie. Westhoff, who in pictures seems to have been about Coulter's age, played an important but as-yet unappreciated role, since he assisted in the design of two of the firm's biggest camps in 1903–4, the Lewisohn Camp on Prospect Point and the Levi P. Morton Camp on Eagle Island. Westhoff continued the practice after Coulter's death, taking young Distin

Otto Kahn Camp, Bull Point, Upper Saranac Lake, 1901–2. William L. Coulter, architect. The main house from circle drive. Half-timbered and eclectic in style with multiple gables and dormers, and a covered walkway. The Adirondack Museum (38271).

Main House, Otto Kahn Camp, 1901–2. Corner facing the lake. The Adirondack Museum (P38292).

back as a partner and moving to Massachusetts about 1917, opening a practice there and retiring in 1937.[20]

A mark of Coulter's work before Westhoff was half-timbering and log slabs laid on birch bark in gable ends that alluded to half-timbering. Commuter towns along rail lines from the city were sprouting houses and apartment buildings that were half-timbered with stucco in-filling, a touch of Old England thought by city people to be suited to suburban life. For the Otto Kahn Camp, Coulter designed a camp in the eclectic style known as Queen Anne, substituting log walls and railings on ground floors and log trim on the floors above for the usual all-over stick-and-board variety of residence at ocean and mountain resorts, as well as in and near towns.

The Coulter and Westhoff partnership produced about a dozen camps and residences in the Adirondacks, in addition to two camps on Lake Sunapee in New Hampshire, and work at the Lake Placid Club and Paul Smith's Hotel. For Adolph Lewisohn they designed two residences, a weekend home at Ardsley, outside New York City; and a very large camp on Prospect Point, on Upper Saranac Lake. A third Lewisohn residence was in the city.

Adolph Lewisohn and his brother Leonard came to America in 1867 from Hamburg, Germany. They were among the group of German immigrants whose influence on business and culture in America far exceeded their comparatively few numbers. In the late 1890s a number of aristocratic Jewish families from New York City began buying property in the Adirondacks, principally on the Saranac Lakes, but also in the vicinity of Loon Lake and Blue Mountain Lake.

An article in *Town & Country* called attention to the "remarkable series of buildings" that Lewisohn "chooses to call a camp" on Upper Saranac Lake.[21] The author, citing rustic effects attained by spruce logs and slabs and "exquisite old birch bark and doors paneled with bark from some monarch of the ancient forest," praised the architect (Coulter and Westoff) for introducing "striking effects" and "all the fanciful ideas of rustic construction." Interior walls were of local spruce and southern pine from North Carolina stained in tan and greens, harmonizing with cocoa rugs, corduroy cushions, and "woodsy" furniture, some made in Saranac Lake.

The central lodge was a Swiss chalet, three stories tall with half-timbering in the gable end of the third floor. Similar half-timbering was used on the boathouse, which may have been the biggest building on the water in the region. William West Durant selected a Swiss chalet for Sagamore Lodge in 1897, perhaps because an open site vis-

Boathouse, Otto Kahn Camp, 1901–2. Dock and basin. The Adirondack Museum (p38280).

Adolph Lewisohn Camp, Prospect Point, Upper Saranac Lake, c. 1903. Coulter and Westhoff, architects. Much altered by Young Life–Saranac Village, a non-denominational Christian organization, which runs it as a regional facility. The Adirondack Museum (P38251).

Boathouse, Adolph Lewisohn Camp, c. 1903. The Adirondack Museum (P38250).

ible from the lake seemed suitable for the singular chalet silhouette. Chalets were a part of the mix-and-match vocabulary of architects like Coulter, so it does not follow that he was influenced by Durant's chalet, which he saw on a visit in 1901. Lewisohn's chalet had split logs in a pattern vaguely Indian under the eaves on the gable end, as well in the gable ends of the boathouse below. The thrust and recession of walls is symptomatic of Coulter's tendency—really that of the architectural taste of the time—to leave no wall unbroken.

Practical advances were incorporated into the camp. Windows in the wall of the dining room dropped into the floor, a spectacular way of bringing the outdoors inside and opening up unobstructed views of the lake at mealtime. The camp had its own electric generator, powered by a sixty horsepower gasoline engine, and telephones were installed in all buildings.

The Lewisohn brothers had made a fortune in copper, managing to keep most of it even though bested by Meyer Guggenheim, another copper magnate. Adolph gave most of his wealth away to charitable causes in New York City by the time of his death in 1938 while at his camp. The camp was bought in the early 1940s by Mr.

Levi P. Morton Camp, Eagle Island, Upper Saranac Lake, built 1903. Coulter and Westhoff, architects. Since 1938 the island has belonged to the Girl Scout Council of Essex and Montclair Counties (N.J.), which uses it for summer campers. Photograph, c. 1910. The Adirondack Museum (P38275).

Mladek Willy, who tried running it as a lodge. Called "Sekon in the Pines," it failed and was purchased in 1951 by Mr. and Mrs. Irving Blum of South Orange, N.J., who ran it as Navarac Girls Camp, an exclusive summer camp for Jewish girls.

Young Life, a nondenominational Christian organization, bought the camp in 1969. Called "Saranac Village," it has been much altered to accommodate hundreds of boys and girls from upstate New York and nearby Canada spending one-week sessions at the camp in summer. Young Life owns about 105 acres of land and five thousand feet of frontage on Upper Saranac Lake.

About the time the Lewisohn Camp was being built, another camp by Coulter and Westhoff was erected on Eagle Island. Built for Levi P. Morton, it replaced Camp Pinebrook, which Coulter had designed for Morton several years earlier. As mentioned above, the main lodge follows the veranda idea that Robert H. Robertson had adopted at Santanoni ten years earlier.

The extent of the camp can be judged from a printed flyer that listed the buildings for prospective buyers after Morton's death in 1920.[22] What are below identified as the main lodge, dining room, and owner's cabin were enclosed within a continuous veranda and roof. The porch, being fifteen feet or so above the rock knoll and grade that drops away to the water, conveys the sensation that the observer is somewhere between earth and sky, in a tree house. The island has a cover of tall trees and shrubs that prevent the camp from being seen from the lake. The descriptions below have been paraphrased by the author.

Main lodge. A living room building, measuring 35 by 26 feet and open to the rafters, with fireplace and chimney breast of stone, stained log walls with white cement in the joints, dark stained floors, and rustic rafters.

Dining room. A building of its own, octagonal in plan with porches around the sides, connected to the lodge by a covered passage. Walls inside were covered with fabric, perhaps painted linen, over which were decorative framing of halved saplings and logs. A truss of stained logs in the ceiling tied the eight sides and conical roof together. A brick fireplace with arched opening filled one wall. Two doors led to a children's dining room and to the service wing with pantry, kitchen, china room, larder, store room, linen room.

Owner's cabin. A two floor lodge, with a sitting room around which were grouped four bedrooms and "three baths and a lavatory" on the first floor. Upstairs were two bedrooms, one large and the other small, together with a dressing room, bath, and balcony.

Launch house (only partly remaining). An "artistic building" containing three motorboats, four canoes, four guideboats, besides "several boats for servant's use." Above the boathouse were three bedrooms and a bath which shared a veranda across the front which looked at the lake and mountains beyond.

Porch with rustic gable end, Eagle Island (Levi P. Morton) Camp. Photograph by Craig Gilborn, 1998.

Porch, Eagle Island (Levi P. Morton) Camp. Looking from the dining building, 1998. The building with shingles, the kitchen, was added by the Girl Scouts. Photograph by Craig Gilborn, 1998.

Fireplace, Eagle Island (Levi P. Morton) Camp. Staff eat in this octagonal room, which opens into the dining hall. Photograph by Craig Gilborn, 1998.

Other buildings. At the rear of the kitchen was a "servants' hall" with servants' dining room and veranda, cook's room, and bath room; on the second floor, were rooms for the valet, footman, butler, and maid. A separate building held the laundry room with washing and ironing rooms, and, on the second floor, three maids' rooms. The guide house had two bedrooms, kitchen, and workroom. The power house had an electric generator and a pump for water supply, and there was an ice house, wood shed, and bathing beach. Next to this veranda camp was an independent cottage, which faced the lake and may have been for guests. It does not seem to have been included in the inventory above, although it is as old as the main building.

Eagle Island Camp was given to a Girl Scout Council in New Jersey in 1937, an early charitable gift of a camp, second to the former Caughnawauga Club which had been donated to Syracuse University in 1932. When seen in 1998, the camp seemed in good condition considering its sixty years of wear and tear from summer campers. It retains much of its original fabric but has lost most of its furnishings.

Today the Adirondack resorts are approaching the
Newport style, and beautiful and costly cottages and
modern architecture have succeeded the rustic camp.

—Newspaper item from Saranac Lake, N.Y.
July 21, 1900

CHAPTER 11

Old Forge and Saranac Lake Architects

William S. Wicks (1854–1919) and Augustus D. Shepard (1869–1955)

WILLIAM S. WICKS, an early member of the Adirondack League Club, drew plans for Mountain Lodge, the clubhouse built on Little Moose Lake in 1892. In plan it resembled a shallow V, a type of plan sometimes called "butterfly" and "sun trap," then used by architects for country houses in Britain, presumably because it afforded views and sun and daylight both front and back.[1] Mountain Lodge and a dining room added later burned in 1913; the replacement that year was designed by Augustus D. Shepard, a younger architect who also belonged to the club and was then designing a number of new cottages and enlargements of older ones for club members. He discarded the V-plan for a rectangular plan in the clubhouse, although the replacement departed little from Wick's plan in layout and detailing. Shepard's clubhouse still stands, although it lost a sizable portion of the dining room wing in an economy move.

Comparison of Wicks's camps and those of Shepard is useful because each approached the camp from the perspective of his own generation. (For biographies and critical examinations of Wicks and Shepard, see Wesley Haynes's article in *The Adirondack League Club,* as well as lists of club buildings and camps attributed to them by Haynes and Edward Comstock, Jr., who edited and produced the book: 196–245, 246–62). Wicks, the older of the two, adhered to an earlier idea of the Adirondack camp as a place unlike a residence in the city or suburb, while Shepard brought a suburban finish to his later camps and in their emphasis that grounds be landscaped.

Wicks attended Cornell University, transferred to the Massachusetts Institute of Technology, from which he graduated, and took courses at the École des Beaux-Arts in Paris.[2] Presumably he was fully capable of designing larger camps, although by some quirk of fate there are no camps known for certain to have been designed by him, though several are attributed to him on the basis of similarities to illustrations

OPPOSITE: *Augustus D. Shepard, in guideboat at the Adirondack League Club, c. 1905–10. Courtesy of The Adirondack League Club, Old Forge, N.Y.*

Camp Oriole (Snyder/Squier Camp), Adirondack League Club, Honnedaga (Jock's) Lake. William S. Wicks, architect. A drawing of the prospective camp and floor plan were in Wicks's book Log Cabins and Cottages, *1889. Built in 1892, the camp burned in 1980. Photograph by Craig Gilborn, 1974.*

in his book *Log Cabins: How to Build and Furnish Them*.[3] The cottages in Wicks's book, as signified by his use of the word "cabin" in the title, were unprepossessing. He wrote for general readers and not tycoons or upper middle class people like those who were building cottages on Little Moose Lake and Honnedaga Lake. This helped sales of the book, which was reprinted a number of times following its appearance in 1889.

Wicks had an attachment to upstate New York, where he was born, in Barneveld, a small town in farm country north of Utica from which the Adirondack hills could be seen. He owned a cobblestone house in Barneveld, Rubble Home, where he was living when his partnership in the firm of Green and Wicks was dissolved in 1917. He died there two years later. He was partner with Edward B. Green for many years, first in Auburn, N.Y., and then in Buffalo.

Augustus D. Shepard designed about twenty camps at the Adirondack League Club and altered or made additions to perhaps forty other camps or buildings, several times the number of projects credited to William S. Wicks by Comstock and Haynes.[4] Early members of the club, the two architects certainly knew one another, although they did not collaborate. Their camps were on separate lakes not in easy communication with one another. Wicks's Rabbit Wild, a camp on Honnedaga Lake and built in 1892, was the nearest of the club's three inhabited lakes to his Barneveld home. Shepard was at the club in the 1890s but does not seem to have had his own

Living and dining room, Camp Oriole. The kitchen was behind the fireplace, veranda to the right, and two rooms originally intended to be bedrooms are behind the camera. Photograph by Craig Gilborn, 1974.

camp until 1914, when he built Witch Hobble on Little Moose Lake, presently identified as the Oswald Camp.[5]

Shepard's background and training are not clear. His obituary said that he graduated from Lawrenceville School in 1889 and that he had studied architecture in the United States and abroad.[6] He was a partner at the age of twenty-five in the New York firm Haydel and Shepard which designed an ornate town house in the city. The house, which sold for $30 million in 1997, was built for Edith Shepard on the occasion of her marriage to Ernesto Fabbri in 1896. She and Augustus would seem to have had fathers who were brothers; in any event, her name appears on a genealogy of the Vanderbilt family through her mother, who was Margaret Louisa Vanderbilt Shepard, a grandaughter of Cornelius Vanderbilt who built an enormous fortune in steamship and rail transportation.[7]

In 1898, Shepard fought in the Spanish-American War. A photograph of about 1905 shows him in shirt and bow tie at the oars of an Adirondack guideboat, his dark hair parted toward the middle and steel-rimmed glasses planted firmly on his nose.

Mabon Childs (Pratt) Camp, Adirondack League Club, Little Moose Lake, 1904 and later. William S. Wicks may have designed the original buildings, including guest house on left, although this attribution is uncertain. A covered walk connects the two buildings. Photograph by Craig Gilborn, 1998.

The only two books about Adirondack camps to be published before 1980 were written by two Adirondack League Club members, both architects. The books had different readers in mind. Shepard's was a large-format book showing interiors, details, and floor plans, aimed, like the camps themselves, at clients with money.[8] A compendium of ideas, the book remains useful to architects and prospective owners who would build a camp today. The two books were different, as might be expected given the forty years that separated their publication, and all that had transpired in the design and construction of camps in the Adirondacks between 1889 and 1931. Wicks's book, intended for the general reader, was more text than illustration, the latter being small line drawings seldom keyed to what was written on the page.

Log Cabins, reprinted after Wicks's death in 1919, was possibly the most widely read "how-to" book on building and furnishing a camp. In it, Wicks recommended that readers consult with an architect, but he did not say that this was essential. His book, conventional in size, was meant to be taken to heart rather than studied, unlike Shepard's book, which combined pictures and text in tandem, and had detailed photographs and drawings of such items as light fixtures for walls and ceilings.

Wicks belonged to an earlier generation of sportsmen whose experiences in the woods affected their notion of what a decorous cottage in the woods should look like—rustic and partially log and not too large. Perhaps representative was the cottage which he designed for Ole Lynn Snyder on Honnedaga Lake, in 1892; it was of log construction but decorous nevertheless, with a bungalow roof sloped to the front, porches on both floors, and an L-shaped main room with low ceiling in which living and dining were combined, centering on an Arts and Crafts–inspired brick fireplace with ornamental ceramic tiles. The camp, which burned to the ground in the winter of 1980, was comfortable and presentable, but it was not a show place. Wicks's camps have either disappeared or been altered, making comparison with Shepard difficult. The main cottage at the camp of J. Mabon Childs, built by 1904, may have been designed by Wicks with additions in later years, possibly by Shepard.[9]

Shepard, fifteen years younger than Wicks, belonged to a different generation of architects. His camps were elegant, as pictures in his book make clear, but they also took a more total approach to camp design. His camps were kindred to the suave country homes that had begun to appear in magazines like *Country Life, Town and Country,* and *Home and Garden,* in articles and also in advertisements for an expanding array of labor-saving appliances for the "modern" home—refrigerators, gas stoves, vacuum cleaners, washing machines, and mangles for pressing sheets, and the like. Indeed, the Hart-Falck Camp of 1925 seems to anticipate the smaller families and staff of American households in the twentieth century.

Shepard camps related buildings to one another, as well as to their site. Landscaping received far greater attention than before, as illustrations in his book demonstrate. Each camp presented a challenge in itself, like a brooch fashioned for a particular wearer and dress. If Shepard were criticized, it might for the suburban sensibility of the camps, which is likely what his clients wanted in the first place.

Dining room of the Childs Camp, looking into the living room. Spaces between planks are behind split pole battens, a wall treatment used by Shepard. Photograph by Craig Gilborn, 1998.

Read Camp
(Three Star Camp)

Little Simon Pond (formerly Lake Wilburt), 1906, Tupper Lake, N.Y. Davis, McGrath and Shepard, architects

The Shepard was B. H. Shepard and not Augustus D. Shepard, as has been believed. For other illustrations, see page 199.

Living room, Read Camp. Photograph, 1906. Courtesy of Peter B. Read.

Lodge, Read Camp. Covered walk to the dining building is to the left. Photograph, 1906. Courtesy of Peter B. Read.

Bedroom, Read Camp, 1998. Indiana hickory chair in corner. The lake is on the far side of the porch railing. Photograph by Craig Gilborn, 1998.

Dining building from Little Simon Pond. Photograph by Craig Gilborn, 1998.

Octagonal dining room, Read Camp. Photograph, 1906. The room is essentially unchanged today. Through the door is the pantry and kitchen. Courtesy of Peter B. Read.

Arthur B. Lawrence Camp, Adirondack League Club, Little Moose Lake, 1916. Augustus D. Shepard, architect. Behind the cottage are service and staff buildings. Photograph by Craig Gilborn, 1998.

Living room, Lawrence Camp. Dining room can be seen through the doorway. Photograph by Craig Gilborn, 1998.

Hitherto, Augustus D. Shepard has been said to be the "Shepard" in Davis, McGrath and Shepard, the New York architectural firm that designed the Read Camp on Little Simon Pond south of Tupper Lake, N.Y. Given the many camps that he designed at the Adirondack League Club, the attribution to Gus Shepard seemed reasonable. Information found by Edward Comstock, Jr., reveals B. H. Shepard as the partner in question. Adding to the confusion is the fact that the two architects attended M.I.T. in the 1890s. A third Shepard was also an architect, and the three seem not to have been related. The Read Camp, which takes its name from William A. Read, for whom it was built in 1906, was Swiss in style and log in construction, with Arts and Crafts interiors and a covered boardwalk connecting the main building to an octagonal dining room and kitchen on a rocky point extending into the lake. In splendid condition and containing original oak furniture possibly by Charles Rohlfs of Buffalo, N.Y., the camp can be ascribed to the firm but not as yet to one of its principals.

William G. Distin (1884–1970)

William G. Distin, student of William Coulter and heir to the camp legacy of William West Durant and Coulter, was as close to being a native Adirondacker as one can get without having been born in the Adirondacks. He lived most of his life in Saranac Lake, N.Y., where he arrived at the age of fourteen. He was absent roughly seven years—three at Columbia, a year or two of apprenticeship in a Chicago firm and travel in Europe, and a year or two in Washington during the First World War. Except for these, Distin spent about sixty years in a career devoted almost entirely designing buildings in the Adirondack region.[10] This was a noteworthy accomplishment because Adirondackers generally have stood in the shadows of people who came to the region with careers already established somewhere else. (For the buildings which Distin designed or to which he claimed a contribution, see the list under his name in appendix B.)

Distin's father, William L. Distin, was a painter who moved to Plattsburgh, N.Y., from Montreal to take charge of decorating sewing machines and safes in a factory there. In 1898, the family moved to Saranac Lake, fifty-five miles to the southwest but served by rail from Plattsburgh. Saranac Lake was already known for its research into tuberculosis and treatment of people suffering from it. William's father was employed by George W. Baldwin, a photographer in town, and young William attended Saranac Lake High School, graduating in 1900.

On graduation, he entered the architectural office of William Coulter where he likely started as apprentices did, at a drafting table. Distin possibly worked in the Coulter office while still in high school. His apprenticeship in any event was thorough, lasting at least six years and perhaps seven to eight, by which time he must have been nearly ready to take an examination for an architect's license. Some architects were licensed without having graduated from an architectural school. William Scopes (1877–1964) opened an office in Saranac Lake in 1903 while taking a correspondence course in architecture. He had a partner, Maurice M. Feustmann (1870–1943), who had graduated from the University of Pennsylvania and studied architecture in Munich, Germany, and at the École des Beaux-Arts in Paris.[11] Notwithstanding, Scopes was the senior partner, receiving his license from the state in 1914.

William G. Distin at the drafting table, possibly in the office of his mentor, William L. Coulter. Distin appears to be in his early twenties. The Adirondack Museum Library, gift of William "Mo" Distin, Jr.

Living room building, Henry H. Blagden Camp (LaJeunesse), Upper Saranac Lake, built 1930. William G. Distin, architect. Photograph undated. This was an addition to an older camp. Adirondack Museum Library.

When interviewed on tape late in his life, Distin said his desire to be an architect dated from the time he was sixteen, which would have been about the time he met Coulter. He soon would be exposed to a second architect, Max Westhoff, who joined the firm in 1902 and became Coulter's partner in 1906. A second draftsman in the firm was John Faulkner. In September, 1907, perhaps because of Coulter's death earlier that year, Distin left Saranac Lake for Columbia University in New York. Perhaps Coulter and Westhoff convinced him of the importance of a formal course of study. He graduated in 1910 and then served a nine-month stint in the office of S. S. Beeman, where he assisted in designing residences for a development in Highland Park, near Chicago. In addition, he took evening art courses at the Art Institute of Chicago. He also spent time abroad. Some of his surviving sketches give an indication of his excellent draftsmanship.

Octogonal living room, 1930, Blagden Camp. A central chimney with multiple hearths, the dining room beyond. Photograph undated.

When Distin returned is not clear, but it must have been 1912 or 1913. He became Westhoff's associate and was made partner some time after, when the firm was known as Westhoff and Distin. In 1917, Distin went to Washington, where he was "Expediting Engineer" for army hospitals being planned and built in the United States. Westhoff closed the Saranac Lake office and moved to Springfield, Mass., where he continued to practice under his name until his retirement in 1937.[12]

Distin reopened the office after the war. His relationship with Westhoff is uncertain, since on February 26, 1921, he wrote a one-page letter to Westhoff showing $3,983.25 in net income for the firm in 1920, closing with the comment, "Hope that the above will enable you to complete your tax income figures."[13] Distin's report was perhaps more a courtesy than a concession of accountability to a former partner.

Distin had practiced architecture for roughly twenty years at the time of his letter to Westhoff; even so, two-thirds of his career lay ahead of him. Events were not auspicious for architecture or architects of second homes; one world war had ended and a world depression and second war lay ahead.

Distin's was a solo practice, although, according to Arthur Wareham, he took a partner by the name of Arthur G. Wilson into the firm in 1926 who would return to his native Scotland in 1932. Three of Distin's best camp commissions came during the

Camp Wonundra (William Rockefeller Camp), Upper Saranac Lake, built 1932. William G. Distin, architect. In fine repair and now called The Point, it has guest rooms in the wing to the right, off an octagonal entrance that enters into a great hall with fireplaces at each end and a master bedroom beyond. The Adirondack Museum Library.

Depression years. In 1930 and 1932, he designed an addition and a camp at two properties on Upper Saranac Lake. The earlier was an octagonal living room building at the camp of Thomas Blagden. Two years later, he designed a new camp for William Rockefeller called Wonundra. His biggest camp was built for Walter and Kathrin Hochschild in 1937–38. There was a second camp or addition at Eagle Nest some years after, perhaps in the 1940s, for Gertrude Hochschild Sergievsky and her husband Boris. He was working on another camp in the area, Minnowbrook, on Blue Mountain Lake, when Arthur Wareham joined the firm. Built in 1948, Minnowbrook is treated in this book as the symbolic last of the "great" or "trophy" camps in the Adirondacks.

In a taped interview with Jack Demattos on January 15, 1970, Distin, who sounds as though he was failing, said his mentor William Coulter was known "by his love of the country and the way he adapted himself [his buildings] to it, so that all his work, which I tried to follow in later years, was designed to fit the site." Distin in effect said that he continued the work of Coulter, a span of years, 1896–1970, that marked the beginning and an end to the construction of large camp properties in the Adirondacks.

In the 1960s, a chapter of the American Institute of Architects in upstate New York placed Distin's name in nomination for a career award from the A.I.A. headquarters in Washington, D.C. Cited by Distin in his portfolio were several camps designed by William Coulter and by the Coulter and Max Westhoff partnership, including the Lewisohn Camp on Prospect Point and the Morton Camp on Eagle Island. That Distin contributed to the design of these camps seems plausible given the three to four years he had been in the firm by 1903–4, as well as the volume of work passing

Hollingshead (Minnowbrook) Camp. Rendering by William G. Distin, architect, 1948. This butterfly-plan camp on Blue Mountain Lake burned in 1988, to be replaced by a similar but more versatile conference facility by Syracuse University. Courtesy Wareham DeLair Architects, 1975.

through the office before Max Westhoff's arrival in 1902, and after it. Each camp was an enclave of six to a dozen or more buildings large and small, with ancillary features, such as covered walks and sheltered nooks, requiring a plan to be followed by the builder and his men. It would not be surprising if Distin at some point contributed original designs for these larger projects.

To Distin's dismay, and the consternation of the chapter that nominated him, the panel for the national A.I.A. did not approve the nomination. Distin, in his seventies, did not know why; of the reasons, the most obvious one was that residences in general and vacation lodges in particular were not seen as specialties from which national reputations were then being made. In an era of steel and glass skyscrapers, Distin's log camps may have been easy to dismiss as regressive. In his résumé, Distin said he had been in "the McKim Atelier" at Columbia University, which may have put him in an academic camp seen as unfashionable because it was not "modern."

The octagonal room is a Distin trademark; it was usually used for his dining rooms, with an exception being the living room building on Upper Saranac Lake with its central chimney with fireplaces and hearths on four sides. The Walter and Kathrin Hochschild camp at Eagle Nest has four octagonal rooms, the number reflecting, she later said, her admiration of Thomas Jefferson and his use of an eight-sided room at Monticello, his home in Charlottesville, Va.[14]

Another Distin feature is the butterfly or sun trap plan, which he used at Camp Wonundra (since called The Point), at the Hochschild lodge, and at Minnowbrook, the lodge built for R. M. Hollingshead on Blue Mountain Lake. William Wicks may have been the first to use the plan in the Adirondacks in his design for the clubhouse

Proposed camp for Walter and Kathrin Hochschild, rendering by William G. Distin, architect, 1937. The finished camp was not this big. Courtesy of the late Mrs. Walter Hochschild.

BELOW: *Boathouse and lodge, Eagle Lake, 1937–38. Mrs. Hochschild's studio was above the boathouse. Photograph by Craig Gilborn, 1978.*

of the Adirondack League Club on Little Moose Lake in 1892. The plan, in which wings extended off an entrance hall to left and right, was used in country residences designed by McKim, Mead and White in the 1880s.

Distin also substituted stone terraces for porches, accessible from the living room and adjoining dining room through double doors. This admitted more daylight to interior rooms and provided a transition between the building and the land around it. He did not do away with the porch entirely but put it at the end of the lodge, as Augustus D. Shepard had done earlier at the Lawrence Camp on Little Moose Lake. At the Walter Hochschild Camp, Distin placed a double polygonal porch, one above the other, at the east end, off the eight-sided dining room and the bedroom above it.

Distin relied less on camp commissions than on other kinds of buildings, such as schools and churches, as indicated by a list of projects in appendix B. Arthur

Wareham became a partner in the firm of Distin and Wareham in 1954. Ronald DeLair, who came to the office in 1968, was made a partner in the short-lived firm of Distin, Wareham and DeLair. The name was changed to Wareham DeLair Architects, which it was in 1998, though Mr. DeLair is the principal architect following his partner's retirement about 1990.

Living room, Walter Hochschild Camp. Photograph by Peter and Rosine Lemon, 1982.

William Scopes (1877–1964) and Maurice Feustmann (1878–1943)

Maurice Feustmann's obituary said that the firm designed "many show-place camps on upper and lower Saranac Lakes and the St. Regis chain of lakes." However, the firm made its reputation in hospital and sanitarium design—several in New England, one in Syracuse, N.Y., and an addition to the Will Rogers Hospital in Saranac Lake. In 1927, they designed the Hotel Saranac, a business venture for which Scopes sold bonds to businessmen and others in the community.[15] A hotel with a hundred rooms and baths was too big for local demand, and it proved to be a near-disaster for Scopes. The firm designed civic and commercial buildings, as well as residences, including Feustmann's home at 28 Catherine Street, built in 1923.

Chief among their known camps is the Kildare Club, the main lodge of which, built in 1906, is as fine as any in the Adirondacks. Fronting on Jordan Lake, the lodge at one end has an L-shaped porch wrapped around the front and side of the dining room. The remainder of the front is without porch and has two bays with windows offering views of the lake from sitting and family rooms inside.

The dining room has a monumental brick fireplace, to the right of which is a door to the kitchen and service wing. The centerpiece of the room is a horn chandelier reminiscent of lodges in seventeenth-century Germany.[16] Found in Europe by one of the owners, it is suspended over the dining table from inside the interior of a cupola on the roof. Made from interlocking deer antlers, it likely weighs several hundred pounds and would finish off a table of family and guests if it ever fell, said the daughter of one of the original owners.

The family room has a pool table. Over it is a barrel-vault ceiling of wood strips applied to frames under the main roof in the attic. Despite the generous proportions of these two principal rooms, the lodge is economical in its use of space, concentrating bedrooms for family and guests on a single floor next to the family room. A lone bedroom is at the top of a stairway and is thought to have been placed there for a nurse or some other care-giver.

At the dining room end of the lodge is the two-story wing containing pantry and kitchen below

Main lodge, Kildare Club, Jordan Lake, built 1906. Scopes and Feustmann, architects. Photograph by Craig Gilborn, 1998.

and rooms for help above. Several small cottages, including one with a flower garden enclosed to keep out deer, were built facing the lake, together with a boathouse and dock. One of the cottages was for Orin Lehmann, commissioner of the Department of Parks, Recreation and Historic Preservation in Albany for many years. He visited the camp less often after the Second World War, partly because a war injury kept him from enjoying the camp as before.

Recreation room, lodge, Kildare Club. The room has a barrel ceiling. Photograph by Craig Gilborn, 1998.

Cottage, Eagle Lake, 1920s. Scopes and Feustmann, architects. Built for Harold K. Hochschild, who founded the Adirondack Museum, Blue Mountain Lake, N.Y. The Adirondack Museum (P7080).

The firm also designed two cottages at Eagle Nest Park on Eagle and Blue Mountain Lakes at different times. The older of the two, built about 1905, belonged to Marcus M. Marks and was illustrated in Henry H. Saylor's *Bungalows,* in which it is said to be a house suited to mountain country.[17] The house is hardly a bungalow, since it has two full floors and no bedrooms on the first floor. It possessed a Swiss or Scandinavian character, with a front porch recessed well back, beneath the second-floor above; porches on the sides each had roofs of their own. The living room inside had a gallery that looked down on the living room from the floor above, an arrangement later altered so kitchen, dining room, and bedrooms above could be heated for winter visits.

The other Scopes and Feustmann cottage at Eagle Nest is of unknown date; it may have been built for Harold K. Hochschild, who, as the eldest child, was heir-apparent to the family's mining and smelting interests. It was a classic bungalow, half-house below and a roof for the upper half-story, the rooms getting light and lake views through dormer windows. The cottage had an exterior stairway for bathers going to and from the lake.

The Distin and Scopes firms shared space for a time. Together they worked on a project at Dannemora Prison in Clinton County. Mary Hotaling says that local work by Scopes and Feustmann came to a halt when construction work "nearly ceased" after 1930. In the 1970s, Arthur Wareham of the Wareham DeLair firm opened a closet containing cubicles with rolled up blueprints and plans that he said had been left by the Scopes and Feustmann firm.

Summary

Distin, along with Robert H. Robertson and Augustus D. Shepard, achieved a breakthrough in developing a style that alluded not at all to historic styles but was configured to the needs of their occupants instead. Coulter and Westhoff could have claimed they had done no less themselves, but their training in the Queen Anne style—an eclectic mishmash of half-timbering, pendants, hanging turrets, many gables, and a hooded appearance created by porches and balconies—is obvious at the Otto Kahn Camp.

The buildings at the Levi P. Morton Camp reveal Coulter to have been fully capable of an innovative approach to camp design, in its spectacular continuous porches that establish their own environment. Architects after Coulter, notably Shepard and Distin, reduced the size and visual importance of the porch so as to brighten interiors made dark by roof porches; they did not eliminate the porch so much as they figuratively moved it to one side.

The Adirondack camp may be innovative by its elevation of the porch to a status equal to interior rooms. Coulter explored the porch as much as any architect. The two-story building that is the restaurant of the Wawbeek Resort looked familiar to the author, although he could not put his finger on just why. It was the double-porch, one stacked over the other and hinting that the building might have been designed by William Coulter, as it was, the confirmation coming from the owner. The porch was part of the "wilderness cure" that made Dr. Trudeau and the village of Saranac Lake famous, so it perhaps it is not surprising the porch was so prominent a feature at camps in the region.

Because Saranac Lake had become a center for research and treatment of tuberculosis, its architects were sought for planning of hospitals and related facilities, not just in the region but in other states as well. Coulter came to Saranac Lake to assist his architectural firm with the expansion of the Adirondack Cottage Sanatorium. In 1906, a year before his death, he was said to have planned a mining town of 350 buildings in Keokee, West Virginia. Distin was an engineering expediter in the construction of hospitals for the army in the First World War, and he later collaborated with Scopes and Feustmann in designing a hospital at Dannemora Prison in Clinton County.

Augustus D. Shepard designed the conventional two-story vacation cottage like its residential counterpart—with porch, living room, and dining room on the first floor and bedrooms on the floor above, as at the Lawrence Camp. But he also could be experimental, as at the Hart-Falck Camp, built in 1925, which consisted of a central story-and-a-half living room and two wings, one a service wing and the other a series of bedrooms like boxcars on a train, giving each room outdoor views in front and back, and access from a door in each to the outside.

Distin was the only person, other than Coulter himself, who was acquainted with *all* of Coulter's Adirondack work. Distin said in effect that he deserved a measure of credit for Coulter's camps and those done in partnership with Westhoff, and this deserves credence. He spent, after all, seven years at Coulter's elbow. However, his degree from Columbia counted for more than his apprenticeship with Coulter insofar as the panel of the A.I.A. was concerned.

Assigning credit is a very sticky process where two or three architects may each have contributed to a building's appearance; most buildings undergo renovation or alteration sometime within living memory, so the predicament is far more common than not. The profession distinguishes between the architect-of-record and the design-architect, the first being the senior partner or partners to whom the practice belongs and the latter being the person who may have had the concept, but whose name may never be known outside the firm itself. Technically, Distin was a draftsman and apprentice for the years 1900–1907. The practice was Coulter's, and he and his partner Westhoff got their names on the plans, not Distin.

Adirondack Camps after Distin

William Distin's death in 1970 ended an era that opened about seventy-five years earlier, in the camps of William West Durant, of 1895–1900, and those of William Coulter, of 1896–1907. Distin took Arthur Wareham into the office in 1946. One of Wareham's first projects was the Hollingshead camp, built on Blue Mountain Lake two years later, in 1948, the year that brought an end—or a pause—to the outsized camp in the Adirondacks. Wareham was made partner in the firm in 1953, and Ronald DeLair, a native of Tupper Lake and a graduate of Rensselaer Polytechnical Institute, became partner in 1969–70. One of Arthur Wareham's last projects before his retirement was the Conference Building which he designed for the Adirondack Museum when the author was director.

Mr. DeLair, who was carrying the work of the firm by the late 1980s, brought young architects into the firm who in time went elsewhere, eventually to open their

"The Beehive" (Reed/Woods Camp), Adirondack League Club, Bisby Lake. Adaptive restoration by Wareham DeLair, Architects, 1988. Courtesy Ronald H. DeLair.

own practices. Two of these, Thomas Chapin and Richard Hanpeter, are mentioned below. The early seventies were slow years for the firm, when inflation and fuel shortages cast serious doubt about the survivability of camps that burned fifty dollars to a hundred dollars worth of fuel a day between December and March even when they were unoccupied.

Work began to pick up toward the end of the decade, in anticipation of the Winter Olympic Games to be held in Lake Placid in 1980. Older buildings were spruced up and new ones built as residents and outsiders figured they would clean up through sky-high rentals to corporations and wealthy individuals during the actual two-week period of the games and the weeks just before and after.

Wareham DeLair Architects, which celebrated its centennial in 1997, is the fifth oldest office in continuous practice in New York State.[18] Other architects began migrating to the region in anticipation of the Oympic games and the expected boost to the economy. The 1998 telephone directory for the Saranac Lake–Lake Placid area had three architectural firms in which at least one principal had "A.I.A." after his name. Five other firms were listed under the Architects heading, three in Lake Placid and one apiece for Keene Valley, Malone, and Plattsburgh, N.Y.

One A.I.A. firm was that of Richard E. Hanpeter who had formerly worked in the Wareham DeLair office but later opened an office of his own, soon gaining a reputation for camp designs. The adaptive restorations of two cottages at the Adirondack Museum—the Bull Cottage and Moodie Cottage—were done by Mr. Hanpeter when he was with the Wareham DeLair firm. Another architect formerly in the office was Thomas Chapin, whose wife, Lisa Chapin, prepared a landscaping plan for the hillside where these cottages were located. Thomas Chapin later designed an octagonal pavilion for the hill as part of his wife's larger plan. In addition, he designed a far

Detail showing log post-and-beam construction of the Marion River Carry Pavilion. Main beams are forty-six feet in length. Photograph by Craig Gilborn, 1998.

larger log and timber pavilion on the pond for public assembly and as a drydock for the museum's steamboat, the *Osprey,* which had suffered after years of being alternately floated for four months on the pond and cradled for eight months when the pond was drained.

This pavilion-on-the-pond was of heroic character and proportions, not exactly camp, to be sure, but exemplary of rustic design and construction, and a demonstration of the universal applicability of wood in any age. Twenty-nine peeled white pine columns about thirty inches in diameter support a system of timber trusses that support a cedar shingle roof that drops, like a bird's wings, close to the water, within reach of an outstretched hand. The pavilion looks bigger than it is, accomplishing for timber and logs what the John Russell Pope's buildings did for stone at Kamp Kill Kare, which is to show these elemental materials at their muscular best, in harness.

The contractor for the job, Tupper Lake Supply, had never dealt with anything like Chapin's system of timber trusses and log columns. Their men fussed over plans and did the cutting on the ground; particularly delicate was hewing two tree trunks into continuous timber beams on the ground, each forty-six feet in length. These were hoisted and tied to the tops of pine columns. It was shortly before Christmas that the men finished their work, five months from the time the drydock had been poured and was ready for the elaborate timber structure that would go over it. While the snow fell around them, two men finished nailing the last of the cedar shingles at the peak or ridge, and a third began picking up scraps of cedar on the ground. Men get work where they can get it in the Adirondacks, in below-freezing weather, a legacy of the woods and living with no more than just enough.

The new big camps of the Adirondacks are unlike the camps of the past in one major respect: the old camps called for indoor and outdoor staff, while their modern descendants increasingly are turn-key operations, requiring only a caretaker, who usually lives in town. Labor is far less arduous than before, thanks to machines: trees are cut by chainsaw and split into firewood by a hydraulic splitter, and cutting ice on the lake is past. (Blocks from New Pond are still put in ice boxes at the Underwood Club for the sake of nostalgia.) Electronic sensors in camps ring the caretaker's telephone if the temperature inside the empty camp falls below 50 or 60 degrees F. These and other devices eliminate the need for around-the-clock surveillance and even for a live-in caretaker.

Camp owners are now doing jobs formerly done by domestic help, proud of their independence on such matters as the preparation of food. Part-time housekeeping and some cooking can be obtained from town, and caterers are available from Paul Smith's College and elsewhere for *soirées*. The modern Adirondack camp, in other words, requires far fewer employees than before, and the consequence of this loss of steady or reliable employment has been a weakening of ties between the owners of the camps and the local people on whom camp owners are as dependent as ever for putting out fires, clearing fallen trees, and carrying people in an ambulance to a hospital in Saranac Lake, Glens Falls, or Utica.

The prodigy camp, of which Kamp Kill Kare, in the next chapter, is the author's only candidate, is extinct; but the trophy camp may be enjoying a revival. A *New York Times* reporter who visited Saranac Lake area in 1997 wrote of a couple of recent projects, one a brand-new lodge of 12,000 square feet, or roughly five times the size of the average American house, and the other a restoration and expansion of Camp Topridge. Perhaps big-time spenders are returning to the Adirondacks. Whether the camp is a haven, as it was for people in business and public life a century ago, or yet another venue for getting and spending is outside the scope of this book.[19]

CHAPTER 12

Kamp Kill Kare: Prodigy Camp

THE LINE inscribed on the outside edge of a log slab mantle of the central stone fireplace in the "Kabin" at Kamp Kill Kare aptly set the note of cheer that would prevail at the camp for the next seventy-five years. The name of the lake was changed from Sumner to Lake Kora, for Cora Eastman Woodruff, and the camp with its *K*s was a place where adults and especially children and youths of two families enjoyed blissful summers in a rustic enclave in the heart of the Adirondacks, each family adding to what it found. Kamp Kill Kare in its early and later guises was the most thoroughly rustic of Adirondack camps, a candidate on anyone's "best" list of fine architecture. It also is the best kept and best documented, which is why Kamp Kill Kare is the finale to this book on Adirondack camps built before 1950.

The Durant Period

The story of Kill Kare begins with William West Durant, who carved three preserves out of two townships that he largely owned at the south end of Raquette Lake. Most of the land would be sold to the state, but the choicest sites he set aside for development, erecting cabins and shelters on them and letting men use them for the favors they could do for him in Albany. Frank S. Black, who was elected governor of New York in 1896, stayed in one of these remote camps, Fish Camp, on Sneed Creek, about three miles from Kamp Kill Kare. It was Governor Black's favorite retreat in the Adirondacks.[1]

Lieutenant Governor Timothy Woodruff, as will be seen, purchased the Sumner Lake preserve from Durant in 1897, the same year that the State Forest Commission, of which Woodruff was chairman, agreed to buy Township 6 from Durant, except for 2,550 acres for two preserves, one for Woodruff and the other for Durant.[2]

A cabin provided a pretext for not including a lake or stretch of water on which it was located in a sale to the state: it signified an "improvement," justifying sequestering the preserve on grounds of its increased value and the state's unwillingness to pay

Camp Omonson (Bear Camp), Sumner Lake (Lake Kora), 1880s. Arpad G. Gerster used the cabin, which was on land belonging to W. W. Durant, who sold the preserve and lake to Timothy Woodruff in 1897. The Woodruffs incorporated this cabin into the rustic lodge are pictured on page 277. Iron shutters kept out hungry bears. The woman and guide are unidentified. The Adirondack Museum, gift of Mrs. Bromley Seeley (P7572).

the selling price. Documentation for this has not been found by the author, but the insinuation of private interests in public life, endemic at this time, led to partial truths that cronies construed as the whole truth. An investigation was conducted by the Moreland Commission into the seeming conflict-of-interest, but its report was issued in 1910, by which time Woodruff had owned Kamp Kill Kare for more than a dozen years, and nothing came of it.

The log cabin on Sumner Lake was built for Dr. Arpad Gerster sometime prior to 1888. Gerster, a friend of Durant's, had owned a camp, Oteetiwi, on Big Island on Raquette Lake since about 1880. Still, the surgeon delighted in camping out, especially in the territory south of Raquette Lake where fish and deer were abundant and the terrain not too steep. The two men likely saw one another in New York City where Gerster was a surgeon at Mt. Sinai Hospital, receiving patients at his brownstone house next to what became the Whitney Museum. The cabin was Durant's but Gerster paid to have it built in return for permission to use it, occasionally with his wife and son, a Hungarian cook, and two guides.

Called "Omonson" on an early photograph and "Bear Camp" elsewhere, the cabin had iron plate shutters at the windows and an equally bear-proof wooden door salvaged off a walk-in cooler. Curious about the power of a bullet, Gerster, using an Austrian-made Mannlicher rifle, fired at one of the shutters and made a "neat hole" in it at seventy-five feet.[3] Durant, he said in his journal, had given him permission for the experiment.

At dinner at Camp Uncas on August 8, 1897, Durant informed Dr. Gerster that the Sumner Lake property had been sold to the lieutenant governor and that the state would buy most of the remainder of Township 6 at what Durant said was an "acceptable price." In his journal, the crestfallen Gerster later wrote, "This is, then, very likely the last season when I shall be permitted to enjoy the beauties of Sumner Lake." The change was "for the better," he observed, though to him it was sad because "that was and is the natural course of events in all the beautiful, lovely places in the woods." Not all was lost, for Durant "cheerfully acceded" to selling him an island on Long Lake.

The Woodruff Period Opens

A month after the dinner, Gerster happened to see his old cabin on Sumner Lake following a call to come to the Woodruff camp. He found Mrs. Woodruff in bed, later writing that she was "a restless inquisitive body," with a perpetual twitch to her lip and cheek. The camp, which he noted "was originally for me," had changed in the time the Woodruffs had taken it over, apparently before his dinner with Durant. They had turned the kitchen into a dining room and made the woodshed into a kitchen. The veranda had been enlarged, now being "ornamented with artistic iron lamps and other city gimcracks," a wonderfully incisive statement by a man with an unerring eye for telling detail.

On August 13, 1898, a year later, he paid a second house call. Met at the landing by a boy, he was taken to what he noted now had the name "Killkare Camp." He was received by Lieutenant Governor Woodruff, who took him into a darkened room

Farm buildings, Kamp Kill Kare, c. 1900. Possibly designed by Charles C. Hiscoe, a retired English naval officer. The quaint rusticity of the early Woodruff period was removed later, perhaps by the Garvans or even the Woodruffs themselves. The Adirondack Museum, gift of Bea Garvan in memory of her husband, Dr. Anthony N. B. Garvan (P62100). Illustrations identified as Adirondack Museum Library were gifts from Mrs. Garvan.

where Mrs. Woodruff, "somewhat indisposed," lay in her bed. Later Gerster confided to his journal that he was favorably impressed by the changes at the camp: "They have built up and extended the old camp, and have done it evidently under the guidance of someone of good taste." He gets to specifics: "A bathroom, hot & cold water, laundry, etc., etc., mark a wide departure from former conditions at Sumner," concluding "they have now a splendid camp." However, the "once abundant deer" had vanished, perhaps because the Woodruffs had cut the bushes around the camp, exposing it to the lake.

The "someone of good taste" may have been Cora Woodruff, who soon would be credited for the "artistic remodeling" of her residence in Brooklyn in an item in the *Brooklyn Eagle* for May 27, 1900, in which her "luxurious" camp in the Adirondacks was also mentioned. An article the next year, in *Town & Country*, confers credit on husband as well as wife, calling the buildings the "outgrowth of the views" and "experiences" of the couple "extending over a number of years." The two, it said, were "artistic in their tastes."[4] In 1903, yet a third writer, Henry Wellington Wack, an Englishman, cited Mrs. Woodruff's "provident hand" in doing "the work of genius" with "taste and forethought."[5] Praise from three different sources lends some credence to the Woodruffs having contributed to Kill Kare's rustic transformation.

Timothy Woodruff (1858–1913) attended Yale for four years and entered business, reorganizing the Worcester Salt Company and then developing a warehousing and wharfage business which he sold, investing the profits in diverse companies. After a brief stint as Park Commissioner in Brooklyn, N.Y., he was elected to three two-year terms as lieutenant governor, beginning in 1896.

The conjurer of rusticity for the Woodruffs was Charles C. Hiscoe, about whom little is known except that he had come from England and was addressed as "Captain," presumably because he had served in the navy.[6] In 1918, when he was last heard from, he was residing in Elmhurst in Queens on Long Island. He assisted in

Woodruff family in front of cottage with the "tree bed," Kamp Kill Kare. Photograph, c. 1909. The former lieutenant governor holds a bamboo fly rod and looks at his wife; he was a widower when they married. To the right is the main building. The Adirondack Museum (P62115).

decorating the rooms at Kamp Kill Kare in 1897–99, and he may have designed ancillary buildings, but not, as seems likely, the main building. He may have returned to Kill Kare for the construction of the island Kabin in 1901, and he almost certainly came following a fire in 1908, designing a combination sitting room and bedroom that was perhaps the most audacious expression of rustic taste in the Adirondacks before or since, centering on a tree-bed fashioned from a tree that was surrounded by other locally made rustic furniture and fitments. A second fire, in 1915, destroyed most of the main building, though not this cottage. Seeing an opportunity, Hiscoe wrote the owners of the camp, Mr. and Mrs. Frances P. Garvan, who had bought the camp that year. He said he had been a friend of the Woodruffs and offered his services to the Garvans in a similar capacity, as a decorator. Captain Hiscoe had been to Kill Kare on as many as three occasions prior to his being hired to return yet again to oversee the reconstruction and furnishing of the lodge, as well as the decoration of new buildings.

By 1898–99, Dr. Gerster's cabin had disappeared into a larger main camp structure comprising four cabins connected by a combination of roofed verandas across the front. An older cabin swallowed by an enlargement had been done elsewhere: a cabin of the 1880s was later integrated into the main building at the camp on Birch Island in Upper St. Regis Lake. But linking log cabins in the manner of boxcars on a train and connecting them by a veranda across the front, was a novel solution to the emerging precept that buildings should follow the grade of a site, merging with it instead of seeming to sit on it like a throne. This approach was never tried again in fashionable camp construction, so far as the author knows.

The modular approach fit the building to its site. As the veranda deck was inches off the lawn for two-thirds of the building, occupants and rooms were in an especially intimate relationship to the land. The remaining third of the camp followed the slope toward the lake, and so was elevated, reached by a series of steps and landings. The

Kamp Kill Kare, Lake Kora (Sumner Lake). The lodge as Mr. and Mrs. Garvan, newly married, likely saw it when they rented the camp, c. 1913. Fires in 1908 and 1915 destroyed sections of the lodge; just where is uncertain. The 1915 fire, which occurred just after the Garvans purchased the camp, ushered in a period of major improvements and additions. The Adirondack Museum (P62162).

Bedroom, main building, Kamp Kill Kare, 1897–99. Attributed to Charles C. Hiscoe, designer. Pedestal table with massive burl top on a stout cedar base with castors; it seems to have survived the fire that destroyed this room in 1908. Peeled log furniture like the bed had appeared at neighboring camps a year or so earlier, c. 1895–97 (see p. 223) The Adirondack Museum (P62127).

camp followed Arts and Crafts precepts about using local spruce and rock and keeping occupants in close proximity to nature, while attaining the horizontal profile preferred for country homes by architects and clients. Dr. Gerster's keen eye noticed these changes and found them altogether agreeable.

Outside chimneys at the early Kill Kare had the squared ashlar stonework of the camps of William West Durant at this time, perhaps because one of his stonemasons, Schuyler Kathan, worked at Kill Kare as well. John Kathan, in an interview with the author in the 1970s, said his father had worked at Kamp Kill Kare for the Woodruffs and later for Mr. and Mrs. Garvan. Indoors, the fireplaces were rough-cut without courses, a departure from the square-cut and relatively smooth and sometimes tooled faces of fireplaces and chimneys of the Durant camps. The early Kill Kare had this squared stonework, but quite different stone, cobblestone, was adopted later, seemingly following the fire in 1908, when a cobblestone chimney appeared in the design bearing that date for the tree-bed cottage. These stones, rendered smooth and rounded by ancient glacial streams and sand, were chosen in 1915 and after, when the lodge was reconstructed and the rest of the camp underwent an extensive enlargement. One can easily distinguish early and later versions of the main building that look exactly the same except for their very dissimilar chimneys.

Photographs of Kill Kare in a 1901 article in *Town and Country* magazine, during the Woodruff period, reveal interiors with a combination of wood and stone—log walls, ceilings with log beams supporting floors above, casement windows—set off by colored curtains and a variety of rugs and carpeting on which were laid animal skins. Rooms had low ceilings, an indication of a floor and rooms above, mostly bedrooms. Rooms were keyed to certain colors: the dining room, which had a large Persian carpet on the floor, had red hangings, while Cora Woodruff's bedroom was green.[7] These were Arts and Crafts interiors, with plank chairs with shaped backs in the manner of folk chairs in Switzerland, and decorative plates and dishes arrayed side-by-side on shelves above the windows with cups and mugs suspended by their handles from hooks. Mr. Woodruff had a room of his own, and the couple had separate baths.

Next to the dining room was an outside dining room with eight sides affording views of the camp and veranda and of the grounds and lake beyond. The dome-like ceiling, an essay in the use of rustic materials, was divided into concentric areas divided by bark-covered saplings separating fields of white birch bark.

The Kabin was built in 1901 for assemblies of people on the first floor with guest bedrooms on the second. On an island in view of the main building, and reached by a long rustic bridge, it had a massive central stone chimney and opposite-facing fireplaces with cobblestone hearths on the first floor. It was for Woodruff and his cronies, though dances were to be held in it, as well. Contained in it were a phonograph and a Ping-Pong table, a library and a "buffet stocked with every 'medicinal comfort' known to mixology," a euphemism for a bar and perhaps cocktails. Hiscoe's hand was likely evident in thematic "corners"—an Indian corner, fishing corner, trapper's corner, as well as "fur, fin and feather" that were mounted on the walls.[8]

Interior of "Kabin," Kamp Kill Kare, built 1901–2. Photograph, c. 1923. The Kabin was for meetings and dancing downstairs and guests upstairs. On an island, it was reached by a foot-bridge several hundred feet long. Inscribed on the mantel of one of two opposite facing fireplaces is "Kare Killed the Kat, Here We Kill Kare." The Adirondack Museum (P62151).

It was used for entertaining associates and guests of the Woodruffs in early November of 1902, when a group of politicians and their wives gathered in Grand Central Station as evening papers carried reports of the reelection of both Governor Benjamin B. Odell and Lieutenant Governor Timothy Woodruff. In the party was a former political reporter, Henry Wellington Wack, who was to write an effusive but informative article about Kamp Kill Kare in the February 1903 issue of *Field and Stream.* The following evening the group was welcomed at the camp by bonfires set along the shore of the lake and on the camp grounds, and by colored lanterns suspended from the railings of the bridge to the Kabin. The effect, according to Mr. Wack, was "weird and beautiful." For the next five days, the men divided into smaller groups, one or two guides to each, and hunted deer, returning to camp by dark.

Woodruff and Garvan brought an interest in American history to Kamp Kill Kare. Woodruff's main building with its undressed logs with bark on the outside was said to have been "modeled in pre-Revolutionary style," while the playhouse built for Mr. Garvan some fifteen years later was assembled from parts of old buildings, perhaps in the manner of the historic interiors that were being reassembled in the American Wing at the Metropolitan Museum of Art. The playhouse contained beams from a century-old mill, pine paneling from another building, and a brick fireplace from an early Colonial house in Connecticut.[9]

Woodruff and Garvan had both been at Yale, though separated by twenty-five years. A third person with Yale credentials was Alfred G. Vanderbilt, who bought Sagamore Lodge in 1900 and would buy Kill Kare from Woodruff or his estate in 1913 and then sell it to Mr. and Mrs. Garvan in 1915.

The camp's amenities and attractions by 1903 included bathrooms with running water, piped from Green Mountain; enclosures for pet deer and a tame bear; the Kabin, said to be "a symposium of sport." In addition to two barns, there was a black-

Camp Topridge

Upper St. Regis Lake, Paul Smiths, N.Y.; 1920s with additions in the 1930s; Ted Blake, architect; Fred Vogel, interior designer.

Boathouse designed by Ben Muncil, who also was builder of the camp. Mrs. Post purchased a stone rubble camp and 207 acres of land from Alvin M. Lathrop about 1923. She replaced much of what had been there, adding a rustic boathouse and two funicular rail cars from the shore to the ridge that gave the camp its name. She moved between Topridge and large homes in Washington, D.C., and Palm Beach, Florida, by season: she spent July and August in the Adirondacks. She died at eighty-six in 1973. American Indian artifacts accepted by Smithsonian Institution traveled to Washington in three moving vans. See pages 180 and 202 for other illustrations.

Great Hall, Camp Topridge. Photograph, c. 1927. Steel beams replaced wood beams, 1938–39. Courtesy of Saranac Lake Free Library.

Dining room, Camp Topridge. Photograph, c. 1927. Courtesy of Saranac Lake Free Library.

Stairway to Great Hall, Camp Topridge. Photograph, c. 1927. Courtesy of Saranac Lake Free Library.

smith's shop where most of the hardware and lighting fixtures had been fashioned. One or two gondolas were shipped to the camp from Italy in 1902, an idea perhaps inspired by the pond in Central Park which also had these boats. Wack said that seventy could be accommodated at the camp, a number that seems high even counting rooms for employees. Bedrooms for family and guests were on second floors of three buildings, the main building, boathouse, and Kabin. There was telephone service by way of a line to Old Forge, N.Y.

An account of an entertainment at Kill Kare in 1899 was written by James S. Whipple, the Clerk of the Senate, and published in an Albany newspaper. If there was any concern about riling up critics who had asked how the lieutenant governor came to own an in-holding surrounded by State Forest Preserve, it is not evident in the story:

> We arrived at Camp Kill Kare just at dark, and as we drove across the ice . . . [of Lake Kora] near the camp, the bright lights hanging in many places among the trees about this beautiful woodland home of the [Lieutenant] Governor, flashed out their evening welcome. As we swung up to the door, the sleighbells jingling out their merry tunes, the guides received us taking the teams and helping us out of the sleigh. Inside the bright fires blazed from great stone fireplaces, and the table was spread with all the delicacies one would expect to find at Delmonico's.[10]

If his entertaining was intended to gain him the nomination for governor, Woodruff was disappointed, for the Republicans did not give it to him in 1904, the year he lost his wife. He remarried a year later, to Isabel Morrison.[11]

The Later Woodruff Period

A fire in 1908 occasioned Kill Kare's next stage of development. The fire started that winter while one of Woodruff's sons, John E. Woodruff, was at the camp with several friends. A newspaper story datelined Boonville, N.Y., for February 13, 1908, reported the loss of a building but not those adjacent to it, and said that some of the furnishings had been saved.

The 1908 fire helps explain a couple of unanswered questions about two buildings that do not appear in the album of photographs of the camp during the Woodruff era. One building was the tree-bed cottage, still standing, close to the main building but detached from it. The second building was the dining room modeled after an English great room in its cathedral ceiling of hewn and dark-stained trusses and rafters, replacing the former dining room with its low ceiling and bedroom above which burned.

The present dining room, which has a cathedral ceiling, may have been built as the replacement at this time. There is no hard evidence for this, although it can be inferred from the construction of the cottage with the tree bed, the design for which bears Hiscoe's mark and the date 1909.

These later buildings, ascribed to 1908–9, were open to the roof a full story above, representing a departure from the earlier buildings, which all seem to have had two

Room with tree bed. Charles C. Hiscoe, designer, 1909. Photograph by James Fynmore, 1960s. The Adirondack Museum (P9562).

floors and rooms with low ceilings, except perhaps for the Kabin. Heat from furnaces may have made cathedral ceilings more reasonable by this time. One of the first had been installed by William West Durant at Sagamore Lodge by the turn of the century. Nearly all of the cottages and residences at Kill Kare had a furnace by 1923.[12] The new dining room had the timber ceiling of a great hall in England during the Middle Ages. The carpentry was joinery of a high order, but it was anomalous in an otherwise all-rustic camp, and defies explanation. Formality at camp may have been a felt need, what with governors and other luminaries staying as guests. The dining room that burned was folkish and not formal, but it was proper all the same. An ar-

chitect certainly designed the English hall, and we might say it was designed by John Russell Pope during the changes made for the Garvans in 1915 and after, except Mrs. Francis P. Garvan, when she spoke with the author in 1974, said she had been puzzled by the absence of the hall in photographs of the camp when it was owned by the Woodruffs. The hall was there when she and her husband rented and then bought the camp.

Hiscoe's presence at Kill Kare is corroborated by several dated de-

Tree bed room. Compare this and the above photograph with Hiscoe's drawing of 1909, following. Photograph by Richard Linke, 1974. The Adirondack Museum (P40384).

Design for a room with a tree bed, "C. C.Hiscoe 09." Captain Hiscoe visited Kamp Kill Kare on four possible occasions—for the Woodruffs in 1897–99, 1902, and 1909; and the Garvans in 1915–17, when he designed and directed the furnishing of interiors for Mr. Garvan. He may have contributed ideas for the detailing of some buildings. The Adirondack Museum Library.

signs, the earliest of which is for the interior of the tree-bed cottage bearing "C. C. HISCOE 09" in the bottom right corner. The drawing is faithful to the room as photographed in subsequent years, down to the author's picture-taking visit in 1977. The fireplace in the drawing shows the same pyramid of rubble stones that appears, in the present bedroom, as though it might collapse and send rocks of bowling ball heft spilling across the floor. The dressing table and desk designed for the corners are still in the room, as are the bench built into the footboard of the bed and the gallery above the window facing the bed. Possibly the room was intended for Woodruff's second wife.

Great hall dining room, Lodge, Kamp Kill Kare, [?]1909. Modeled after the "Grete Hall" of a medieval manor house, this room is unlike any other room in its historicism; such rooms were replicated by architects for wealthy American patrons aspiring to upper class English pretentions. Photograph by James Fynmore, 1960s. The Adirondack Museum (P9571).

The Garvan Era

A second fire broke out at Kill Kare shortly after the Garvans had bought it from Mr. Vanderbilt. The Garvans, married in 1910, were introduced to the Adirondacks by Robert J. Collier, publisher of *Collier's Weekly* and owner of the former Stott camp at Bluff Point on Raquette Lake. The couple stayed at the Antlers one summer but rented Kamp Kill Kare from Vanderbilt in 1913 and 1914, buying it the next year. Mrs. Garvan, in her eighties when the author spoke with her, said that the superintendent, Dennis Linnehan, grabbed dynamite and set it off where the main building was burning, blowing out the fire and saving the cottage with its tree bed and the great hall for dining. A snapshot of the camp with smoke still rising shows nothing but three tall chimney stacks standing.[13] The dining room building and bedroom building cottage, which would be far left and far right, cannot be seen; that the person with the camera did not choose to include them in the picture is the obvious explanation.

Mrs. Garvan said that Captain Hiscoe wrote her husband to offer his assistance in restoring the camp. She said he re-did the Indian Room and the furniture which had been destroyed in the fire. Correspondence and designs from Hiscoe to her husband reveal a wider role for Hiscoe than the Indian Room, as will be seen.

"Indian Room," main building, Kamp Kill Kare, possibly as reconstructed by C. C. Hiscoe. Photograph, 1915–20. Wrought iron hardware and rustic furniture, like the pieces shown here, were produced in shops at Kamp Kill Kare. The Adirondack Museum Library.

"Original Sketch for Proposed Indian Room. By C. C. Hiscoe," dated, 1915. The Garvans asked Hiscoe to re-create the room as they had known it before it burned. The finished room thus owes something to the Woodruffs. Hiscoe may have painted the footboards. The Adirondack Museum Library.

Hiscoe was but one of several key figures who share credit for Kamp Kill Kare as it emerged, beginning with Francis Garvan, who was a man of taste, like the Woodruffs, but with a passion for making the camp a place for displaying some of the American art and antiques that he had only started to collect at the time of the fire. He was still collecting in 1930 when he promised his collection to Yale, where it now fills a museum.[14] Very much in charge, Mr. Garvan chose John Russell Pope as an architect. Pope, a fashionable New York architect, would later design the National Gallery of Art in Washington, as well as the railroad station in Plattsburgh, N.Y. An architectural firm from Utica was hired to oversee the carrying out of Pope's plans. Contractors and foremen were in charge of workmen at the site. Construction continued for some years, just how many is uncertain; publication of an article about the camp, in December, 1923, suggests that work was finished by then, eight years after the fire.[15]

Kamp Kill Kare during re-construction and expansion, 1915–17. John Russell Pope, chief architect. Compare the cobblestone chimneys with ashlar chimneys of the lodge before the fire (p. 277). The lodge seems rebuilt, but the new boathouse is still under construction. Photograph by H. M. Beach. Visible to the right is the footbridge to the Kabin on the island. The Adirondack Museum (P9424).

Hiscoe's job may never have been defined; as decorator, a term used by him, he was to restore the rusticity of the camp as the Garvans had known it from the one or two summers they had spent in it, in 1913 and 1914. They kept the alliterative K-names of the lake and the camp and its buildings when they might have changed them all. However, they drew a line on the obsessive rusticity of the camp, in which the walls of smaller farm or service buildings were fashioned from poles nailed to boards, sometimes in patterns. We do not know that this superfluity of rusticity had been Hiscoe's doing earlier, when

he was working for the Woodruffs; in any event, the early rustic buildings disappeared, to be replaced by John Russell Pope's stone barn and stable.

We do know that Hiscoe submitted a design for a chapel at Kill Kare, and that it was rejected and seems to have led to a falling-out between him and Garvan. Hiscoe's relationship to John Russell Pope, the design architect for the entire camp, including an elegant Norman chapel in a clearing in the woods, is uncertain. It is apparent from correspondence that Hiscoe was working for Garvan and not Pope; how agreements were reached among Garvan, contractors, Hiscoe, and the firm Warren & Clark, Pope's architects on the site, remains to be seen.

Farm building, Kamp Kill Kare. John Russell Pope, architect. Photograph by James Fynmore, 1960s. The Adirondack Museum (P9571).

Papers recently donated to the Adirondack Museum by Bea Garvan, widow of Anthony N. B. Garvan, reveal that Hiscoe was one of three or four men in authority at the camp at this time. Hiscoe drew a proposed alteration to the stairway between first and second floor porches of a log building and sent it to Mr. Garvan. On the sketch he wrote that several others had approved it, including "Mr. Rogers," likely Garry Rogers, who had been the superintendent for William West Durant at Sagamore Lodge in 1897–99.[16] From this it seems Rogers was a foreman at Kill Kare in 1917.

Hiscoe's rapidly drawn but sure ink sketches reveal an artistic ability. In his letters to Garvan he gives no sign that he is or thinks he is in charge of anyone at the site; but his alleged background as a naval officer and especially his writing ability gave him an advantage over the others with responsibilities comparable to his own. He was a bearer of news to Garvan, typing long letters that are circumspect and leave much to be concluded by Garvan, whom he treats like a patron—no suggestion proffered that could not be withdrawn: he gossiped while denying any intent to do so.

Writing from Kill Kare on June 8, 1917, he says that he spoke to Rogers about the plans and elevations for the barns, which he found so "thoroughly good as to be above criticism from me." These were Pope's barns of cyclopean stone, and his praise reflects good judgment. He tried hanging the African horns that Garvan had sent in the apartment that was to be Garvan's quarters in the boathouse, but they were "too many" and "monotonous," giving the "general effect of a bone-yard." He weeded some out and combined the best of the weapons with them, with "a few bits of brass and copper and pottery on the shelves," which made for an "artistic ensemble."

He speaks of rugs and carpets for various rooms and says he is glad to learn that Garvan had found some lanterns, the arrival of which Hiscoe awaits with "pleasurable anticipation," since he is to be allowed to place them around the camp as he thinks best. He has not gotten to the "decorative work" in the Casino and the Island Camp (Kabin), but those tasks can be dispatched rapidly. He photographed the trench for the new sewage system and will send pictures when he receives the proofs. (An outbreak of typhoid fever at Kill Kare in 1916 is unmentioned.) The window shades at John Wanamaker's are awfully expensive, he agrees, but he understands Mr. Garvan's dilemma and supposes they should be ordered anyway, since more than 100 are needed.

He reports that George Wilson replied that he could grow red and white gardenias in the greenhouse as well as any other flower, and then, in a finely penned note inserted between typed lines, remarks that Wilson "now says there are no *'red'* garde-

"As now" and "As suggested," sketch showing proposed alterations to a building at Kamp Kill Kare. C. C. Hiscoe to Frances P. Garvan, dated May 3, 1917. The Adirondack Museum Library.

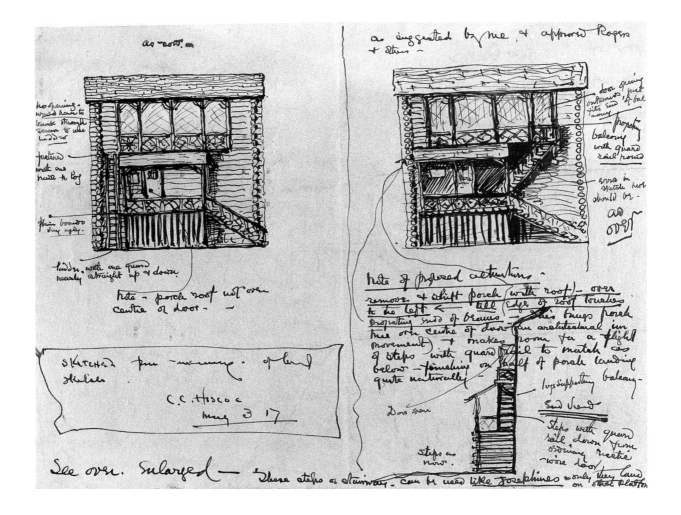

nias," as in no-such-thing. Wilson and Hiscoe were not friendly, as this small contretemps suggests; elsewhere Hiscoe complained to Garvan that Wilson was a "loafer." Hiscoe stood out among the workers at Kamp Kill Kare: he was English while many of the others may well have had parents from Ireland. Indeed, Mr. and Mrs. Garvan were Irish American (she was a Brady), and Wilson was said to have been Scottish.

Ambling on, Hiscoe recites an episode in which Garvan's black team of horses were agitated in a rainstorm and wanted to "rush to their stable." Hiscoe was standing by when he overheard a fellow named Devine comment that the blacks "were the meanest team you had, afraid of [an] automobile and with a tendency to lose their heads." It was "only gossip but perhaps worthy of mentioning," Hiscoe wrote, that Devine remarked that the gray pair was "gentle as kittens and afraid of nothing" and "much better for children" than the blacks.

Garvan exercised considerable taste or judgment at Kill Kare despite his absence and his appointment as Chief of the U.S. Bureau of Investigation and Alien Property Custodian in New York City when the United States declared war on Germany in 1917. It seems he cautioned Hiscoe about overcrowding, for Hiscoe concludes his four-page single spaced typed letter by asking Garvan not to worry, but that excessive "decorations" could be weeded out if desired.

Meddlesome as he may have been, Hiscoe's hand is very evident in those interiors for which he chiefly seems to have been responsible—the lodge or main building, especially the Indian Bedroom, and the cottage next door with its spectacular rustic interior after his design of 1909. From what he wrote, he seems to have arranged furnishings in many if not most of the buildings, both older ones as well as the new ones being built. The selection of objects may have been as much or more a matter of Garvan's doing than his own.

Hiscoe could not have gotten the effects he did without assistance from men who could make the furniture from his designs. Indeed, a writer for the Pope firm acknowledged this in the 1923 article in *Country Life,* in which the buildings, being of "logs, with irregular roofs," were built by workmen "after sketches" sent up from the firm's office in the city. The "atmosphere of informality" at the camp likely derived from "the fact that they [the buildings] were built by native labor that evolved the details as the work progressed." The outcome, the unidentified writer said, "would have been very different had the artisans been required to follow details laid down in a city office." Similar praise could be made for the improvisational abilities of Adirondack men at other camps.

There were several types of furniture in the camp—plain country stuff for the superintendent's house and antique furniture, including a quantity of Windsor chairs, in guest cottages.[17] But much of the furniture was rustic, some dating from the first years of the camp, to judge from photographs of the late 1890s; more of it was produced for the Garvans in the expansion of 1915–23, "made on the spot" by local workmen and consisting largely of tables and beds fashioned from whole and half logs.

One maker not previously known to the author had the name Stickney, "a darned

good man . . . clever, quick and full of enthusiasm," according to Hiscoe, sounding like a naval officer. Log furniture could be made in quantity and was far easier to clean than bark-covered furniture. There was ornamental rustic furniture—tables with burl tops that took a polish that brought out their spectacular graining. The half-spherical tops were so heavy that bird-cage pedestals or tree roots were needed to hold them up. Much of the furniture and furnishings remained with the camp when it was sold in 1980.

In the fall of 1917, when he was remodeling rooms of the Garvan children at their home in New York, Hiscoe seems to have angered Garvan, the reason later forgotten or buried. He complained in a letter of December 20 to James Hamill, who may have been Garvan's secretary, of a "rebuke," either from Garvan or Hamill. The following February, he got termination notice in a letter dated the nineteenth from Osborne, Lamb & Garvan, a law firm at 115 Broadway in the city. Agreement on severance terms came the following June in a document offering $2,000 in exchange for Hiscoe's return of plans and correspondence still in his possession.

In 1930, in the first year of the Great Depression, an insurance agent gave the best idea of the extent of the camp in a report that is edited for brevity.[18] There were, he

Living room of lodge ("Casino"), Kamp Kill Kare. This room and the building enclosing it were likely rebuilt by John Russell Pope, 1915–16; compare these windows with their counterparts outside in the Woodruff family group portrait (p. 276). Early photograph. The pool table was made at the camp. The Adirondack Museum (P62135).

said, ten to twelve employees in winter and thirty to forty in summer. The fish hatchery below the dam at Kill Kare had been removed by 1930.

The Main Camp. Consisting from the front, l. to r., Mrs. Garvan's cottage with its tree bed (1909); and, in four buildings connected by passageways, a living room or casino with cathedral ceiling (possibly John Russell Pope, c. 1915); a cottage with the Indian Room on the first floor and bedroom above (c. 1915); a play room and library for children, possibly with bedrooms above (c. 1915); the dining room on the lines of a medieval English hall, with trussed cathedral ceiling (c. 1909); an octagonal dining pavilion. Behind the dining room were kitchen, laundry, other service areas and servants' quarters (c. 1915).

Boathouse and Residence. John Russell Pope, architect, 1917. Mr. Garvan's library, living room and bedroom, plus several guest bedrooms. A theater for showing movies was on the boathouse level.

Kabin. 1901. Two floors with assembly room and bedrooms for guests. Removed was the 300 foot rustic bridge to the island that was built c. 1917. The Kabin still on the island was neglected, according to Mrs. Garvan in 1974.

Two Cottages. John Russell Pope, architect, before 1923. One cottage was for the camp superintendent.

Playhouse. John Russell Pope, architect, before 1923. An early American tap-room and collections of pewter and antique furniture on the first floor and various firearms, powder horns, and weaponry—2,000 items—on the second. Also two bowling alleys and squash court with skylight.

Norman Chapel. John Russell Pope, architect, c. 1918. Stone, with a slate roof, authentic except for its reduced scale.

Three Cottages. For resident electrician and other employees, the largest cottage contained a kitchen, big dining room, laundry, and pump house that was the camp's source of water until a remote pond was tapped.

Barn Complex. John Russell Pope, architect, 1917–18. Constructed of massive unfinished quarried stone, this contained a tower with gateway, a barn for cows, dairy, stable for horses, wagon and carriage rooms, plus a playroom, and shops for a carpenter and blacksmith.

Kamp Keen Kut. From Woodruff era, formerly for men guests but used for dances in 1930.

Greenhouse and *Gardener's Cottage.* Before 1923.

Two Ice Houses, Cooler and Dairy.

Woodshed. 100 by 30 feet, containing about 500 cords of wood.

Two lean-tos. Partially filled with balsam boughs.

Generator House and Light Plant.

Pump House. 1917. For sewerage system.

Small Boat House. Open on four sides with storage for row boats and canoes.

Miscellaneous. Silo, two "farm buildings," hog house, tool house, storage building for chemicals and dynamite, spring house.

Neither the Woodruffs nor the Garvans harvested the thousand-acre preserve, and the buildings inventoried above were largely confined to a few dozen acres.

Later Life at Kill Kare

Seven children were born to Mr. and Mrs. Garvan (one, Patricia, died of diphtheria when a small girl). The entire Yale baseball team often stayed at the camp and played against a team from Raquette Lake. Kill Kare in summer was a place alive with young people. Tony Garvan, the next to the youngest of seven siblings, was born at Kill Kare. He spoke of his carefree years at Kill Kare and the piquancy of life there, part of which lay in making life in the woods look easy.

As a professor of American architecture and culture, he was conscious that the joyous life at Kill Kare had been a passing moment, barely two generations long, and that it was made possible by infusions of money. By the 1960s, it was fading as a way of life, likely to disappear at his mother's death, which it did, in 1979. He inquired, without much hope, whether the Adirondack Museum might be interested in taking the camp. A small endowment might help defray the costs, but it would not, as he implied without saying so, be sufficient to keep the camp occupied and in repair. The matter was moot, in any event, since there were some thirty-four beneficiaries whose interests had to be consulted.

Kamp Kill Kare was one of three neighboring trophy or prodigy camps, each having a connection to William West Durant, who seems to have introduced a spirit of cooperation among the owners and staffs at the three properties which continued long after his departure from the region in 1901–2. Services and even employees were exchanged among the camps, and teams from the camps got together in friendly competitions, especially between Kill Kare and Sagamore Lodge, which each had bowling alleys and facilities for recreation missing at Camp Uncas.

Dana Winslow, a grandson of the senior Garvans and now a judge on Long Island, remembers sitting at the knee of "Uncle George" at a baseball game at Kill Kare, a reference to General George Marshall, the former five-star general who was then, in 1949, U.S. Secretary of State.[19] Marshall and his wife, together with Madame Chiang Kai-shek, of Nationalist China, were guests of Margaret Emerson at Camp Uncas, which Mrs. Emerson had bought a year or two earlier from the Morgan family.[20] Mrs. Emerson stayed at her camp, Sagamore Lodge, three miles distant.

Judge Winslow shared his recollections of his grandmother's camp to which he was brought as a baby (he was born in 1939) and continuing nearly every summer until 1979. Kill Kare's team was semi-professional, and it divided into two teams, the Punkies and Horseflys, which competed against one another when not playing outside teams, such as the one in Raquette Lake. Team manager was Francis P. Garvan, Jr., a son of Mr. and Mrs. Garvan. Winslow pinch-hit for the team in the early fifties, he said. Dan Topping, owner of the Yankees baseball team, was a visitor with his family.

Aerial view of Kamp Kill Kare, 1980. Buildings from bottom to top: Boathouse, Lodge, Tree Bed Cottage. Kitchen and service building are to the right of the lodge in this photograph. Roofs reveal a composite of individual but attached buildings. Photograph by Peter and Rosine Lemon, 1980.

A priest conducted mass in the chapel at eight on Sunday mornings, after which, at nine, campers and priest ate breakfast. Afternoons might be spent fishing or bowling. Children got to eat with adults when they reached their mid-teens. Winslow slept in the Children's Cottage until he was seventeen, after which he moved to a bedroom in the boathouse and then to family quarters off the casino in the main building. They made many visits to the camp in winter, he said.

Staff numbered approximately thirty-five in the sixties and included at least five employees who generally accompanied Mrs. Garvan to her four New York residences at Millbrook, Old Westbury, the Adirondacks, and in Manhattan: a butler, a chef, a personal maid, a personal assistant, and a chauffeur. Four college students worked as bellboys each summer through 1965, and a man was posted at the dock. Leo Small was superintendent in the 1960s, and he was replaced in the seventies by Al Smith, whose wife, Dorothy, was a cook. There was an executive chef and *sous chef,* plus two cooks and two assistants to prepare food for family, guests, and staff in the kitchens at the camp. The superintendent and his wife lived year-round at the camp, as did a man named Riley Parsons who had been an electrician at Kamp Kill Kare for over thirty-five years. Riley's son Ricky attended schools in Raquette Lake and Old Forge for twelve years and never missed a single day.

Two men traveled and camped for almost three months in the Adirondacks in the 1850s. Emblematic of their "small pecuniary outlay," less than $100, was a woodcut of a banknote with a hole framing mountains, lakes, and trees, illustrated in an account in *The Great Republic Monthly* for April 1859.

Appendixes

Notes

Bibliography

Index

"Great" Camps and Their Care

Historic Preservation Comes to the Adirondacks

The earliest *public* acknowledgment of large Adirondack camps may have occurred in 1978 with dissemination of "Great Camps of the Adirondacks," a research report prepared by the Preservation League of New York State, a private consortium of preservation groups in the state. The earliest unofficial use, and possibly the first by a scholar, was in 1970 when Arnold Lehman, then a graduate student at Yale, undertook a study of the camps and called his manuscript "Great Camps of the Adirondacks: A Wilderness Architecture," a copy of which, with photographs, is in the library at the Adirondack Museum.[1]

I objected to the use of the word "great" by the Preservation League for reasons given below but could not offer a credible alternative when my book *Durant* was published in 1981. When *Great Camps of the Adirondacks* was published the next year, by Harvey Kaiser, an architect and facilities administrator at Syracuse University, the term was further buttressed; long in print, "Great Camp" had become a part of the vocabulary of architectural historians.

Despite my caveats, the reader will find the locution in this book. "Great Camp" comes trippingly off the tongue of almost everybody, preservationists among them. In 1998 Paul Malo used "Prodigy," as in "Prodigy Log Interior," pointing the way to an alternative which might introduce clarity or nuance in our conversations and writings about Adirondack camps.[2] Kamp Kill Kare is a Prodigy Camp, at least to my way of thinking, which is why it was awarded the last chapter in this book. Camps that are significant but fall short of Kill Kare's artistic innovativeness might be termed, as I have done on these pages, "Trophy Camps," the title of chapter 10 and applicable to the camps cited in chapter 11 as well. Camps designed by architects were "Decorous Camps," a larger category enclosing Trophy Camps, which itself enclosed the more-exclusive Prodigy Camp.

My objection to "great" is that it is self-validating, and so, being incapable of discriminating one great camp from another, shuts off analysis before it can get started:

"Great Camp" can be trumped only by "greater" and "greatest," so a camp's merits are ratified before it can be analyzed. Dr. Kaiser's *Great Camps,* for those who read the text, has as much to do with the celebrity status of owners as with the architecture of the camps themselves.

The Preservation League and Dr. Kaiser both found "Great Camp" useful because as a concept it was quickly grasped by people who knew little about the particulars of the camps but needed a common point for discussion to begin. This led to the appearance of consensus that was useful in efforts to attract attention to the camps in the 1970s and 1980s. "Great Camp," instantly grasped by legislators and administrators, served as the major premise that the camps were worth saving.

Neither the Preservation League nor Harvey Kaiser examined "Great Camp" with rigor, saying in effect that the camps were communities with many buildings and retinues of family, guests, and staff in the woods, and leaving it at that. Glibness can be partially explained by the newness of the Adirondack region to historic preservation issues. Awareness that the camps were vulnerable came late, in 1975, when Syracuse University announced it was selling Sagamore Lodge, both the camp and farm buildings, and a preserve of some 1,500 acres of forest land. These had been given to the university as a gift from Margaret Emerson about twenty years earlier, to be used as part of the university's program in continuing education.

A result was a conference on cultural properties in the Adirondacks that was held at Camp Topridge in 1978 largely as an initiative of Lieutenant Governor Mary Ann Krupsak. It was the first gathering on historic preservation in the Adirondack Park, and Sagamore was fresh in everybody's minds, the urgency being that if a college or university, regarded as the best societal steward of cultural properties, could now treat them as part of an investment portfolio, then the camps were in real jeopardy.

Preservation in the Adirondacks is a special case: buildings on Forest Preserve land cannot be repaired or used, according to the State Constitution. Court rulings have upheld the "forever wild" provision that bans nonconforming structures—including camps—on state land inside the Adirondack Park. Excepted are state lands needed for management or administrative purposes, an admitted loophole that environmentalists watch like hawks.

Support for the camps came mostly from outside the Adirondack Park. Some of these were camp owners: Anthony Garvan and his wife, Bea, of Philadelphia, one a college professor and the other a curator, at Kamp Kill Kare, and Howard Kirschenbaum and Barbara Glaser, educators from Saratoga Springs. Joan Davidson, formerly chairman of the New York State Council on the Arts and later appointed by Governor Cuomo to the Department of Recreation and Historic Preservation, facilitated a foundation grant that helped in the formation of Adirondack Architectural Heritage (AARCH) in 1989, principally on Dr. Kirschenbaum's initiative. Officials in government were supportive, as when the 1978 conference was followed by a letter from Peter Berle, the commissioner of the Department of Environmental Conservation, acknowledging that the buildings at Santanoni were of "indisputable" cultural and architectural significance.[3] The conference and its report sent a go-slow message on the acquisition of land that happened to have camps. Environmental organizations like the Adirondack Conservancy, an intermediary between buyers and sellers, learned that a constituency of preservationists now had to be consulted.

It seems to have worked: mutuality of concern was reciprocated among state agencies, environmentalists, and historic preservationists for twenty years, although seeming agreement was never seriously tested. The region has its own home-grown preservation organization in AARCH, which has an educational program, newsletter, an office and director in Keesville, N.Y., and a board drawn largely from inside the Adirondack Park.

Origin of Great

The closest the writer has come to a source for "Great Camp" is an article, "The New Adirondacks," which appeared in *The Outlook* magazine for 1916. In it, Raymond Spears criticized "dilettantish people who built huge mansions and called them 'camps.'" Hundreds of men had been called out, he wrote, "to save the great 'camp'" from fire on occasion.[4] A "grete lodge" is cited in the Oxford English Dictionary for the year 1465, in which the term may derive as much from the status of the owner as from the building.

Certainty as to the attributes of a Great Camp dissolves as we get to particulars. The camps were not as big as people would believe; country houses in the Berkshire Mountains of Massachusetts were more expansive at that time. American country houses did not come close to matching the splendor of country houses in Britain, as a reading of Gervaise Jackson-Stops's *The English Country House: A Grand Tour* may reveal to the reader.[5]

Another attribute of the Great Camp is its multiple buildings—guest cottages and dependencies in proximity to a central or main building. But camps of guides had clusters of cabins, bark lean-tos, and tents arrayed on shorefronts on Blue Mountain Lake, Raquette Lake, and Smith's Lake (now Lake Lila), as the author tried to point out in chapters 3 and 7. These camps predated Camp Pine Knot, the first of the Great Camps. Pine Knot was totally unlike field camps used by guides, as its inventory of china, glass, and silver makes clear, but it was not the first multi-building camp in the Adirondacks.[6]

Artistic intent is a difference. This was noted in the Preservation League's *Research Report* of 1978, in which it is said that Great Camps "demonstrate a singular design response to the wilderness environment" created through "deliberate, aesthetic choices." The word "deliberate" implies that Durant and others chose local materials in preference to others that might have been used but were not. Qualification is needed here, for gentry always have dressed summer rooms and cottages with wildflowers, Japanese fans, family pictures, picture postcards, and similar ephemera. Lady Mary Wortley Montague, in a farmhouse that she rented the summer of 1748 near Brescia, Italy, said she had "fitted up" one of the rooms for herself, strewing the floor with rushes, covering the chimney with moss and branches, and placing bouquets of flowers in earthenware containers around it. Her only furniture was a couch bed and "some straw chairs."[7] This is what genteel Americans began to do when they came to the Adirondacks not so much to extract something from it—deer and fish—as to be spectators of its beauties and renewed in mind and body. Accordingly, reticence, and not greatness, as in grandeur, was William West Durant's object at Camp Pine Knot.

Camps as Institutional White Elephants

"Out of sight, out of mind" accounts for the neglect of camps in institutional hands, a consequence of their remoteness from the offices where decisions are reached. It is difficult to make a case for repair of a camp when administrators who make decisions affecting the camps are hundreds of miles from the camps and every day see much that needs to be done in their own backyard.

The camps were useful as a bookkeeping device: some overhead and staffing costs incurred at the main office could be assigned to the camp, a bookkeeping tactic that virtually guaranteed that Adirondack camps would appear to operating executives and boards of trustees to be a bigger financial drain on the parent organization than they really were. The camps were like step-children; their welfare was in the hands of a home office.

The camps have always suffered from benign neglect, and this originates in uncertainty about their institutional role. Inexperience with camps is a reason, although plant maintenance and adherence to preservation standards, one would think, should be no mystery to a college or university. (Syracuse University did a better job of keeping Sagamore Lodge and its roads in good repair than did most other institutional owners.) Without a plan other than to house and feed numbers of people, the physical plant and even the furnishings were at the mercy of complacent managers and conference registrants and campers who stayed at the camps and had little more regard for them than the chain-owned conference centers and motels found on the outskirts of most American cities.

Their legacy of wealth and privilege made it easier to neglect or even dismiss the camps; what viable message could possibly be extracted from these rustic playgrounds? The perception in the early 1970s was that the camps had little permanent or lasting value, a perpetual interim status the equivalent of limbo: those who managed them behaved as though the fate of the camps would be decided by their successors and not by them.

Set alongside the majesty of the "forever wild" clause of the State Constitution, appeals to save the camps seemed frivolous. Camps as toys of a class and era satirized by writers and discredited by historians thus was a subtle rationalization for neglect. By definition, as implied in the introduction to this book, camps were a transitory phenomenon—each had its moment in the sun but was fated to succumb to the forest. Permanent camps are intrusive to those who hold the idea of the primacy of wilderness.

The argument might be more convincing had the camps damaged the preserves of which they were, after all, a small part—perhaps twenty acres of buildings plus another fifty or so acres of farm and pasture land, or seldom more than one or two percent of cleared land out of forest preserves of a thousand acres of forest land. Private families and clubs have been good stewards of the woods, wildlife, and waters in their care. At the time of the Sagamore sale in the mid-seventies, however, no one was ready to make that argument.

Preservation

Syracuse University received Sagamore Lodge in 1953–55 from Margaret Emerson, second wife and the widow of Alfred G. Vanderbilt, for the purposes of continuing education. In 1974, citing financial need, the university announced it was seeking a buyer for the preserve. It already had disposed of a second Adirondack camp, Camp Pinebrook, on Upper Saranac Lake. The university promised it would keep a third camp, Minnowbrook, on Blue Mountain Lake, as its commitment to continue its presence in the Adirondacks.

Sagamore's main enclave with the Swiss Chalet at its center was acquired by Howard Kirschenbaum and Barbara Glaser, who operated the National Humanistic Foundation, which ran conferences and workshops similar to those conducted by the university. This was a welcome outcome, as was the acquisition by New York State of nearly all the 1,500 acre preserve, including most of the frontage on Sagamore Lake. A problem soon became apparent: the farm buildings now were in state hands, the buyers of the main camp having been reluctant to take responsibility for the upkeep of a dozen farm buildings along with the dozen or so they already owned.

The omission of the farm was soon seen to be an oversight, since the farm had allowed the show-part of the camp to exist. Among its buildings were two staff cottages and a schoolhouse for the five children of Richard Collins, who had worked for William West Durant in the late 1890s and was superintendent at Sagamore Lodge from the 1920s to 1933, when he opened the Hedges, the former Duryea house, as a hotel on Blue Mountain Lake.

Sagamore's farm buildings were saved when the Preservation League of New York State gave assurances of its backing, and Dr. Kirschenbaum began a campaign to acquire the farm by exchanging it for land more suited to the Forest Preserve somewhere else. The process was enormously complicated, requiring an amendment to the State Constitution which had to gain approval in two successive sessions of the Legislature followed by voter approval in a ballot measure in a November election. This was accomplished, and tours of Sagamore now include the restored farm buildings, as well as the main camp.

The university auctioned off many of the furnishings, a loss that diminished the ability of the camp's educators to interpret the camp to the public. The university also retained the "stumpage" on the land—the marketable trees on the preserve. This decision was accepted by the Department of Environmental Conservation, which preferred a tract without most of its standing timber so sun would promote new growth and attract deer and other wildlife. The amount paid by the state was reduced by the value of the timber recouped by the university.

Its interest in the Adirondacks has been in land and not buildings, but the state has found itself holding good buildings like Camp Santanoni, along with minor structures of little merit. Santanoni, an important employer from 1900 to 1940, is one of the few cultural attractions remaining in Newcomb, N.Y. Aware of this, government officials and even a few environmentalists have been reluctant to enforce the "forever wild" provision at Santanoni, an instance in which good can come from bureaucratic foot-dragging.

Still, many small buildings have been removed by the Department of Environmental Conservation on newly acquired Forest Preserve land. Cabin owners were notified and given time to move their structures. This happened with the log cabin on Buck Lake, which was moved to the Adirondack Museum in 1990. A number of hunting camps on formerly leased tracts that had been sold to the state were destroyed. The state razed Forest Lodge, which had been designed by Robert H. Robertson for the Webb family.

Camp Topridge has had a quixotic history. It was offered to and turned down by C. W. Post College on Long Island, even though Marjorie Merriweather Post, heir to the cereal fortune and married four times, had been the college's benefactor. After her death in 1973, two other Post homes, one in Washington, D.C., and the other in Florida, were slow to find takers. Hillwood was turned down by the Smithsonian Institution, which deemed the endowment with it would be inadequate for its maintenance. The Palm Springs residence, which she called the "cottage" despite its one hundred rooms, was accepted and then turned back by the National Park Service, perhaps because gold plated fixtures in bathrooms carried no socially redeeming message.

New York State ended up with Mrs. Post's Adirondack camp, which consisted of some forty-five buildings and 207 acres with two ponds and frontage on Upper St. Regis Lake, which had perhaps a greater concentration of old money than any lake in the Adirondacks (a camp fetched $12,000 in rent for six weeks one summer in the 1890s). A hundred acres was transferred to the Forest Preserve, with the remaining land reserved for the camp enclave.

Initially, the thinking in Albany was that the facility might be owned by the state but operated locally, either by a town government or by Paul Smith's College. Public tours were offered by the Saranac Lake Chamber of Commerce, and occasional conferences and dinners were catered by the college, which taught hotel management and culinary arts along with forestry at the campus nearby. The college was operating the Hotel Saranac, so adding Camp Topridge as a complementary hospitality venue was a logical fit. Jobs were needed in the region, and the mutuality of interest among the parties—state, college, and the communities of Paul Smiths and Saranac Lake—seemed obvious.

Mrs. Post never intended that the camp be part of the Forest Preserve, which may have been why the Governor Carey administration went around the Department of

Environmental Conservation, placing the camp under the jurisdiction of the Office of General Services, which oversees the state's sprawling empire of buildings and structures. A shortage of housing was expected during the Winter Olympics that was to be held in Lake Placid in 1980, so Topridge seemed eminently suited to be a hospitality center for the state, which was to be official host during the month-long preparations and the playing of the Olympic events.

But it was the press and not environmentalists that spoiled plans for a multi-use public and private facility at Topridge after the Olympics. Stories about the use of the camp by Governor Carey and his family turned Topridge into a hot potato. The headline of the *Lake Placid News* for October 7, 1977, was typical: "Care of 'White Elephant' Costs State $70,000 a Year." Coverage of this kind, habitual in the region, warned local elected officials not to go to bat for this venture, or any others involving local tax expenditures. The *Saranac Lake Daily Enterprise* was selective in its coverage, never complaining about taxpayers' millions being poured into Lake Placid and Saranac Lake and vicinity. Elected officials responded as the area's two newspapers prescribed—local taxpayers should not contribute to Topridge's upkeep.

When Mario Cuomo became governor, he ordered that Topridge be auctioned. The state put conditions in the deed, including a prohibition on selling alcoholic beverages, a restriction unsatisfactory to some buyers. Another condition, which the state later seems to have dropped, required an owner to open Topridge to public visitation for a brief period each year. The winning bid of $911,000 in 1985 was a bargain given an assessment of $3 million for the camp in 1977.

The buyer was Roger Jacubowski, formerly a resident of Camden, N.J., who had made money selling hot dogs on the boardwalks of Atlantic City and Ocean City. Roger, as he liked to be called, made good newspaper copy, as when a *New York Times* reporter compared him to Mrs. Post, to which he demurred, saying he was a "Polish kid from Camden." Mrs. Post took a cereal fortune from her father in 1914 and built it into the General Foods Corporation and a still bigger fortune.

Mr. Jacubowski in time bought the ski slope and a radio station in Tupper Lake, using the WRGR call-letters as a play on his first name. He bought land around Lake Ozonia and Valcour Island, a historic island on Lake Champlain near Plattsburgh, both purchases arousing fears of development. The island had been the site of a burial for sailors killed in a battle of the War of 1812, and it additionally had a historic lighthouse. Warming to these attentions, Mr. Jacubowski told reporters he had bested the state when he got Camp Topridge and the island: bureaucrats would never be a match for men of vision and daring like himself. Not long after, he was declared bankrupt, many of his assets were dispersed, and local reporters previously eager for interviews no longer sought him out.

Camp Topridge was sold by his creditors in the early 1990s to Harlan Crow, a real estate developer from Texas. A *New York Times* writer raised a troublesome issue, whether renovations to buildings designated as essential to the integrity of Topridge by the Office of Parks, Recreation, and Historic Preservation, as stated in the deed that conveyed the property to Mr. Crow, had been altered or even removed.[8]

Camp Uncas adjoining Sagamore has had a checkered history. Bought by the investment banker J. Pierpont Morgan from William West Durant in 1895, it passed to his children, Jack and Anne Morgan, in 1913. Both enjoyed outdoor sport and were frequent visitors. It was sold to Margaret Emerson, owner of neighboring Sagamore Lodge, and she seems to have donated it to a medical foundation in New York City in 1953. The foundation did not hold it for long, since the property was bought by Uncas Estates, Inc., a name that implied a future subdivision for the 1,500 acre preserve and Mohegan Lake. The camp was opened briefly as a museum, but it was sold again, this time to directors of the Rockland (N.Y.) County Council of the Boy Scouts of America.

Scouts camped in tents in a distant clearing while their supervisors slept in the Manor House, and bathed, as one Scout leader boasted to the writer in 1973, in Mr. Morgan's capacious bathtub. In 1975, in poor repair and depleted of furnishings sold at auction, the buildings and land under them were purchased by Howard Kirschenbaum and Barbara Glaser, who were instrumental in acquiring Sagamore Lodge at roughly the same period. They and a third party own the camp, while nearly all of the Uncas Preserve was purchased by the state and is now part of the Forest Preserve.

The storied Lake Placid Club resembled an impoverished aristocrat out of a Russian novel when the author stayed in it for a few days during a meeting of the Garden Clubs of America in 1973; it was a shadow of what it had been in its glory days. Business people in Lake Placid looked to the club's restoration in the upcoming 1980 Winter Olympics. However, the prospects of the facility were hardly better and perhaps worse after the event than before, except for time-sharing condominiums that were built on club grounds.

Even if it had been restored and retrofitted, the building would always have been a fire hazard given the amount of wood that went into its construction. The club's owner, Melvil Dewey, understood this, for, consistent with his policy to keep the club largely independent, he installed hydrants on the grounds and in the Clubhouse, and employed men who patrolled for fire around the clock. Hopes were raised when Gleneagles, a partnership that included Guinness Brewery of Britain, proposed to fix up the grounds, renovate a portion of the clubhouse, rebuild the golf courses, and construct modern condominiums off the fairways. Reaction predictably was divided: environmentalists said the development was both too intensive and too intrusive, a position generally taken by the Adirondack Park Agency, which reviews high-impact development proposals in the region. A few residents and neighbors of the village, already familiar with congestion on the town's narrow and winding streets, asked how the town, a quarter of a mile away, would cope with additional traffic and the extra burden on town services.

Business people were euphoric over the prospect, since a revitalized L.P.C. was seen as the engine to revive the tiny mountain community so it would be a world-class winter resort once again. Renewal required deep pockets and management with a commitment to excellence. After months of exchanges between supporters and opponents, plus reviews by the Adirondack Park Agency, the Gleneagles partnership called it quits and withdrew, buying a languishing resort hotel in Manchester, Vermont, the Equinox, spending millions of dollars, and turning it into a first-class hotel.

The departure of Gleneagles dashed the club's hopes. Ten arson attempts were made on club buildings in under ten months; the eighth, in 1992, led to the demolition of much of the main lodge, violating a 1988 agreement between an earlier owner who wanted to tear it down on safety grounds and the National Advisory Council on Historic Preservation.[9] Subsequently, the six Tiffany windows, in the custody of an insurance company, were removed from the chapel by specialists and placed in storage for safe-keeping. The Lake Placid Club complex was purchased by a family corporation, Placid Gold. Refurbished golf courses and tennis courts were components of what was advertised as the Lake Placid Resort, but the assembly areas called the Agora, consisting of auditorium and chapel, and the hotel building, all designed by William G. Distin in 1924, were boarded up in 1998, which was their status when this book went to press.[10]

APPENDIX B

Projects of W. W. Durant, William Coulter, and William Distin

William West Durant (1850–1934)

Durant was not an architect, although he owned draftsman's tools and is known to have had R. Newton Brezee (1851–1929), a Saratoga Springs architect, finish his drawings. For more information, the reader is advised to consult the author's *Durant: The Fortunes and Woodland Camps of a Family in the Adirondacks* (1986), as well as Harold K. Hochschild's *Township 34* (1951).

DURANT FAMILY PROJECTS

The following three camps were built by the sons of Charles Wright Durant, brother of Dr. Thomas Clark Durant and uncle of William West Durant. William West Durant may have had a role in the construction of the camps.

Charles Durant's *Camp Fairview,* Osprey Island, Raquette Lake, 1879–84. Main building burned on August 13, 1938.

Frederick Clark Durant's *Camp Cedars,* Forked Lake, 1880. Demolished following Blowdown of 1950. Sunset Cottage moved to Adirondack Museum. F. C. Durant's Prospect House was built on Blue Mountain Lake in 1881–82. It accommodated 500 guests.

Howard Durant's *Little Forked Camp,* Little Forked Lake, by 1885. It became part of the camp of Mr. Cornelius Vanderbilt Whitney, whose widow owned it in 1998.

Camp Stott. Bluff Point, Raquette Lake, 1878 and later. Built by Frank H. Stott, whose daughter, Janet, married W. W. Durant in 1884. Still standing.

The following camps are credited to William West Durant:

Camp Pine Knot, Long Point, Raquette Lake, 1877–1900. Small preserve and farm. An outdoor education center belonging to Cortland College since 1948. A fire destroyed several original buildings in 1981 that were replaced by replicas. The fabric of the camp, including farm buildings, remains remarkably intact.

Camp Uncas, Mohegan Lake, 1893–95. Preserve and farm, 1,500 acres. Sold to J. Pierpont Morgan and still standing with recent modifications by three owners. Designs for the camp at the Adirondack Museum Library indicate that Grosvenor Atterbury was W. W. Durant's architect.

Sagamore Lodge, Sagamore Lake, 1897–99. Preserve and farm, 1,526 acres. Sold to Alfred G. Vanderbilt and open to the public.

Arbutus Lodge (a.k.a., Mossy Camp), Arbutus Lake, 1898–99. Preserve and farm, 1,536 acres. Sold to Archer Huntington. Camp buildings much reduced about 1939 for purposes of the College of Environmental Science and Forestry, Syracuse.

OTHER W. W. DURANT CAMPS

Camp Omonson (*Bear Camp*), Sumner Lake, before 1888. This cabin with iron shutters to keep out bears was part of the 1,030 acre preserve sold to Timothy Woodruff and his wife Cora in 1897. The lake was renamed Lake Kora, and the Woodruffs built a splendid rustic camp, *Kamp Kill Kare,* on the cabin site.

Fish Camp, Sneed Creek, Hamilton County, about 1893. Cabin.

Camp on Aluminum Pond

Goodnough Mountain, Newcomb, N.Y., 1890s. Cabin on tract purchased by Archer Huntington, about 1900.

Camp Togus, an uncertain Durant connection. It was on property of the Hamilton Park Club, of which Howard Durant was president, in which the Norwood Manufacturing Co., a maker of hardwood rollers, also had an interest. William C. Whitney, who visited the area in 1896, bought this land along with Howard's Little Forked Camp.

Eagle's Nest Country Club, Eagle Lake, 1899–1901. This had a nine hole golf course, four tennis courts, a clubhouse for members, and various cottages and service buildings including a "Swiss Cottage" on its own lot which was intended for Durant's own use.

William L. Coulter (c. 1864–1907)

Below are buildings credited to Coulter in an obituary written by his friend and business partner. It is edited here and may contain omissions and errors of spelling and attribution.

COULTER ALONE (1897–1902)

Warren and Coleman Cottages; the Coulter Building; studied the development of Highland Park and Miller properties.

Coulter designed the following cottages and residences:

Saranac Lake Village: MacIntosh cottage; residences of F. L. Creesey, C. F. Aldrich, George V. W. Duryea.

Lake Placid: Camps for Miss Florence Kilpatrick, Charles J. Gallagher, Mr. Olmsted, John R. Kane, Rev. W. W. Moir, James Harie, John W. Naylor.

St. Regis Chain of Lakes: Camps for Mrs. Hoe, W. W. McAlpin, John Seeley Ward, William Hall Penfold.

Saranac Lakes: Knollwood Club; Kahn Camp on Bull Point.

Elsewhere: Recreation Hall at Sagamore Lodge near Raquette Lake, N.Y.; "Valuable residential property" in Schenectady, N.Y.

COULTER WITH MAX WESTHOFF (1902–1907)

Camps: Mr. Henry and Mrs. Henry Smith, A. L. White, Schuyler Merritt, W. C. Floyd-Jones, George H. Daniels, John A. Hamlin, Victor Herbert, Theodore A. Ely, Carrol Berry, and "many others."

Prospect Point Camp of Adolph Lewisohn

Camp of Levi P. Morton, Eagle Island

Lake Placid Club

Plans for the new Paul Smith's

A "new mining town, Keokee, W.Va.," 350 buildings

Weekend home for Mr. Lewisohn at Ardsley, N.Y.

William G. Distin (1884–1970)

Below is Distin's own list of projects. It accompanied his nomination for a lifetime achievement award by a regional chapter of the American Institute of Architects. It is edited for clarity, but inconsistencies in information provided that are Distin's are retained for whatever they're worth. "Camp" often means a building or an addition, and not an entire complex of buildings. Most of the camps and lodges are still standing.

Camps and Lodges by Distin

R. M. Hollingshead, Blue Mountain Lake [Camp Minnowbrook]

Walter Hochschild, Blue Mountain Lake [Eagle Nest]

Mrs. Boris Sergievsky, Blue Mountain Lake [Eagle Nest]

William A. Rockefeller, Upper Saranac Lake [Wonundra]

John Dimick, Lake Placid

Frederick W. Marks, Lake Placid

George M. Holley Ranch, Lake Placid

Dr. Philip Cole Ranch, Lake Placid [Last Chance Ranch]

Peter S. Paine, Willsboro

William A. Van Alstyne, Westport

Arthur Rodszinsky, Lake Placid

George Hamlin Chalet, Lake Placid

Waddill Catchings, Lake Placid

Distin Additions and Renovations

J. S. Bache, Camp on Upper Saranac Lake

Thomas Blagden, Washington, D.C., Camp on Upper Saranac Lake

Mrs. Alfred Belo, Camp near Saranac Inn

Caesar Cone, Camp on Lake Placid

W. C. Floyd-Jones, Lower Saranac Lake

Robert Garrett, Baltimore, Md., Camp on Upper St. Regis

Henry Goldman, Goldman Sachs, Camp on Upper St. Regis

Daniel R. Hannah, Cleveland, Ohio, Camp on Lower Saranac Lake

Victor Herbert, Camp at Lake Placid

Edmond Guggenheim, Boat House on Lower Saranac Lake

Harold K. Hochschild, American Metals Co., Clubhouse, etc., at Eagle Nest, Blue Mountain Lake

George M. Hendee, Indian Motorcycle Co., Camp on Lake Sunapee, N.H., and country house at Springfield, Mass.

Henry L. Bowles, Camp on Lake Sunapee, N.H.

Mrs. C. V. Whitney, Camp on Little Forked Lake, Sabattis, N.Y.

W. W. Armstrong, of Oyster Bay, N.Y., Camp on Big Wolf Lake

Robert G. Merrill, Syosset, L.I., Camp on Big Wolf Lake

Hon. O. Byron Brewster, Residence at Elizabethtown, N.Y.

Mrs. Whitelaw Reid, Camp on St. Regis Lake

Mrs. Merriweather Post, Camp "work" on St. Regis Lake

Dr. F. B. Trudeau, Camp on St. Regis Lake

Thomas B. Aldrich [poet], Residence at Saranac Lake

Walter E. Cluett [formerly Cluett Peabody Co.], House in Saranac Lake

DISTIN "IN ASSOCIATION WITH COULTER & WESTHOFF"

The Adolph Lewisohn Camp, Upper Saranace Lake

The George Hendee Camp, Lake Sunapee, N.H.

The H. L. Bowles Camp, Lake Sunapee, N.H.

Lodge on Upper Saranac Lake for Lt. Gov. Levi P. Morton

D. Henry Smith Camp, Lower Saranac Lake

Victor Herbert Lodge, Lake Placid

DISTIN CHURCHES AND CHAPELS

St. John's-in-the-Wilderness, Paul Smiths

St. Barnard's Catholic Church, Saranac Lake

Presbyterian Church, Fort Covington

St. Eustace Episcopal Church, Lake Placid

Pilgrim Holiness Church, Lake Placid

Island Chapel, Upper Saranac Lake

Chapel at Lake Placid Club

Methodist Church, Ausable Forks

Presbyterian Church, Gabriels

DISTIN HOTELS, EXTENT NOT INDICATED

Whiteface Inn on Lake Placid: hotel, auditorium, cottages

Saranac Inn on Upper Saranac Lake: main buildings, cottages

Lake Placid Club: main building, cottages, chapel, auditorium

Bartlett Carry Club, Upper Saranac Lake

SCHOOLS

Saranac Lake Junior-Senior High School

Grade schools in Gabriels, Lake Clear, Lake Colby

Northwood School, Lake Placid

Banks

Saranac Lake National Bank

Bank of Ausable Forks

Citizen's National Bank, Malone

Miscellaneous

1932 Olympic Arena, Lake Placid

N.Y. State National Guard Armory, Saranac Lake

Mining Village, Mineville

Notes

Foreword

1. Historian Dixon Ryan Fox framed the cultural divergence of New England and New York in *Yankees and Yorkers* (New York: New York Univ. Press, 1940).

2. Perry Miller, *Nature's Nation* (Cambridge: Harvard Univ. Press, 1967), 152–53.

3. Alan Gussow, *A Sense of Place: The Artist and the American Land* (San Francisco: Friends of the Earth/Seabury Press, n.d.), 27.

Introduction

1. *Oxford English Dictionary.* 2 vols. Compact edition (Glasgow: Oxford Univ. Press, 1971).

2. E. B. White, "Once More to the Lake," *One Man's Meat* (New York: Harper & Brothers, 1950), 246–53.

3. Henry H. Saylor, *Bungalows* (New York: McBride, Winston & Co., 1911). See also Clay Lancaster, *The American Bungalow, 1880–1930* (New York: Abbeville Press, 1985), 239–43.

4. Stephen E. Ambrose, *Undaunted Courage* (New York: Simon and Schuster, 1996).

5. *Oxford English Dictionary,* citing Catherine Parr Traill, *Backwoods of Canada* (1836), 6:9.

6. Samuel Eliot Morison, *The Story of Mount Desert Island* (Boston: Little Brown, 1960).

7. Clive Aslet, *The Last Country Houses* (New Haven: Yale Univ. Press, 1982), 59.

8. Martin Van Buren Ives, *Through the Adirondacks in Eighteen Days* (New York & Albany: Wyncoop, Hallenbeck Crawford Co., 1899), 95.

9. Walter Howe, comp., *The Garden Considered in Literature* (New York: E.P. Putnam's Sons, 1890), 45–46.

10. Rose Standish Nichols, *English Pleasure Gardens* (New York: Macmillan, 1902), 275.

CHAPTER I
The Log Cabin as American Symbol

1. See Hans Huth, *Nature and the American: Three Centuries of Changing Attitudes* (Berkeley: Univ. of California Press, 1957), 107. The Paulding quotation is from Huth's book.

2. Roland Van Zandt, *The Catskill Mountain House* (New Brunswick, N.J.: Rutgers Univ. Press, 1966), 19, 27.

3. Warder H. Cadbury and Henry F. Marsh, *Arthur Fitzwilliam Tait: Artist in the Adirondacks* (Newark, Del.: American Art Journal/Univ. of Delaware Press, 1986), 129.

4. Chilson D. Aldrich, *The Real Log Cabin* (New York: Macmillan Co., 1928), dedication page.

5. Henry David Thoreau, *Walden* (Boston: Ticknor and Fields, 1854). In *Walden and Other Writings by Henry David Thoreau,* ed. and with intro. by Joseph Wood Krutch (New York: Bantam Books, 1989), 140.

6. Jo Ann W. Weiss, *Clarence Cook: His Critical Writings* (Baltimore: Johns Hopkins Univ. Press, 1976), 13. University Microfilm Facsimile.

7. Timothy Dwight, *Travels in New-England and New-York . . . in Four Volumes* (1822; Cambridge, Mass.: The Belknap Press, 1969), 3:252.

8. Samuel H. Hammond and L. W. Mansfield, *Country Margins and Rambles of a Journalist* (New York, Boston: J. C. Derby, Phillips, Sampson & Co., 1855), 338–56.

9. Krissa Johnson, "Tree Houses," *Adirondack Life* 17 (Jan./Feb. 1986): 46–48.

CHAPTER 2

Adirondack Guides and Caretakers

1. William H. H. Murray, "In Memorium," *Woods and Waters* 4 (Summer 1901): 7–8. See also Harry V. Radford, "The Sportsman and His Guide," *Field & Stream* 7 (Feb. 1903): 691–94.

2. Hallie E. Bond, *Boats and Boating in the Adirondacks* (Blue Mountain Lake, N.Y.: The Adirondack Museum; Syracuse: Syracuse Univ. Press, 1995), 66, 226n. 17.

3. Harold K. Hochschild, *Township 34: A History with Digressions of an Adirondack Township in Hamilton County in the State of New York* (New York: Privately printed, 1952), 154. Another account held that the dog bit Buntline, who then shot him between Dunning's legs.

4. Craig Gilborn, *Durant: The Fortunes and Woodland Camps of a Family in the Adirondacks* (Sylvan Beach, N.Y.: North Country Books, 1981; reprint, Blue Mountain Lake, N.Y.: The Adirondack Museum, 1986), 13.

5. William H. H. Murray, *Adventures in the Wilderness; Or, Camp-Life in the Adirondacks* (1869; reprint, edited by William K. Verner with an introduction and notes by Warder H. Cadbury, Blue Mountain Lake, N.Y.: The Adirondack Museum; Syracuse: Syracuse Univ. Press, 1970), 32–40. Alice Wolf Gilborn discerned that Charles Dudley Warner's humorous sketch "The Adirondacks Verified," one of a series written by Warner for the *Atlantic Monthly* in 1878, was a burlesque of Murray's book. See her introduction in a book of Warner's essays, *In the Wilderness* (Blue Mountain Lake, N.Y.: The Adirondack Museum; Syracuse: Syracuse Univ. Press, 1990), vii–xx. The veracity of Murray's book, even allowing for literary license, was questioned from the start. Murray himself cast doubt on it twice, in an affidavit taken from him in 1904 in an ejectment suit brought by New York State against the owner of Camp Fairview on Osprey Island. Asked about a statement in the book, Murray replied, "When you strike the book, you strike fiction largely." Elsewhere he repeats this, saying, "I tell you that there isn't much truth in the book." Murray, who was on his death bed at his Guilford, Conn., home, may have been trying to keep the interview short. He died that year. Supreme Court, Appellate Division, Third Division, *The People of the State of New York Against Jennie H. Ladew and Joseph H. Ladew. Case on Appeal* (Wilton, N.Y.: 1920), 460. Copy at Adirondack Museum Library, MS 65-26, Box 6, p.460.

6. Murray, "In Memorium," 7–8.

7. Alfred L. Donaldson, *A History of the Adirondacks* (1921; reprint, Fleischmanns, N.Y.: Purple Mountain Press, 1996), 2:83.

8. Commission of State Parks, *First Annual Report,* Senate Document No. 102 (Albany, 1873), 14.

9. Marc Cook, *The Wilderness Cure* (New York: William Wood & Co., 1881), 55.

10. "Camp Building in the Adirondacks," *The Decorator & Furnisher* 7 (Oct., 1885): 8.

11. Edith Pilcher, *Up the Lake Road: The First Hundred Years of the Adirondack Mountain Reserve* (Keene Valley, N.Y.: Adirondack Mountain Reserve, 1987), 105.

12. Snyder Papers, vol. 5, 243. Adirondack Museum Library, MS 65-26.

13. Ibid., 317.

14. Cook, *The Wilderness Cure,* 89–91.

15. Thomas G. King, "Adirondack Guides," *Recreation* 17 (Sept. 1902), 183–84.

16. This was on July 15, 1998.

17. On Oct. 19, 1998.

18. David Fitch Remington, *History of Matamek Corporation at Ragged Lake* (Still River, Mass.: Privately printed, 1997), 22–24.

CHAPTER 3
Open Camps and Shanties

1. William H. H. Murray, *Adventures in the Wilderness*, 52–53. Df. of vernacular: *The Random House Dictionary of the English Language* (New York: Random House, 1967).

2. W. E. Wolcott, "The Walton Club," *Forest and Stream* 48 (May 22, 1897): 402–3.

3. William Charles Redfield, "Some Accounts of Two Visits to the Mountains in Essex County, New York, in the Years 1836 and 1837," *The Family Magazine* 5 (1838): 345–54.

4. Supreme Court, *State of New York Against Jennie H. Ladew and Joseph H. Ladew*, 196–210.

5. New York State Commission of Fisheries, Game and Forests, *Eighth and Ninth Reports of . . . [1902 and 1903]* (Albany: Wyncoop Hallenbeck Crawford Co., n.d.), 277.

6. Amelia Matilda Murray, *Letters from the United States, Cuba and Canada* (London: John W. Parker & Son; New York: Putnam, 1856), 2:266. Kate Field, "In and Out of the Woods," *The Atlantic Almanac for 1870* (N.p.): 48–53.

7. C. C. Hiscoe to Francis P. Garvan, June 8, 1917. Adirondack Museum Library.

8. Manuscript in possession of David and Sally McAlpin, Hewitt Lake, Minerva, N.Y.

9. A. Judd Northrup, *Camps and Tramps in the Adirondacks* (Syracuse: Davis, Bardeen & Co., 1880), 168–69.

10. 8 above.

11. Bradford Wykoff Sherwood, Autobiographical Recollections, 1859–1939. Typed transcript. Adirondack Museum Library, MS 62-221.

12. Hochschild, *Township 34*, 151.

13. Sherwood, Autobiographical Recollections.

14. Hochschild, *Township 34*, 151.

15. W. W. Ely, "Ampersand Mountain, A Bird's Eye View of the Adirondacks," *Forest and Stream* 1 (Sept. 18, 1873): 84.

16. "An August Sporting Tour," *Frank Leslie's Illustrated Newspaper* (Nov. 13, 20, 1858): 346.

17. Henry B. Auchincloss, "Suggests Open Camps to Solve Problem of Cheaper Sanatorium Construction," *Journal of Outdoor Life* 3 (Aug. 1906): 260–76.

18. Samuel H. Hammond, *Wild Northern Scenes; Or, Sporting Adventures with the Rifle and the Rod* (New York: Derby & Jackson, 1860), 282–83.

19. *St. Lawrence Plaindealer* (August 24, 1881). The story also appeared in the *New York Evening Post*.

20. H. L. Ziegenfuss, "Lake Piseco Trout Club," *Forest and Stream* 18 (Feb. 16, 1882): 44–45. Mortimer Norton, "Old Lobb of Piseco Lake, *Fur-Fish-Game* 53, no. 7 (Jul./Aug. 1958): 13, 22–23; no. 8 (1958): 28–32.

21. Supreme Court, *State of New York Against Jennie H. Ladew and Joseph H. Ladew.* The Ladew record, printed in book form in 1920, contains cumulative testimony following the state's ejectment suit of Sept. 1, 1897.

22. Jervis McEntee, Diary, June 12–Aug. 17, 1851. Transcript by William K. Verner, Adirondack Museum Library, MS 67-19. MF 4.50.

23. Hochschild, *Township 34*, 155.

24. Hammond, *Wild Northern Scenes*, 282.

25. "Sporting Tour in August, 1858," 395.

26. Sherwood, Autobiographical Recollections.

27. Peter C. Welsh, *Jacks, Jobbers, and Kings: Logging the Adirondacks* (Utica, N.Y.: North Country Books, 1995), 35–37.

28. Hammond and Mansfield, *Country Margins and Rambles of a Journalist*, 317–19.

CHAPTER 4

Log Cabin, Log House and Home into Hotel

1. Jeanne Robert Foster, *Neighbors of Yesterday* (Boston: Sherman, French & Co., 1916; reprint, Schenectady, N.Y.: Riedinger & Riedinger, 1963), 23.

2. Douglass C. Reed, *Log Cabin Mythology* (Hagerstown, Md.: Creative Printing, 1977), 5–6.

3. Thomas Cole, Diary, original in the New York State Library, Albany. Excerpt at Adirondack Museum Library, MS 68-7.

4. Geraldine Collins, *The Brighton Story, Being the History of Paul Smiths, Gabriels and Rainbow Lake* (Larchmont, N.Y.: North Country Books, 1977), 3.

5. [John Patterson Lundy], *The Saranac Exiles: A Winter's Tale of the Adirondacks. Not by W. Shakespeare* (Philadelphia: Privately printed, 1880), 122.

6. *Census of the State of New York, 1855.*

7. McEntee, Dairy, 1851.

8. *Census,* 1855.

9. Supreme Court, *State of New York Against Jennie H. Ladew and Joseph H. Ladew.*

10. "Sporting Tour in August, 1858," 343.

11. John Todd, *Long Lake,* ed. J. Brace, Jr. (1845; reprint, Harrison, N.Y.: Harbor Hill Books, 1983), 43.

12. Quoted by Amy Godine in "The Peopling of the Adirondacks" (1997). Adirondack Museum Library.

13. Francesca Moran Fiore and Judith M. Jacob, "The Rustic Use of Wood in Adirondack Camp Architecture, 1875–1929: An Inventory of Fifteen Camps" (Dec. 1993), 16. Adirondack Museum Library, MS 95-15.

14. A. E. Leavenworth, "The Lakes of the Wilderness," *The Great Republic Monthly* 1 (Apr. 1859): 347.

15. Anonymous account of a visit to a cabin on Cedar River near Indian Lake, N.Y. The writer, a girl, is unknown. The typescript, in the Adirondack Museum Library, says that the account was published in the *Glens Falls Republican* in 1859 and gives a "Cedar River, Township 17" location, which is west of Indian Lake village.

16. Alice Gilborn, "Cabin Coming," The Adirondack Museum *Guide-Line,* no. 20 (Nov. 1995), 6.

17. The author visited Mr. Leadley at his home in 1993.

18. "Sporting Tour in August, 1858," 343.

19. Joseph W. Stickler, ed. and comp., *The Adirondacks as a Health Resort* (New York: G. P. Putnam's Sons, 1886), 155.

20. Hochschild, *Township 34,* 190.

21. "Visit to the Chateaugay Lakes," *The Spirit of the Times* (July 15, 1848): 247–48.

22. Cadbury and Marsh, *Arthur Fitzwilliam Tait,* 68.

23. Adirondack Lakes Survey Corporation, *Adirondack Lakes Survey* (Ray Brook, N.Y.: Adirondack Lake Survey Corp., 1984–87), ES-2.

24. William H. H. Murray, *Adventures in the Wilderness,* 47–48.

25. Hugh Fosburgh, *A Clearing in the Wilderness* (New York: Doubleday & Co., 1969), vii–ix. Leila Fosburgh Wilson, *The North Woods Club, 1886–1986* (Minerva, N.Y.: Privately printed, 1986), 1–5.

26. Arpad Gerster, Chronicles of Camp Oteetiwi, Raquette Lake, Beginning November 6, 1896, Ending September 1898. Adirondack Museum Library, MS 71-6.

27. Raymond Hopper, "Primeval Adirondacks," *Forest and Stream* 36 (June 18, 1891): 432–33.

28. William Chapman White, *Adirondack Country* (New York: Alfred A. Knopf, 1970), 130–35.

29. Interview conducted Class of 1988, James Briggs, teacher. Adirondack Museum Library.

CHAPTER 5

Land and the Formation of Private Preserves

1. From an extract of the Hon. David McClure's speech in "Our Forest Preserves," *Forest Leaves* 1 (Spring 1904), 37–42. The Pownall extract is quoted in Philip G. Terrie, *Contested Terrain: A New History*

of Nature and People in the Adirondacks (Blue Mountain Lake, N.Y.: The Adirondack Museum; Syracuse: Syracuse Univ. Press, 1997), 5.

2. Norman J. Van Valkenburgh, *The Adirondack Forest Preserve* (Blue Mountain Lake, N.Y.: The Adirondack Museum, 1979), 12–15.

3. John Brinkerhoff Jackson, *Discovering the Vernacular Landscape* (New Haven: Yale Univ. Press, 1984), 15.

4. John Perlin, *A Forest Journey* (Cambridge, Mass.: Harvard Univ. Press, 1989), 25–31.

5. John Hildebrand, "Coming Home: Hunting Squirrels and Tigers with the Hmong," *Harper's Magazine* 297 (Oct. 1998), 73.

6. John C. Gerster to Kenneth Durant, October 29, 1962, Adirondack Museum Library, MS 65-4, Box 2.

7. McClure, "Our Forest Preserves," 38.

8. Terrie, *Contested Terrain,* 13, 94–95. Eleanor Brown, *The Forest Preserve of New York State: A Handbook for Conservationists* (Glens Falls, N.Y.: The Adirondack Mountain Club, 1985), 27.

9. Assembly Document, 1850, 68.

10. Hochschild, *Township 34,* 171–76.

11. Gilborn, *Durant,* 11.

12. Frank Graham, Jr., *The Adirondack Park: A Political History* (New York: Alfred A. Knopf, 1978), 68. Graham identified the editor as Charles Loring Brace. Another prescient editor was Henry Jarvis Raymond, founder of the *New-York Daily Times* which later evolved into the *New York Times.* In 1855, in a series of four letters signed "H. J. R." and appearing under the title "A Week in the Wilderness," Raymond told of a one-week trip which he and others took as guests of business interests who wanted to bring the benefits of a railroad to public attention. The letters were published on June 19, June 26, July 7, and July 14 in the *Daily Times.* They were published in 1952 in *Township 34,* in an "Addendum to Chapter 13" inserted only in comparatively few copies of the book, following page 170 and numbered page 170-A through page 170-X. In an introduction to the addendum, Harold K. Hochschild said that William Chapman White had unearthed the letters in the files at the *New York Times.*

13. Gilborn, *Durant,* 12.

14. Ibid, 10.

15. Roger C. Thompson, "The Doctrine of Wilderness: A Study of the Policy and Politics of the Adirondack Preserve-Park" (Ph.D., diss., Syracuse Univ. College of Environmental Science and Forestry, 1962), 77.

16. Phineas Lounsbury to George Thompson, Sept. 1, 1901, Adirondack Museum Library.

17. Hochschild, *Township 34,* 314.

18. Ibid., 306–7. Gilborn, *Durant,* 108.

19. Terrie, *Contested Terrain,* 113–14.

20. Van Valkenburgh, *The Adirondack Forest Preserve.* 65. The list of estates in 1893 appears in Thompson, "The Doctrine of Wilderness," 461–63.

21. Seaver Asbury Miller, "The Sporting Clubs in the Adirondacks," *Outing* 32 (Aug. 1898): 480–81. Similar phrasing was used by Alice Kellogg in "Luxurious Adirondack Camps," *Broadway Magazine* (Aug. 1908): 207–12.

22. John W. Stock, "Litchfield Park: Stories from an Adirondack Great Camp" (North Port, Fl., c. 1998), photocopy.

23. White, *Adirondack Country,* 148.

24. Graham, *The Adirondack Park,* 138–41.

25. Raymond G. Hopper, "Primeval Adirondacks," 432–33.

26. Cook, *The Wilderness Cure.*

27. Raymond D. Masters, *A Social History of the Huntington Wildlife Forest (Which includes Rich Lake and the Pendleton Settlement)* (Newcomb, N.Y.: Newcomb Historical Society, 1993), 64–65.

28. Remington, *History of Matamek Corporation at Ragged Lake.*

29. Ibid., 207.

30. Ibid., 216. See also Edward Comstock, Jr., "The Role of Private Preserves in the Adirondack Park," *Adirondack Journal of Environmental Studies* 2 (Fall/Winter 1995): 32–39.

CHAPTER 6

Clubs

1. Paul Schullery, *Fly Fishing in America, A History* (New York: Lyons & Burford, 1987), 16.

2. T. B. Thorpe, "A Visit to John Brown's Tract," *Harper's New Monthly Magazine* 19 (July 1859), 171–72.

3. Paul Schullery, "'A Sportsman's Paradise': Fishing and Hunting on the 'Preserve,'" in *The Adirondack League Club*, ed. and comp. by Edward Comstock, Jr. (Old Forge, N.Y.: The Adirondack League Club, 1990), 112–13.

4. Graham, *The Adirondack Park,* 19–20.

5. Arthur H. Masten, *The Story of Adirondac* (New York: Privately printed, 1923; reprint, Blue Mountain Lake, N.Y.: The Adirondack Museum; Syracuse: Syracuse Univ. Press, 1968).

6. Masters, *A Social History of the Huntington Wildlife Forest,* 45–54.

7. Leila Fosburgh Wilson, *The North Woods Club,* 11.

8. Ibid., 21.

9. In *The Adirondack League Club,* 115–16.

10. Ibid., 23–24.

11. Hochschild, *Township 34,* 371–78.

12. Philip G. Terrie, "'The Grandest Private Park': Forestry and Land Management," in *The Adirondack League Club,* 76–77. Also see Graham, *The Adirondack Park,* 119–20.

13. Donaldson, *A History of the Adirondacks,* 2: 159–60.

14. Harold Evans, *The American Century* (New York: Alfred A. Knopf, 1998), 77. Evans prints a table which estimates that $150 in 1890 was worth $2,089 in 1989 dollars, a multiple of almost fourteen, which seems a little high.

15. Pilcher, *Up the Lake Road,* xiii, 43.

16. Ibid., 174–75.

17. Ibid., 50.

18. Roger Yepsen's essay "Camp and Camp Life" in *The Adirondack League Club,* 19–71, nicely shows the effort of the club to adapt to the desires and needs of the three lodges, each of which had a distinct history apart from the others and a personality it wanted to preserve (p. 61).

19. Wayne A. Wiegand, *Irrepressible Reformer: A Biography of Melvil Dewey* (Chicago: American Library Association, 1996).

20. White, *Adirondack Country,* 135–39.

21. From Morris T. Longstreth's book, *The Adirondacks* (New York: The Century, 1917), 240–54, excerpted in Donaldson, *A History of the Adirondacks,* 1: 366–74.

22. Wiegand, *Irrepressible Reformer,* 374.

23. "Early History" on sheet accompanied by a letter from Bruce W. Kirkpatrick, President, Gooley Club, Inc., to the author, Oct. 2, 1998.

24. Telephone conversation with Mr. Naylor at his office in Glens Falls, Oct. 8, 1998.

CHAPTER 7

Transitional Camps and Tents

1. J. M. M. [John M. MacMullen (1818–1896)]. Diary. Adirondack Museum Library, typescript. Trip taken by two young men in 1843, printed in the *St. Lawrence Plaindealer* for Aug. 24, 1881. MacMullen graduated from Columbia in 1837 and became a college professor.

2. Abstract of Title of Township 39, including copy of the patent of Mar. 21, 1851, patent conveying the township to Benjamin Brandreth by the People of the State of New York. Modern typescript, 33 pages. Collection of author.

3. "Brandreth Park," Adirondack Land Owners Association *News* 6 (Aug. 1996): 5–6.

4. Rev. Henry Smith Huntington, Diary, entry for July 21, 1853. Adirondack Museum Library, MF 4.60.

5. Benjamin B. Brandreth, Sing Sing, N.Y., Dec. 28, 1874, to Reuben Cary, Long Lake, N.Y., Adirondack Museum Library, MS 76-25, photocopy.

6. Abstract of Mar. 21, 1851. Photocopy of typescript of letter accompanied by a note dated July 27, 1976, to the author from Franklin B. Brandreth.

7. Edwin McAlpin to Reuben Cary, Dec. 8, 1880, on stationery of D. H. McAlpin & Co., "Tobacco Manufacturers," New York City, Adirondack Museum Library, MS 76-25, photocopy.

8. [W. A. Rogers], "Camping Out as a Fine Art," *Harper's Weekly* (Nov. 17, 1883): 731.

9. Donaldson, *A History of the Adirondacks,* 2:92. Seneca Ray Stoddard, *The Adirondacks, Illustrated* (Albany: Charles Van Benthuysen & Sons, 1880), 122.

10. Timothy Dwight, *Travels in New-England,* 2:252.

11. John Ellis, "Diary of a Trip to the Adirondacks, 1879, 1880." Manuscript in The New-York Historical Society.

12. The towered camps are discussed in Gilborn, *Durant,* 50–56.

13. Leila Fosburgh Wilson, "One Hundred Years in the Adirondack Wilderness," *The Conservationist* (May/June 1989): 40–46.

14. Wilson, *The North Woods Club,* 9.

15. Ibid., 19.

16. Pilcher, *Up the Lake Road,* 5.

17. Graham, *The Adirondack Park,* 43.

18. Elizabeth Putnam McIver, *Early Days at Putnam Camp* (Elizabethtown, N.Y.: Privately printed, 1941).

19. Donaldson, *A History of the Adirondacks,* 2:25.

20. Obituary of Henry van Hoevenberg by Godfrey Dewey: Mar. 1, 1918; reprinted in *The Lake Placid News,* Mar. 20 and Mar. 27, 1975.

21. Stickler, *The Adirondacks as a Health Resort,* 35.

22. Donaldson, *A History of the Adirondacks,* 1:377–78.

23. John R. Stilgoe, *Common Landscape of America, 1580–1845* (New Haven: Yale Univ. Press, 1982), 235. Stilgoe cites B. Weed Gorham, *Camp Meeting Manual* (Boston: 1854), 125–30.

24. Floyd and Marion Rinhart, *Summertime: Photographs of Americans at Play, 1850–1900* (New York: Clarkson N. Potter, Inc., 1978), 166, 169.

25. Amelia Murray, *Letters,* 2: 279.

26. E[dwin] R. Wallace, *A Descriptive Guide to the Adirondacks . . . ,* rev. and corrected (N.Y.: The American News Co., 1875–1900). Issued annually, Wallace's first guide was published in Smith's *Modern Babes,* note 30 below.

27. Hochschild, *Township 34,* 150–51.

28. Bond, *Boats and Boating in the Adirondacks,* 62.

29. McEntee, Diary, June 12–Aug. 17, 1851.

30. H. Perry Smith, *Modern Babes in the Wood; Or, Summerings in the Wilderness* (Hartford, Conn.; Syracuse, N.Y.: Columbian Book Co., 1872), 104.

31. Stilgoe, *Common Landscape of America,* 235.

32. Mildred Phelps Stokes Hooker, *Camp Chronicles* (Blue Mountain Lake, N.Y.: The Adirondack Museum, 1964), 36.

33. William Nathaniel Banks, "The Wesleyan Grove Campground on Martha's Vineyard," *Antiques* (July 1983): 104–15. See also Rinhart, *Summertime,* 96, 182–83.

34. Cook, *The Wilderness Cure,* 53.

35. Kate Field, "In and Out of the Woods," *The Atlantic Almanac for 1870,* 52.

36. New York Commission of Fisheries, Game and Forests. *Eighth and Ninth Reports of . . .[1902 and 1903].* The photograph is part of the article "Fishes and Fishing in the Adirondacks" by A. Judd Northrup, 277–78. The earlier practice of using bark had been proposed by him in his book *Camps and Tramps in the Adirondacks and Grayling Fishing in Northern Michigan.*

37. Smith, *Babes,* 104–5.

38. "Camp Building in the Adirondacks," *Decorator & Furnisher,* 8.

39. Hochschild, *Township 34.*

40. Telephone conversation, August 6,1998, Region 5 office.

41. Wilson, *The North Woods Club,* 20.

42. Lewis Spence, "A Mountain View" (Cranbury, N.J., n.d. [c. 1995]).

43. Gilborn, *Durant,* 162.

CHAPTER 8

Decorous Adirondack Camps

1. Harvey Ellis, "An Adirondack Camp," *The Craftsman* 4 (July 1903): 281.

2. Seneca Ray Stoddard, *The Adirondacks, Illustrated* (Glens Falls, N.Y.: Published by the author, 1888), 206.

3. Gilborn, *Durant,* 135–36.

4. Hochshild, *Township 34,* 119–23.

5. Fosburgh, *A Clearing in the Wilderness.* Anne LaBastille, *Woodswoman* (New York: E. P. Dutton & Co., 1976).

6. Jackson, *Discovering the Vernacular Landscape,* 63.

7. Graham, *The Adirondack Park,* 20–22.

8. Ellis, "An Adirondack Camp," 281–83.

9. Eileen Boris, "The Social Ideas of the Arts and Crafts Movement," in Wendy Kaplan, ed., *"The Art That Is Life": The Arts & Crafts Movement in America, 1875–1920* (Boston: A New York Graphic Society Book and Little Brown, 1987), 208–22.

10. Robert Judson Clark and Wendy Kaplan, "Arts and Crafts: Matters of Style," in Kaplan, ed., *"The Art That Is Life,"* 80.

11. Hochschild, *Township 34,* 208–17.

12. Ellis, "An Adirondack Camp," 283.

13. Craig Gilborn, *Adirondack Furniture and the Rustic Tradition* (New York: Harry N. Abrams, 1987), 261–97.

14. Catherine Zusy, "Gustav Stickley and the Craftsman Workshops," in Kaplan, ed., *"The Art That Is Life,"* 243.

15. "An Adirondack Camp," *International Studio* 38 (July 1909): xxv.

16. The best source of information about Adirondack furniture, its background and makers, is Gilborn, *Adirondack Furniture.*

17. Hiscoe to Garvan, Oct. 31, 1917, Adirondack Museum Library.

18. Gilborn, *Adirondack Furniture,* 325–26.

19. Kathrin S. Hochschild with Alice Gilborn, *The Walter Hochschild Camp at Eagle Nest* (Blue Mountain Lake, N.Y.: Privately printed, 1975), [5].

20. Lillie Hamilton French, "Adirondack Camps," *Harper's Bazaar* 32 (Sept. 16, 1899): 775–77.

CHAPTER 9

Other Features of the Decorous Camp

1. Seneca Ray Stoddard, *The Adirondacks, Illustrated* (Glens Falls, N.Y.: Published by the author, 1893), 204.

2. Rebecca Harding Davis, "Boston in the Sixties," *Concord Saunterer* (Fall 1995): 76.

3. Comstock, ed., *The Adirondack League Club,* 14–15.

4. Augustus D. Shepard, *Camps in the Woods* (New York: Architectural Book Publishing Co., 1931).

5. "An Adirondack Camp," *International Studio* 38 (Autumn 1909), xv.

6. Kathrin Hochschild, *The Walter Hochschild Camp.*

7. Harvey Kaiser, *Great Camps of the Adirondacks* (Boston: David R. Godine, 1982), 209.

8. Gilborn, *Durant,* 97.

9. Ibid., 94.

10. Interview with Basil Cheney, Aug. 4, 1998.

11. Dana Winslow, responses in margin of letter and draft from author dated Sept. 24, 1998.

12. Hochschild, *Township 34,* 208–12.

13. Ibid., 387–90, 549–55.

14. Ibid., 390.

15. Gilborn, *Durant,* 104–7.

16. Comstock, ed., *The Adirondack League Club,* 26–27.

17. Beverly Bridger to the author on Oct. 12, 1998.

18. Gilborn, *Durant,* 100–103.

19. Wesley Haynes, "HSR Complete for Santanoni Farm," Adirondack Architectural Heritage *Newsletter* 5 (Nov. 1996): 1, 3–4.

20. Hooker, *Camp Chronicles,* 9–11.

21. Pieter Litchfield to the author, Litchfield Park, Aug. 10, 1998.

22. Hochschild, *Township 34,* 550.

CHAPTER 10

Trophy Camps and Their Early Designers

1. William Frederick Dix, "Summer Life in Luxurious Adirondack Camps," *The Independent* 55 (July 2, 1903): 1556–57.

2. Gilborn, *Durant,* 100.

3. Stoddard, *The Adirondacks, Illustrated* (1888).

4. Gilborn, *Durant,* 1–14.

5. Mary B. Hotaling, "Robert H. Robertson: Architect of Santanoni," Adirondack Architectural Heritage *Newsletter* 5 (June 1996): 1, 3.

6. The bark shanty but not its painted designs was described in G. M. Hoppin, "The Adirondack Lakes," *Broadway, A London Magazine* N.S. 2 (Mar. 1869): 263–69.

7. Roger Hale Newton, "Our Summer Resort Architecture—An American Phenomenon and Social Document," *Art Quarterly* 4, no.4 (1941): 308–10.

8. J. Watson Webb to Dennis April, Aug. 22, 1998, a copy of which Mr. Webb sent to the author.

9. Florence Adele Sloan, *Maverick in Mauve* (Garden City, N.Y.: Doubleday, 1983), 96.

10. New York State, *Report of the Forest Commission . . . 1893* (Albany: Wyncoop Hallenbeck Crawford, 1893), 1:178–79.

11. William Alanson Borden, "Veranda Houses," *Indoors and Out* 4 (June 1907): 110–13.

12. *Report of the Forest Commission . . .1893,* 178.

13. Paul Malo, "Inventing the Adirondack Log Villa: From Woodsman's Cabin to Rustic Lodge," Association for Preservation *Bulletin* 29, no. 2 (1998): 27–34. Malo suggests without saying so that Robert C. Pruyn favored log construction and the configuration of the lodge at Santanoni because of its resemblance to architecture in Japan where part of his youth had been spent. Malo develops this and other ideas related to Japanese influences in a second article: "Nippon in the North Country: Japanese Inspiration in Form and Philosophy," *Adirondack Life* 29, no.7, Special Collectors Issue (1998): 50–56. A projected book on Santanoni was being readied while this book was being prepared for publication in 1998. Co-authors were Robert Engle, Howard Kirschenbaum, and Paul Malo, and the working title was "Santanoni: From Japanese Temple to Adirondack Great Camp."

14. Haynes, "HSR Complete for Santanoni Farm," 1, 3–4.

15. Santanoni stands because individuals and governmental agency heads refused to let it be torn down or disintegrate from neglect. George Canon, Newcomb Town Supervisor, and Howard Kirschenbaum, merit mention. It was Kirschenbaum who introduced public tours that brought Santanoni to public attention, passing on responsibilities for this to a regional preservation organization, AARCH, which he founded in 1989. Winthrop Aldrich, a deputy executive in the Department of Environmental Conservation, spoke up for camp and historic preservation inside an agency whose mission was environmental conservation and not historic preservation. A 1976 loan exhibit, "Adirondack Rustic: Camp Furniture, 1876–1926," at the Adirondack Museum, drawing public attention to the region's rustic arts for the first time, helped the preservation cause.

16. Obituary, undated [1907], from a Saranac Lake, N.Y., newspaper, in author's possession and received from Bruce Coulter, son of William L. Coulter.

17. The author is indebted to Mary Hotaling, who has continued her work on Coulter and other architects in Saranac Lake, where she has been active as a preservation historian. The author has had an interest in Coulter, corresponding with Bruce Coulter, the architect's son, who visited the author at the Adirondack Museum in 1977. Bruce, who was born in 1897, about the time his father opened his Saranac Lake office, taught English at Cranbrook Academy.

18. Seaver Asbury Miller, "Adirondack News and Notes," datelined Saranac Lake, N.Y., with a July 21, 1900, date. Unsourced, copy in author's possession.

19. See Appendix B.

20. Mary B. Hotaling, "Framing a Legacy," *Adirondack Life* 28 (Mar./Apr. 1997): 32–39. See also her "William L. Coulter: Adirondack Architect," Preservation League of New York State *Newsletter* (Fall 1989): 4–5.

21. Kenneth Goldthwaite, "A Quaint Lodge in the Adirondacks," *Town & Country,* no. 3036 (July 23, 1904): 18–21.

22. The flyer, for "Camp Adirondack," is in the Adirondack Museum Library. Kaiser, *Great Camps of the Adirondacks,* 136–37. Morton sold Pinebrook to Mitchell Levy in 1903, which was the year Coulter was directing construction on Eagle Island.

CHAPTER II
Old Forge and Saranac Lake Architects

1. Epigraph is from a photocopied newspaper clipping that is unsourced but is datelined Saranac Lake, N.Y., July 21, 1900. For butterfly plans, see Clive Aslet, *The Last Country Houses,* 74–76, 246.

2. Wesley Haynes in Comstock, ed., *The Adirondack League Club,* 207–12, 246–47.

3. William S. Wicks, *Log Cabins and Cottages: How to Build and Furnish Them* (1889. 9th, revised ed.: New York: Forest and Stream, 1928).

4. Haynes, in Comstock, ed., *The Adirondack League Club,* 197–257.

5. Ibid., 249.

6. Obituary for Augustus D. Shepard, *New York Times* (Oct. 2, 1955).

7. Published but unsourced genealogy, "from the Files of Dennis J. Brown, Lakewood, N.J." Author's files. The sale of the town house appeared in the *New York Times* (Dec. 3, 1997), 31.

8. Shepard, *Camps in the Woods.*

9. Comstock, ed., *The Adirondack League Club,* 261. Haynes and Comstock did not say who designed the Childs Camp in the book, although they now believe that Wicks designed the original cottage, with additions possibly by Shepard.

10. Distin Papers. Collection of papers given to the author, who turned them over to the Adirondack Museum, a gift from Distin's son, William "Mo" Distin. Interview with William G. Distin on Jan. 15, 1970, by Saranac Lake historian Jacques DeMattos, who gave a copy to the author.

11. Hotaling, "Framing a Legacy," 32–39.

12. Ibid.

13. William G. Distin (unsigned) to W. H. Westhoff, Feb. 21, 1921. Copy in author's possession.

14. Kathrin Hochschild, *The Walter Hochschild Camp at Eagle Nest,* 5.

15. Mary B. Hotaling, "Architects and Builders in the Adirondacks," Adirondack Architectural Heritage *Newsletter* 1 (May 1992), 5–8.

16. Simon Jervis, "Antler and Horn Furniture," Victoria and Albert Museum *Yearbook* (London: V & A Museum, 1972).

17. Henry H. Saylor, *Bungalows* (New York: McBride, Winston & Co., 1911), 52.

18. Committee for the Preservation of Architectural Records, Inc. *Directory of Historic American Architectural Firms* (New York: American Institute of Architects Foundation, 1979).

19. Patricia Leigh Brown, "Out-Twigging the Neighbors," *New York Times,* House & Home Section (Oct. 23, 1997): 1, 7. For other developments, see *Adirondack Life,* Special Collector's Edition, 1998–99.

CHAPTER 12
Kamp Kill Kare: Prodigy Camp

1. Henry Wellington Wack, "Kamp Kill Kare," *Field and Stream* 7 (Feb. 1903): 656–61.

2. Gilborn, *Durant,* 108–12.

3. This and other quotations from the Gerster journal appear in *Durant* above. A version of Arpad Gerster's journals was being edited for publication by Sidney Whelan, Jr., in 1998.

4. "'Kamp Kill Kare': Lieutenant-Governor Woodruff's Preserve," *Town & Country* (Nov. 2, 1901): 57–60.

5. Wack, "Kamp Kill Kare," 656–57.

6. Information about Hiscoe is from correspondence and drawings in the Adirondack Museum Library, gift of Mrs. Anthony N. B. "Bea" Garvan.

7. "Kamp Kill Kare," *Town & Country,* 6–11.

8. Wack, "Kamp Kill Kare," 656.

9. "Kamp Kill Kare," *Country Life* (Dec. 1923): 57–60.

10. Gilborn, *Durant,* 97.

11. Cora Woodruff obituary, *New York Times,* Mar. 29, 1904. Timothy Woodruff obituary, *New York Times,* Oct. 19, 1913.

12. "Kamp Kill Kare," *Country Life,* 57–60.

13. Illustrated in Gilborn, *Durant,* Fig. 98.

14. Gerald W. R. Ward, "A Wide View for American Art," *Francis P. Garvan, Collector* (New Haven: Yale Univ. Gallery of Art, 1980), 10. Yale's Garvan Collection now numbers over 10,000 objects.

15. "Kamp Kill Kare," *Country Life,* 57–60. Eleven photographs by John Wallace Gillies accompany the article.

16. Hochschild, *Township 34,* 331, 333, 510.

17. "Kamp Kill Kare," *Country Life.*

18. E. C. Saxe, insurance agent, Malone, N.Y., Adirondack Museum Library, MS 63.240.

19. Judge Dana Winslow, various fax transmissions in response to questions posed by the author on Sept. 24, 1998, etc.

20. Hochschild, *Township 34,* 306.

APPENDIX A
"Great Camps" and Their Care

1. Preservation League of New York State, *Great Camps: A Century of Adirondack Architecture* (Albany, N.Y.: Preservation League, 1992). Arnold Lehman, "Great Camps of the Adirondacks: A Wilderness Architecture," 1970, Adirondack Museum Library, MS 73.11.

2. Malo, "Inventing the Adirondack Log Villa," 31.

3. Peter Berle, Commissioner, Department of Environmental Conservation, to Orin Lehman, Commissioner of Parks and Recreation, Dec. 27, 1978.

4. Raymond S. Spears, "The New Adirondacks," *The Outlook* (May 24, 1916): 191, 193.

5. Gervaise Jackson-Stops, *The English Country House: A Grand Tour* (New York: Little, Brown, 1985). Aslet, *The Last Country Houses.*

6. Gilborn, *Durant,* 157–66.

7. In Walter Howe, comp., *The Garden Considered in Literature* (New York: G. P. Putnam's Sons, 1890), 164.

8. Patricia Leigh Brown, "Preserving Adirondack Great Camps," *New York Times,* House & Home Section (June 12, 1992). Brown, "Out-Twigging the Neighbors."

9. "Arson at the Lake Placid Club," *Adirondack Life* 24 (Jan./Feb. 1993): 8. "News & Notes," Adirondack Architectural Heritage *Newsletter* 7 (Spring 1998): 9.

10. "Demolition of Most Remaining Lake Placid Club Cottages Proposed," AAH *Newsletter,* 10.

Bibliography

Manuscripts

Clark, Mrs. Henry M. Diary, 1897–1901. Adirondack Museum Library. MF 4.51.

> *The family operated a hunting lodge in the Cranberry Lake area.*

Cole, Thomas. Diary, original in the New York State Library in Albany. Excerpt at Adirondack Museum Library, typed. MS 68-7.

> *Visit to Schroon Lake with Asher B. Durand "in search of the picturesque" in 1837.*

Distin, William G. Miscellaneous drawings, blue prints of camps, etc., relating to his architectural career, c. 1910–1970. Adirondack Museum Library. MS 76-41; 81-16; 88-13; 89-14.

Domblewski, Mary Ellen. "The Adirondack Camp of the Last Quarter of the Nineteenth Century: A Wilderness Architecture." Master's thesis, Cornell Univ., 1974. Adirondack Museum Library.

Ellis, John. "Diary of a Trip to the Adirondacks, 1879, 1880." Manuscript. The New-York Historical Society.

> *Ellis seems to have been acquainted with the Durants.*

Fiore, Francesca Moran, and Judith M. Jacob. "The Rustic Use of Wood in Adirondack Camp Architecture, 1875–1929: An Inventory of Fifteen Camps." Dec. 1993. Adirondack Museum Library. MS 95-15.

Gerster, Dr. Arpad. Chronicles of Camp Oteetiwi, Raquette Lake, Nov. 6, 1896–Sept. 1898. Adirondack Museum Library. MS 71-6.

> *Vivid scenes and marginal drawings by a New York surgeon.*

Hotaling, Mary B. "W. L. Coulter: Adirondack Architect." Master's thesis, Univ. of Vermont, 1995.

Huntington, Rev. Henry Smith. Diary, 1852–1854. Adirondack Museum Library. MF 4.60.

> *Author, a resident of Rome, N.Y., was at Princeton Seminary.*

Jacobs, Ward S. Letter of Apr. 9, 1929, to W. G. Distin. Adirondack Museum Library. VF "Camps."

> *Mr. Jacobs, writing from Hartford, Conn., said that their architect, Mr. Bassette, thought Distin's proposal for an Adirondack Room in their new house "quite radical." He asked Distin to develop his ideas but asked they be less strongly "Adirondack."*

Johnson, Ruth Ann. "A Quaint Lodge in the Adirondacks," student paper for Dr. Everest's history 203 class, typewritten and dated Dec. 9, 1977. Author's possession.

Adolph Lewisohn's camp on Prospect Point, Upper Saranac Lake.

Kelly, C. Lise. "Private Camps and Cottages at the Blue Mountain House." Research report, 1985. Adirondack Museum Library. Archives.

Leavenworth, A. E. "Journal of a Surveying Excursion to Raquette Lake & Vicinity, August, 1851." Adirondack Museum Library. MF 4.25.

The journal, written by a University of Vermont student, is in the library at Yale.

Lehman, Arnold. "Great Camps of the Adirondacks: A Wilderness Architecture," 1970. Adirondack Museum Library. MS 73.11.

Descriptions and photographs of Adirondack camps by a graduate student at Yale.

Longstreth, Richard. "Summer Architecture in the Adirondacks: Hamilton, Franklin and Essex Counties." Author's possession.

Prepared for the Domestic Study Tour of the Society of Architectural Historians, 1996.

Lux, Karen, and Karen Creuzinger. "Architectural Survey of Minor Adirondack Camps." Karen Lux and Karen Creuzinger, 1985. Adirondack Museum Library. MS 83-16.

Selection of camps on Raquette Lake and four lakes west.

M., J. M. [John M. MacMullen (1818–1896)]. Diary. Adirondack Museum Library. Typescript. VF.

Trip taken by two young men in 1843, printed in the St. Lawrence Plaindealer for Aug. 24, 1881. MacMullen graduated from Columbia in 1837 and became a college professor.

Martin, Nancy. "Food in the Adirondacks," Aug. 22, 1985. Adirondack Museum Library. Typed report with footnotes and bibliography. VF.

Preservation League of New York State. "Research Report on the Great Camps of the Adirondacks," June 1978. Albany: The Preservation League of New York State. Author's possession.

McEntee, Jervis. Diary, June 12–Aug. 17, 1851. Transcript by William K. Verner. Adirondack Museum Library. MS 67-19. MF 4.50.

McEntee and his companion Joseph Tubby, also an artist, saw many kinds of shelters, including Billy Wood's shanty, illustrated in this book.

Null, Janet A. "Historic Survey of the Lake Placid Club." Lake Placid, N.Y.: Lake Placid–North Elba Preservation Commission, 1989. Author's possession.

Perdue, Martin Clay. "The Log Cabin in American Art and Architecture, 1840–1890." Masters thesis, School of Architecture, Univ. of Virginia, 1985. Author's possession.

Pruyn, Mrs. John V. L. Account from her diary of a visit to Camp Pine Knot in 1894. Adirondack Museum Library. MS 61-32.

Shepard, Augustus D. 570-plus drawings, mostly of camps at the Adirondack League Club. Adirondack Museum Library. MS 89-1.

Sherwood, Bradford Wycoff. Autobiographical recollections. Adirondack Museum Library. MS 62-221.

Summers of 1881 and 1882 on Raquette Lake by a Hamilton College student who became a physician, written shortly before his death in 1939.

Spence, Lewis. "A Mountain View." Manuscript. Cranbury, N.J.: n.d. [c. 1995].

Boyhood years in the early 1930s at Camp Woodwil, built for his grandfather on Upper Saranac Lake in 1926.

Stock, John W. "Litchfield Park: Stories from an Adirondack Great Camp." Manuscript. North Port, Fl.: n.d. [c. 1998].

> *A professional forester, the author was employed at Litchfield Park from 1955 until his retirement in 1983.*

Supreme Court, Appellate Division, Third Division. *The People of the State of New York Against Jennie H. Ladew and Joseph H. Ladew, Case on Appeal.* Walton, N.Y., 1920. Adirondack Museum Library. MS 65-26, Box 6.

People of the State of New York Against George H. Carlin, Cooperstown, N.Y. [c. 1919].

> *The Ladew record, printed in book form in 1920, contains cumulative testimony following the state's ejectment suit of Sept. 1, 1897.*

Thompson, Roger C. "The Doctrine of Wilderness: A Study of the Policy and Politics of the Adirondack Preserve-Park." Ph.D diss., Syracuse Univ. College of Environmental Science and Forestry, 1962.

Books

Ackerman, David H. *Lake Placid Club, 1895–1980: An Illustrated History.* Lake Placid, N.Y. Lake Placid Educational Foundation, 1998.

Adirondack Lakes Survey Corporation. *Adirondack Lakes Survey.* Ray Brook, N.Y.: Adirondack Lake Survey Corp., 1984–87.

Adirondack Mountain Club. *Adirondack Bibliography. A List of Books, Pamphlets and Periodical Articles Published Through the Year 1955.* Dorothy A. Plum, ed. Gabriels, N.Y.: Adirondack Mountain Club, Inc., 1958.

———. *Adirondack Bibliography Supplement, 1956–1965.* Edited by Dorothy A. Plum, with an introduction by William K. Verner. Blue Mountain Lake, N.Y.: The Adirondack Museum.

> *Ms. Plum, assisted by seven who submitted annotated notes, compiled and edited both volumes, in which there are some 10,601 entries. The 31-page introduction to the Supplement by William K. Verner, who was curator at the Adirondack Museum, is a useful overview of the literature to 1965.*

Aldrich, Chilson D. *The Real Log Cabin.* New York: Macmillan Co., 1928.

> *An architect, Aldrich was a member of Page and Hill in Minnesota, which manufactured log cabins from his designs.*

Ambrose, Stephen E. *Undaunted Courage.* New York: Simon and Schuster, 1996.

Andrews, Malcolm. *The Search for the Picturesque.* Stanford, Calif.: Stanford Univ. Press, 1989.

Aslet, Clive. *The Last Country Houses.* New Haven: Yale Univ. Press, 1982.

> *Houses in Victorian Britain that Americans tried to emulate.*

Beard, D. C. *Shelters, Shacks and Shanties.* New York: Charles Scribner's Sons, 1914. Reprint, with an introduction by Paul Cardwell, Jr., 1972.

Bicknell, A. J. and Co. *Specimen Book of One Hundred Architectural Designs.* New York: A. J. Bicknell, 1879.

> *Rustic pavilion on lake.*

Bierstadt, Edward. *The Adirondacks: Artotype Views Among the Mountains and Lakes of the North Woods.* New York: E. Bierstadt, 1886.

> *Durant family members likely cleared the way for Bierstadt, brother of the painter, to take his pictures. Frederick Clark Durant received no. 1 of forty-five special copies of the book, given years later to the Adirondack Museum by Harrison Durant.*

Bodine, Samuel T., and William T. Hord, comps. *Church of the Ascension: The First 100 Years.* Saranac Inn Post Office, N.Y., 1984.

Booklet, history of log church at Saranac Inn.

Bond, Hallie E. *Boats and Boating in the Adirondacks.* Blue Mountain Lake, N.Y.: The Adirondack Museum; Syracuse: Syracuse Univ. Press, 1995.

A history of outdoor recreation and camping, focusing on boats.

Brimmer, Frank Everett. *Camps, Log Cabins, Lodges and Clubhouses.* New York: D. Appleton, 1925.

Brown, Eleanor. *The Forest Preserve of New York State. A Handbook for Conservationists.* Glens Falls, N.Y.: The Adirondack Mountain Club, 1985.

Useful chronology and primer on the Forest Preserve.

Bruette, William A., ed. *Log Cabins and Cottages, How to Build and Furnish Them.* New York: G. Howard Watt, 1934.

Acknowledges borrowing from William Wicks and Robert Gardner.

Cable, Mary. *Top Drawer: American High Society from the Gilded Age to the Roaring Twenties.* New York: Atheneum, 1984.

Cadbury, Warder H., and Henry F. Marsh. *Arthur Fitzwilliam Tait: Artist in the Adirondacks.* Newark, Del.: American Art Journal/ Univ. of Delaware Press, 1986.

Cardinal, Roger. *Outsider Art.* New York: Praeger, 1972.

Carley, Rachel. *Cabin Fever: Rustic Style Comes Home.* New York: Simon Schuster Editions, 1998.

[Carpenter, Geo. B., & Co.]. *Tents.* Chicago: Geo. B. Carpenter & Co., 1895.

Catalog, tents for every purpose including "Regular Wall Tents," "Square Hip Roof Tents," both common in the Adirondacks.

Clark, Nancy L., and Doris A. Crofut and Elizabeth O. Lawrence, comps. *History of Ragged Lake . . . Continued. Written by Members of the Fitch Family.* Rochester, N.Y.: Lawrence W. Smith, Xerox Corp., [1980]. Illustrated. Copy signed by Nancy L. Clark and given to the Adirondack Museum Library.

Recollections of a family camp since the 1880s, bracketed by histories written by Morton Cross Fitch and David Remington, below.

Clarkson, Elisabeth Hudnut. *An Adirondack Archive: The Trail to Windover.* Utica, N.Y.: North Country Books, 1993.

Camp Foxlair and Camp Windover near North Creek.

Collins, Geraldine. *The Brighton Story, Being the History of Paul Smiths, Gabriels and Rainbow Lake.* Larchmont, N.Y.: North Country Books, 1977.

Camps, hotels, and guides by librarian at Paul Smith's College.

Committee for the Preservation of Architectural Records, Inc. *Directory of Historic American Architectural Firms.* New York: American Institute of Architects Foundation, 1979.

Comstock, Edward, Jr., ed. and comp. *The Adirondack League Club, 1890–1990.* Old Forge, N.Y.: The Adirondack League Club, 1990.

Contributors' articles on Camp and Camp Life, Land and Forest Management, Boats and Boating, Rustic Architecture, to which useful maps and ownership histories of various properties are appended.

Comstock, William T. *Bungalows, Camps and Mountain Houses.* New York: William T. Comstock, 1908.

Bungalows were easily adapted into camps, as revealed here. The Read Camp on Little Simon Pond is illustrated.

Conklin, Henry. *Through "Poverty's Vale," A Hardscrabble Boyhood in Upstate New York, 1832–1862.* Edited by Wendell Tripp. Syracuse: Syracuse Univ. Press, 1974.

Outdoor life as the companion of poverty.

Cook, Marc. *The Wilderness Cure.* New York: William Wood & Co., 1881.

Describes a camp for convalescents, skills of the guide. Cook had tuberculosis.

Cortland College. *Cortland College Essays: Outdoor Education Reflections.* Edited by Norbert Haley and George McDermott. Cortland, N.Y.: SUNY College at Cortland, 1983.

Essays on the 35th anniversary of the Outdoor Education Center at Camp Pine Knot, the first great camp.

Covey, Frances Alden. *The Earl Covey Story.* New York: Exposition Press, 1964.

Builder of lodges, chapels, and camps, written by his wife.

Cross, Amy Willard. *The Summer House: A Tradition of Leisure.* Toronto: Harper Collins Publishers, 1992.

Author's summer home in Canada, an evocation on its many facets, each with a correlative place in the heart. No illus.

Curl, Donald. *Mizner's Florida: American Resort Architecture.* Cambridge: The MIT Press, 1984.

White Pine Camp on Osgood Pond, Paul Smiths, N.Y.

Dana, William S. B. *The Swiss Chalet Book.* New York: William T. Comstock, 1913.

Articles from Architecture and Building, 1911–12.

DeSormo, Maitland C. *The Heydays of the Adirondacks.* Saranac Lake, N.Y.: Adirondack Yesteryears, Inc., 1974.

———. *John Bird Burnham.* Saranac Lake, N.Y.: Adirondack Yesteryears, 1978.

Burnham was founder and builder of the Crater Club, Essex, N.Y., in 1900.

———. *Seneca Ray Stoddard: Versatile Camera-Artist.* Saranac Lake, N.Y.: Adirondack Yesteryears, Inc., 1972.

Camps and hotels by the region's preeminent photographer, whose career spanned more than four decades.

———. *Summers on the Saranacs.* Saranac Lake, N.Y.: Adirondack Yesteryears, 1980.

Insufficiently documented as they are, DeSormo's books are full of incident drawn from his own researches and collection of historic photographs.

Donaldson, Alfred L. *A History of the Adirondacks.* 2 vols. 1921. Reprint, Fleishmanns, N.Y.: Purple Mountain Press, 1996.

The region's first history, indispensable because Donaldson's sources included people who remembered and made that history.

Downing, A. J. *The Architecture of Country Houses.* New York: D. Appleton & Co., 1850. Reprint, New York: Dover Publications, 1969.

Rural homes for tasteful Americans of moderate means.

———. *Rural Essays.* New York: Putnam, 1853. Reprint, New York: Da Capo Press, 1974.

Essays by Downing, published after his death in 1852, from the influential magazine The Horticulturist, *which he edited.*

———. *A Treatise on the Theory and Practice of Landscape Gardening, Second Supplement by Henry Winthrop Sargent.* New York: Orange Judd, Co., 1875. Reprint, Little Compton, R.I.: Theophrastus Publishers, 1977.

This includes changes by Downing to his 1841 edition.

Dunham, Harvey L. *Adirondack French Louie: Early Life in the North Woods.* Privately printed, 1952. Reprint, Saranac Lake, N.Y.: North Country Books, 1970.

Dwight, Timothy. *Travels in New-England and New-York . . . In Four Volumes.* Privately printed, 1822. Reprint, Cambridge, Mass.: The Belknap Press, 1969.

Dwight, a traveler on Lake George in 1802 and 1811, prophesized "villas of opulence" on its shores in the future.

Dwyer, C. P. *The Immigrant Builder; Or, Practical Hints to Handy-Men.* Philadelphia: Claxton, Remsen & Haffelfinger, 1872.

Popular, since the 10th edition was published in 1884.

Essai sur la Composition et L'Ornement des Jardins; ou Recueil de Plans de Jardins de Ville et de Compagne. Paris: Chez Audot, 1823.

Pavilion of hewn log with a Palladian profile, pl. 42.

Evers, Alf. *The Catskills: From Wilderness to Woodstock.* New York: Doubleday & Co., 1979.

Finley, James B. *Autobiography of James B. Finley; Or, Pioneer Life in the West.* Cincinnati: Methodist Book Concern, 1854.

Pioneer life on the frontier.

Folwell, Elizabeth, and Amy Godine. *Adirondack Odysseys: Exploring Museums and Historic Places from the Mohawk to the St. Lawrence.* Blue Mountain Lake, N.Y.: The Adirondack Museum; Lee, Mass.: Berkshire House Publishers, 1997.

Historic sites and camps open to the public.

Fosburgh, Hugh. *A Clearing in the Wilderness.* New York: Doubleday & Co., 1969.

Baker's Clearing, now the North Woods Club, Minerva, N.Y.

Foster, Edward Halsey. *The Civilized Wilderness: Backgrounds to American Romantic Literature, 1817–1860.* New York: The Free Press, 1975.

Ideas that informed the Adirondack experience.

Fowler, Albert, ed. *Cranberry Lake from Wilderness to Adirondack Park.* Blue Mountain Lake, N.Y.: The Adirondack Museum; Syracuse: Syracuse Univ. Press, 1958.

Judge Vann's camp on Buck Island, other camps.

France, Jean R. "Harvey Ellis: Architect," in *A Rediscovery—Harvey Ellis: Artist, Architect.* Exhibition catalogue. Rochester, N.Y.: Memorial Art Gallery and Margaret Woodbury Strong Museum, 1973.

Francis, Dennis Steadman. *Architects in Practice New York City 1840–1900.* New York: Committee for the Preservation of Architectural Records, 1979.

Germann, Georg. *Gothic Revival in Europe and Britain.* Trans. by Gerald Onn. Cambridge, Mass.: MIT Press, 1973.

Gilborn, Craig. *Adirondack Furniture and the Rustic Tradition.* New York: Harry N. Abrams, 1987.

———. *Durant: The Fortunes and Woodland Camps of a Family in the Adirondacks.* Sylvan Beach, N.Y.: North Country Books, 1981. Reprint, Blue Mountain Lake, N.Y.: The Adirondack Museum, 1986.

W. W. Durant's camps and a few others besides are treated in detail, along with Durant family travails.

Gilpin, William. *Remarks on Forest Scenery.* 3 vols. London: R. Blamire, 1791.

> By conditioning Europeans and American travelers to see countryside like a scroll being unfolded, books such as this made nature in its wilder guises seem more approachable, less alien.

Glassie, Henry. *Patterns in the Material Folk Culture of the Eastern United States.* Philadelphia: Univ. of Pennsylvania Press, 1968.

> Log cabins and the Cape Cod House and their plans.

Good, Albert H., ed. *Park and Recreation Structures.* 3 vols. U.S. Department of the Interior, National Park Service. Washington, D.C.: U.S. Printing Office, 1938.

> A rich compilation of rustic buildings, plans, and accessories for national and state parks.

Gowans, Alan. *Styles and Types of North America Architecture: Social Function and Cultural Expression.* New York: Icon/Harper Collins, 1992.

> Colonial to modern times, Dr. Gowans looks at housing in terms of styles and social context, an interesting synthesis. See for example his classification of architectural styles and types in North America at the back of the book.

Grady, Joseph F. *The Adirondacks: Fulton Chain–Big Moose Region.* 2nd ed. Old Forge, N.Y.: North Country Books, 1966.

> First published in 1933, this good history includes camps and hotels west of Raquette Lake.

Graham, Frank Jr. *The Adirondack Park: A Political History.* New York: Alfred A. Knopf, 1978.

Graves, Richard H. *Bush Hutmaking: Thatched Huts, Rammed Earth, Log Cabins.* Sydney: J. M. Graves, 1952.

Hamlin, Huybertie Pruyn. *An Albany Childhood.* Edited by Alice C. Kenney. Albany: Washington Park Press, 1990.

> Author's visits to Camp Santanoni, built by a relative.

Hammond, Samuel H. *Wild Northern Scenes; Or, Sporting Adventures with the Rifle and the Rod.* New York: Derby & Jackson, 1860.

Hammond, Samuel H., and L. W. Mansfield. *Country Margins and Rambles of a Journalist.* New York: J. C. Derby, Phillips, Sampson & Co., 1855.

> The end of the forest is seen in abandoned loggers' shanties and lands cleared for lumber.

Hanks, Charles Stedman. *Camp Kits and Camp Life.* New York: Charles Scribner's, 1906.

> Kit meant articles carried, as on a camping trip.

Headley, Joel Tyler. *The Adirondacks; Or, Life in the Woods.* New York: Baker and Scribner, 1849. Reprint, Harrison, N.Y.: Harbor Hill Books, 1982.

Herrmann, Wolfgang. *Laugier and Eighteenth Century French Theory.* London: A. Zwemmer, 1962.

> The "primitive hut" as source for the paragon of Western civilization, the temples of Greece and Rome.

Hewitt, Mark Alan. *The Architect and the American Country House, 1890–1940.* New Haven: Yale Univ. Press, 1990.

Hochschild, Harold K. *Township 34: A History with Digressions of an Adirondack Township in Hamilton County in the State of New York.* New York: Privately printed, 1952.

> A meticulously researched history that encompasses shanties and large camps, along with diverse subjects centering on the people who stayed and those who visited.

Hochschild, Kathrin S., with Alice Gilborn. *The Walter Hochschild Camp at Eagle Nest.* Blue Mountain Lake, N.Y.: Privately printed, 1975.

Holly, Henry Hudson. *Holly's Country Seats.* New York: D. Appleton and Co., 1863.

Housing in "savage Meccas for pale pilgrims."

Holt, Charles. *Adirondack Frontier: Stories of Keene Flats after 1776.* Elizabethtown, N.Y.: Denton Publications, 1976.

Party trapped in a leaky shanty.

Hooker, Mildred Phelps Stokes. *Camp Chronicles.* Blue Mountain Lake, N.Y.: The Adirondack Museum, 1964. Reprint, with Afterword by Whitelaw Reid, 1992.

Circulated to friends in 1952, this small book is a first-hand account of how the well-to-do summered on the St. Regis Lakes before 1900. Dr. Jamieson's introduction is brief but insightful.

Howe, Walter, comp. *The Garden Considered in Literature by Certain Polite Writers.* New York: G. P. Putnam's Sons, 1890.

Hubka, Thomas C. *Big House, Little House, Back House, Barn.* Hanover, N.H.: Univ. Press of New England, 1984.

A precedent for free-standing and connected buildings can be found in houses in New England.

Hunt, W. Ben. *How to Build and Furnish a Log Cabin: The Easy-Natural Way Using Only Hand Tools and the Woods Around You.* New York: Macmillan, 1974.

Combines Hunt's two previous books published in 1939 and 1947.

Huth, Hans. *Nature and the American: Three Centuries of Changing Attitudes.* Berkeley: Univ. of California Press, 1957.

Hyde, Floy S. *Water Over the Dam at Mountain View in the Adirondacks.* Binghamton, N.Y.: Vail-Ballou Press, Inc., 1970.

Bellmont, N.Y., on both sides of the Adirondack Park boundary in the north.

Ives, Martin Van Buren. *Through the Adirondacks in Eighteen Days.* New York and Albany: Wynkoop, Hallenbeck, Crawford Co., 1899.

A legislative report enlarged for a wider audience, it showed larger camps as evidence of the region's development.

Jackson, John Brinkerhoff. *Discovering the Vernacular Landscape.* New Haven: Yale Univ. Press, 1984.

Jackson-Stops, Gervaise. *The English Country House: A Grand Tour.* New York: Little, Brown and Co., 1985.

Jamieson, Paul. *Adirondack Pilgrimage.* Glens Falls, N.Y.: The Adirondack Mountain Club, Inc., 1986.

Essays. See "The Lean-to, Then and Now."

————, ed. *The Adirondack Reader.* 2nd. ed. Glens Falls, N.Y.: The Adirondack Mountain Club, 1982.

Excerpts from diverse sources in ten groups, each introduced by Dr. Jamieson. See sections on guides and shelters.

Jones, Barbara. *Follies & Grottos.* London: Constable, 1953.

Kaiser, Harvey H. *Great Camps of the Adirondacks.* Boston: David R. Godine, 1982.

Kaplan, Wendy, ed. *"The Art That Is Life": The Arts & Crafts Movement in America, 1875–1920.* Boston: A New York Graphic Society Book and Little, Brown, 1987.

The design and furnishing of Adirondack camps was an aspect of the Arts and Crafts Movement. This is the catalogue for the exhibition organized by the Museum of Fine Arts, Boston.

Katonah Museum of Art. *Forever Wild: The Adirondack Experience.* Katonah, N.Y.: Katonah Museum of Art, 1992.

Catalogue of exhibition celebrating Centennial of the Adirondack Park with essays by Anthony N. B. Garvan, Craig Gilborn, Paul Malo, and Robert L. McGrath.

Keith, Herbert F. *Man of the Woods.* Blue Mountain Lake, N.Y.: The Adirondack Museum; Syracuse: Syracuse Univ. Press, 1972.

Lumber camps, hotels, and hunter's cabins, Wanakena, N.Y.

Kemp, Oliver. *Wilderness Homes: A Book of the Log Cabin.* New York: The Outing Publishing Co., 1908.

Book version of articles in Field and Stream.

LaBastille, Anne. *Woodswoman.* New York: E. P. Dutton & Co., 1976.

Building a cabin and acquiring outdoor skills are told in this classic of a modern woman, first in a series by this ecologist.

Lancaster, Clay. *The American Bungalow, 1880–1930.* New York: Abbeville Press, 1985.

Author falls short of a definition that embraces his examples, but that is justified by his grasp and their scope.

———. *The Japanese Influence in America.* New York: Walton H. Rawls, 1963.

Log Cabin Office. *The Log-Cabin Song-Book. A Collection of Popular and Patriotic Songs Dedicated to the Friends of Harrison and Tyler.* New York: The Log Cabin Office, 1840.

Log cabin as a symbol of national destiny is evident here.

Longstreth, Thomas Morris. *The Adirondacks.* New York: Century, 1917.

Lossing, Benson John. *The Hudson, from the Wilderness to the Sea.* New York: Virtue & Yorston, 1866.

First published in The Art Journal of London in 1860–61, this depicted an industrious yet scenic river valley prophesized fifty years earlier by Timothy Dwight (see above).

Lowndes, G. R. *Gypsy Tents and How to Use Them.* London: Horace Cox, 1890.

[Lundy, John Patterson]. *The Saranac Exiles: A Winter's Tale of the Adirondacks. Not by W. Shakespeare.* Philadelphia: Privately printed, 1880.

A sardonic miscellany, half-fact and half-fiction, as in his caricature of the Saranac guide.

Mason, Bernard S. and Frederic H. Kock. *Cabins, Cottages, and Summer Homes.* New York: A. S. Barnes & Co., 1947.

Masten, Arthur H. *The Story of Adirondac.* New York: Privately printed, 1923. Reprint, Blue Mountain Lake, N.Y.: The Adirondack Museum; Syracuse: Syracuse Univ. Press, 1968.

McIntyre Iron Works and the Tahawus Club, to which the author had family connections.

Masters, Raymond D. *A Social History of the Huntington Wildlife Forest (Which includes Rich Lake and the Pendleton Settlement).* Newcomb, N.Y.: Newcomb Historical Society, 1993.

Caughnawauga Club and Arbutus Lodge and Preserve.

McAllester, Virginia, and Lee McAllester. *A Field Guide to American Houses.* New York: Alfred A. Knopf, 1986.

McClelland, Linda Flint. *Preserving Nature: The Historic Designs of the National Park Service, 1916 to 1942.* Washington, D.C.: U.S. Printing Office, 1993.

    See George Good, above.

McIver, Elizabeth Putnam. *Early Days at Putnam Camp.* Elizabethtown, N.Y.: Privately printed, 1941.

    Outdoor and indoor exercises of body and mind pursued by intellectuals of Boston and Cambridge, Mass.

McMartin, Barbara. *To the Lake of the Skies: The Benedicts in the Adirondacks.* Canada Lake, N.Y.: Lake View Press, 1996.

Meinecke, Conrad E. *Your Cabin in the Woods, A Compilation of Cabin Plans and Philosophy for Discovering Life in the Great Out Doors.* Buffalo: Foster & Stewart, 1945.

Morison, Samuel Eliot. *The Story of Mount Desert Island.* Boston: Little Brown, 1960.

Mott, George, and Sally Sample Aall. *Follies and Pleasure Pavilions.* New York: Harry N. Abrams, 1989.

Murray, Amelia Matilda. *Letters from the United States, Cuba and Canada.* 2 vols. London: John W. Parker & Son; New York: Putnam, 1856.

    Her Elizabethtown to Boonville trip is the first trans-Adirondack trip recorded by a woman. See vol. 2: 264–87.

Murray, William H. H. *Adventures in the Wilderness; Or, Camp-Life in the Adirondacks.* 1869. Reprint, edited by William K. Verner with introduction and notes by Warder H. Cadbury, Blue Mountain Lake, N.Y.: The Adirondack Museum; Syracuse: Syracuse Univ. Press, 1970.

    Credited with starting the "rush to the wilderness" the year of publication; in 1904, the author said the book was "fiction largely," a comment he repeated two more times. He was ill and died soon after.

———. *Lake Champlain and Its Shores.* Boston: De Wolfe, Fiske & Co., 1890.

    Murray proposes that the forest across northern New England and New York be pre-served and called "the Great National Park."

Nabokov, Peter, and Robert Easton. *Native American Architecture.* New York: Oxford Univ. Press, 1989.

    Indians routinely used bark shanties before settlers from Europe.

National Architects' Union. *Picturesque Homes for Forest and Shore.* Philadelphia: National Architects' Union, c. 1891.

Newhouse, S. *The Trapper's Guide; A Manual of Instructions.* 3rd ed. New York: Oakley Mason & Co., 1869.

    Illus. of "The Home Shanty."

New York State. Chapter 831, An Act for the Protection of Private Parks and Grounds, and to Encourage the Propagation of Fish and Game. Passed April 28, 1871. *Laws of New York: Ninety-Fourth Session.* Albany: Argus Co., 1871.

    Encouraged formation of private preserves and clubs.

———. Commission of Fisheries, Game, and Forests. *First Annual Report of . . . [1895].* Albany: Wyncoop Hallenbeck Crawford, 1896.

    State support for large landowners: laying out, posting, and trespass on private grounds, 310–16.

———. Commission of Fisheries, Game, and Forests. *Second Annual Report of . . . [1896].* Albany: Wyncoop Hallenbeck Crawford, 1897.

Occupants of state lands, 341ff; lands purchased, 371ff.

———. Commission of Fisheries, Game, and Forests. *Eighth and Ninth Reports of . . . [1902 and 1903].* Albany: Wyncoop Hallenbeck Crawford, n.d.

Private preserves: 36ff.

———. Commission of State Parks. *First Annual Report,* Senate Document No. 102. Albany: Weed, Parsons & Co., 1873.

Largely the work of Verplanck Colvin, the Commission recommended that forest lands be protected by placing them in a state park.

———. *Report of the Forest Commission . . . 1893.* 2 vols. Albany: Wyncook Hallenbeck Crawford, 1893.

Nichols, Rose Standish. *English Pleasure Gardens.* New York: Macmillan, 1902.

[Nichols, William B.] *Life in the Adirondacks.* New York: Privately printed, 1876.

Copy at the New-York Historical Society, New York City.

Nickl, Peter, ed. *Banke In Park Und Garten.* Edition Minerva. Muchen: Minerva Hermann Farnung, 1998.

Park and garden furniture.

Norberg-Schulz, Christian. *Architecture: Meaning and Place.* New York: Rizzoli, 1986.

Northrup, A. Judd. *Camps and Tramps in the Adirondacks and Grayling Fishing in Northern Michigan.* Syracuse: Davis, Bardeen & Co., 1880.

Camping narrative in the southwest quarter of the Adirondack Park.

Nowlin, William. *The Bark-Covered House; Or, Back to the Woods Again.* Detroit: Privately printed, 1876. Facimile copy: Ann Arbor, Mich.: Univ. Microfilms, 1966.

Family that moved from Putnam Co., N.Y., to southern Michigan where they erected a house with bark roof in 1834.

O'Brien, Kathryn E. *The Great and the Gracious on Millionaire's Row.* Sylvan Beach, N.Y.: North Country Books, 1978.

O'Leary, Ann Stillman. *Adirondack Style.* New York: Clarkson Potter, 1998.

Oxford English Dictionary. 2 vols. Compact edition. Oxford Univ. Press, 1971.

Owens, Carole. *The Berkshire Cottages: A Vanishing Era.* Englewood Cliffs, N.Y.: Cottage Press, Inc., 1980.

Shadow Brook, a summer lodge completed in 1893 with 100 rooms, made Adirondack camps seem not so "great" in terms of size.

Parker, J. B. *Vacation Cabins.* Minnesota: J. B. Parker, 1932.

Company catalogue of prefabricated vacation cabins.

Perkins, George F. *Journeys to the Adirondacks for the Years 1879, 1892, 1883, 1885.* N.p., privately printed, 1956.

Extracts from diaries by president of the Hollywood Club.

Perlin, John. *A Forest Journey.* Cambridge, Mass.: Harvard Univ. Press, 1989.

Pilcher, Edith. *Up the Lake Road: The First Hundred Years of the Adirondack Mountain Reserve.* Keene Valley, N.Y.: Adirondack Mountain Reserve, 1987.

History of land management by AMR and the Ausable Club. The two bodies have similar boards.

Prance, Anne E. *Bark: The Formation, Characteristics and Uses of Bark Around the World.* Portland, Oregon: Timber Press, 1993.

Preservation League of New York State. *Great Camps: A Century of Adirondack Architecture.* Albany, N.Y.: Preservation League, 1992.

Multilithed summary distributed at the conference held at Sagamore Lodge on July 24–26, 1992.

Reed, Douglass C. *Log Cabin Mythology.* Hagerstown, Md.: Creative Printing, 1977.

Reed, William. *Life on the Border, Sixty Years Ago.* Fall River, Mass.: Robert Adams, 1882.

Derelict log cabin near Adirondacks became home in 1820s for a family from Newport, N.H.

Remington, David Fitch. *History of Matamek Corporation at Ragged Lake.* Still River, Mass.: Privately printed, 1997.

See citations to Fitch and Clark above.

Ricauti, T. J. *Rustic Architecture.* London: 1842.

His designs, he says, should appeal to Americans.

Richards, T. Addison. *American Scenery, Illustrated.* New York: Leavitt and Allen, 1854.

Lake George and the Adirondacks.

Rinhart, Floyd and Marion. *Summertime: Photographs of Americans at Play, 1850–1900.* New York: Clarkson N. Potter, Inc., 1978.

Rivinus, Willis M., comp. *The Cabins of the Huron Mountain Club.* N.p., privately printed, 1969.

Booklet illustrating camps in a Michigan club. Adirondack Museum Library.

Roy, Robert. *Book of Cordwood Masonry Housebuilding.* New York: Sterling Publishing Co., 1981.

That's right, a house of cordwood.

Rutstrum, Calvin. *The Wilderness Cabin.* New York: The Macmillan Co., 1961.

Rykwert, Joseph. *On Adam's House in Paradise: The Idea of the Primitive Hut in Architectural Theory.* Cambridge: MIT Press, 1981.

Sampson, W. H. *Mohican Point on Lake George.* New York: Privately printed, 1913.

Summer homes and resort hotel "Mohican House" in Bolton and vicinity.

Saylor, Henry H. *Bungalows.* New York: McBride, Winston & Co., 1911.

Two Adirondack camps, the Read Camp designed by Davis, McGrath and Shepard, New York City, and a "country home" by Scopes & Feustmann, Saranac Lake.

Schneider, Paul. *The Adirondacks: A History of America's First Wilderness.* New York: A John McRae Book/Henry Holt & Co., 1997.

Schullery, Paul. *Fly Fishing in America, A History.* New York: Lyons & Burford, 1987.

Especially good on clubs and sporting books and periodicals of the nineteenth century.

Schuyt, Michael, and Joost Elffers and George Collins. *Fantastic Architecture.* New York: Harry N. Abrams, 1980.

Scully, Vincent. *The Shingle Style and the Stick Style: Architectural Theory and Design.* Rev. ed. New Haven: Yale Univ. Press, 1971.

Sheldon, George William. *Artistic Country-Seats: Types of Recent American Villa and Cottage Architecture with Instances of Country Club-Houses.* 1884. Reprint, with introductory essay by Arnold Lewis, "Sheldon and *Artistic Country-Seats.*" New York: Dover Publications, Inc., 1982.

Lewis analyzes residences by owner, architect, and region, offering insights into a patronage comparable to wealthier camp owners in the Adirondacks.

Shepard, Augustus D. *Camps in the Woods.* New York: Architectural Book Publishing Co., 1931.

Camps designed by Shepard between c. 1902 and 1930 at the Adirondack League Club for fellow members.

Sherman, Joe. *The House at Shelburne Farms.* Middlebury, Vt.: Paul S. Eriksson, 1986.

The architect was the same for Dr. and Mrs. Webb's Vermont farm and estate and their camp and preserve in the Adirondacks.

Sloan, Florence Adele. *Maverick in Mauve.* Garden City, N.Y.: Doubleday, 1983.

Vanderbilt family.

Smith, H. Perry. *Modern Babes in the Wood; Or, Summerings in the Wilderness.* Hartford, Conn.; Syracuse, N.Y.: Columbian Book Co., 1872.

E. R. Wallace's first descriptive guide to region: 239ff.

Springer, John S. *Forest Life and Forest Trees.* New York: Harper & Bros., 1851.

Logging and logging camps in Maine.

Steinback, Elsa Kny. *Sweet Peas and a White Bridge on Lake George When Steam Was King.* Burlington, Vt.: Privately printed, 1974.

Adirondack Lodge, Knapp Estate, and other attractions.

Stickler, Dr. Joseph W., ed. and comp. *The Adirondacks as a Health Resort.* New York: G. P. Putnam's Sons, 1886.

Stickley, Gustav. *Craftsman Homes.* 1909. Reprint, New York: Dover Publishing Co., 1979.

———. *More Craftsman Homes.* 1912, Reprint, New York: Dover Publishing Co., 1982.

Stilgoe, John R. *Common Landscape of America, 1580–1845.* New Haven: Yale Univ. Press, 1982.

Stoddard, Seneca Ray. *The Adirondacks, Illustrated.* Albany: Weed, Parsons, 1874.

Guide to the region, published annually, 1874–1913.

———. *The Adirondacks, Illustrated.* Glens Falls, N.Y.: Privately printed, 1893. 25th ed. in 1895.

Strombeck, Janet and Richard. *Gazebos and Other Garden Structure Designs.* New York: Sterling Publishing Co., 1983.

Sylvester, Nathaniel Bartlett. *Historical Sketches of Northern New York and the Adirondack Wilderness.* 1877. Reprint, Harrison, N.Y.: Harbor Hill Books, 1973.

[Taylor, Frank H.] *Birch Bark from the Adirondacks; Or, From City to Trail.* New York: Adirondack Railway Co., 1888.

Taylor, Robert. *Saranac: America's Magic Mountain.* New York: Paragon House Publishers, 1986.

Personalities in the rise of Saranac as a tuberculosis treatment center and playground for the rich and famous, including Mrs. Post and her Camp Topridge.

Terrie, Philip G. *Contested Terrain: A New History of Nature and People in the Adirondacks.* Blue Mountain Lake, N.Y.: The Adirondack Museum; Syracuse: Syracuse Univ. Press, 1997.

Adirondack lands and conflicting views by a college professor formerly on the staff at the Adirondack Museum.

————. *Forever Wild: Environmental Aesthetics and the Adirondack Forest Preserve.* Philadelphia: Temple Univ. Press, 1985. Reprint, *Forever Wild: A Cultural History of Wilderness in the Adirondacks,* Syracuse: Syracuse Univ. Press, 1994.

————. *Wildlife and Wilderness: A History of Adirondack Mammals.* Fleischmanns, N.Y.: Purple Mountain Press, 1993.

Hunters and camping, including "Murray Fools" of 1869.

Thevoz, Michel. *Art Brut.* New York: Rizzoli, 1976.

Thiede, Arthur, and Cindy Teipner. *American Log Homes.* Layton, Utah: Gibbs Smith, 1992.

Thomas, Lester St. John. *Timber, Tannery and Tourists: Lake Luzerne, Warren County, New York.* Lake Luzerne, N.Y.: Committee on Publication, 1979.

Thoreau, Henry David. *Walden; Or, Life in the Woods.* Boston: Ticknor and Fields, 1854.

Thoreau's experiment on Walden Pond, in which he built a one-room "house" for $28 and lived in it, was followed by his book Walden, *holy grail for dreamers of a cabin in the woods ever since.*

Todd, John. *Long Lake.* Edited by J. Brace, Jr. 1845. Reprint, Harrison, N.Y.: Harbor Hill Books, 1983.

Rev. Todd's mission took him to Long Lake in 1841, 1843, and 1844. Log houses.

Townshend, F. Trench. *Ten Thousand Miles of Travel, Sport and Adventure.* London: Hurst & Blackett, 1869.

Trudeau, Edward Livingston. *An Autobiography.* Philadelphia: Lea & Febinger, 1916.

Dr. Trudeau wrote about churches and camps and advocated exposing tubercular patients to open air, rest, and a good diet.

U.S. Department of Agriculture. *Plans of Farm Buildings for Northeastern States.* Misc. publication No. 278. Washington, D.C., 1937.

Split-log barn, 42.

Van Zandt, Roland. *The Catskill Mountain House.* New Brunswick, N.J.: Rutgers Univ. Press, 1966.

Van Valkenburgh, Norman J. *The Adirondack Forest Preserve.* Blue Mountain Lake, N.Y.: The Adirondack Museum, 1979.

"A narrative of the Evolution of the Adirondack Forest Preserve" by the former head of lands and forests for New York State.

Vaux, Calvert. *Villas and Cottages.* New York: Harper & Brothers, 1857.

Vaux and the late A. J. Downing had been partners in Newburgh, N.Y.

Waddell, William Coventry Henry. *A Paper Read before the American Geographical and Statistical Society, November 2, 1854.* New York: Putnam, 1855.

Based largely on an 1840s report written by a civil engineer, Abraham Franklin Edwards, for the Sackett's Harbor and Saratoga Railroad Co.

Wallace, Edwin R. *A Descriptive Guide to the Adirondacks, Revised and Corrected.* 8th ed. Syracuse, N.Y.: Privately printed, 1880.

See H. Perry Smith, Modern Babes in the Woods; Wallace's guides, 1875–1900.

Ward, Gerald, et. al. *Francis P. Garvan, Collector.* New Haven: Yale Univ. Art Gallery, 1980.

Weiss, Jo Ann W. *Clarence Cook: His Critical Writings.* Baltimore: Johns Hopkins Univ. Press, 1976.

Cook, a cultural critic and advocate of public parks along with his influencial brother-in-law, A. J. Downing.

Welsh, Peter C. *Jacks, Jobbers, and Kings: Logging the Adirondacks.* Utica, N.Y.: North Country Books, 1995.

Weslager, C. A. *The Log Cabin in America: From Pioneer Days to the Present.* New Brunswick, N.J.: Rutgers University Press, 1969.

Wheeler, Gervase. *Rural Homes or Sketches of Houses Suited to Country Life.* New York: Charles Scribners, 1851.

Wheeler, Llewellan R. *Ornamental Rustic Work.* Orange, N.Y.: Llewellan R. Wheeler, 1931.

   Illustrated sales catalog for firm "Established 1865."

White, Charles D. *Camps and Cottages, How to Build Them Yourself.* New York: Thomas Y. Crowell, 1946.

   By an architect, this was the first revised edition.

White, E. B. *One Man's Meat.* New York: Harper & Brothers, 1950.

   See "Once More to the Lake," first published in August 1941.

White, Steward Edward. *The Cabin.* London: Thomas Nelson & Sons, 1912.

White, William Chapman. *Adirondack Country.* New York: Alfred A. Knopf, 1954. Rev. ed. New York: A.A. Knopf, 1970.

   Readable and reliable, by the retired reporter and columnist at the Herald Tribune and New York Times.

Wicks, William S. *Log Cabins and Cottages: How to Build and Furnish Them.* 1889. 9th rev. ed. New York: Forest and Stream, 1928.

   The best-read book of its kind to judge by reprints. Wicks was an architect and member of the Adirondack League Club.

Wiegand, Wayne A. *Irrepressible Reformer: A Biography of Melvil Dewey.* Chicago: American Library Association, 1996.

Wilkinson, Elizabeth and Marjorie Henderson. *The House of Boughs or Decorating Eden.* San Francisco: Chronicle Books, 1992.

Wilson, Leila Fosburgh. *The North Woods Club, 1886–1986.* Minerva, N.Y.: Privately printed, 1986.

   A well-written, documented history of the Baker Farm and the club that followed it.

Winslow, C. A. *The Life of Hermann M. Biggs.* Philadelphia: Lea & Febiger, 1929.

   Platform tents.

Withey, Henry F., and Elsie Withey. *Biographical Dictionary of American Architects, Deceased.* Los Angeles: Hennessy & Ingalls, 1956. Reprint, Detroit: Omni-Graphics, 1996.

Woodward, George E. *Woodward's Country Homes.* New York: Privately printed, 1865.

Periodicals

Adams, Samuel Hopkins. "William Rockefeller, Maker of Wilderness." *Colliers* (Apr. 22, 1905): 15–18.

   Residents of Brandon, N.Y., being evicted from land bought for a game preserve.

"An Adirondack Camp." *International Studio* 38 (July 1909): xxv.

   Camp Ziegler on Loon Lake.

"An Adirondack Lodge." *House and Garden* 12 (Dec. 1907): 203–7.

   William Read Camp on Lake Wilbert (now Little Simon), designed by Davis, McGrath & Shepard.

Adirondack Mountain Reserve. "The First One Hundred Years of the Adirondack Mountain Reserve." Poster, n.d. [c. 1986].

Parallel chronologies of AMR and Town of Keene, 1887–1987.

"Adirondack Style Shopping." *Elle Deco,* no.22 (Feb. 1996): 98–115.

Produced in Japan in Japanese with illustrations from the Adirondack Museum.

Ames, Joseph B. "Building a Log Cabin." *Country Life in America* 20 (May 15, 1912): 62, 82.

"Association for the Protection of the Adirondacks, The. By 'Adirondack.'" *Woods and Waters* 5 (Autumn 1902): 12–14.

Auchincloss, Henry B. "Suggests Open Camp[s] to Solve Problem of Cheaper Sanatorium Construction." *Journal of Outdoor Life* 3 (Aug. 1906): 260–67.

Bailey, M. Kennedy. "A Forest House." *The Craftsman* 12 (May 1911): 205–7.

Banks, William Nathaniel. "The Wesleyan Grove Campground on Martha's Vineyard." *Antiques* (July 1983): 104–16.

Cabins resembling tents and tiny picturesque cottages.

Bauer, Peter. "New Houses, Old Ideas." *Adirondack Life* 19 (Sept./Oct. 1988): 63–67, 95–96.

Barrows, John E. "Earl Covey, Adirondack Builder." *Fine Homebuilding* 40 (June/July 1987): 38–42.

Covewood Lodge, Twitchell Lake Inn, Chapel at Big Moose Lake.

Beals, Jessie Tarbox. "An Open Camp in the Woods." *Country Life in America* 18 (June 1910): 204.

Lean-to built by "three young men in four days," Big Moose Lake.

———. "Bungalows of All Types for Hill and Dale." *Country Life in America* 22 (Sept. 1914): 38–41.

Binney, Marcus. "Luxury in the Wilds." *Country Life in America* (Apr. 2, 1981): 866–69.

Continuation of the article below.

———. "Two Great Camps of the Adirondacks." *Country Life in America* (March 26, 1981): 794–97.

Uncas and Sagamore Lodge.

Bliss, Carmen. "The Ghost House: A Quiet Day in the Catskills." *The Craftsman* 5 (June 1906): 279–84.

Bordon, William Alanson. "Veranda Houses." *Indoors and Out* 4 (June 1907): 110–13.

Stairless houses dominated by wrap-around porches.

Boyd, [Charles Vaughn]. "Blue Mountain Lake, Adirondacks." *Forest and Stream* 2 (July 2, 1874): 323.

Chauncey Hathorn's shanty hotel under construction. See below.

———. "The Old-Fashioned Log Cabin." *Woman's Home Companion Picture Section* (May 1916): 46.

See above.

Brown, Patricia Leigh. "Out-Twigging the Neighbors." *New York Times.* House & Home section (Oct. 23, 1997).

Camp construction and restoration by the new-rich.

———. "Preserving Adirondack Great Camps." *New York Times*. House & Home section (June 12, 1992).

Burly, James. "A Comfortable Camp in the Woods." *House and Garden* (June 1914): 449–51, 480–81.

"Hukweem," Loon Lake.

Burnham, John B. "Back to Log Cabin Days." *House and Garden* (June 1933): 37, 62.

Burroughs, Julian. "How I Built My Own Country House." *Country Life in America* 9 (Feb. 1906): 415–17.

His father, famed naturalist-writer John Burroughs, also built a log cabin.

"Camp Building in the Adirondacks." *Decorator & Furnisher* 7 (Oct., 1885): 8.

Reveals early grasp of region's lake character and "ensemble" camps. Locale was possibly Upper St. Regis Lake.

Carpenter, Warwick S. "How to Build a Recreation Log Cabin." *Recreation* 25 (July 1909): 17–19, 32–33.

Practical text with variety of examples, of which one was a remodeled cabin and another a "Reclaimed Chopper's Cabin."

Comstock, Edward, Jr. "The Role of Private Preserves in the Adirondack Park." *Adirondack Journal of Environmental Studies* 2 (Fall/Winter 1995): 32–39.

Cook, Clarence. "The Late A. J. Downing." *The New York Quarterly* (Oct. 1852).

Cook, an advocate of parks and rustic adornment, was brother-in-law to A. J. Downing.

Corthell, Wendell G. "The Use of Wood in Switzerland." *The Craftsman* 5 (Oct. 1903): 31–41.

Coulter, William L. "Three Little Cabins in the Woods." N.p., c. 1905.

Fragment of an article by a Saranac Lake, N.Y., architect. Adirondack Museum Library.

"Craftsman Lodge for the Wilderness, A." *The Craftsman* 12 (Oct. 1916): 82–88.

Crosby, Ernest. "A Century of Ugliness." *The Craftsman* 5 (July 1904): 409–10.

Complaints of modern life in a magazine that showed alteratives—Craftsman designs and a vigorous outdoor life.

Curtis, Natalie. "The New Log House at Craftsman Farms." *The Craftsman* 12 (Nov. 1911): 508–11.

Abraham Lincoln and romantic associations with log houses.

Davis, Matthews E. "The Floating Camp for Summer." *Winter Life at Saranac Lake* (1912): 16.

"Floating bungalow" in a booklet promoting the village. Adirondack Museum Library.

"Destruction of Young Spruce for Rustic Architecture, The." *Woods and Waters* 6 (Winter 1903–4): 14–15.

Dix, William Frederick. "Summer Life in Luxurious Adirondack Camps." *The Independent* 55 (July 2, 1903): 1556–62.

Sees camps as "a highly significant phase of American life."

Ellis, A. Raymond. "Bungalows of Logs." *Indoors and Out* 3, no.6 (1906): 300–304.

———. "The Cheapest House—The Log Cabin." *Country Life in America* 14 (April 15, 1912): 39–41.

Ellis, Harvey. "An Adirondack Camp." *The Craftsman* 4 (July 1903): 281–84.

Ely, W. W. "Ampersand Mountain: A Bird's Eye View of the Adirondacks." *Forest and Stream* 1 (Sept. 18, 1873): 84.

"Excursion to the Adirondack Mountains, in the Summer of 1861, An." *Friend's Intelligencer* 18–20; 650–52; 665–67; 699–701; 715–17; 726–28; 742–43.

   Article in six issues.

Fernald, Bejamin G. "The Decorative Possibilities of Birch and Cedar Bark." *Country Life in America* 13 (Aug. 1, 1911): 53–54.

Field, Kate. "In and Out of the Woods." *The Atlantic Almanac for 1870* (1870): 48–53.

   Field sounds like Thoreau, whom she admired, in giving advice, namely that women be as independent in the woods as men.

Fisher, Theodore M. "Rustic Architecture at Its Best." *Country Life in America* 11 (April 1909): 643–44.

"Folingsby's Pond." *Hours at Home* 9 (Aug. 1869): 427–35.

   Follensby is the current spelling.

"Forest Bungalow, A." *The Craftsman* 5 (June 1904): 305–9.

Freeman, Allen. "Call of the Wild." *Historic Preservation* 46 (Nov./Dec. 1994): 28–35, 86–88.

   Historic preservation in the Adirondacks.

French, Lillie Hamilton. "Adirondack Camps." *Harper's Bazaar* 32 (Sept. 16, 1899): 775–77.

   Adirondack camps viewed with a decorator's eye.

G., C. S. "An Ideal Game Preserve." *Recreation* 14 (April 1901): 263–65.

   Litchfield Park.

Gadsky, Mary Ellen. "Sagamore: A Prototypical Adirondack Great Camp." Preservation League of New York State *Newsletter* (Jan./Feb. 1983): 3–5.

Gaut, Helen Lukens. "The Charm and Usefulness of a Mountain Camp." *The Craftsman* 12 (Aug. 1911): 593–96.

Gilborn, Craig. "Oh for a Lodge in Some Vast Wilderness." *Nineteenth Century* 2 (Summer 1976): 22–29.

   Adirondack camps.

Goldthwaite, Kenneth. "A Quaint Lodge in the Adirondacks." *Town & Country*, no. 3036 (July 23, 1904): 18–21.

   Adolph Lewisohn's camp, designed by William Coulter.

[Hallock, Charles]. "The Raquette Club." *Harper's Magazine* 41 (Aug. 1870): 321-38.

   With satirical engravings.

Harrigan, Anthony. "Ned Harrigan's Summer House." *National Review* (July 18, 1975): 779–80.

   Summer home on Schroon Lake of author's grandfather, a theatrical figure who wrote, "Now I'm Schroon Jake from Schroon Lake."

Harris, William Laurel. "Rustic Life and the Furniture It Demands." *Good Furniture* (Oct. 1915): 228–32.

Haynes, Wesley. "HSR Complete for Santanoni Farm." Adirondack Achitectural Heritage *Newsletter* 5 (Nov. 1996): 1, 3–4.

Hewitt, Mark A. "Living with Antiques: The Pavilion, Ticonderoga, New York." *Antiques* (July 1988): 130–41.

Hildebrand, John. "Coming Home: Hunting Squirrels and Tigers with the Hmong." *Harper's Magazine* 297 (Oct. 1998): 72–80.

Hinds, Michael deCourcy. "Adirondack Survivors: Rustic Grand Camps." *New York Times.* Home section (Aug. 27, 1981).

Eagle Nest Park and Kamp Kill Kare.

Hopper, Raymond. "Primeval Adirondacks." *Forest and Stream* 36 (June 18, 1891): 432–33.

LaMont's hotel for sportsmen on Smith Lake, which Hopper said had telephone service to Lowville, N.Y., outside the Adirondacks.

Hoppin, G. M. "The Adirondack Lakes." *Broadway, A London Magazine* N.S. 2 (Mar. 1869): 263–69.

Hotaling, Mary B. "Architects and Builders in the Adirondacks." Adirondack Architectural Heritage *Newsletter* 1 (May 1992): 5–8.

———. "Ben Muncil, Master Builder." Adirondack Architectural Heritage *Newsletter* 6 (June 1997): 1, 3–4.

———. "Framing a Legacy. *Adirondack Life* 28 (Mar./Apr. 1997): 32–39.

William Coulter and successor architects in the firm he started in Saranac Lake, N.Y., in 1897.

———. "Robert H. Robertson, Architect of Santanoni." Adirondack Architectural Heritage *Newsletter* 5 (June 1996): 1,3.

———. "William L. Coulter: Adirondack Architect." Preservation League of New York State *Newsletter* (Fall 1989): 4–5.

Hunter, George Leland. "Summer Furniture." *Country Life in America* 15 (May 15, 1912): n.p.

Wicker and other natural materials for camp furniture.

"In the Camps and on the Lakes of the Adirondacks." *New York Times* (Aug. 15, 1909): n.p.

St. Regis camps illustrated in Sunday edition. The predecessor of Camp Topridge is among them.

Iovine, Julie V. "Raising Arizona in Manhattan." *New York Times.* House and Home section (Jan. 4, 1996).

Fake log cabin atop a brownstone in the city.

Jervis, Simon. "Antler and Horn Furniture." Victoria and Albert Museum *Yearbook* (London: V & A Museum, 1972).

Johnson, Krissa. "Tree Houses." *Adirondack Life* 17 (Jan./Feb. 1986): 46–48.

Practical information about logs and log construction by a builder.

K., E. D. "A Millionaire's Adirondack Camp." *The Mail and Express Illustrated Saturday Magazine* 64 (Aug. 25, 1900): 3.

Huntington's Camp Pine Knot in an English periodical.

"Kamp Kill Kare." *Country Life* (Dec. 1923): 57–60.

Fine photographs by John Wallace Gillies, who was photographer for the book by Augustus D. Shepard.

"'Kamp Kill Kare,' Lieutenant-Governor Woodruff's Preserve." *Town & Country* (Nov. 2, 1901): 6–11.

Kellogg, Alice M. "Luxurious Adirondack Camps." *Broadway Magazine* 21 (August 1908): 207–12.

Excellent portrait of trophy camps.

———. "Recent Camp Architecture." Parts 1 and 2. *International Studio* 25 (1905): 73–76; 26 (1906): 6–10.

    Camps of Adolph Lewisohn, Reginald Vanderbilt, O. H. Kahn, and Levi P. Morton.

Kelly, Florence Finch. "How to Furnish a Bungalow." *Indoors and Out* 4 (Aug. 1907): 217–20.

Kidney, Walter C. "The Dragons and the Swiss: An Earlier International Style?" *Nineteenth Century* 1 (Winter 1975), 21–28.

King, Thomas G. "Adirondack Guides." *Recreation* 17 (Sept. 1902): 183–84.

    Unfavorable comparison of present-day guides with those of a generation earlier.

Kirschenbaum, Howard. "Endangered Architecture." *Adirondack Life* 16 (Sept./Oct. 1985): 13–14.

    Great camps at risk and their potential.

———. "Thirty-Four or More?" *Adirondack Life* 16 (May/June 1985): 9–12.

    "Great Camp" definitions and 34 camps that might qualify.

"Lake George." *Harper's New Monthly Magazine* 361 (Aug. 1879): 321–39.

Lay, Charles Downing. "Gazebos and Summer Houses." *Indoors and Out* 2, no.3 (1906): 129–32.

"Log Cabin Club House." *The Craftsman* 30 (Aug. 1916): 523–24.

    Haverford, Pa., designed by architect D. Knickerbocker Boyd.

Leonbruno, Frank. "The Knapp Estate on Lake George." *The Chronicle* (May 8–15, 1997): 16, 17.

Mabie, Hamilton Wright. "Winter in the Adirondacks." *Scriber's Magazine* 4 (Dec. 1888): 641–56.

    Winter sport was still a novelty when this appeared.

Macqueen, Peter and J. Hyatt Smith. "Life in the Adirondacks." *Munsey's Magazine* 8 (Feb. 1893): 479–93.

Malo, Paul. "Inventing the Adirondack Log Villa: From Woodsman's Cabin to Rustic Lodge." Association for Preservation Technology *Bulletin* 29, no. 2 (1998): 27–34.

———. "Nippon in the North Country: Japanese Inspiration in Form and Philosophy." *Adirondack Life* 29, no. 7, Special Collectors Issue (1998): 50–56.

Marshall, James Collier. "Furnishing the Bungalow." *Country Life in America* 16 (Sept. 1914): 45–48.

McClure, David. "Our Forest Preserves." *Forest Leaves* 1 (Spring 1904): 37–42.

    Excerpts from his speech at the Constitutional Convention, 1894.

[McEntee, Jervis]. "The Lakes of the Wilderness." *The Great Republic Monthly* (April 1859): 335–50.

    Illustration of Wood's shanty on Raquette Lake, after a drawing by Jervis McEntee.

Merrill, Fannie B. "Life at Paul Smith's." *Forest and Stream* 41 (June 18, 1891): 435–36.

    Vivid portrait of a "fashionable hostelry."

Miller, Seaver Asbury. "The Sporting Clubs in the Adirondacks." *Outing* 32 (Aug. 1898): 475–82.

    Larger clubs and their preserves.

Murray, William H. H. "In Memorium." *Woods and Waters* 4 (Summer 1901): 7–8.

    Eulogizes "Honest" John Plumley.

Newton, Roger Hale. "Our Summer Resort Architecture—An American Phenomenon and Social Document." *Art Quarterly* 4, no. 4 (1941): 297–321.

Pioneering study inspired by exhibition organized by Talbot Hamlin at the Avery Architectural Library, Columbia University.

Oettinger, Brenda. "Historic Preservation Bills." *New York Environmental News* 9 (June 30, 1982): 6–7

Sagamore land exchange and positions taken, including DEC's posture of "benign neglect."

"Our Artist in the Adirondacks." *Appleton's Journal of Literature, Science and Art* 8 (Sept. 1872): 323–25.

Amusing woodcut sketches of people, including Mother Johnson.

"Our Great Summer Playground." *Munsey's Magazine* 15 (June 1896): 258–84.

Pike, Horace L. "Building a $600 Log Cabin." *Country Life in America* 9 (Jan. 1906): 333–34.

Priestman, Dorothy Tuke. "Furnishings for the Bungalow." *Country Life in America* 13 (Feb. 1911): 321–23.

Radford, Harry V. "The Lewis and Clark Exposition from the Viewpoint of the Sportsman." *Woods and Waters* 8 (Summer 1905): 11–13.

The Forestry Building at the Portland, Ore., exposition measured 205 feet by 108 feet and used two miles of unfinished logs, three to six feet in diameter.

———. "The Seventh Annual Sportsman's Show." *Woods and Waters* 4 (Summer 1901): 9–10.

———. "The Sportsman and His Guide." *Field & Stream* 7 (Feb. 1903): 691–94.

Address delivered at the annual banquet of the Brown's Tract Guides' Association, reprinted in Radford's Woods and Waters 7 *(Spring 1904), 16–19.*

———. "The World's Fair." *Woods and Waters* 7 (Summer 1904): 20–22.

Louisiana Purchase Exposition at St. Louis, 1904, including New York display with "Camp Adirondacks" built by Frank Sperry.

Randolph, Wayne. "Wilderness Architecture: A Trapper's Cabin Survey." (N.p., n.d.): 6–8.

Written by a graduate of the Cooperstown Program, in author's files.

[Raymond, Henry Jarvis.] "A Week in the Wilderness, Notes on a Tour of Observation Through the Wilderness of Northern New-York." *New-York Daily Times* (June 19, 26; July 7, 24, 1855).

Signed "HJR." Raymond's interest and support of the Adirondacks was continued by the New York Times, successor to Raymond's newspaper.

"A Real Lesson in House Building." *The Craftsman* 7 (June 1906): 408–12.

Redfield, William Charles. "Some Accounts of Two Visits to the Mountains in Essex County, New York, in the Years 1836 and 1837." *The Family Magazine* 5 (1838): 345–54.

Reiff, Daniel D. "Architectural History and the Great Camps." *Nineteenth Century* 10, no.2 (1991): 14–19.

———. "Small Camps of the Adirondacks." *Nineteenth Century* 12, no. 2 (1993): 23–29.

By "Pleasant Lake" the author may mean Lake Pleasant, Hamilton County.

Residents' Committee to Protect the Adirondacks. "Whitneys Push 15,000-Acre Development Around Little Tupper Lake." *Newsletter* 3 (Winter 1997): 1–2, 4–5.

In 1998, New York State purchased this 15,000 acre tract, which left 36,000 acres still in the Whitney Estate.

Roberts, Russell G. "Architect-Author William S. Wicks." Adirondack Architectural Heritage *Newsletter* 6 (Dec. 1997): 1, 6.

[Rogers, W. A.] "Camping Out as a Fine Art." *Harper's Weekly* 27 (Nov. 17, 1883): 731.

Woodcut illustrations from drawings made by W. A. Rogers at Camp Pine Knot.

Rozhon, Tracie. "New York Begs for its Orphans: Houses Taken by the State, Then Left Out in the Cold." *New York Times.* House and Home section (Feb. 5, 1998).

Schermerhorn, C. E. "Adirondack Cabin: An Ideal Summer Home." *Beautiful Homes* (c. 1909): 13

Item in possession of Paul Maloney, owner of this camp on Blue Mountain Lake.

Schopfer, Jean. "Swiss Chalets." *Architectural Record* 7 (1898): 33–61.

Chalets no longer are farm houses but are summer residences for "moneyed classes."

——— "Wooden Houses in Switzerland." *Architectural Record* 6 (April–June, 1897): 415–28.

Shaw, Christopher. "The Caretakers." *Adirondack Life* 19
(Nov./Dec. 1988): 58–62.

People who look after Adirondack camps.

Shoumatoff, Alex. "Camp Life." *Vanity Fair* (May 1997): 158–68, 188–94.

Camps as playgrounds for the rich.

Spears, Raymond S. "Adirondack Camp Troubles." *Forest and Stream* 70 (May 30, 1908): 856–57.

Thievery and damage to vacant camps, written by a camp owner.

———. "The New Adirondacks." *The Outlook* (May 24, 1916): 191–200.

Land grabbing and the automobile and other forces bring about changes to the region.

"Sporting Tour in August, 1858." *Frank Leslie's Illustrated Newspaper* (Nov. 13–20, 1858): 378–80; 394–96.

"The Spread of the Country Life Idea." *Country Life in America* 14 (April 15, 1912): 19–20.

Credo of magazine. Ideas beckon Americans no less today.

Stallknecht, F. S., and Charles E. Whitehead. "An August Sporting Tour." *Frank Leslie's New Family Magazine* 6 (Nov. 13–20, 1858): 337–40.

Humorous account and illustrations, the latter by Whitehead.

"A Summer Home for Five Hundred Dollars." *The Craftsman* 5 (May 1904): 305–9.

Surprenant, Neil. "The Great Camp No One Knows." *Adirondac* (May 1989): 21–23.

White Pine Camp on Osgood Pond, near Paul Smiths, N.Y.

Thorpe, T. B. "A Visit to John Brown's Tract." *Harper's New Monthly Magazine* 19 (July 1859): 160–78.

Woodcut illustrations of open camp shelters.

"Types of Woodland Camps." *Town and Country* (Aug. 22, 1908): 12–13.

"Vacation Houses: Charles Nutt." *Architectural Record* 90 (July 1941): 66–68.

Summer home and guest cottage, Silver Bay, Lake George.

Vallingdigham, E. N. "Summer Camps in Northern Woods." *Indoors and Out* 2 (Aug. 1906): 205–12.

Van Court, Robert H. "Vacation Homes in the Woods." *The Independent* 72 (June 6, 1912): 1239–46.

Camps and outdoor camping for children.

Vane, Henry. "Adirondack Days." *Harper's New Monthly Magazine* 63 (Oct. 1881), 678–91.

Wack, Henry Wellington. "Kamp Kill Kare." *Field and Stream* 7 (Feb. 1903): 651–61.

> *Best publication showing this camp during Woodruff period.*

Whiton, L. C. "The St. Regis Camps." *Forest and Stream* 36 (June 18, 1891): 435.

Wilson, Leila Fosburgh. "One Hundred Years in the Adirondack Wilderness." *The Conservationist* (May/June 1989): 40–49.

> *North Woods Club.*

Wilson, Michael. "The Uses of Bog River's Ruins: The Adirondacks as a Cultural Landscape." *Adirondack Joural of Environmental Studies* 2 (Fall/Winter 1995): 18–31.

Wing, Ralph K. "A Damp Journey On a Down Grade." *Outing* (Nov. 1888): 111–24.

> *Desiring a roof, two young men hid their canoe and asked a farmer if they could sleep in his barn.*

Wolcott, W. E. "The Walton Club." *Forest and Stream* 48 (May 22, 1897): 402–03.

> *What camping was like fifty years earlier.*

Wright, Richardson, ed. "Summer Camps & Cottages." *House and Garden* 75, section 2 (June 1939): 1–37.

> *Special supplement surveys "modern" camps of 1930s, including a cabin designed by Charles L. Nutt in the Adirondacks.*

Ziegenfuss, H. L. "Lake Piseco Trout Club." *Forest and Stream* 18 (Feb. 16, 1882): 44–45.

> *A look back at an Adirondack sporting club started in 1834.*

Index

Italic page numbers denote illustrations.